THE EARLY HISTORY OF EASTERN INDIA

the early history of eastern india

(*From the Earliest Times to the Muslim Conquest*)

Vol. I.

PROMODE LAL PAUL

Forwarded by :
Dr. R.C. MAJUMDAR

SHARADA
Sharada Prakashan
DELHI-110052
1990

Paul, Pramode Lal.

The early history of Bengal : from the earliest times to the Muslim Conquest / by Pramode Lal Paul; with foreword by R.C. Majumdar. Delhi : Sharada Prakashan, 1990.

2 v. in 1, map; 23 cm.

Reprint. Originally published : Calcutta : Indian Research Institute, 1939.

Includes bibliographical referenc

ISBN : 81-85320-10-1

1. India Eastern—History—Ar India Eastern—Antiquities.

First Published : 1939
Reprinted : 1990

ISBN : 81-85320-10-1

Published by
SHARADA PRAKASHAN
E-239, Shastri Nagar,
DELHI-110052
Phone : 516539

Printed by
MOHINDRA OFFSET PRESS
308/B, Shahzada Bagh,
DELHI-110035

To

Hon'ble Moulvi A. K. Fazlul Huq

Chief Minister of Bengal.

As a token of my deep respect for his untiring efforts for the educational uplift of the masses and the rural regeneration of the province.

Foreword

The Early History of Bengal by Mr. Pramode Lal Paul is a noteworthy attempt by a young Bengali scholar to bring together the known facts regarding the political history of Bengal during the Hindu period. It undoubtedly marks a distinct advance over the existing books on the subject. The author has studied the subject critically, and presented the facts in a detached spirit, free from prejudices and predilections for any particular point of view. It may not be possible to accept all his opinions and conclusions but there can be no question of his thoroughness of study and an honest endeavour to judge every question from all possible points of view. A critical study of the history of Bengal is of recent origin, and scanty as our materials are, many years must elapse before we can sketch a fairly complete outline of its main stages of evolution. But it will be impossible to achieve this end if we do not occasionally take stock of our knowledge in the shape of preliminary sketches such as the present book professes to be. Mr. Paul has no ambition to write the history of Bengal. But he was facilitated the task of the future historian by a painstaking study of the relevant materials and the results achieved by him are certainly both creditable and encouraging. There are many important problems regarding the political history of Bengal which at present defy solution. Mr. Paul has presented them in all their aspects. As the Sanskrit proverb says, 'Vāde Vāde jāyate tatvabodha.' So further discussions on the problems so clearly presented before us are likely to help us in arriving at a correct solution. Mr. Paul would regard his labour amply justified if this book paves the way for a fuller and better treatment of history of Bengal. He puts no higher claim, and I have no doubt that his humble attempt fully deserves the encouragement and and appreciation from students of Indian History.

R. C. MAJUMDAR.

Author's Preface

Thanks to the recent progress of archæological studies and to the untiring researches of a band of enthusiastic scholars, it is now possible to write a history of ancient Bengal. In this volume, an attempt has been made to sketch the outline of political history from the earliest times to the Muslim conquest. The next volume dealing with cultural and social history will be shortly out.

In preparation of this volume I am thankful to many friends. I must express my thankfulness to Dr. R. C. Majumdar under whose guidance this work was undertaken and from whom more than anyone else I have learnt how to handle the sources of ancient history. To Dr. N. K. Bhattasali I am indebted to a degree for which no amount of thanks would suffice. He has taken a keen interest in the progress of the work, has readily helped me in every possible way with his expert knowledge in the subject and has kept the Dacca Museum Library open for me, day and night, sometimes to his great inconvenience. I have to tender my heartfelt thanks to Prof. V. Bhattacharyya, Dr. D. C. Ganguly and Dr. R. G. Basak for some helpful suggestions and to my friends Mr. A. K. Shom and Mr. A. J. Bhattacharrya for encouragement. I record hereby my grateful appreciation of the assistance I have received in going through the manuscript and the proofs to Babu Mati Lal Paul B. A., Headmaster, Tarkibandar Victory H. E. School, and to Messrs M. N. Roychowdhury M. A., Nani Lal Sengupta M. A., Chittaranjan Das B. A. and Jyotish Chandra Paul B. A., In fine, I owe a deep debt of gratitude to Mr. Satis Chandra Seal M. A., B. L., the young and energetic Secretary of the Indian Research Institute, but for whose help it would have been impossible to bring out the book.

I crave the indulgence of the readers for a few serious misprints that have crept in. An index and a map, so invaluable to a work of this kind, will be added in the next volume.

15TH APRIL, 1939. P. L. PAUL.

A Note

With the publication of the Early History of Bengal by Mr. P. L. Paul M. A., the Indian Research Institute presents before the scholarly world the second number of the Indian History Series. The object of taking up this series is to bring out a comprehensive religious, cultural, political and social History of India by publication in separate volumes of the history of its places and provinces. The first number of the series was a Monograph on Gaya and Buddha Gaya by Dr. B. M. Barua M. A. D. Lit. (Lond.) which is a Holy Shrine to the Hindus and the Buddhists alike from ancient times.

As has been pointed out by Dr. R. C. Majumdar M. A., Ph. D., the Vice-Chancellor of the Dacca University in his Foreword to this volume, it serves as an outline of a comprehensive history of early Bengal. It will be complete in two volumes and the political history is dealt with in the first volume. The second volume will give the religious, cultural, and social history and we expect to bring it out at an early date.

Lastly I appeal once again to all lovers of history and Indology, public libraries and directors of public instructions of different provinces to extend to us their valuable co-operation by liberally subscribing to this and other publications of this Institute, each of which deals with a particular aspect of Indian Civilisation and Culture.

1st Vaiśākha 1346 B. S.
THE INDIAN RESEARCH INSTITUTE
170, Maniktala Street, CALCUTTA.

SATIS CHANDRA SEAL

Contents

	Pages
Foreword by Dr. R. C. Majumdar	
Author's Preface	
Publisher's Note	
Introduction ...	I—VIII
Chapter I—From the earliest times to the Gupta period	1—14
Chapter II—From the fall of the Guptas to the rise of the Pālas	15—32
Chapter III—The Pāla dynasty ...	33—51
Chapter IV—The Pāla dynasty (continued) ...	52—73
Chapter V—Independent dynasties in Vaṅga and Rāḍha	76 – 85
Chapter VI—The Sena dynasty ...	86—100
Chapter VII—Administrative System ...	111 – 152

Appendices

Appendix A – Pāla Chronology ...	73 – 75
Appendix B – Sena Chronology ...	101 – 101
Appendix C – Lakṣmaṇsena Era	101 – 107
Appendix D – Doubtful Invasions of Bengal ...	107 – 110

THE EARLY HISTORY OF BENGAL

INTRODUCTION

ANCIENT GEOGRAPHICAL DIVISIONS—It is indeed a very difficult task to describe the boundaries of geographical divisions and localities of ancient Bengal, as there is no clue to determining the location of some of them. It may be surmised that in ancient Bengal, as in the present time, the natural boundaries were generally the rivers whose beds had been constantly shifting. Our difficulty is further enhanced by the fact that some localities seem to have been included within, or conterminous with, the bigger and well-known geographical units, and the boundaries changed with political circumstances also. In the fourth Jaina Upāṅga, the Pannavaṇā,[1] Tāmralipti (Tamluk in modern Midnapore) is included in Vaṅga, and Koḍivarṣa (Koṭivarṣa in modern Dinajpur) is mentioned as the chief city of Lāḍha (Rāḍha). This seems to refer to a very early period, when the political expansion of Vaṅga and Rāḍha was at its zenith. In the Pāla and Sena periods two broad and commonly known geographical divisions were Gauḍa and Vaṅga.

Gauḍa included both Rāḍha and Varendra. In the Haraha inscription of Iśānavarman,[2] dated in 554 A. D., Gauḍas have been described as 'Samudrāśrayān.' It is stated in the drama 'Prabodhacandraodaya'[3] that Rāḍha was included in Gauḍa. It is known from an inscription of the Madras Presidency that Dakṣiṇa (southern) Rāḍha was within Gauḍadeśa.[4] All these

1. IHQ, 1932 pp. 521ff.

2. EI, XIV, pp. 117ff.

3. For the correct reading of the passage in question, see IHQ, 1932, pp. 521ff.

4. Rangachariar, 'Ins. of the Madras Presidency' I, p. 353; see IHQ. 1937, pp. 162.

go to show that Gauḍa comprised Rāḍha. Rāḍha is roughly represented by the modern Burdwan Presidency, and it is quite probable that some portion of the Manbhum and Hazaribagh districts were also included within it. Rāḍha was divided into Dakṣiṇa Rāḍha and Uttara Rāḍha by the river Ajaya,[1] and these two divisions were also known as Suhma and Brahma respectively[2]. From the Tirumalai inscription of Rājendra Cola and from the Irda grant of the Kamboja king Nayapāladeva[3] it seems that Daṇḍabhukti comprised the south-western part of the Midnapore district and some portion of the Balasore district and it was a separate geographical unit from Rāḍha. Tāmraliptikas are mentioned as a tribe or people in ancient literature, and in Yuan Chwang's time Tāmralipti was one of the principalities of Bengal visited by him.

The ancient name of northern Bengal was Puṇḍravardhana and the identification of its capital Puṇḍranagara with Mahasthan in the Bogra district is certain after the publication of the Mahasthan inscription in Old Brahmi script.[4] It was one of the famous cities of ancient India. In the inscriptions of the Gupta period Puṇḍravardhana-bhukti seems to have comprised northern Bengal, whereas it is definite that this 'bhukti' in the Pāla and Sena periods included some portion of eastern Bengal also.[5] Later northern Bengal was known as Varendra. From the Silimpur inscription[6] Varendra seems to be mentioned as a tract within the Puṇḍra country. The earliest mention of Varendra is found in a

1. JRAS, 1935, pp. 73ff.
2. IHQ, 1932, pp. 521ff.
3. EI, XXII, pp. 153ff.
4. IHQ, 1934, pp 57ff.
5. JRAS, 1935,, pp. 73ff. It is quite possible that the country of the Puṇḍras comprised some portion of Burdwan Divition also. See 'Deśāvalī-vivṛti' written by Jagamohona Pandit. 'Descriptive Cat. of Sans. Mss. in the Govt. Collection, History and Geography,' p. 63. It is said in this book that there were seven deśas in Puṇḍradeśa, vix. Gauḍa, Varendra, Nivṛti, Suhma, Vardhamāna, Varāhabhuma, Jaṅgala Jhārikhaṇḍa. Also see JASB, 1897, pt. I, pp. 85-112.
6. EI, XIII, pp. 283ff.

south Indian inscription[1] of 967 A. D., in which a Brahman immigrant has been described as 'Gauḍa-cūḍāmaṇi' and 'Vārendra-dyoti-kāriṇa.' It is therefore likely that the name Varendra was well-known by the tenth century. Varendra is roughly represented by the Rajshahi Division excluding perhaps Jalpaiguri and Darjeeling districts. Some portions of the Purnea district might have been included within it.

It is not possible to define the boundary of Vaṅga with any degree of accuracy and preciseness. At the present state of our knowledge the rivers Hoogly and Brahmaputra seem to be the western and eastern boundaries, and on the north was Varendra and to the south, the Bay of Bengal. It is difficult to say whether Harikela and Samataṭa were included within Vaṅga. In the "Mañjuśrī-Mūlakalpa"[2] these three countries are mentioned side by side in the description of the countries where 'asura' speech was prevalent. In view of this evidence we think that the identification of Vaṅga with Harikela by the lexicographer Hemacandra[3] should be accepted with some reservation and it is also to be noted that Hemacandra wrote in the 12th century from Guzrat. Mention may be made of the fact that in the two Mss[4] of the

1. EI, XXI, p. 260ff, Prof, Bhandarkar in his 'Aśoka' (second edition, pp. 36-37) conjectures that Pārimdas of the Girnar inscription of Aśoka may be identical with Vārendras. But it is far from being certain.

2. Edited by Ganapati Shastri, 22nd 'Paṭala' pp. 232-233,

3. Hemcandra writes, 'Campāstu Aṅgā Vaṅgāstu Harikelīyā.' In order to explain the obvious difficulty Dr. H. C. Roy Chowdhury suggested that the term Vaṅga was used in a broader and narrower geographical sense and it is in its narrower sense identical with Harikela. But there is no evidence to show that there was a broader Vaṅga and a narrower one. We agree with Dr. Roy Chowdhury in regarding Harikela as a small principality, compared with Vaṅga ('Mānasī-O-Marmavāṇī', 1935-36, B. S, pp. 566ff). In the Chittagong plate of Kāntideva Harikela is called a 'maṇḍala.'

4. I am thankful to Mr. S. C. Banerjee, keeper of the Dacca University Mss., for drawing my attention to these two Mss. They are (1) No. 2141B, named 'Rudrākṣa-māhātya,' folio I, and (2) No. 1451, named 'Rupa-cintāmoṇi-koṣa' by Yādavānanda Dāsa, composed in 1515 S. E., folio 15A.

Dacca University collection Harikola (= Harikela ?) is synonymous with Śrīhaṭṭa (Sylhet), adjacent to Kāmarūpa. According to I-tsing and Tan-Kang, Harikela was the eastern limit of eastern India,[1] and Yu-he writes that it was 30 days' journey from Ceylon and 100 yojanas from Nālandā. From the Rampal plate of Śrīcandra it appears that it was contiguous to Candradvīpa and Harikela might have included some portion of Bakerganj and Noakhali districts. It was a coastal country and there was direct communication between Harikela and Ceylon.

The word Samataṭa implies that it was a coastal country. Cunningham[2] is of opinion that Samataṭa is to be identified with the delta of the Ganges including the Sunderbans between the Huranghata river and Bakerganj. In the Barrackpore plate of Vijayasena it is stated that in the Khāḍi-maṇḍala of Puṇḍravardhana-bhukti land was measured according to the 'Nala' standard prevalent in Samataṭa. Khāḍi is at present the name of a 'pargana' in the Diamond Harbour Sub-division and it can be suggested that this part of thea 24-Parganas was included in Samataṭa[3]. The Baghaura image inscription of the 3rd year of Mahīpāla I shows that some portion of modern Tippera was included in Samataṭa[4].

Candradvīpa was another locality in south-eastern Bengal and is still a 'pargana' in the Bakerganj district. It might have included some portion of Khulna[5] and Noakhali[6] districts.

Dr. H. C. Roychowdhury expressed the opinion that Vaṅga and Vaṅgāla are two separate countries and suggested that Vaṅgāla was probably identical with Candradvīpa.[7] We differed from Dr. Roychowdhury because the only evidence which goes to

1. Takakasu, 'I-tsing,' p xlvi ; Chavanes, 'Memore de Religione Eminents,' p. 106, pp. 144-5.

2. 'Ancient Geography of India,' pp. 501-03.

3. IB, p. 61.

4. EI, XVII, pp. 353ff.

5. S. Mitra, 'History of Jessore and Khulna' (in Bengali), p. 140

6. P. C. Bagchi, Intro., 'Kaulajnāna-Nirṇaya,' pp. 25ff.

7. 'Mānasī-O-Marmavāṇī,' 1335-6 B. S., pp. 566ff.

support his view is the Ablur inscription of Vijjala[1] and because the particular invasion of Bengal by this Kalacurya king has no historical basis at all.[2] The poet might have meant to repeat the same incident by referring to the conquest of Vaṅga and by alluding to the killing of the king of Vaṅgāla. Vaṅga and Vaṅgāla cannot be regarded as two separate countries on the strength of this evidence alone. We therefore observed that Vaṅgāla seems to be an etymological variation of Vaṅga, probably made by the southerners and foreigners. In a short note[3] Dr. N. N. Chaudhury says that Vaṅga is derived from the Tibetan word 'bans' and means marshy and moist. The second part of Vaṅgāla, the Dravidian 'ālam,' is a verbal derivative from the root āl, meaning to possess. Therefore Vaṅgālam means marshy and moist region.

In course of further study of the subject we find Bangala (=Vaṅgāla) has been mentioned in many south Indian inscriptiions.[4] In two records, as in the Ablur inscription, Vaṅga and Vaṅgāla have been mentioned, thereby showing that they were probably two separate countries.[5] Again, in the Hāmmīra Mahākāvya of Nayacandra Sūri (composed before 1496 A. D.) Banga and Bangala have been mentioned side by side[6]. It must be noted that exploits in Vaṅga and Vaṅgāla in these four records seem to be vague generalisations and poetic exaggerations. But the fact that in four separate records Vaṅga and Vaṅgāla are to be found side by side goes to strengthen Dr. Roychowdhury's opinion. It is also to be noted that we do not find any mention of Vaṅgāla in any record before the 10th century.

Mr. R. C. Banerjee locates the Vaṅgāla country to the east of the Brahmaputra river[7]. Attention may be drawn to Marco Polo's account of the Bangala country. The king of Mien

1. IHQ, XII, p. 77, fn 61. 2. Ibid., XI, p. 769.

3. 'Modern Review,' September, 1936,

4. 'Epigraphia Carnatica,' V Intro. 14n, 19 ; Cn, 179 ; VI, Cm 137 ; VII, Intro. 30 sk, 119 ; IX Bn. 96 ; IA, IX, pp. 333ff.

5. 'Epigraphia Carnatica,' V, Cn, 179, Eng. p. 202. IA, IX! pp. 333ff.

6. IA, 1879, p. 58. 7. IC, II, pp. 756 ff.

(Burma) is also called the king of Bangala (=Vaṅgāla)[1]. As regards its geographical position, Yule remarks[2]: "Marco conceives of Bangala, not in India, but as being like Mien, a province on the confines of India, as lying to the south of that kingdom, and as being at the (south) western extremity of a great traverse line which runs (north-east) into Kweichan and Sze-ch'wan. All these conditions point consistently to one locality ; that, however, is not Bengal but Pegu......And possibly the name of Pegu may have contributed to this error, as well as the possible fact that the kings of Burma did at this time claim to be kings of Bengal, whilst they actually were kings of Pegu." This does not preclude the possibility of locating Vaṅgāla as a separate country to the east of the Brahmaputra. In the eleventh and twelfth centuries the kings of Burma had important political and social relations with this part of Bengal. Anoratha (1044-77 A. D.), one of the most powerful kings in Burmese history, extended his conquests as far as Bengal[3]. A prince of Paṭṭikerā (still a 'pargana' in Tippera) married the daughter of the Burmese king, Kyanzittha (1084-1112 A.D.). The next king Alaungstthu (1112-87 A.D.) married a princess of Paṭṭikerā. The Mainamati plate of Raṇavaṅkamalla[4] bears testimony to the Burmese influence in that region. This perhaps explains in a way why the kings of Burma and Pagan were also called kings of Bangala by Marco.

ADMIXTURE OF DIFFERENT RACIAL BLOOD—Opinions of scholars are divided on the question of different racial elements in Bengal, but the fact that the present Bengali population is the admixture of different racial bloods seems to be conceded by many. Sylvian Levi[5] believes that Aṅga-Vaṅga, Kaliṅga-Triliṅga, Oḍra-Puṇḍra, Pulinda-Kulinda, Kośala-Tosala belong to 'Munda, Kol' and 'Mon-khemar' group of languages whose traces are found in the

---

1 The account of Marco Polo translated by Yule. Yule takes Bangala to refer to the entire province of Bengal Vol. II, p. 98., note 99, 100 ; for the account of the Bangala country, see pp. 114 ff. 2 Ibid., p. 128.

3 Phare, 'History of Burma,' p.37. 4 IHQ 1933, p.285. 5 P. C. Bagchi, 'Pre-Dravidian and Pre-Aryan in India', Part III 'Vicitrā', 1340 B. S., pp. 413 ff.

Khasia hills of Assam, upper and lower Burma, Nicobar islands and Malaya Archipelago. These languages are denoted by the general term *Austric*. The common ethnic origin of Aṅga, Vaṅga, Puṇḍra, Kaliṅga and Suhma has perhaps found expression in the legendary story of their origin in the Mahābhārata, Purāṇas and the Harivaṁśa as the sons of 'Ṛṣi' Dīrghmanta through his union with Sudoṣṇā, wife of the demon king Bali. Risley described the Bengali type "as a blend of Dravidian and Mongolian elements with a strain of Indo-Aryan blood in the higher groups." This theory has been challenged by some scholars but has not been replaced by a better one. Thus Dr. B. S. Guha considers the Malas of Santal-Parganas, Bankura and Midnapore as Austroloid and finds traces of Alpine race in the Brahmanas and Kāyasthas, and Mongolian element in the Brahmaputra delta.[1]

As regards Aryan immigrations, Oldenberg, Hoernle and and Grierson hold that there was a previous migration of a band of Aryans before the coming of the Vedic Aryans, and the earlier ones were pushed into the outlying provinces of northern India like Bengal, Behar, Assam, Maharastra and Guzrat. According to R. P. Chanda, the Outer Aryans came later across the tableland of Central India, when the Inner Aryans lived in the Kuru-Pāñchala country. The theory of Outer and Inner Aryans has been questioned recently by Dr. N. K. Datta[2] who is of opinion that there were two types of culture—the older of the Panjab and the later of the Midland. "It is the former type that spread in Eastern India and later the Midland culture began to conquer its way in the east." Scholars who have gone deep into the question are thus at variance. But it seems clear from the stray references to Aṅga, Vaṅga, Puṇḍra and Kaliṅga in the 'Aitareya Brāhmaṇa,' 'Aitareya Āraṇyak' and 'Baudhāyana-sūtra' that the peoples or tribes of eastern India were different from those who composed these books[3]. The predominant non-Aryan character of the population perhaps accounts for the popularity of the non-Brahmanical

---

1 'Prabāsī,' 1340 B. S., pp. 257

2. 'Aryanisation of India,' Ch. II, Previous opinions summarised and criticised.

3. Vide infra.

religions like Buddhism and Jainism in eastern India. These two factors seem to have combined to prevent the rapid Brahmanisation of Bengal and from that standpoint perhaps the migrations of Brahmanas from the midlands were welcome to the followers of their faith even in the later periods.

MANY UNEXPLORED SITES—Many ancient sites and localities have not been explored yet. Even the few sites declared as protected area by the Ancient Monuments Preservation Act have not been excavated. The rich finds at Paharpur, Mahasthan and Rangamati should remove the old notion that ancient sites of Bengal are not worth excavating. Paharpur finds alone can in many ways interpret the artistic and religious evolution of ancient Bengal and they have enriched our knowledge about those phases to an unexpected degree. The undertaking of the excavation of Banagarh by the Calcutta University is expected to throw light on many disputed events. It is the city of the demon king Bāṇa of the Purāṇas, the headquarter of the Koṭivarṣaviṣaya of the Gupta period, the site of the mysterious pillar of a Kamboja king and the mounds of this place have been described as "second only to those at Paharpur." The tours[1] undertaken by a student of archaeology in Dinajpur, Malda and Bogra districts have revealed the fact that most of the important villages abound in images of iconographic interest. The 'Bīrbhūma-Vivaraṇa'[2] contains imperfect reproductions of some images which are of great iconographic importance and exhibit high artistic excellence. Its author for the first time drew attention to the Paikore pillar inscription of Kalacuri Karṇa which proves beyond doubt that he penetrated in the very heart of Bengal in course of his invasion which was so long doubted, as the information was from the Tibetan source and as the 'Rāmacarita' gives a different story. There cannot be any denying the fact that some of the disputed events and gaps of the early history of Bengal cannot be explained unless fresh materials throw some light on them. Explorations and excavations of important sites are, therefore, of paramount importance and imperative necessity.

1. JASB, 1932, pp, 151. 173. 185.
2. Published by Hare Krishna Mukherjee.

THE EARLY HISTORY OF BENGAL

CHAPTER I

From earliest times to the Gupta period

There is no mention of any part of Bengal in the Ṛg-Veda. In the 'Aitareya Brāhmaṇa'[1] it is said that the Puṇḍras, Andhras and Śabaras live on the border of the Ārya country and the bulk of them are Dasyus. In the 'Aitareya Āraṇyaka'[2] Vaṅgas, Vagadhas (=Magadhas) and Ceras have been compared with birds. Baudhāyana[3] quotes older authorities (Bhallavins) to show that any one visiting Puṇḍra, Vaṅga and Kaliṅga had to perform some purificatory sacrifices. It seems that in the later Vedic period Bengal was inhabited by tribes or peoples who belonged to a different stock of population from these Brạhmanical writers and contact with these tribes was avoided by them as far as possible.

Manu[4] refers to the Pauṇḍrakas as one of the Kṣatriya tribes or peoples who had degraded themselves to the status of the Śūdras for their neglect of the sacred rites and for not consulting the Brahmanas. The 'Anugītā'[5] mentions the Pauṇḍras as one of the Kṣatriya tribes who fled into the mountains and other inaccessible places in fear of Jāmadagni and neglected their prescribed duties. The legendary story of the five sons of Bali, Aṅga, Vaṅga, Kaliṅga, Puṇḍra and Suhma, may be construed to mean that the ruling princes and high dignitaries were coming into contact with the Aryans. All these references perhaps point to the fact that in a subsequent period when the Aryan settlements were

---

1. VIII, 18.
2. II, 1. I.
3. 1, 2, 14.
4. SBE, XXV, p. 412,
5. SBE, VIII, p. 295,

growing, they tried to connect these tribes with them by some stories and legends. They were not yet strictly conforming themselves to Aryan rites and customs and hence they were called degraded Kṣatriyas and Śūdras. Anyway, the Aryans were coming into contact with Bengal in post-Vedic period and could not neglect the power of the original tribes of the country.

We learn from the 'Mahābhārata' that Vaṅga and Puṇḍra were subject to Jarāsanda of Magadha. In course of Bhīma's expedition[1] he is said to have defeated Vāsudeva of Puṇḍra, Samudrasena of Vaṅga and an unnamed king of Suhma. In addition to the above mentioned tribes or peoples we know the existence of many others from the description of his victories. Prasuhmas are mentioned along with Suhmas and seem to have occupied adjacent territories. Tāmraliptakas and Karvaṭas[2] also seem to have been peoples of western Bengal. The seacoast and islands of the Bay were inhabited by the Kirātas and Mlecchas.

The description of the kingdom of Aṅga in the 'Mahābhārata' and Buddhist literature goes to indicate that some portions of Bengal were sometimes included within it. Karṇa, king of Aṅga, brought troops from Aṅga, Vaṅga, Puṇḍra and Kaliṅga in support of the Kauravas. The Buddhist literature bears ample testimony to the greatness of the Aṅga kingdom.[3] It tops the list of the sixteen great kingdoms in the 'Aṅguttara-Nikāya.' The 'Kathāsaritasāgara' alludes to the fact that the kingdom of Aṅga at one time extended to the sea and one of its cities, Viṭaṅkapura, was situated on the seaside. It continued a long struggle with Magadha until it was finally annexed to the Magadhan empire by Bimbisāra.

The inculsion of Aṅga within the Magadhan empire perhaps did not mean the annexation of Bengal also. The existence of a powerful kingdom in south-western Bengal, called Gangaridai,

---

1. Śānti Parva, Ch. 30, (Calcutta edition)
2. For their location see IHQ., VIII, pp. 521 ff; SPP. 1340 B. S. 55 ff.
3. For full references, see Dr. H. C. Roychowdhury, PHAI, pp. 75ff: Dr. Majumdar, The Early History of Bengal. pp. 6ff.

at the time of Alexander's invasion is attested by the classical writers.[1] Diodorus (49 B. C.-A. D. 14) says that it was reported to Alexander, "Beyond these (the Indus, the desert and the Ganges) were situated the dominions of the nation of the Braisioi (Prasii) and the Gangaridai, whose king, Xandrames, had an army of 20,000 horse, 200,000 infantry, 2000, chariots and 4,000 elephants trained and equipped for war. Poros confirmed the report and further informed Alexander that the king of Gangaridai was thought to be the son of a barber and was not much respected. His father won the affection of the queen who murdered the old king treacherously. In this way the ruling king's father became king. Speaking of Indian nations as a whole in a very general way, Diodorus says that "India is inhabited by very many nations, among which the greatest of all is that of the Gangaridai against whom Alexander did not undertake an expedition, being deterred by the multitude of their elephants. This region is separated from farther India by the Ganges, the greatest river in those parts." Cuntius Curtius says that the lower Gangetic country is occupied by two nations, the Gangaridai and Prasii, whose king, Agrammes, commanded an army of almost above strength. The only difference is that Curtius refers to the number of the elephants as 3,000, whereas Diodorus gives the number as 4,000.

Plutarch says that the opposition of Alexander's army against further advance was due to the report that "The kings of Gangaridai and Prasioi were waiting for him with an army of 80,000 horse, 200,000 foot, 8,000 war chariots, and 6,000 fighting elephants." Plutarch assures that there is no exaggeration in the description of the army of the two nations. Pliny writes, "The tribes called Kalingæ are nearest the sea, and higher up are the Mandæi and the Malli, in whose country is mount Mallus, the boundary of all that district being the Ganges......the final part of its course is through the country of the Gangarides. The royal city of Kalinga is called Parthalis. Over their king 60,000 foot

1. We follow McCrindle's translations in quotations.

soldiers, 1,000 horsemen and 7,000 elephants keep watch and ward." Another alternative reading makes Gangarides-Kaliṅga a people, having a king, a capital city and a military force of their own.[1] Pliny adds that Prasii surpasses in power and glory every other power of India. Ptolemy says that all the country about the mouths of the Ganges was occupied by the Gangaridai whose capital was Gange. This city is said to have been at the junction of the Ganges leading to Mega (great) and Kamberikhon mouths respectively. The author of the 'Periplus' mentions the port Gange at the mouth of the Ganges.[2]

It is clear from the accounts of these writers that the country of the Gangaridai was to the east of the Prasii with their capital Palibothra or Pāṭaliputra. The Ganges most probably flew into the sea, as it does at present, into many channels, the two important branches being the Hooghly and the Padma. The suggestion[3] that the Indian name of the country of the Gangarides is Gaṅgārāṣṭra (i. e. the country of the Ganges) seems to be near the mark. Their country seems to have comprised Burdwan, Presidency and Dacca Divisions. The power and prestige of this kingdom reached the ears of Alexander and its rise may be placed sometime earlier. It is a significant fact that no writer definitely calls Gangaridai subordinate to Prasii. Such a conclusion held by many scholars has been therefore questioned.[4] Late Mr. Monahan rightly observed, "It is not certain whether the two peoples at that time (of Alexander's invasion) formed one state or a confederation, but the evidence seems on the whole to point to two states with separate kings and forces, but united in a close confederation—so close that the population of both was sometimes included under one name, as Parsii or as Gangarides." It is noteworthy that Diodorus definitely calls Xandrames king of Gangaridai. This king has

1. Monahan, The Early History of Bengal, p. 5.
2. Schoff, 'Periplus', p. 47.
3. IHQ. III. p. 728 ; Ibid, IV, pp. 44. 234.
4. Dr. R. C. Majumdar, The Early History of Bengal, p. 10.

generally been identified with Mahāpadma Nanda of the Nanda dynasty, who seems to be the ruler of both the nations. It is not again certain that Candragupta Maurya, who supplanted the the Nanda dynasty from Magadha, brought Gangaridai under his authority. He is sometimes called king of Prasii but nowhere that of Gangaridai. It is clear from Pliny's account that the countries of the Gangarides and Kaliṅgas were adjacent territories. His description of Kaliṅgas deserves more than a passing notice. He mentions one tribe called Maccokalingæ and another called Modokalinga inhabiting an island in the Ganges. We have already referred to the fact that one interpretation of a text of Pliny makes out Gangarides-Kaliṅga, and from this Viven de Saint-Martin concluded that they were three branches of the Kaliṅgas. Their country was nearest to the sea and their capital was called Parthalis which has been identified with Purvasthālī, a large village about 20 miles from the present Burdwan town.[1] The common ethnic character of Aṅga, Vaṅga, Kaliṅga, Puṇḍra and Suhma has already been emphasised. It is therefore likely that a branch of the Kaliṅgas also inhabited some part of western Bengal and were allied with the Gangarides. The great Kaliṅga expedition of Aśoka was perhaps meant against the powerful combination of the Kaliṅgas and Gangarides. The huge loss of human lives and havocs of the Kaliṅga war, so vividly described in the Thirteenth Rock Edict, may be better explained in this way, for the subjugation of a province like modern Orissa did not possibily require so much effort of the powerful Maurya emperor.

Whatever may be the case, it seems that Bengal was brought under the Aśokan empire. Yuan Chwang saw many Aśokan topes at Puṇḍravardhana, Samataṭa, Tāmralipti and Karṇasuvarṇa (in the Murshidabad district). This positive evidence is corroborated by the fact that while the kingdoms of the extreme south like Cola, Cera, Keralaputra and Sātiyaputra have been mentioned in the inscriptions as frontier kingdoms, no part of Bengal so near

1. IHQ. IV, p. 55.

to Pāṭaliputra has been mentioned as such. The geographer Ptolemy writing in the 2nd century A. D. refers to the country of the Gangarides, and their capital Gange[1] was a port of considerable importance in the first century A. D., as the evidence of the 'Periplus' shows. It is quite probable that the Gangarides cast off the Magadha yoke during the rule of the weak successors of Aśoka or after the break-up of the Maurya empire and their country continued an independent political existence at least up to the time of Ptolemy.

The history of Bengal from the fall of the Mauryas to the rise of the Guptas is almost dark. Ptolemy places a people called Marundai "on the left bank of the Ganges, south of the Gogra, down to the top of the delta." But it would not be very safe to trace their extension of power so far east and south as the delta of the Ganges on the authority of Ptolemy whose geographical knowledge was often defective.[2] The 'Purāṇas' state that the Muruṇḍas will rule over large tracts of the Ganges valley.[3] Jaina books call Maruṇḍarāja ruler of Kānyakuvja and residing in Pāṭaliputra.[4] The Chinese records also confirm the existence of a tribe called Meouloun (=? Muruṇḍas) in the Gangetic valley.[5] It is not easy to determine who these Muruṇḍās were. Sten Konow says that the word Muruṇḍa has been used in Kushana inscriptions in the sense of overlord.[6] If the words Śaka-Muruṇḍas of the Allahabad Pillar inscription of Samudragupta should be taken to mean as two separate peoples and not as Śaka chiefs, the Muruṇḍas seem to be a foreign horde like the Śakas who invaded India in the early centuries of the Christian era.

---

1. It has been sought to be located in the Jessore and Dacca districts (IA, 1884, p. 365) and identified with Saptagrāma in the Hooghly district (IHQ, IV, pp. 234ff). Its identification is not certain.
2. Monahan, The Early History of Bengal, pp. 8-13.
3. DUS, I, No. 2, p. 47.
4. Allan, Catalogue of Indian Coins, p. XXIX.
5. Prof. Sylvian Levy first drew attention to this, Ibid.
6. IA, XXXVII, p. 33 ; JASB, XIX, pp. 343ff.

According to the Purāṇas, Devarakṣitas ruled over Kośalas, Andhras, Pauṇḍras and Tāmraliptas and countries on the sea-shore before the rise of the Guptas. Nothing is known about Devarakṣitas from any other source.[1]

Gupta Rule in Bengal—The establishment of Gupta authority over north-western Bengal can be traced from the time of Samudragupta. In the famous Allahabad pillar inscription we find that his 'pratyanta' (frontier) kingdoms in the east were Samataṭa, Davāka and Kāmarūpā. The location of Davāka is uncertain,[2] but the positions of the other two are more or less certain. These three kingdoms also obeyed his suzerainty and paid taxes to him and they seem to have been within the spheres of his influence. The evidence of the Allahabad praśasti read along with the Damodarpur plates suggests that north-western Bengal was included within the empire of Samudragupta. The suggestion[3] that Candravarman of the Susunia Rock inscription is to be identified with Candravarman mentioned in that praśasti as one of the kings of Āryāvarta whose power was exterminated by Samudragupta rests on strong grounds and is perhaps to be accepted.

It is known from the Meharauli Iron pillar inscription that a king named Candra subjugated his enemies who gave a united front in Vaṅga and he also inflicted a defeat on the Bāhlikas by crossing the seven mouths of the Indus. The identification of king Candra has led to much discussion among scholars and the subject needs fresh treatment in the light of recent discoveries about the imperial Gupta history. Fleet[4] emphasised the early characters of this inscription but it must be observed that being a record on

1. Dr. R. C. Majumdar is of opinion that they belonged to the kingdom of Devarāṣṭra (mentioned in the Allahabad pillar inscription of Samudragupta) which was situated in the Vizagapatam district. Op, it. p. 13, also see DUS, I, No. 2, pp. 62-63.

2. IHQ, I, pp. 250ff. 3. PHAI, p. 364 fn. vide in fra.

4. CII. III. pp. 139-142.

an iron pillar, it is 'sui generis' and does not bear comparison with other contemporary records. Three sets of opinions have come out of previous discussions.

(a). Mm. H. P. Shastri[1] expressed the opinion that Candra of the Meharauli pillar did not belong to the Gupta dynasty but was a king of Puṣkaraṇa in Rajaputana, who tried to found an all-India empire before Samudragupta. The Mandasor inscription of 404 A,D. describes Naravarman as a powerful king of Puṣkaraṇa and son of Simhrvarman and grandson of Jayavarman. The Susunia Rock inscription in the Bankura district of Bengal records that a wheel of Viṣṇu was set up by Candravarman, son of Simhavarman and king of Puṣkaraṇa. Mm. H. P. Sastri on the strength of the identity of the name Simhavarman of the Mandasor and Susunia inscriptions took Candravarman and Naravarman to be brothers and identified Candravarman with Candra of the Meharauli pillar. But Pokharana is the name of a place not far off from the findspot of the Susunia inscription. It may be regarded almost certain after what Mr. K. N. Dikshit has written about the ancient ruins of this place that Candravarman was the king of Pokharana (whose sanskritised form is Puṣkaraṇa) and as such he has been regarded as a local king.[3] It is not known whether Simhavarman, father of Naravarman of the Mandasor inscription, had any son of the name of Candravarman. The identification of Candravarman of the Susunia inscription with a man of unknown existence is hardly tenable and there is no definite clue whatsover to the identification of Candravarman with Candra of the Meharauli pillar.[4]

1, EI. XIII. p. 133 ; XII. pp. 315ff. He is supported by R. D. Banerjee (EI, XIV. pp. 368-71.)

2, ASIR, 1927-28, pp. 188-9, 3, PHAI, p, 364 fn,

4, Dr. N. K. Bhattasali supports this identification by pointing out a solitary reference to one Candravarman whose Koṭa or fort formed the boundary of the land granted to a Brahmana by Samācārandeva in the 6th century A. D. (EI, XVIII p, 84), But it is very difficult to say who was this Candravarman whose fort is referred to in the inscription of Samācāradeva. He might be Candravarman of the Susunia inscription.

(b). Fleet expressed the opinion that Candra of the Meharauli pillar might be Candragupta I of the Gupta dynasty, and this has been supported by Dr. R. G. Basak and Prof. S. K. Aiyangar. Dr. Basak[1] accepts the identity of Siṁhavarman of the Susunia inscription and of the Mandasor inscription but would not concede that Candravarman came to Vaṅga on a campaign of conquests and would presume that Candravarman might have gone to the Susunia hill on a pilgrimage.[2] But this presumption is contradicted by Dr. Basak himself when he brings Candravarman in Bengal owing to the political vicissitudes of the Varman family of Malwa. He writes, "Siṁhavarman and Jayavarman might have ruled independently and when Samudragupta reduced the Malwa power, it is not unlikely that the elder brother was driven away from Malwa towards the east. This may in a way explain why he came to the Susunia hill"[3] Prof. S. K. Aiyangar argues the case of this identification with greater ardour[4] and lays down three conditions which shou'd be satisfied in solving the controversy regarding Candra of the Meharauli pillar.

(i) The person Candra must have been a man of achievement by his own efforts, acquired a vast kingdom, and held rule over it for a length of time.

(ii) He must have fought two actions against enemies across the wide stretch of India, such as western front of Bengal and western frontier of Sindh on the western side.

(iii) The enemies thus overthrown along the western frontier of Sindh [more properly on the other side of the Indus] are stated to be Bālhikas.[5]

1. History of North-Eastern India, p. 14.

2. Ibid, pp. 17-18.

3. Ibid, pp. 27-28.

4. JIH, VI, Studies in Gupta History, pp. 14-22 ; the Vākaṭakas and their place in Indian History, Ibid pp. 1-12.

5. Bālhikas are known as ruling in the Panjab with Sakāla (present Sialkot) as their capital (Mahābhārata, Karṇaparva, Ch. 37-38). Varāha-Mihira mentions Bāhlikas as a northern people.

2

But Prof. Aiyangar has failed to cite any definite evidence and known event of Candragupta I's reign to satisfy any one of these three conditions. The Purāṇas make him rule over Magadha, Sāketa and Prāyāga.[1] His name is omitted from the list of imperial Gupta kings in the 'Mañjuśrī-Mūlakalpa'.[2] The above-mentioned three conditions are rather in complete agreement with certain events of Candragupta II's reign. To emphasise the identification of Candra of the Meharauli pillar with Candragupta I is to ignore some definitely known events of the reign of Candragupta II.

(c) The identification with Candragupta II was proposed by Hœrnle[3] and V. A. Smith,[4] but the latter gave up his own proposition and accepted Mm. H. P. Shastri's identification.[5] The existence of a hitherto unknown king, named Rāmagupta,[6] elder brother of Candragupta II, seems now to be accepted, and the drama 'Devī Candragupta' acquaints us with a hard and keen struggle between Candragupta II and the Śakas. Allan's remark[7] that "the enemies who had united against him (i. e. Candra of the Meharauli pillar) in the Vaṅga country were probably peoples who had taken the opportunity of his absence in the west to cast off the yoke under which his father had laid them" is applicable to Candragupta II. It seems that the paramountcy established by the arms of Samudragupta was going to be lost during the rule of Rāmagupta but was re-established by the prowess of Candragupta II. It is quite clear from the epigraphic, literary and numismatic evidence of his reign that Candragupta II came into conflict with the Śaka Satraps.

If the identification of Candra of Meharauli pillar with Candragupta II is to be accepted, it seems certain that the Vaṅgas

1. Pargiter, Dynasties of the Kali Age, Intro. p. xii.
2. K. P. Jayaswal, An Imperial History of India, sl. 645.
3. IA, XXI, p.43. 4. JASB, 1897, pp. 1-18.
5. EHI, (4rth ed.) p. 290, fn. I.
6. JBORS, XIV, pp. 223-253 ; Malaviya Commemoration Volume, 1932, pp.189 ff ; IC, IV, p.216.
7. Catalogue of Indian Coins, (Gupta Dynasties) p. XXXVI. It is to be noted that Allan rejected the identification with Candragupta II.

tried to cast off the Gupta yoke but the attempt was frustrated by the valour of Candragupta II. Whoever this Candra might be, it is certain that the people of Vaṅga fought with a king who was in a position to overrun the territory between eastern Bengal and the Indus.

The Dhanaidaha, Baigram, Paharpur and five Damodarpur plates record land sales by different district (viṣaya) governments of the Puṇḍravardhana-bhukti within the period between 432 and 544 A. D. and clearly indicate that northern Bengal was under the Gupta emperors almost upto the middle of the sixth century A. D. The Dhanaidaha, Baigram and Damodarpur plates Nos. 1 and 2 of 113, 128, 124, 128 G. E respectively fall within the reign of Kumāragupta I. In the Damodarpur plates Nos. 1 and 2 'uparika' Cirātadatta and 'kumārāmātya' Vetravarman are mentioned as the governors of the Puṇḍravardhhana-bhukti and of the Koṭivarṣaviṣaya respectively during the sovereignty of Kumāragupta I. The name of the emperor has not been mentioned in the Baigram plate but the date shows that it is a record of the reign of the same monarch when 'kumārāmātya' Kulavṛddhi was in charge of the Pañcanagarī-viṣaya.

We need not enter into the controversial question regarding the successor or successors of Kumāragupta I. Something may be said for or against the three theories viz. [i] after the death of Kumāragupta I his sons set up independent kingdoms in different parts of the empire,[1] [ii] he was succeeded by his son Skandagupta who was followed by his brother Puragupta and his descendants[2] and [iii] there were two rival lines—one represented by Skandagupta, Kumāragupta II [?] of the Saranath inscription of 154 G. E. and Budhagupta, and the other[3] represented by Puragupta, Narasiṁhagupta and Kumāragupta III [?] of the Bhitari seal inscription. Each of these theories should be regarded as

1. IA. 1918, pp. 161-67 ; JASB. 1921, pp. 249-55.
2. Dr. H. C. Roychowdhury, PHAI, pp. 386 ff.
3. Dr. R. G. Basak, History of North-Eastern India, pp. 72 ff.

tentative, and no conclusion is possible unless further light is thrown on the controversy by fresh data. No epigraphic record of the reigns of Skandagupta, Puragupta, Narasiṁhagupta and his son Kumāragupta II [?] has been discovered in Bengal but it is to be noted that coins of Skandagupta have been found in different districts[1] and coins of Narasiṁhagupta and Kumāragupta [II ?] have been found in the large Kalighat hoard.[2] The Damodarpur plates Nos. 3 and 4 mention two governors of the Puṇḍravardhana-bhukti, Brahmadatta and Jayadatta by name, during the sovereignty of Budhagupta. The Paharpur plate of 159 G. E. does not mention the name of the emperor but it falls within his reign-period. These three plates read along with the Eran pillar inscription[3] and the Saranath image inscription of 157 G. E.[4] go to indicate that his authority was acknowledged in Central Provinces, United Provinces and Northern Bengal. Even if it is to be conceded that the Gupta empire was parcelled out among the sons of Kumāragupta I, it seems that Budhagupta ruled over a wide extent of territory and he cannot be regarded as the local ruler of Malwa and that he perhaps re-united the Gupta empire under his authority.

The Gunaighar grant of Vainyagupta,[5] dated in 508 A. D., raises some important problems. It was issued from the camp of victory situated at Kṛpura at the request of the dependent Mahārāja Rudradatta. It records grant of land in the Gunaik-āgrahāra which is to be identified with Gunaighar, the find-spot of the plate, in the Tippera district. The dūtaka of the grant was Mahāsāmanta Mahārāja Vijayasena whose high-sounding titles

1. One gold coin from each of the following districts, viz,. from Mahanad in Hoogly, Faridpur and Midnapore and a few silver coins from Muhammadpur in Jessore. BI, p. 71 ; JASB, XXI, p. 401.

2. Allan. Catalogue of Indian Coins, Intro. p. CXXVI.

3. Fleet, CII, III, p. 88.

4. IA, 1918, p. 162,

5. IHQ. 1930, pp. 40 ff.

'pañcādhikaraṇoparikapratyuparika [1] and 'puraloparika' [2] imply that he was a man of considerable importance in the kingdom. In this record Vainyagupta himself is styled only 'Mahārāja' and 'Paramaśaiva' and this has led Mr. D. C. Bhattacharyya to infer that he was a Gupta prince who declared independence during the troubled times of Huṇa invasions. Dr. R. C. Majumdar,[3] who contends that after the death of Kumāragupta I Gupta princes set up independent kingdoms in different parts of the empire, finds additional support from this record in favour of his view. Dr. D. C. Ganguli[4] has correctly attributed the coins with the legend 'Dvādaśāditya' on the reverse to Vainyagupta (hitherto attributed to Candragupta III), and his heavy gold coins, similar in type to those of the imperial Guptas, lead him to infer that he belonged to the same dynasty and was not a local ruler of Samataṭa. Mention may be made of the fact that a seal of Vainyagupta with the title 'Mahārājādhirāja' has been found at Nālandā along with the seals of Budhagupta, Kumārgupta (II ?) and Bhāskaravarman.[5] The inclusion of Vainyagupta in the imperial Gupta line means that in the first decade of the sixth century Gupta empire included Samataṭa or a part of it, which was an outlying kingdom at the time of Samudragupta. The late Mr. R. D. Banerjee[6] was of opinion that even in the Gupta period Puṇḍravardhana-bhukti comprised some part of eastern Bengal as in the Pāla and Sena periods.

Unfortunately the name of the Gupta emperor in the Damodarpur plate No. 5 is lost. Dr. R. G. Basak suggested the name to be (Bhānu ?) gupta.[7] We are rather inclined to

1. Mr. D. C. Bhattacharyya renders it as "President of five (district) court judges." Ibid.

2. Rendered by the same scholar as "President of city Governors." Idid.

3. IHQ, IX, pp. 989ff. 4. Ibid, pp. 784ff ; x, pp. 154ff.

5. ASIR, 1930-34, p. 230. 6. BI, p. 63.

7. EI, XV. p. 144 ; Jayaswal thinks him to be Kumāragupta III, Imperial History of India, p. 67.

to identify him with Viṣṇugupta, a large number of whose coins have been found in the Kalighat hoard with the legend on the reverse reading 'Candrāditya'.[1] If this is to be accepted, Viṣṇugupta seems to be the last known Gupta king of Bengal. The title of the governor of the Puṇḍravardhana-bhukti in this plate is 'Mahārājaputra-rājaputradeva-bhaṭṭāraka and his name seems to be lost, though it is not unlikely that his name was Rājaputradeva. The epithets 'Mahārājaputra' and 'Bhaṭṭāraka' perhaps imply that he was a prince of the royal blood. Yuan Chwang and the 'Mañjuśrī-Mūlakalpa'[2] state that the Huṇa chief Toramāna was captured in the marshy land in the east and Gauḍa. It seems that when western provinces were passing into the hands of the Huṇas and Yaśodharman was rising in Malwa, the last stronghold of the Guptas was Bengal. The proud boast of the court-poet that Yaśodharman's songs of victories resound on the bank of the Lauhitya[3] perhaps refers to his fight with a Gupta king in Bengal.

CHAPTER II

From the Fall of the Guptas to the Rise of the Pālas

The Gupta empire finally broke up about the middle of the sixth century and there arose independent dynasties like the Maitrakas of Vallabhī, the Maukharis and the Later Guptas in different parts of the empire. The four Faridpur plates acquaint us with the names of three Mahārājādhirājas, viz., Gopacandra, Dharmāditya and Samācāradeva, who seem to have been, as Dr. N. K. Bhattasali[1] points out, "related to one another and formed a dynasty." After the publication of the Mallasarula plate of Mahārāja Vijayasena[2] it cannot perhaps be maintained that the kings of the Faridpur plates (at least Gopacandra) were rulers of eastern Bengal only. Palæographically these five plates belong to the same period, i. e., the sixth century A. D. Though two letters just after the name 'Gopa' are lost in the new plate, Mahārājādhirāja Gopa is perhaps to be identified with Gopacandra of the Faridpur plate C of Pargiter. The existence of two Mahārājādhirājas with the same name in the same period is hardly a tenable proposition in the absence of some positive proof. By this plate land transaction was made in the Vardhamāna-bhukti which, roughly speaking, comprised modern Burdwan Division. Further, if the identification of Mahārāja Vijayasena of this record with the Mahārāja of the same name of the Gunaighar grant is to be accepted, the chronological order of the kings of the Faridpur plates, as worked out by Pargiter[3] after careful palæographical examinations, needs be changed. In that case Gopacandra seems to have preceded Dharmāditya, unless the vassal king Vijayasena lived an unusually long life to serve three kings, Vainyagupta

1. EI, VIII, p. 84
2. SPP, 1344 B. S., pp. 17 ff.
3. IA, 1910, pp. 193 ff.

Dharmāditya and Gopacandra, if not more others. If the identification is to be accepted, it seems that Gupta authority in Bengal was supplanted by Gopacandra.

The invasions of Bengal by the Maukhari king Iśānavarman and the Cālukya king Kīrtivarman I most probably took place during the reigns of the three kings of the Faridpur plates. The Haraha inscription[1] of 554 A. D. records that the Gauḍas were compelled by Iśānavarman to take shelter on the sea shore. The Mahakuta inscription,[2] dated in 602 A. D., states that Kīrtivarman I, son of Pulakeśin I, defeated the kings of Aṅga, Vaṅga and Kaliṅga. No other event of the reigns of Gopacandra, Dharmāditya and Samācāradeva is known. Their rise as well as fall remains shrouded in mystery. Two coins in the Indian Museum with the legend 'Narendrāditya' on the reverse may be attributed to Samācāradeva, as the reading of the legend 'Samāca' on the obverse appears to be almost certain.[3]

The chronological position of Mahārājādhirāja Jayanāga of the Vappaghoṣavaṭa grant is not very easy to determine. The alphabets seem to be earlier than those used in the Ganjam plate of Mādhavarāja of 619 A. D. and in the Nidhanpur plates of Bhāskarvarman. It is for the upright character of the letters used in Vappagoṣavaṭa grant that Dr. R. G. Basak[4] is inclined to place Jayanāga before Śaśāṅka. But it must be noted that the 'Mañjuśrī-Mūlakalpa' places Jayanāga immediately after Śaśāṅka. It is difficult to say anything definitely on the chronological position of these two kings from palæographical consideration, as the interval between them appears to be very short. The Vappaghoṣavaṭa grant was issued from Karṇasuvarṇa and records grant of land to Bhaṭṭa Brahmavīrasvāmin by Sāmanta Nārāyaṇabhadra who was in charge of the Audumbarika-viṣaya which has been identified with

1. EI, XIV, pp, 110 ff.
2. IA, XIX, p, 16.
3. EI. XVIII, pp. 79-80 ; Allan, Op. Cit. pp. 149-50.
4. History of North-Eastern India, p. 139.

Audumbar pargana in the Murshidabad district.[1] The coins with the legend 'Jaya' on the obverse and 'Prakāṇḍayaśaḥ' on the reverse may be attributed to Jayanāga.[2]

ŚAŚĀNKA—Śaśāṅka played an important rôle in the history of north-eastern India in the first half of the seventh century. His activities are known in some details from contemporary sources. Bāṇabhatta calls him king of Gauḍa and Yuan Chwang refers to him as ruler of Karṇasuvarṇa which has been identified with Rangamati in the Murshidabad district.

Some scholars attempt to show Śaśāṅka's connection with the Guptas. Buhler noticed in one of the Mss. of the 'Harṣacarita' the name of the king of Gauḍa as Narendragupta.[3] Dr. R. G. Basak[4] is of opinion that the word 'Narendra' has been used by Bāṇa under the garb of a pun to refer to Śaśāṅka, The same provanence and the similar style of the coins of Śaśāṅka with those of the Guptas led R. D. Banerjee[5] to go so far as to assert that he was a son or nephew of Mahāsenagupta. All that can be said is that he seems to have 'Narendra' as his 'virūda' but there is no positive evidence to prove his Gupta lineage. But if Gupta heredity cannot be claimed for him, his heritage was the Gupta imperial tradition which he tried to emulate.

The Rotasgarh seal matrix[6] found in the Shahabad district of Bihar bears an inscription reading "Śrī-mahāsāmanta-śaśāṅka-devasya" [of the illustrious Mahāsāmanta Śaśāṅkadeva]. For palæographical reasons this Mahāsāmanta is to be identified with Śaśāṅka, the rival of Harṣavardhana. The testimony of the Rotasgarh seal-matrix is so great a commentary on his early life that its significance cannot be ignored. To all intents and purposes, it appears that Śāśaṅka began his career as a subordinate chief. The question of finding out the overlord whom he served in his early life is not very easy. The Haraha inscription of Iśāna-

1, EI, XIX, p. 286,
2, Allan, Op, Cit, pp. 150-51,
3. EI. I, p. 70,
4, Op, cit, p, 138,
5. BI, p. 105.
6. CII, III, p, 284,

varman of 554. A. D. and the Deobaranark inscription[1] of Jīvitagupta II indicate the suzerainty of the Maukhari kings Iśānavarman, Sarvavarman and Avantīvarman over Bihar. The latter record clearly shows that the authority of Sarvavarman and Avantīvarman was acknowledged in the Shahabad district. This would indicate that Śaśāṅka was a feudatory of the Maukharis. But it is known from the Apshad inscription of Adityasena[2] that his grandfather Mahāsenagupta described by Bāṇa as king of Mālava defeated Susthitavarman on the bank of the Lauhitya, who is to be identified with the king of Kāmarūpa of that name. Mahāsenagupta's son Mādhavagupta, Susthitavarman's son Bhāskaravarman and Harṣavardhana were contemporaries. Therefore Mahāsenagupta fought with the Kāmarūpa king during the close of the sixth or during the opening years of the seventh century A. D.. Śaśāṅka might have been a feudatory of Mahāsenagupta in the train of whose invasion he came. This may in a way also explain the Rotsgrah seal-matrix of Śaśāṅka.

But the chief sphere of his activities was Gauḍa, as it is clear from Bāṇabhaṭṭa and Yuan Chwang. It is not known how he made himself master of Gauḍa. If Jayanāga preceded him, most probably Śaśāṅka established himself at Karṇasuvarṇa by ousting him or his descendants. At the time of his siege of Kanouj after the death of the Maukhari king Grahavarman and before the accession of Harṣavardhana, Śaśāṅka must have made himself independent and held Gauḍa and Magadha under him. His supremacy over Orissa, which is proved by the Ganjam plates[3] of Mādhavarāja II, dated in 619 A.D., might have been established before his rupture with the Puṣyabhutis of Thāneśvara, by defeating Śambhūya of Patiakella grant, dated in 602 A.D. The prophetic statement in the Mañjuśrī-Mūlakalpa[4] that king Soma (Śaśāṅka) will rule

1. Ibid, p. 218
2. Ibid, No. 42 ; IHQ, XII, p. 457.
3. EI, VI, p. 143 ; IHQ, XII, pp. 459 ff. also EI, XXIII, pp. 197ff,
4. Imperial History of India, p. 49-50, Sl. 715-16.

over the Gangetic valley up to Benares may be taken as implying the north-western boundary of his kingdom in the normal circumstances. According to Yuan Chwang[1], his influence was felt in Kuśīnagara. Śaśāṅka seems to have brought under him the whole of eastern India excepting perhaps Kāmarūpa and Vaṅga. Śaśāṅka's rising importance in the political arena of northern India is also clear from Bāṇa[2] who refers to Śaśāṅkamaṇḍala in describing the meeting of Rājya and Harṣa after former's return from the battle with the Huṇas during the life-time of Prabhākaravardhana.

The use of the word 'Maṇḍala' in this connection is very significant, and if it is to be interpreted in the light of the 'Artha-Śāstra,'[3] it would mean the circle of states headed by Śaśāṅka. In any case, it means the rising importance of this king in the political horizon even before the death of Prabhākaravardhana. This would strengthen the view that there was an alliance between Śaśāṅka and the Mālava king[4] against the Maukharis and the Puṣyabhutis. If there was any connection between the Mālava king Mahāsenagupta and him in his early career, the almost simultaneous marches of a Mālava king and of Śaśāṅka indicate something like a joint operation, which was not perhaps accidental. But the important point against this view is that in the 'Harṣacarita' Rājyavardhana received the news of the death of the Kanouj king Grahavarman, his brother-in-law, caused by the Mālava king who was advancing towards Thāneśvara, and he at once started with 10,000 horsemen to meet the enemy. The only enemy that he knew of at that time

1. Watters, II, p. 43.   2. Harṣacarita, Ch. VI.

3. Kauṭilya, Bk. VII, Ch. II.

4. As regards the identity of this Mālava king, scholars so long took him to be Devagupta who has been mentioned as one of the kings defeated by Rājyavardhana (Madhuvan inscription, EI, VI, 210). Recently Dr. D. C. Ganguli has expressed the opinion that the Mālava king was Kalacuri Budharāja, son of Saṅkaragaṇa. There is no doubt that these two kings were in possession of Ujjayinī and western Mālava. But it may be that Devagupta was a king of eastern Mālava (EI, IX, p. 285 ; JBORS, XIX. pp. 405 ff ; IHQ, XII, p. 461).

was the Mālava king and Bāṇabhaṭṭa does not at all allude to the activities of Śaśāṅka. The next news from Kanouj was that though the Mālava army had been easily routed, Rājyavardhana "was allured to confidence by false civilities on the part of the king of Gauḍa, and then weaponless, confiding, and alone, despatched in his own quarters". It is also clear from the 'Harṣacarita' that Rājyavardhana found Kanouj besieged by Śaśāṅka, as the Gauḍa trouble has been definitely mentioned by Bāṇa. The march of Śaśāṅka on Kanouj from Karṇasuvarṇa must have taken a long time, and if there was a concerted action, it seems that the Mālava king was earlier to arrive at the scene of action and did not wait for his ally. But it must also be said that the court of Thāneśvara was unaware of any such joint action, and Rājyavardhana after defeating the Mālava army sent the trusted general Bhaṇḍī with the booty and a part of his army and himself proceeded towards Kanouj without any knowledge of the impending danger from the Gauḍa king. This would indicate that the actions of Śaśāṅka and Mālava king were not connected in any way.

The Śaśāṅka-Rājyavardhana episode has been discussed by many scholars and two sets of opinions have come out of previous discussions. Mr. C. V. Vaidya[1], Dr. R. G. Basak[2] and Dr. D. C. Ganguli[3] accept the statement of Bāṇa (mentioned above), who further says[4] that the death of Rājyavardhana was due to carelessness on his part. In this connection he cites the examples of some careless kings of ancient times and their dealings with women. These scholars find corroboration of Bāṇa, when Saṅkara, one of the commentators of the 'Harṣacarita' in the fourteenth century, explains those passages by introducing Śaśāṅka's marriage proposal of his daughter to Rājyavardhana and says that he was murdered, while enjoying a feast in the former's camp. Further corroboration is to be found, in their opinion, in Yuan Chwang's account

1. Medieval India, I, p. 4.
2. History of North-Eastern India, pp. 144-50.
3. IHQ, XII, pp. 462-64.
4. Cowell, Eng. Trans. of Harṣacarita, p. 192.

and Harṣavardhana's inscription. The Chinese pilgrim records, "Śaśāṅka addressed his ministers in these words,[1] 'If a frontier country has a virtuous ruler, this is the unhappiness of the mother kingdom.' On this they asked the king to a conference and murdered him." Harṣavardhana's inscription[2] records that "he gave up his life in his enemy's house, owing to his adherence to his promise (satyānurodhena)".

Rai Bahadur R. P. Chanda, R. D. Banerjee and Dr. R. C. Majumdar[3] are of opinion that both Bāṇa and Yuan Chwang were biased against Śaśāṅka who was the adversary of their patron Harṣavardhana, and therefore much reliance cannot be placed on their accounts in this particular matter. Rājyavardhana had a small army with him after his fight with the Mālava king and was defeated in a fair fight and there was nothing unfair in his death. It may be said in support of their view that there is some force in their argument. Bāṇa does not refer to Śaśaṅka in very honourable terms when he calls him 'vile Gauḍa' ('Gauḍādhama') or the serpent of Gauḍa' (Gauḍa-bhujaṅga). It is not known what was the source of information of the commentator Saṅkara's reference to the marriage proposal. If the remarks of Bāṇa on Śaśāṅka are to be doubted, the veracity of the comentator to explain them by referring to a marriage proposal in an abnormal circumstance can be further questioned.

A mystery hangs over this episode and it is rather difficult to be definite. It is clear that Saśāṅka must have marched on Kanouj at the head of a large army and there is nothing to show that he went with the intention of staging a marriage ceremony of his daughter (at least there is no scent of it in the 'Harṣacarita' and Yuan Chwang's accounts). We would rather suggest that the death of Rājyavardhana is to be sought in the rash and hasty policy pursued or in his 'carelessness', as Bāṇa puts it. He was not

1. Beal, Records, pp, 210-211 ; Watters, I, p, 343 ; Life, p. 83.
2. EI, VI p, 210,
3. Gauḍarājamālā, pp, 8-10 ; Early Hist, of Beng, pp, 17-18 ; BI, p, 107,

aware of Śaśāṅka's plan and most probably unprepared to fight with him, which would have meant defeat, and therefore agreed or was forced to meet the Gauḍa king in a 'conference', as Yuan Chwang reports. What happened in that conference is not known but he was perhaps asked to give up the Maukhari alliance, which he could not do, confirmed as it was by the marriage of his sister Rājyaśrī with the Maukhari king Grahavarman. After the death of the Maukhari king he also could not put back the claim of his sister to the throne of Kanouj. This perhaps brought about his death, which has been described in Harṣavardhana's inscription as "due to adherence to his promise." The political union of Thāṇeśvar and Kanouj was certainly a dread to a king who aspired after the overlordship of northern India and the campaign of Śaśāṅka was undertaken with that object in view. This may also in a way explain why Bāṇabhaṭṭa and Yuan Chwang could not specifically mention the cause of Rājyavardhana's death, for it would not reflect any credit on his political sagacity and wisdom, and they have refered to it as due to carelessness and murder in a conference.

What happened after the death of Rājyavardhana is not known[1] and why Śaśāṅka retired from Kanouj cannot be explained. The news of the death of his brother enraged Harṣavardhana and the Thāneśvara court. He prepared himself with a large army to

1, Dr. D C. Ganguli is inclined to identify the noble man of the name Gupta with Devagupta who, according to him, occupied Kanouj, Śaśāṅka was between the two enemies and got out of the critical situation by murdering Rājyavardhana in an unfair way. But Dr. Ganguli does not explain who this Devagupta was and how he occupied Kanouj. It is also to be noted that then Śaśāṅka had to fight with Devagupta after Rājyavardhana's death. There is nothing to indicate that Śasāṅka fought with Davagupta The Mālava army was routed by Rājyavardhana after whose death Devagupta, (whom we have suggested to be a ruler of eastern Mālava) and Śasāṅka were perhaps in possession of Kanouj, if there was an alliance between them. It should also be said there is no strong reason to identify the noble man of the Gupta family with Devagupta. He might have been an officer under the Gauḍa king under whose orders Rājyaśrī was released from prison.

fight with Śaśāṅka with the vow "unless in a limited number of days I clear this earth of the Gauḍas, and make it resound with fetters on the feet of all kings who are excited to insolence by the elasticity of their vows, then will I hurl my sinful self, like a moth, into an oil-fed flame." He ordered Bhaṇḍī to advance as he himself had to search for his sister. After the rescue of his sister from the Vindhyā forest we find him receiving an envoy of the Kāmarūpa king. A close study of the 'Harṣacarita' reveals the fact that Harṣa like Rājya did not hastily proceed against Śaśaṅka. In spite of the grandiloquent description of the vows of revenge, calumniations and fulminations of the court of Thāneśvara it is clear that Harṣa first consulted the trusted counsellors and veterans of war. Though it is difficult to say at whose initiative the alliance with Kāmarūpa took place, it is clear from the manner in which Haṁsavega, the Kāmarūpa envoy, was presented before Harṣa and from the discussions between the two parties that the latter was no less eager than the other side to form this 'entente', as both were in dread of the aggressive policy of the Gauḍa monarch.

The late Mr. R. D. Banerjee[1] was of opinion that Harṣa and Bhāskaravarman occupied Karṇasuvarṇa by defeating Śaśāṅka immediately after which he retired to Ganjam. But the Ganjam plate of 619 A. D. rather shows that Śaśāṅka was in full enjoyment of his imperial power upto that date. We are rather inclined to accept the opinion of Dr. D. C. Ganguli[2] that Harṣa had to undertake two campaigns against Gauḍa. In his first campaign during the life-time of Śaśāṅka he could not achieve anything tangible. Bāṇa is silent on the result of this campaign against the Gauḍa king, though he refers to his conquest of Sindh and the Himalayan countries.[3] Yuan Chwang says that after the anti-Budhistic activities of Śaśāṅka in Magadha Purṇavarman, the last descendant of Aśoka, was on the throne of Magadha. The pilgrim

1. History of Orissa, I, p. 129. 2. IHQ, XII, pp. 465-67.
3. Cowell, Op. Cit. p. 76.

visited Magadha for the first time in 637 A. D. and refers to Śaśāṅka as a recent king.[1] All these go to show that the Gauḍa king could successfully hold himself against Harṣa. But in another connection he reports[2] that "Śīlāditya held his court here (Kajangala), cut grass to make huts and burned these when leaving." If the author of the "Mañjuśrī-Mūlakalpa" is to be believed, Harṣa even advanced upto Puṇḍra, to the great distress of the people. This seems to have happened on the occasion of another campaign in the east, otherwise this cannot be satisfactorily reconciled with the evidence of the Ganjam plate and the account of Yuan Chwang. It must also be noted that nothing is known of Śaśāṅka after 619 A. D. excepting that Yuan Chwang refers to him as a recent king in 638 A. D. It is also clear from the pilgrim's account that he died a natural death.

The bull symbol of his coins shows that Śaśāṅka was a Śaiva. Both Yuan Chwang and the author of the "Mañjuśrī-Mūlakalpa"[3] are vehement in their accusation of persecution of the Buddhists by this king. The Chinese pilgrim says that Harṣa got an oracle from the image of a Bodhisattva to the effect that he should accept the throne to save Buddhism from the ruin brought about by Śaśāṅka. But Bāṇa would make us believe that Harṣa consented to ascend the throne only to avenge the foul murder of Rājya by the Gauḍa king. Speaking of Kuśīnagara, the pilgrim reports that the groups of the brethren were broken up. Further, he is said to have cut the Bodhi Tree, destroyed its roots down to the water and burnt what remained. He also destroyed the foot-prints of Buddha at Pāṭaliputra. These are the specific charges mentioned by Yuan Chwang, and for his anti-Buddhistic activities he had to die a very miserable death and was even taken to task in hell. But when speaking of Puṇḍravardhana, Karṇasuvarṇa and Tāmralipti and other places of Magadha which were also included in his dominion, Yuan Chwang does not refer to any oppression and

1. Ibid, p. 183.
2. Watters. II, p. 115.
3. Op. Cit.

finds Buddhism in flourishing condition. If there would have been a wholesale persecution, there is no reason why the Buddhists of Bodh-Gaya and Kuśinagara were singled out. Rai Bahadur R. P. Chanda and R. D. Banerjee[1] expressed the opinion that most probably the Buddhists of those places conspired against Śaśāṅka and had sympathy with Harṣavardhana who was after all a pro-Buddhist king. These two scholars therefore hold that the motive behind the persecution was rather political necessity than religious conviction. Similar cases are not wanting in Indian history. When describing Hiranaparvata[2] (near Mongyr), Yuan Chwang says that in recent times the king of a neighbouring country had deopsed the ruler and given the capital to the Buddhist brethren. It is not known why the ruling king was deposed and who was the deposer. But the very fact that the capital was given to the Buddhist brethren rouses a suspicion of conspiracy by the Buddhists with the neighouring king against the ruler of the locality. In 1581 A. D. during the reign of Akbar[3] mosques of Bengal and Guzrat became centres of political meetings and Akbar was even declared deposed. There was no other way but to close the mosques and even in some cases they were demolished. These extreme measures were regarded by the orthodox Mussalmans of his time as anti-Islamic and nothing more than that. In reality, political necessity compelled Akbar to take these measures. The real motive behind the anti-Buddhistic activities of Saśāṅka cannot be judged, until we know of them from other sources. To Yuan Chwang all these were sacrilegious and the 'Mañjusrī-Mūlakalpa' is an out-and-out Buddhist book in which everything has been put in the mouth of Lord Buddha in the form of prophecy.

Such in outline is the career and reign of Śaśāṅka. The details are still lacking. But in spite of the charge of treacherous murder of Rājyavardhana and accusation of the persecution of the

1. Gauḍārājamālā, pp. 11-13 ; BI, p. 110
2. Watters, II, p. 178
3. V. A. Smith, Oxford History of India, p. 358

Buddhists, he was no less a dazzling and important figure than his great rival Harṣa. It is clear that his account comes from the manifestly hostile camp. The key-note to his character was the ambition of founding an empire and he succeeded considerably in realising it at first, but his plan was upset by a combination of Harṣa and Bhāskaravarman.

The Period of Anarchy—Yuan Chwang visited five principalities of Bengal viz., Kajangala (north-eastern part of Santal parganas and Rajmahal), Puṇḍravardhana, Samataṭa, Karṇasuvarṇa and Tāmralipti. He does not refer to any ruling kings and to their political status. From this it has been concluded by some writers that Bengal formed a part of Harṣa's empire. But the view that Bengal was under the Kāmarūpa king Bhāskaravarman seems to rest on a stronger basis. The land granted by the Nidhanpur plates has been definitely located in Pañcakhaṇḍa in the Sylhet district.[1] These plates were issued from the camp of victory situated at Karṇasuvarṇa. Bhāskaravarman has been called the king of 'eastern India' and he promised safe conduct to the pilgrim up to Tāmralipti.[2] All these point to the establishment of his authority over Bengal. This seems to be more reasonable than the other view which rests on the general statement of Yuan Chwang that Harṣa conquered five Indies.[3] Whoever might have exercised suzerainty, it seems clear that after the death of Śaśāṅka his kingdom was divided into many petty principalities.

1. JASB, 1935, pp. 419 ff.

2. IC, II, p. 38 ; IA, 1880, p. 20 ; IHQ, XII, p 73 ; Beal, Life, p. 188.

3. Scholars differ as to the time of the occupation of Karṇasuvarṇa by Bhāskaravarman. Dr. Basak holds that Harṣa conquered Karṇasuvarṇa with his help and handed it over to him. R. D. Banerjee expressed the opinion that Harṣa and Bhāskaravarman occupied the capital of Śaśāṅka by joint operation. Dr. Majumdar is of opinion that Bhāskaravarman occupied Karṇasuvarṇa after the death of Harṣa in 647 A. D. who would not have allowed his ally to be dangerously powerful (see History of North-Eastern India, pp. 153, 227 ; History of Orissa, I, p. 122 ; Early History of Bengal, p. 20)

The Tippera grant of Lokanātha is to be palæographically assigned to the seventh century.[1] This record introduces us to a Nātha family who ruled as feudatories[2] for three generations before Lokanātha. The first member of the family is called 'Ādi-Mahārāja but his name is lost. His son was Srīnātha whose son Bhàvanātha was of religious temperament and took to ascetic life. Lokanātha was placed in charge of administration but it is not clear whether he was the son or brother's son of Bhavanātha. Verses 7-9 describe the exploits and achievements of Lokanātha. The army of the 'Parameśvara' (his suzerain) met with discomfiture repeatedly at his hands. He fought a successful fight against one Jayatuṅgavarṣa who seems to be a local chief like Lokanātha himself but cannot be identified. Another chief named Jīva-dharaṇa is said to have given up hostilities against Lokanātha in consideration of his success against Jayatuṅgavarṣa, his confirmation by a royal charter (most probably by the suzerain) and the love and affection of his subjects towards him. Jīvadharaṇa followed the principle that prudence is the better part of valour, as there was perhaps very little chance of success against Lokanātha, but the composer of the praśasti in a clever way eulogised his patron by putting everything through the mouth of the adversary of Lokanātha. The land granted by the Tippera plate was situated in the Suvvaṅga-viṣaya which cannot be located and it may be provisionally held that this family ruled in Tippera or in a neighbouring locality.

1. The plate bears a date. Dr. Basak read it as 44 at first. But just before the letters signifying 44 the word 'adhika' occurs. Prof. Bhandarkar suggested that the date is 144 and Dr. Basak now reads 344 and refers it to the Gupta era. We are inclined to accept this and this would place it in 663-4 A.D.

2. The seal attached to the plate bears an inscription reading 'kumārāmātya' but it is written in early Gupta script. Dr. Thomas concluded that it "was issued from the office of the 'kumārāmātya' of Lokanātha's overlord and only countersigned by Lokanātha." (EI, XV, p. 303 fn). But Dr. Basak maintains that the opening words 'kumārāmātya'in prose portions refers to the feudatory chief Lokanātha himself. The fact remains that Lokanātha and his ancestors were feudatories. (History of North-Eastern India, p. 95).

The Asrafpur plates of the Khaḍgas and the Deulbadi Sarvāṇī image inscription of Queen Prabhāvatī supply the information about another dynasty ruling over at least some portion of Dacca and Tippera districts. These records have been palæographically examined by the present writer[1] in details, and it has been shown that the alphabets represent an earlier variety then those used in the Khalimpur plate of Dharmapāla. The Khaḍgas ruled for four generations and therefore can be assigned to the period between 625-725 A. D.[2] The Asrafpur plates were issued from Karmāntavāsaka which has been identified with Baḍkamta in the Tippera district.[3] The first known member of the family is Khaḍgodyama who has been discribed in the Deulbadi inscription as 'nṛpādhirāja' and as a great conqueror. It may be that the family rose into political importance under him. His son Jātakhāḍga is said to have defeated his enemies whose son Devakhaḍga donated land to the Buddhist monastery of Saṁghamitra for the longevity of his son Rājarājabhaṭa. The prince after his accession confirmed the grant and is to be identified with Rājabhaṭa, the devout Buddhist king of Samataṭa, who was highly spoken of by the Chinese traveller Sen-chi during his visit towards the close of the seventh century. The fact that the name Khaḍga sounds un-Indian and that a caste of that name can be traced in Nepal in the 14th century led Dr. R. C. Majumdar[4] to presume "that the Khaḍga dynasty came to eastern Bengal in the trains of the Tibetans and the Nepalese during the troublesome days that followed the death of Harṣavardhana."

1. DUS. 1. No. p 54.

2. Dr. Basak rightly says that the first symbol of the two letters signifying the year of the second Asrafpur plate remains a puzzle and cannot be satisfactorily explained unless we agree with Dr. Majumdar to read it as 73 or 79 by following Bendall's chart of numerical symbols. 'History of North-Eastern India,' p. 203 ; JASB 1928. pp. 375ff.

3. EI, XVII. pp. 357ff.

4. Early History of Bengal, p. 124

But it must be said that there is no proof to connect the Khaḍga dynasty with Nepal.

In the Tippera plate there is a reference to Lokanātha's defiance of the authority of the suzerain whose army was many times defeated by this feudatory chief. In the second Asrafpur plate there is a reference to the 'Bṛhatparameśvara' and the higest officials whom the Khaḍgas could command were the 'viṣayapatis'. From these it appears that Samataṭa in the latter half of the seventh century was divided into many principalities under a suzerain power. The dynasty which exercised overlordship over Samataṭa is not known. It has been asserted that Bengal was under Kāmarūpa kings from Bhāskaravarman's occupation of Karṇasuvarṇa to the time of Harṣa of the Bhagadatta dynasty, who has been described as the lord of Gauḍa, Oḍra, Kaliṅga and Kośala in the Pasupati temple inscription of 759 A. D.[1] It may be argued that the Later Guptas from the reign of Ādityasena exercised overlordship over some portion of Bengal, as it is clear from the Apsadh (Gaya district) Shahpur (Patna district) and Mandar (Bhagalpur district) inscriptions that there was a great revival of his power in north-eastern India.[2]

While eastern Bengal was parcelled into many small principalities fighting among themselves and setting at naught the shadowy authority of the overlord, the condition of Gauḍa was perhaps not better in any way. The 'Mañjuśrī-Mūlakalpa'[3] correctly records that after the reign of Śaśāṅka the 'Gauḍatantra' (system) was paralysed. It refers to many kings of Gauḍa most of whom are mentioned by initials only and therefore they connot be identified, as they are otherwise unknown. What deserves particular notice is that the reigns of most of them lasted for months and days and not even a year. During the reign of one king named Śiśu it

1. IC, II, pp37-45.
2. IHQ, XII, p. 74 ; History of North-Eastern India, pp. 125-26.
3. Imperial History of India, sl. 735-58.

is said that the influence of women would be felt and he would rule for a fortnight and then would be killed. To crown the misery of the people, it is predicted that a severe famine would visit the eastern country. This certainly points to the absence of any stable government in Gauḍa. Might was right and there was disorder and anarchy, and this is just the state of things which has been very appropriately described in the Khalimpur plate of Dhamapāla as 'matsyanyāya'. By this significant term the ancient writers used to express the extreme state of anarchy and chaos. Tārānātha describes the condition of Bengal just before the election of Gopāla in the following way, "There was no longer any member of it (the royal family of the Candras) a king ; in Oḍivisa, in Bengal and the other provinces to the east, each Kṣatriya, Brahman, and merchant constituted himself king of his surroundings, but there was no king ruling the country."[1]

The weakness of the political power of Gauḍa naturally invited many foreign invasions by neighbouring powerful potentates. Three or four invasions of this period are definitely known. It is stated in the Ragholi plates that a king of Śailavaṁśa killed the king of Puṇḍra. The first known member of the family is Śrīvardhana I and his son Pṛthuvardhana attacked Guzrat. In that family was born Sauvardhana (his exact relationship with Pṛthuvardhana is not known). Three sons of Sauvardhana played havoc on three kingdoms. One killed the king of Puṇḍra. Another conquered the king of Kāśī and Jayavardhana I defeated the king of Vindhyā. His son was Śrīvardhana II, and his grandson, Jayavardhana II, who was the donor of the grant and is to be assigned in the last part of the eighth century A. D. Therefore Jayavardhana I and his brothers may be placed in the first part of the eighth or in the last part of the seventh century. It was in this period that the king of Puṇḍra was killed. It is not known whether the unnamed Śaila prince established himself on the throne of northern Bengal.

2. IA. IV. pp. 365-66.

Vākpati in his 'Gauḍa-vaho' narrates the defeat and slaughter of the king of Gauḍa by his patron Yaśovarman of Kanouj. The important point to notice in that book is that the king of Gauḍa has been called 'Magadhanātha'[1] also. This shows that in the second quarter of the eighth century Gauḍa and Magadha were politically united. Vākpati further informs that Yaśovarman defeated the king of Vaṅga. Most probably Magadha was annexed to the dominion of the Kanouj king. The Nālandā inscription[2] of Mālaḍa, a son of the minister of Yaśovarman, records some gifts to the temple of Bālāditya at that famous monastery there. Even during the time of Devapāla there was a towu called Yaśovarmapur in Bihar.

But the Kanouj king could not long enjoy the fruits of his victory as he was defeated by the Kāśmīra king Lalitāditya,[3] and Kalhaṇa says that in course of his 'digvijaya' the Kāśmīra king reached the sea-shore. But it is doubtful whether Lalitāditya conquered Bengal. We are told that after the defeat of Yaśovarman Lalitāditya's army proceeded with ease to the eastern ocean and reached Kaliṅga. Numerous elephants joined him from the Gauḍa country, as if attracted by friendship for their comrades.[4] This rather implies friendly assistance by the Gauḍa king to Lalitāditya in his Kaliṅga expedition. The poet narrates a heroic episode connecting the Kāśmīra king and an unnamed Gauḍa king and a band of thirty loyal followers and it may be that there is some historical truth in this episode, though it does not prove definitely the authority of Lalitāditya over

1. Dr. R. C. Majumdar points out that Yaśovarman first met his eastern enemy near the Vindhyās and this he explains by suggesting that a branch of the Śaila family which ruled over northern Bengal had settled itself in the Vindhyā region and the Gauḍa king who added Magadha to his dominions sided with his kinsmen. Early History of Bengal, p. 25.). The defeated king of Gauḍa may be also identified with Jīvitagupta II of the Later Gupta dynasty.

2. EI, XX, p. 37.

3. Rājataraṅgiṇī, IV. 144.

4. Ibid, IV, vs. 146-48.

Gauḍa. The Gauḍa king visited Kāśmīra on his request and on the promise of safety of his own person in Kāśmīra, the image of Viṣṇu Parihāsakeśava being made surety of Lalitāditya's faith. But the Gauḍa king was treacherously murdered by Lalitāditya. Thirty loyal and brave followers of the Gauḍa king went to Kāśmīra on the pretext of pilgrimage and had their revenge fulfilled by breaking the idol of Viṣṇu Rāmasvāmin which they mistook for that of Parihāsakeśava. They fought bravely when the army came from the capital and died a glorious and heroic death. Kalhaṇa[1] exclaims, "Even the creator cannot achieve what the Gauḍas did on that occasion. Even to this day the temple of Rāmasvāmin is empty, whereas the whole world is filled with the fame of Gauḍa heroes." The fact that Kalhaṇa pays so eloquent a tribute to the Gauḍa heroes because of the great impression it produced in the eighth century indicates that there was some truth in this episode. The story of Jayapīḍa's stay in disguise at the house of a courtesan in the city of Puṇḍravardhana, the revelation of his identity on his killing a fierce lion, his marriage with Kalyāṇadevī, daughter of the Gauḍa king Jayanta, and his conquest of Pañca-Gauḍas for his father-in-law, reads like a romance, and it is to be doubted if there is any historical truth in this romantic tale.

Another invasion of Gauḍa was by Harṣadeva. The Pasupati temple inscription of Jayadeva,[2] dated in 759 A. D., describes his father-in-law Harṣadeva of the Bhagadatta dynasty as lord of Gauḍa, Oḍra, Kaliṅga and Kośala. As the kings of Kāmarūpa claim descent from the epic hero Bhagadatta, Harṣadeva may be regarded as a king of Kāmarūpa.

The extent of the depredations and devastations of these invasions can be better understood with reference to the results of the excavations at Paharpur and Mahasthanagar. The excavated sites have revealed the existence of magnificent buildings of the Gupta and post Gupta periods at both these places. The remains are enough to show that the old structures were desolated in the subsequent period and on their ruins new ones were erected in the Pāla period. This was perhaps due to a calamity like the depredations of a foreign army.[3]

1. Ibid, IV. Vs. 332, 335. 2. IA, IX. p. 178 ; IHQ. 1931, p. 664.

3. IC. II, pp. 518 ff. ; Mr. A C. Banerjee is of opinion that the invasion of the Saila king was more serious and disastrous in consequences.

CHAPTER III

The Pāla Dynasty

In their inscriptions the Pālas do not claim descent from any mythical figure or epic hero like contemporary dynasties. The Khalimpur plate of Dharmapāla informs us that Gopāla I, the founder of the dynasty, was the son of 'khaṇḍitārāti (killer of enemies) Vapyaṭa and grandson of 'sarva-avadāta' Dayitaviṣṇu. From this it seems that before Gopāla I this family was not of much importance. Mm. H. P. Shastri found in the end of the 32nd chapter of the commentary[1] on 'Aṣṭasāhasaikā-Prajñāpāramitā' by Haribhadra that Dharmapāla has been described as 'Rājabhaṭādi-vaṁśa-patita'. The Ms. is in a Katmandu library and is written in the 11th or 12th century script in the Traikūṭa-vihāra. Scholars have generally taken this Dharmapāla to be the second Pāla king and tried to establish some connection of the dynasty with Rājarājabhaṭa of the Khaḍga family of Samataṭa. But there is difference of opinion about the meaning of the expression, 'Rājabhaṭādi-vaṁśa-patita'. Mm. H. P. Shastri was of opinion that it denotes remote connection with Rājabhaṭa and rendered the passage to mean that Dharmapāla belonged to the family of a military officer of some king. Mr. N. N. Vasu[2] is of opinion that Dharmapāla came of the family of Rājabhaṭa, while another writer[3] thinks that the Pālas were connected with him through the female line. It appears strange that

1. The śloka runs thus :--

   Rājye Rājabhaṭādi-vaṁśa-patita Śrī Dharmapālasya vai
   Tattva-loka-vidhāyinī viractia sat-panjikeyam mayā

   See MASB, III, p. 6

2. VJI, Rājanya Kāṇḍa, p. 147

3. IHQ, VII, p. 533 ; see for some interesting suggestions on this point by the present writer, IC, II, pp. 795 ff.

if there had been any such connection of the Pālas with a previous ruling dynasty, the court-poets failed to mention that in their panegyrics. It is therefore reasonable to hold that Gopāla I came of a 'plebian' family.

Recently there have been some discussions about the caste of the Pālas. Their inscriptions are silent on this point. The Mañju-śrī-Mūlakalpa'[1] calls Gopāla I a 'śūdra'. According to Abul Fazl, the Pālas were Kāyasthas.[2] Mr N. N. Vasu accepts the statement of Akbar's court historian, but, for the history of the Hindu period his statements are not much valued. The 'Rāmacarita' of Sandhyākaranandī describes Dharmapāla as 'Samudra-kula-dīpa,'[3] and in the commentary of the same verse he is compared with Ikṣvāku. It is stated in the Kamauli plate of Vaidyadeva that the Pālas belonged to the solar dynasty (Mihirasya-vaṁśa).[4] Sandhyākaranandī and Vaidyadeva flourished in the 12th century and were intimately connected with the Pāla court. In a passage of the Udayasundarī-kathā of the Guzrat poet Soddhala of the 11th century it seems that Dhrmapāla has been described as belonging to the Māndhātṛ-vaṁśa.[5] Mr J. C. Ghose[6] says that mythologically the sea-god and Māndhātā belonged to the family of the sun and therefore concludes that the Pālas belonged to the solar dynasty, as there is agreement in the above accounts. Ghanarāma in his 'Dharmamaṅgala', written in 1713 A. D., narrates that Devapāla was the illegitimate son of Dharmapāla through the union of his wife with the sea-god. R. D. Banerjee[7] was of opinion that most probably the Pālas came from the sea and in the absence of any plausible account of their ancestry, they became known in popular tradition as the children of the sea-god. It must be said that the Pālas were

---

1. Vs. 683-90.

2. Jarret, 'Ain-i-Akbari,' II, pp. 145 ; N. N. Vasu, 'Rājanya-Kāṇḍa, p' 151

3. 1/4.

4. Kamauli plate, verse 2.

5. Kathañcana valīyasa saptāṅga-samagren-Ottarapathasvāmina Māndhātṛ-vaṁśa-prabhavena bhubhṛta Dharmapālena saha vigraho dīrghatām-āvāpa. published in G. O. S., p. 4.

6. IHQ, IX, pp. 479 ff.

7. BI, I, p. 163.

Buddhists and it is not to be expected that they should mention their caste like the Brahmanical ruling dynaties. But though their inscriptions are silent, Sandhyākaranandī and Vaidyadeva tried to prove the Kṣatriyahood of their masters. For about four centuries the Pālas performed the functions of the Kṣatriyas and contracted matrimonial relationship with the Rāṣṭrkūṭas and Kalacuris. If they were not 'de jure' Kṣatriyas, 'de facto' Kṣatriyahood can be claimed for them, although it is to be noted that their religious system did not recognise the caste divisions of the Brahmanical religion.

Tāranātha says that Gopāla was elected to the vacant throne of Vaṅga some years after the rule of the Candra dynasty. His evidence is not reliable unless it is corroborated by some other sources. Sandhyākaranandī's 'Rāmacarita'[1] and the Kamauli grant[2] refer to Verendra as the 'Janakabhū' (fatherland) of the Pālas, and from this it would seem that northern Bengal was their original home. The Tibetan historian further records that Gopāla extended his power over Magadha. The extension of power from Varendra to Magadha was natural rather than from Vaṅga to Magadha.

It is pretty sure that Gopāla must have given ample proof of his military ability and political wisdom before his election to the throne by the 'prakṛtis' (which we are inclined to take in the light of Śukra's interpretation of the term as denoting chief officers of the state—at most the sane and sober section or the leaders of the people[3]) at the most critical juncture when the very existence of the kingdom was at stake. This unmistakably shows that he was the only man who was thought competent to cope with the situation. It is quite probable that Gopāla might have come into prominence by warding off one of the foreign invasions that preceded his rise. It has been suggested[4] that in the first verse of

1. 1/38 ; 1/50. 2. 4th verse. 3. See Ch. on Administration.

4. IHQ, VII, pp. 533 ff.

Jitvā yah kāmakāri-prabhavem abhibhavam śāśvatīm prāpa śāntim
Sa Śrīmān Lokanātha jayati Daśavalonyaśca Gopāldevaḥ.

the Bhagalpur grant of Nārāyaṇapāla a pun has been used on the word 'kāmakāri', and in case of Buddha it refers to Māra, while it may refer to king Harṣa of Kāmrūpa in case of Gopāla. Tārānātha most probably confused Harṣa of Kāmrūpa with Harṣa of Kāśmīra who, according to him, was a contemporary of Gopāla.[1] He must have been a man of unusual abilities which commanded respects from his contemporaries.

The spirit of the inscriptions points out that he proved himself equal to the occasion and the confidence that was reposed in him was amply justified. We do not know who were the enemies against whom he had to fight, but his military preparations and campaigns are alluded to in the Mongyr plate of Devapāla, which further records that he extended the boundary of his kingdom upto the sea-coast. If Tārānātha is to be believed, Magadha was also annexed. If he cannot be credited with any great political achievement, it seems that peace and order was restored after a period of misrule and anarchy, and a strong consolidated kingdom was left, thus making the task of his successor Dharmapāla easier in order to take an active part in north-Indian politics. According to Tārānātha, Gopāla ruled for 45 years. It seems that he was sufficiently advanced in age before his election. The 'Mañjuśrī-Mūlakalpa'[2] records that he died at the age of eighty after a reign of 27 years. He was succeeded by his son Dharmapāla.

The outstanding political fact of the period from 750 to 950 A. D. was the tripartite struggle among the three great powers, the Prathihāras, the Pālas and the Rāṣṭrakūṭas, for imperial suzerainty of northern India and for the possession of Kanauj, the imperial city of the time. Dharmapāla inherited a consolidated kingdom, and it seems that his ambition was to make Bengal the suzerain power in northern India. Naturally he turned his attention to the west. It is not known which were the powers with whom he had to fight at first for the westward expansion of his kingdom. The

1. Schienfner, Tārānātha, pp. 195 ff,

2. Vs. 683-90.

Gawalior praśasti[1] informs that Pratihāra Vatsarāja wrested the sovereignty of Kanauj from Bhaṇḍīkula. Dharmapāla must have regarded him as a rival, but in the encounter the Pāla king was defeated. We know from the Wani and Radhanpur plates[2] that Rāṣṭrakūṭa Dhruva defeated Vatsarāja who had inflicted a defeat on the Gauḍa king. But though defeated in his first attempt, Dharmapāla did not give up his imperial ambition and made further attempts to occupy Kanauj, because not long after this we find him in the possession of the Ganges-Yamuna Doab. The Sanjan plates of Amoghavarṣa record that the Gauḍa king was defeated by Dhruva in the Ganges-Yamuna valley[3] and this is confirmed by the Baroda and Surat plates of Karkarāja.[4] Chronologically it stands thus that in the westward expansion of his kingdom Dharmapāla received two checks—first from Vatsarāja and next from Dhruva. Dhurva attacked Vatsarāja in C. 789 A. D., and therefore Dharmapāla was defeated by Vatsarāja before that. Durva died before May, 794 A. D.,[5] and he must have defeated the Pāla king before that date.

But nothing could arrest the political expansion of Bengal, reinvigorated and regenerated as it was from the political turmoil after the election of Gopāla. The Pālas were determined to assert themselve in north Indian politics and make Bengal a first class political power. The Pratihāra king was driven into the desert by Dhurva and the next Rāṣṭrakūṭa king Govinda III was engaged in a fratricidal war for succession with his brother Stambha,[6] and thus the time was opportune for Dharmapāla. The 7th verse of the Mongyr plate of Devapāla states that his (Dharmapāla's) army in course of 'digvijaya' visited Kedāra (in the Himalayas) and Gokarṇa which has been sought to be identified with Gokarṇa-tīrtha

1. EI, XVIII, p. 101
2. Ibid, VI, p. 244 ; IA., XI, p. 157.
3. EI., XVIII, p. 250
4. IA., XII, p. 160 ; EI., XX, p. 145
5. Dr, Altekar, The Rāṣṭrakūṭas and their times p. 56.
6. Ibid., p. 61.

in Nepal, Gokarṇa in the Bombay Presidency and in Orissa.[1] The 12th verse of the Khalimpur plate enumerates the countries that actually acknowledged his overlordship. It is told that "with a sign of his gracefully moved eyebrows he installed the illustrious king of Kānya-kubja, who readily was accepted by the kings of Bhoja (Vidarbha), Matsya (Jaipur), Madra (E. Panjab), Kuru (Delhi region), Yadu (Mathurā),Yavana (W.Panjab), Avantī (Malwa) Gāndhāra (Taxila) and Kīra (Kangra valley),[2] bowing down respectfully with their diadems trembling and for whom his own golden coronation jar was lifted by the delighted elders of Pāñcāla'.[3] Further light on the whole situation is thrown by the 3rd verse of the Bhagalpur plate of Nārāyāṇapāla. It is known therefrom that Dharmapāla took possession of Kanauj from Indrarāja[4] and installed his own 'protege' Cakrāyudha on its throne by calling an imperial assembly. His overlordship was acknowledged, and the war of 'digvijaya' he had to undertake for this purpose speaks of the stupendousness of the task. The supreme political achievement was sanctified by holding the imperial assembly at Kanauj.

The undisputed sovereignty of Dharmapāla over northern

1. 'IC,' IV, pp. 264-67.

2. The Kīra country has been identified with Kīragrāma or Bajinath in the Kangra district by Dr. R. C. Majumdar '(IHO, IX, p, 11.)

3. Two interpretations of this verse are possible. According to the other, it seems that Dharmapāla himself was installed on the throne of Kanauj.

4. Dr. R. C. Majumdar identified Indrarāja with the prince of that name, younger brother of Govinda III, who was in charge of Lāṭeṣvaramaṇḍala which denotes, according to him, the whole northern possession of the Rāṣṭrakūṭas '(Journal of the Department of Letters, X, 1923,. p. 37 fn,) But some scholars identify Indrarāja with Indrāyudha of Jaina 'Harivaṁśa,' the ruler of the north, who was ruling contemporaneously with Vatsarāja. (BI, p. 180 ; Dr H. C. Ray, DH, I. p. 285) If this identification is to be accepted, it may be conjectured that Indrāyudha and Chakrāyudha were of the same family and the cause of the latter was probably championed by Dharmapāla. Chakrāyudha has been described as one 'whose lowly demeanour is manifest because of his dependence on others' in the Gwalior praśasti and as 'begging of Dharmapāla' the crown of Kanauj in the Bhagalpur plate. Is it because of his seeking the throne of Kanauj from Indrāyudha with the help and support of Dharmapāla ?

India and his handling of the situation according to his pleasure did not go unchallenged. The invasion of Dhruva did not crush the Pratihāra power but only gave a temporary blow to its vigorous rise. Nāgabhaṭa II, son and successor of Vatsarāja, once more tried to consolidate the Pratihāra power in order to make another trial of strength with the Pālas. Before actually taking the fiield, he came to a close understanding with the kings of Sindhu, Andhra, Vidarbha and Kaliṅga[1] thus making a strong confederacy of states which, as Dr. Majumdar points out, "formed a central belt right across the country bounded in the east by the empire of the Pālas and on the south by that of the Rāṣṭrakūṭas." Thus strengthening his position, Nāgabhaṭa II most probably first directed his attention to his eastern rival and defeated Cakrāyudha, Dharmapāla's nominee on the throne of Kanauj. This was nothing but a challange to the suzerainty of Dharmapāla and necsssarily brought him on the field. This fight between Nāgabhaṭa II and Dharmapāla for the overlordship of northern India was one of the most fiercely contested battles of the period and in all probability both the parties were equally matched. The epigraphic records of the vassals of the Pratihāras claim victories over the Gauḍa emperor, implying that they followed Nāgabhaṭa in his campaign. In an inscription of Avantīvarman II, great grandson of Vāhukadhavala and a feudatory of Mahendrapāla, it has been claimed that Vāhukadhavala defeated in battle[2] king Dharma who may be identified with Dharamapāla. Again, from the Catsu inscription of Bālāditya it is known that Saṅkaragaṇa, the Guhilot prince, conquered Bhaṭa, king of the Gauḍa country, and made a present of his kingdom to his overlord.[3] It is known from the Jodhpur inscription of Bauka

1. EI, XVIII, pp. 101 ff ; JDL, X, p. 38

2. EI, IX, pp. 2 ff.

3. Dr. Majumdar has adduced good reasons to prove that Bhaṭa refers Dharmapāla and the overlord to Nāgabhaṭa II. Op. Cit. Also see IHQ. IX, pp. 479 ff.

that his father Kakka won distinction by fighting with the Gauḍas at Mudgagiri.[1]

Though no details regarding the preparations of Dharmapāla are known, yet from the nature of the vast and elaborate preparations of his rival from every possible quarter and from the description of the array of the mighty hosts of the lord of Vaṅga in the Gawalior praśasti, it can be presumed that the Pāla emperor must have equipped himself fully well to meet the formidable enemy. If Kakka's fight with the Gauḍas refers to Nāgabhaṭa II's fight with Dharmapāla, the Pratihāras advanced as far as Mongyr and the victory of this severe battle was also on their side. But the victory, so strenuously and valliantly won, could not offer to the Pratihāra king the desired overlordship. Once more the Rāṣṭrakūṭas under Govinda III appeared on the scene and the Radhanpur plates record that the Pratihāra king "in fear vanished no body knew wither". Govinda III overran the Pratihāra territorry and advanced as far as the Himalayas. The Sanjan plates inform us that Dharmapāla and Chakrāyudha submitted to the Rāṣṭrakūṭa monarch of their own accord. In the Nilgund inscription it is mentioned that Govinda III fettered the people of Gauḍa.[2] Mr. R. D. Banerji suggested from this that Dharmapāla and Chakrāyudha

1. It appears that the Jodhpur inscription of Bauka is dated in Samvat 4, and it is dated in his regnal year and not in V. E. 894, as Drs. Bhandarkar and Majumdar read it (EI, XVIII, p. 99). Kakka, father of Bauka, had another son named Kakkuka whose Ghatiyala inscription is dated in V. S. 918-861 A. D. There is no reason to take, as Mr. R. D. Banerji does, the Jodhpur inscription later than the Ghatiyala inscription, nor can we accept his opinion that Kakka, father of Bauka and Kakkuka, cannot be regarded as a contemporay of Nāgabhaṭa II and Dharmapāla. If it is not accepted that Kakka fought for Nāgabhaṭa II, he must have fought for Bhoja, as there is no evidence to show that Rāmabhadra, the immediate successor of Nāgabhaṭa II, could advance to Mudgagiri to fight with the Pālas. It is also not likely, as we shall presently see, that in the first part of the 9th century Bhoja could fight with Devāpala at Mudgagiri, Thus it is quite reasonable to hold that Kakka fought for Nāgabhaṭa II against Dharmapāla. '(JBORS,' 1928. pp. 489 ff.)

2. EI, VI, p. 105.

invoked the assistance of Govinda III against Nāgabhaṭa II. Though it cannot be definitely ascertained, it seems quite probable that Dharmapāla after his defeat by Nāgabhaṭa II did not risk another encounter with the Rāṣṭrakūṭas and thought it wise to submit to Govinda III.[1] From a comparision of the Wani and Radhanpur grants the northern invasion of Govinda III can be assigned to the period between 807 and 808 A. D. It is therefore clear that the reverses of Dharmapāla must have taken place before that date.

Dharmapāla is one of the greatest kings of the Pāla dynasty and takes an honourable place among the great kings known to Indian history. He assumed the highest imperial titles of those days, viz. Paramabhaṭṭāraka, Parameśvara and Mahārājādhirāja, while his father was styled only Mahārājādhiaāja.[2] His name and fame was not confined within his kingdom. The Guzrat poet Soddhala of the eleventh century calls him Ottarapathasvāmin. He assumed the title Vikramaśīla either to signalise his might or

1. Mr. N. N. Das Gupta tried to prove with considerable force of arguments that (I) there was an encounter between Dharmapāla and Govinda III and (2) this was anterior to the defeat inflicted by Nāgabhaṭa II (JBORS., XII, p-361). As regards the first point, in the Sanjan plates it is said that Dharmapāla and Cakrāyudha voluntarily submitted to Govinda III's prowess. The possession of the Ganges and the Yamuna valley alluded to in the Baroda plates of Karkarāja II does not seem to mean permanent occupation. In course of his northern campaign up to the Himālayas he must have for the time being occupied some portion of the Ganges valley. The relation between Dharmapāla and Govinda III may not have been one of amicability, but it is likely that the former did not risk a battle with the Rāṣṭrakūṭas (if we interpret in the light of the Rāṣṭrakūta records). If there have been any alliance between them against Nāgabhaṭa II, as has been suggested by R. D. Banerjee, it seems from the evidence of the Nilgund inscription that the position of Dharmapāla was an inferior one. As regards the second point, Mr. Das Gupta's assertion is based on the 10th verse of the Gwalior praśasti. We prefer Dr. Majumdar's translation. It must be pointed out that in the Sanjan plates the submisaion of Dharma aud Cakrāyudha has been mentioned after the defeat of Nāgabhaṭa II.

2. Khalimpur plate.

to commemorate the foundation of the Vikramaśīlā monastery. The Somapurī-mahāvihāra[1] also owed its origin to the great Pāla king. The second verse of the Bhagalpur plate of Nārāyaṇapāla records certain facts which throw light on his administration and the liberality of the man himself, and these seem to be corroborated by other sources too. Though himself a devout Buddhist, he was very particular in following the policy that his subjects should be governed in accordance with their respective śāstric rules. This is alluded to in the 5th verse of the Mongyr plate of his son. That this tolerance was not a thing to be boasted of in the praśastis is attested by the Mahābodhi inscription or Keśava praśasti of the 26th year of Dharmapāla's reign, which records the setting up of a Caturmukha-liṅga of Mahādeva in the great Buddhist holy place. It is further recorded in the Bhagalpur plate that incidence of his taxation was equitable and just. Many kings sought his protecting shelter which he gladly accorded to them.[2] The defeated kings were not uprooted but reinstated on their thrones and a friendly policy was adopted towards them. It is no wonder that a monarch with such brilliant achievements to his credit, whose government was based on so just and benign principles, should win the love and respect of all classes of his subjects. His court-poet[3] records that his praises were sung by the cowherd boys, hermits, village folk, traders and the rich alike. He ruled at least for 32 years.

It is known from the Khalimpur plate that the crown prince Tribhuvanapāla was the dūtaka of that grant. Most probably he died during the life-time of his father. Dharmapāla was succeeded by Devapāla, his son by the Rāṣṭrakūṭa princess Raṇṇādevī. During the reign of Devapāla the Pāla arms were crowned with success everywhere. It is stated in the Mongyr plate that in course of his 'digvijaya' he advanced as far as the Vindhyās and the Kamboja country. This is confirmed by the 13th

1. Vide Ante
2. Mongyr plate, Vs. 8.
3. Khalimpur plate, Vs. 18.

verse of the Badal Pillar inscription where Devapāla's victories in the Vindhyās and Kamboja country have been alluded to. It seems that he fought with the Rāṣṭrakūṭas during the interregnum and the period of minority of Amoghavarṣa I. It is not precisely known where the Kambojas lived at this time.[1] Thus the statement in the Badal Pillar inscription that by the wise counsel and policy of his minister the whole tract bounded by the Vindhyās and the Himālayas and by the eastern and western seas paid tribute to Devapāla was not a mere political exaggeration but an actual fact.

These achievements in the said praśasti have been attributed to Darbhapāṇi, but it is also stated therein that by the policy and counsel of Kedāramiśra (who also served Devapāla) the Gauḍa king "eradicated the race of the Utkalas, humbled the pride of the Huṇas and shattered the conceit of Drāviḍa and Gurjara kings." It seems that the victories and supremacy won during the first part of his reign were challenged, and Devapāla had to undertake another expedition to curb their power and maintain Pāla supremacy. That the two rival powers, the Prathihāras and Rāṣṭrakūṭas, tried to assert their power is also hinted at in their own records, though they are scrupulously silent of their own defeats. The Gwalior inscription of Vailabhatta indicates that Gwalior was the bouudary of the Prathihāra kingdom at the time of Rāmabhadra and in the early part of the reign of Bhoja. The 12th verse of the Gwalior praśasti of Bhoja seems to imply that Rāmabhadra freed his country from the yoke of foreign soldiers, and, as Dr. Majumdar points out, it seems likely that the "band of foreign soldiers by driving whom Rāmabhadra got back the lost fame belonged to the Pālas, for the other rival power, viz., the Rāṣṭrakūṭas are not known to have advanced as far as the Gurjara kingdom at

1. At the time of Aśoka the Kambojas were a Himālayan tribe in N. W. India. It is known from the Irda plate of king Nayapāladeva that there was a Kamboja ruling family in south western Bengal in the 10th century. Did Devapāla fight with this family or a Himālayan tribe ? (EI., XXII, pp. 150 ff.)

this period.[1]" The evidence of Daulatpura plates and Ghatiyala inscription goes to show that some time before 843 A. D. the Pratihāras under Bhoja made an attempt to reassert their power, and though it met with some initial success, his power was again checked some time before 861 A. D. This is in complete agreement with what we know from the Pāla records.

Amoghavarṣa I was the Rāṣṭrakūṭa contemporary of Devapāla. During the period of his minority and anarchy Devapāla victoriously advanced as far as the Vindhyās in course of his first expedition. It is stated in the Sirur[2] and Nilgund grants that the kings of Aṅga, Vaṅga and Magadha paid homage to Amoghavarṣa, but there are reasons to hold that the Rāṣṭrakūṭas advanced through Orissa after the conquest of Veṅgi.[3] Amoghavarṣa finally crushed the power of the Veṅgi ruler Vijayāditya II sometime before 866 A. D., the date ot the issuing of the Sirur grants. It seems, therefore, that the Rāṣṭrakūṭa invasion of Bengal should be placed after 860 A. D., and that Devapāla defeated the Rāṣṭrakūṭas sometime before that date in course of his second expedition, when Amoghavarṣa was perhaps engaged in wars with his Guzrat cousins and in putting down risings of the rebellious chiefs.

It is not known who was the contemporary Utkala king defeated by Devapāla.[4] The conquest of the Utkalas is corroborated by the Bhagalpur plate in which it is recorded that Jayapāla, cousin and general of Devapāla, drove away the Utkala king from the throne. Huṇamaṇḍala in northern Malwa has been mentioned in an inscription of the Paramāra king Vākpati-Muñja.[5] The Bhagalpur plate also records that Jayapāla defeated the king of

1. Dr. Majumdar, Op. Cit.
2. EI., VII, pp. 104-5
3. The Rāṣṭrakūtas and their times, pp. 76, 84. A march through Bagelkhand and Bihar without coming into serious conflicts with the rising power of the Pratihāras under Bhoja does not seem likely. The Rāṣṭrakūṭa grants do not indicate that Amoghavarṣa I marched against Bhoja.
4. The king of Utkala may be a member of the Kara family.
5. EI., XIII, p. 102

Prāgyotiṣa (Kāmarūpa). The Kāmarūpa king defeated by Jayapāla was most probably Harjaravarman whose Tezpur rock inscription is dated in 829 A. D., or his successor Vanamāla.[1]

The Nālandā inscription of the 39th year of Devapāla reveals the fact that there was constant intercourse between the Pāla kingdom and the Indian colonies in the Pacific Ocean, specially Java and Sumatra. The object of the inscription was to grant five villages for the upkeep of the Buddhist monastery built by the Śailendra king Bālaputradeva of Suvarṇadvīpa and Yavadvīpa at the instance of his mother Tārādevī. He requested Devapāla to grant the income of five villages for its maintenance. This request was gladly and readily complied with, thus showing that his wide charities compared with those of Bali, Karṇa and Vikramāditya were not vague flattery of the court-poet.[2] This religious contact must have been accompanied by brisk commercial activity, as the testimonies of Fā-hien, I-tsing and other Chinese travellers point to such a state of things even before the rise of the Pālas.

The history of the Pālas at the height of their power remains incomplete without some reference to the part played by Vākpāla and Jayapāla, and Garga and Darbhapāṇi. We learn from the Bhagalpur plate that Vākpāla was to Dhamtpāla what Lakṣmaṇa was to Rāmacandra, and this able and trusted brother was mainly responsible for his conquests. Again, Devapāla owed many of his victories to the consummate generalship of Jayapāla. The Badal or Garuḍa pillar inscription informs that the Brahmana minister Garga was to Dharmapāla what Bṛhaspati was to Indra, and it was through his counsel that Dharmapāla, lord of the east, became the master of the west also. No less helpful were the services of Darbhapāṇi and Kadāramiśra. Darbhapāṇi's policy brought the tract between the Himālayas add the Vindyās under Devapāla, and Kedāramiśra's advice was responsible for his victories over the Utkalas, Huṇas, Drāviḍas and Gurjaras. The successes of Dharma-

1. DH. pp. 244-45
2. Mongyr plate Vs, 14

pāla and Devapāla were no doubt to a certain extent due to their own abilities and personality. But the way in which bold claims have been made in the Bhagalpur grant and in the Badal praśasti reflects no mean credit on the successful generalship of Vākpāla and Jayapāla, veterans of many battle-fields, and the competent ministers like Garga, Darbhapāṇi and Kedārasamiśra,[1] shrewd in diplomacy and wise in counsel.

The dūtaka of the Mongyr plate was the crown prince Rājyapāla, but Devapāla was succeeded by Vigrahapāla. The Badal inscription places Śūrapāla between Devapāla and Nārāyaṇapāla, and therefore it can be accepted that Śūrapāla was a virūda of Vigrahapāla I. The relation of Vigrahapāla with Devapāla cannot be ascertained, and the opinions of the scholars are divided on this point. The Bhagalpur plate after describing the achievements of Dharmapāla introduces his brother Vākpāla and states that from him ('tasmāt') was born Jayapāla (Vs. 4 & 5). In the next verse Devapāla has been described as 'pūrvaja' referring to Jayapāla. Mr. A. K. Maitra interpreted the word to mean elder brother and took Devapāla and Jayapāla as brothers. It may be said that the word 'pūrvaja' does not necessarily mean elder brother and may also mean 'elder in age'. If strict Sanskrit grammar is to be followed, 'from him' refers to the immediate preceding noun i.e., to Vākpāla and in that case Jayapāla is to be regarded as the son of Vākpāla. Again, in the sixth verse the achievements of Jayapāla on behalf of Devapāla have been recorded, and in the next verse it

---

1. The question as to whether Kedāramiśra was the minister of Devapāla or Śūrapāla is not so difficult to answer as it appears to be. The 15th verse makes him a minister of Śūrapāla. But in the 13th verse the conquest of a Gauḍeśvara over Orissa, Kāmarūpa, the Hunas, Drāviḍas and Gurjaras has been attributed to his counsel. It does not seem that Śūrapāla had such millitary success. Devapāla enjoyed a long reign (at least of 39 years). Nothing specifically has been said of Darbhapāṇi's son Someśvara who most probably died at a compratively young age. It is therefore quite possible that both Darbhapāṇi and his grandson Kedāramiśra served Devapāla.

is said that from him was born Vigrahapāla. If strict grammar is to be followed in this case, 'from him' refers to Devapāla, but it must be said that in the sixth verse Devapāla has been incidentally mentioned and the main theme of the verse was the exploits of Jayapāla. Dr. Horenle wrote in the Centenary Review of the Asiatic Society of Bengal[1], "It seems clear from this (Amgachi) grant that Vigrahapāla was not a nephew but a son of Devapāla, for the pronoun 'his son' (tat-sūnuḥ) must refer to the nearest preceding noun which is Devapāla. In the Bhagalpur grant this reference is obscured through the interpolation of an immediate verse in praise of Jayapāla, which makes it appear as if Vigrahapāla were a son of Jayapāla". Mr. A. K. Maitra[2] accepted this view and went so far as to identify Rājyapāla, the 'dūtaka' of the Mongyr grant, with Vigrahapāla or Śūrapāla. Kielhorn[3] was of opinion that Vigrahapāla was the son of Jayapāla and grandson of Vākpāla, and R. D. Banerjee[4] accepted this view. In all fairness, the question should be kept open and two genealogies are possible.[5] The

1. Appendix II, p. 206
2. Gauḍalekhamālā, p. 37, fn.
3. E I., VIII, Appendix, p. 17.
4. BI, p. 218
5. (a) Gopāla
   - Dharmapāla
     - Tribhuvanapāla.
     - Devapāla
       - Rājyapāla
       - Vigrahapāla.
         - Nārāyanapāla
   - Vākpāla.
     - Jayapāla,

   (b) Gopāla
   - Dharmapāla
     - Tribhuvanapāla
     - Devapāla,
       - Rājyapāla,
   - Vākpāla
     - Jayapāla
       - Vigrahapāla
         - Nārāyaṇapāla

most important point in the controversy is that three is no mention of Vākpāla and Jayapāla in the grants of Dharmapāla and Devapāla, whereas in the grants of subsequent Pāla kings the victories of those two reigns have been ascribed to Vākpāla and Jayapāla. Although it may be argued that the praises of Vākpāla and Jayapāla in the public records might have made them popular heroes and that after their death the subsequent Pāla kings did not feel jealous to give due credit to the two distinguished generals of their own family, yet the way in which the names of Vakpāla and Jayapāla have been introduced cannot be overlooked, and it suggests that Vigrahapāla and Nārāyaṇapāla were probably directly connected with them and not with Dharmapāla and Devapāla.

Dr. H. C. Ray[1] suspects the liklihood of a palace revolution in the case of the accessions of Devapāla and Vigrahapāla I. It may be pointed out that there is not the slightest hint in the Pāla records of a palace revolution or fratricidal war. The same scholar admits that Devapāla succeeded peacefully, as the evidence of the Mongyr plate is definite and clear (v. 12). His son Rajyapāla was alive at the time of the issue of the Mongyr plate of his 33rd regnal year, but the 'dūtaka' of the Nālandā grant of the 39th year was Bālavarman, the lord of the Vyāgraṭī-maṇḍala. It seems that Rājyapāla died by this time during the life-time of his father and the same was perhaps the case with Tribhuvanapāla, brother of Devapāla, and the 'dūtaka' of the Khalimpur grant of 32nd year of Dharmapāla's reign.

The short reign of Vigrahapāla I was not without political significance. The king of Aṅga, Vaṅga and Magadha who paid homage to Amoghavarṣa I was very likely Vigrahapāla I, as it has already been pointed out that the Rāṣṭrakuṭa invasion took place after 850 A. D. The acceptance of an ascetic life by him by shirking all responsibilities to his son might have been due to defeats by the foreign invaders and humiliation consequent thereon It cannot be clearly stated whether Vigrahapāla I suffered defeats

1. DH., I. pp, 29o, 296

at the hands of Bhoja, though the probability is strongly so. The Pāla records are significantly silent over the Pratihāra invasions of the time. But the gradual extension of the Pratihāra empire at the cost of the Pālas can no longer be doubted. Bhoja, like his grandfather, made extensive preparations in his Bengal campaign. It is known from the Kalha plates of Soḍhadeva that the Kalcuri chief Guṇāmbodhideva who ruled in Kālañjara got some territories from Bhoja and took away the fortune of Gauḍa by a warlike expedition.[1] The evidence of the Benares and Bilhari inscriptions[2] has been generally construed to imply that Bhoja was most probably assisted by the Kalacuri king Kokkaladeva against the Pālas. After the publication of the Amoda plates[3] that view is perhaps to be changed, and it seems that Kokkaladeva I raided Vaṅga on his own account most probably during the reign of Vigrahapāla I or that of his successor.

Though no record has yet come to light to show the subjugation of Magadha and adjacent countries by Bhoja, the discovery of the inscriptions of the early part of the reign of his son Mahendrapāla and the absence of Pāla records in that region indicate that the expansion of the Pratihāra power over Magadha might have taken place in the reign of Bhoja. In the 7th and 9th

1. EI VII p. 86. 2. Ibid. II pp. 297 302.

3. Ibld, XIX, pp 7ff. The Bilahari inscription states that Kokkala conquered the whole earth by planting Bhojadeva and Kṛṣṇarāja as his columns of fame in the north and south respectively, who were to be identified with the Pratihāra king Bhoja I (c.836-90 A.D.) and the Rāṣṭrakūṭa king Kṛṣṇa II (c.78-915 A.D.). Kokkala was the father-in-law of the latter and may be assigned to the first part of the latter half of the ninth century. The Benares plates inform that Kokkala granted freedom from fear to Bhoja, Ballabharāja Srī-Harṣa, king of Citrakūṭa and the king Saṅkaragaṇa. It is known from the Amoda plates that he raided the treasuries of Karṇāṭa, Vaṅga, Gurjara, Koṅkaṇa and Śakāmbhari king and also those born of the Turaṣka and Raghu families. The king of Karṇāṭa and the king, born of the Raghu family, have been identified with Kṛṣṇa II and Bhoja I respectively (See IHQ, XII, p, 132 ff.) This goes against the view that Kokkaladeva helped Bhoja.

years of the reign of Nārāyaṇapāla the Pāla sway was acknowledged in Gaya, and his Bhagalpur grant was issued in his 17th regnal year from Mongyr, and it seems that Magadha was included in the Pāla empire in c. 880 A.D. Bhoja died in c.890 A.D.. The evidence of the Ram-Gaya, Guneria and Itkhauri inscriptions[1] goes unmistakably to show that some portion of Magadha was included in the Pratihāra empire in the last decade of the 9th century. The discovery of the Paharpur pillar inscription of the 5th year of the reign of Mahendrapāla[2] shows further expansion of the Pratihāra power. It is quite likely that the Pratihāras advanced along the northern bank of the Ganges and occupied the very citadel of the Pālas. Thus in the long struggle with the Pratihāras the Pālas were ousted for the time being from their 'janakabhū' Varendrī. There is nothing to be wondered at how the name of Mahendrapāla has been included by the Tibetan historian Tārānātha in the list of the kings of Magadha and Gauḍa. It is known from the Catsu inscription[3] that the Guhilot king Guhila II, son of Harṣarāja, defeated the Gauḍa king and levied tributes from princes in the east. Harṣarāja was a contemporary of Bhoja, and his son therefore may be regarded as a contemporary of Mahendrapāla. This Guhilot family was a loyal feudatory one and rendered valuable services to the Pratihāras. Another invasion that took place about this time was by the Rāṣṭrakūṭa king Kṛṣṇa II who, after defeating a Gurjara king, raided Gauḍa, Aṅga, Kaliṅga and Magadha[4]. Kṛṣṇa II ascended tne throne in c.880 A.D., and as he was engaged in the first part of his reign with the Veṅgi ruler and with the Pratihāra emperor Bhoja, his expedition in the east was probably undertaken towards the close of the 9th or begining of 10th century.

It is not known how long the Pratihāra occupation of Magadha and northern Bengal lasted. In the 54th year of Nārā-

---

1. The plates have been published in 'The Pālas of Bengal.'
2. ASIR, 1927-8, pp. 101 ff.
3. EI, XII, p. 11.
4. EI., V, p. 191. Ibid., IV, p. 287.

yaṇapāla (i.e., about the second decade of the 10th century) an image was set up at Nālandā which goes to show that south-eastern Magadha was under the Pālas. Inscriptions of Rājyapāla[1] and Gopāla II have been found at Nālandā, Bodh-Gaya, and in northern Bengal.[2] After the death of Mahendrapāla the Pratihāra empire began to break up. The Rāṣṭrakūṭas under Indra III dealt a crushing blow to the Pratihāras in c.916 A.D., and it is not unlikely that the Pālas might have attempted during this truobled time of the Pratihāras to recover some of their lost possessions. It must be noted that no record of the Pālas from the time of Nārāyaṇapāla to Mahīpāla I (both exclusive) has yet been found in northern Behar. The Pāla kingdom was considerably reduced during the weak rules of Vigrahapāla I, Nārāyaṇapāla, Rājyapāla, Gopāla II and Vigrahapāla II, and during their reigns many foreign invaders took the opportunity of carrying on their depredations in Bengal. It is known from two Kalacuri[3] inscriptions that the Cedi king Yuvarāja I and his son Lakṣmaṇarāja invaded Gauḍa and Vaṅgāla respectively. Yuvarāja I was the father-in-law of Amoghavarṣa III, the Rāṣṭrakūṭa king, whose reign commenced in c. 935 A. D. Therefore Yuvarāja I and his son seem to have reigned in the first half of the 10th century, whose Pāla contemporaries were probably Rājyapāla and Gopāla II. Yuvarāja I carried on raids on many countries far and near, viz., Gauḍa, Karṇāṭa, Lāṭa, Kāśmīra and Kaliṅga. Lakṣmaṇarāja defeated the Vaṅgālas, Pāṇḍyās, Gurjaras and Kāśmīra. Nor was the other central Indian power sitting inactive. The Khajuraho inscription[4] of Candella Yaśovarman, dated in 954 A. D., informs us that he defeated the king of Gauḍa. Another Khajuraho inscription,[5] dated in 1001 A. D., records that the wives of the kings of Kāñchī, Andhra, Rāḍha and Aṅga lingered in the prison of his son Dhaṅgadeva.

1. IA., 1918, p. 111.
2. Recently a plate of Gopāla II has been found in the Malda district. (Bhāratavarsa), 1344, B.S., Sravana isaue, p. 274.
3. EI., II, p. 297, Bilhaṛi and Goharwa plates ; Ibid., xi, XI, p. 142.
4. EI., i, p. 123. 5. Ibid.

CHAPTER IV

The Pāla Dynasty (Continued)

The Pālas must have been passing their most critical days in in the 10th century. It seems now certain that in south-eastern and south-western Bengal two independent kingdoms were established by the Candras and Kambojas[1] respectively. The evidence of the Dinajpur pillar inscription goes to show that the Pālas were dispossessed of Varendra by a Kamboja chief who styled himself Gauḍāḍhipa.[2] Palaeographically this record is to be assigned to the period between 950-1050 A D. Most probably this king belonged to the Kamboja family of the Irda plate of Nayapāladeva. The Bangar grant of Mahīpāla I records that he recovered his paternal throne which was occupied by a usurper (pitryaṁ rāijyam anadnikṛta) who is to be identified with the Kamboja king of Gauḍa. How Mahīpāla I recovered the paternal throne from him still remains unknown.

With the accession of Mahīpāla I there seems to have been a revival of the Pāla power. The Baghaura image inscription shows that Samataṭa was included within his kingdom in his third regnal year.[3] The Imadpur image inscription goes to show that northern Bihar was under his possession.[4] If the date Samvat 1076 of the colophon of the Rāmāyaṇa is to be referred to the Vikrama era, it seems that Mahīpāla I came into conflict with Kalacuri Gāṅgeyadeva, though it has been doubted by

---

1. See Infra., Chapter V.

2. We agree with Dr. R. C. Majumdar that the expression "Kuñjaraghaṭāvarṣeṇa" of the inscription is to be taken as an epithet of Gauḍāpati and not as a chronogram to mean 888, which is to be referred to the Śaka era. See "Vaṅgavāṇi," 1330 B. S., p. 250 ; BI., p.243.

3. EI. XVII, p.353.

4. IA., XIIV, p. 165.

some scholars.[1] It is stated in the Goharwa plates that Gāṅgeyadeva conquered as far as the sea of Utkala and vanquished the king of Aṅga which was included within Mahīpāla's kingdom. The most formidable invasaion during his reign was from the south. It is known from the Tirumalai rock inscription of Rājendracola that in c. 1325 A. D. his general defeated Mahīpāla.[2]

Mahīpāla's foreign policy has been severely criticised by Messrs R. P. Chanda[3] and R. D. Banerjee,[4] because he did not join the rulers of northern India against the Muslims. The learned author of 'Gauḍarājāmlā' observes that Mahīpāla, like the emperor Aśoka after the Kaliṅga war, sheathed his sword and devoted all his eneregies to pious and religious works after the recovery of northern Bengal from the Kamboja chief. Like all historical comparisons it is far from being exact and it is also a mis-statement of facts. With any stretch of historical imagination Mahīpāla I cannot be compared with the great Maurya emperor either in power and prestige or in religious and moral fervour. R. D. Banerji remarks that Mahīpāla could not make common cause with other kings because of his envy and religious bigotry. Mahīpāla, a devout Buddhist though he was, granted a village in the Puṇḍravardhana-bhukti to the excellent Brahmana Bhaṭṭaputra Kṛṣṇādityaśarman in the 9th year of his reign, and many Brahmanical gods

1. The colophon was copied in Samvat 1076 when Tīrabhukti was ruled over by "Mahārājādhirāja Puṇāvaloka Somavaṁśodbhava Gauḍadhvaja Śrīmad Gāngeyadeva." Bendall referred the date to the Vikrama era and identified the king with Kalacuri Gāṅgeyadeva. Objections have been raised by Sylvain Levi and Mr. R. P. Chanda (summarised in IHQ., 1931, pp. 679 ff). But they do not seem to be very strong in view of the evidence of the Goharwa plates. Dr. R. C. Majumdar suggests that the date 1076 is to be referred to the Śaka era and the king is to be identified with Gāṅgeyadvea, successor of Nānyadeva on the throne of Mithilā. This solves all difficulties, no doubt, but it must be said that the facsimile has not been published and therefore cannot be palaeographically examined. The date of the colophon rests on a statement of Bendall who examined it in Nepal. See IHQ., XII, pp. 469 ff.

2. EI, IX., pp. 232-33 ' also see Chapter V.

3. Gauḍarājamālā, p. 41. 4. BI, p. 256.

and goddesses were installed in his reign. The charge of bigotry has no basis at all, as it is disproved both by official and private records. His reign cannot in any sense be called a period of military inactivity and religious asceticism. He was beset with difficulties from the very beginning of his reign. He had to recover the paternal throne from a usurper. The Candras were carving out a kingdom in eastern Bengal and his suzerainty was acknowledged in that region. The Cedis under Gāṅgeyadeva were making great strides in the east and most probably Mahpāla had to fight with him. If the exploits of Mahāśivagupta Yayāti, the Somavaṁśī king of Kośala, as described in his Maranja-Mura charter, are to be believed in its entirety, he seems to have invaded Gauḍa, Rāḍha and Vaṅga during Mahīpāla's reign. He had not only to re-establish the Pāla power but also to cosolidate it which was tottering during the reign of his father. It will be an anachronism to judge the foreign poticy of Mahīpāla in the light of later history or of modern times. If he did not entangled himself in the turmoil of northern Indian politics because of the unlimited liability involved in that course of action and adopted the policy of 'safety first', it shows his foresight and political sagacity. His position was weak in own territory and his kingdom was vulnerable from every quarter. When dangers came from unexpected quarters, his energy and resources were spent in repelling them. If his resources were spent in checking the Muslim imvasions, the Pāla kingdom might have ended with the shock of the Cola invasion, and anarchy and discorder, previous to the rise of the Pālas, might have been the result.

The restoration of the Pāla power by Mahīpāla I and the stability of political power over northern Bengal and Magadha made their influence felt in other spheres also. In the 11th year of his reign one Bālāditya, an emigrant from Kauśāmbī and an inhabitant of Tiladhaka (modern Telāra), rebuilt a temple at

1. JBORS. II pp. 45 ff. ; for his date see DH, 1, pp. 401 ff. Dr. Ray assigns to the first quarter of the 11th century.

Nālandā, which was burnt down by a conflagration.[1] Sthirapāla and Vasantapāla, two brothers of Mahīpāla, restored Dharmarājika and Sāṅgadharmacakra and built the temple of Gandhakuṭi at Sarnatha[2] in 1026 A.D. Many important tanks in northern Bengal are associated with his name.[3] All these must have made him very popular and his name is perhaps still remembered in the popular saying that Mahīpāla's praise is to to be sung when husking the paddy. He was succeeded by his son Nayapāla.

After the fall of the Pratihāras, the Kalacuris were the most active enemies of the Pālas. The invasions Kokkala, Yuvarāja, Lakṣmaṇarāja and Gāṅgeyadeva have already been referred to. The Kalacuri power rose to its height under Karṇa, son of Gāṅgeyadeva, and most of the contemporary northern Indian kings felt the brunt of his power. The Tibetan biographer[4] of Atīśa Srījñāna Dīpankara records the meditation of hostilities that ensued between Nayapāla and Karṇa. If the Tibetan account is to be believed in its entirety, the Kalacuri army was successful at first and besieged the holy city of Gaya but was ultimately defeated by the Pāla army. There is nothing improbable in the account that after hostilities a treaty was brought about through the good offices of the great Buddhist patriarch. With the exception of the articles of food that were destroyed at the time of war, all other things were either restored to or compensated for. The treaty concluded by Atīśa seems to have proved to be a truce. The evidence of the Paikore image inscription[5] and of the 'Rāmacarita'[6] goes to show that a second campaign against the Pālas was undertaken by Karṇa. In this expedition Karṇa advanced as far as Paikore (in the Birbhum district) and set up a

1. JASB, 1908, pp. 106-7 ; Gauḍalekhamālā, p. 101.
2. ASIR, 1903-4, p. 222 ; AI., XIV, p. 139 ; Gauḍalekhamālā, p. 104.
3. Gauḍarājamālā, p. 104 ; Mahīsantoṣa in Dinājpur, Mahipālera Dighi (tank) in Bogra and in Murshidabad.
4. JBTS., I, p. 9.
5. ASIR., 1921-22, p. 78.
6. Rāmacarita 1/9.

column there perhaps as a mark of his victorious march, where an image was carved by a ceriain sculptor by the order of the Cedi king. Karṇa's invasion of Bengal has also been alluded to in the Bheraghat inscription of Ahlaṇādevī[1] and in the Karanabel inscription of Jayashmia[2] It is stated in the 'Rāmacarita' that Vigrahapāla III, son and successor of Nayapāla, though he defeated Karṇa, did not uproot him and that Karṇa's daughter Yauvanaśrī was married to him. It is difficult to believe that the Cedi king who carried extensive conquests far and wide was compelled to give his daughter in marriage with Vigrahapāla. In the height of his power he overran the whole of northern India, but in the latter part of his reign he suffered many defeats. From various sources comes the story of his defeats by Candella Kīrtivarman,[3] Paramāra Udayāditya[4] and Cālukya Someśvara.[5] It is known from the 'Prabodha-candrodaya' that Karṇāṭa first almost annexed the Candella kingdom during the weak ruie of Devendravarman, but the same drama records how his brother Kīrtivarman with the help of his Brahmana minister Gopāla restored the Candella kingdom after vanquishing Karṇa's power. Faced in the south and west by the Cālukyas and the Paramāras, the rising power of the Candellas was still a greater danger to the power of Karṇa. It is therefore quite possible that the motive behind this matrimonial alliance with Vigrahapāla III was a lasting peace with the Pālas.

The 'Vikramāṅkacarita' which narrates the exploits and military expeditions of Vikramāditya VI, son of Cālukya king Someśvara I, records that when a Yuvarāja, Vikramāditya made a raid on Gauḍa and Kāmarūpa.[6] It is stated in the inscriptions of the reigns of Someśvara I,[7] Someśvara II[8] and Vikramāditya VI[9] that the

1. E.I. II, p. 11. 2. IA., XVII, p. 217.
3. EI., p. 222; Prabodha-candrodaya, pp. 11, 12, 14.
4. EI., II, p. 185.
5. 'Uber das Lebender Jaina monchs Hemacandra' by George Buhler, p. 69; IA., V, p. 317, Vikramāṅkadevacarita.
6. Ibid. 7. EI., XV, p. 86. 8. Ibid., p. 97.
9. Ibid., p. 104.

Cālukyas shattered the pride of many countries among whom the names of Gauḍa and Vaṅga occur. The invasion of Someśvara I must have taken place before 1053 A. D., because his Mahāsāmanta Bhogadevaraṣa of the Kelwadi inscription[1] raided Vaṅga and seems to have followed him. As the invasion of Bengal is mentioned in the records of three successive Cālukya kings and in the 'Vikramāṅkacarita,' it is quite possible that there might have been more than one Cālukya invasion in the eleventh century.

It is a rare thing in ancient Indian history to have an account of a period from a contempoıary writer. The 'Rāmacarita' by Sandhyākaranandī, the "Vālmikī of the Kali Yuga", as he styles himself at the end of his work, describes the achievements and glories of the reign of Rāmapala who was, in the eye of the author, the Rāma of his age. A great portion of the work is devoted to the account of the struggle for the recovery of Varendra by Rāmapāla from the Kaivarta king Bhīma. The author's father Prajāpatinandī, was the 'Sāndhivigrāhika' of Rāmapāla. Sandhyākaranandī therefore must have had a first-hand knowledge of the Pāla court and the political vicissitudes of the Pālas, and in his early age he might have witnessed them. His account and specially the commentary on his work are, therefore, of unique importance for the history of Bengal in the last half of the eleventh century.

The real cause of the Kaivarta revolution is not known. Vigrahapāla III had three sons, Mahīpāla II, Śūrapāla II and Rāmapāla. Mahīpāla II succeeded his father to the throne. After his accession he began to follow an unrighteous course of action against the advice of the ministers.[2] Śūrapāla and Rāmapāla were put into prisons, because it was reported by evil mongers and designing men that Rāmapāla was respected by all and would

1. 'EI.,' IV, p. 259.

2. Com. 1/31 Prathamaṁ pūrvaṁ pitari Vigrahapāla uparate sati Mahīpāle bhrātari kṣamabhāraṁ bhubhāraṁ vibhrati sati anītikārāmbharate anītike nītivirudhe ārambhe udyame rate sati Mahīpālaḥ śāḍguṇaśalyasya mantrino guṇitamaguṇayan upaṣṭambhāra bhaṭimātrādisatgrahaṇena.

occupy the throne by killing him.[1] This apprehension led Mahīpāla to devise ways and means for the death of Rāmapāla who was kept in a solitary underground prison.[2] Most probably taking advantage of this internal dissension in the royal family and the general discontent thereon, the Kaivarta chief Divvoka raised the standard of revolt. Mahīpāla suddenly marched with a hastily collocted force to meet the insurgents whose number was increased by the combined army of the Sāmantas of the kingdom. This was done against the express wishes of the ministers and the result was, as the ministers foresaw, defeat. Mahīpāla himself was defeated and killed, and Varendra was occupied by the Kaivarta chief.

At the time of the outbreak of the revolt Śūrapāla and Rāmapāla were in prison. It is not known how they managed to get free. The Rāmacarita does not mention Śūrapāla as a king but, according to the 13th verse of the Manahali plate, Śūrapāla ruled for however short a period it might have been. The suspicion of R. D. Banerjee[3] that Śūrapāla was murdered at the instigation of Rāmapāla is unwarranted, as there is not the slightest hint of it anywhere. The purpose of the author was not to write a dynastic history of the later Pālas but to glorify the achievemants of Rāmapāla, and his silence over Śūrapāla's reign was probably due to the fact that it was a very short reign in which there was nothing worth recording. It is not known where he ruled and what was the boundary of the territory under him. The Kaivartas were in possession of Varendra, and Divvoka was succeeded by his brother Rudoka who was followed by his son Bhīma. It was most probably at the time of the unsteady political state that Gauda was invaded by the Paramāra king Lakṣmadeva,[4] and the invasion of

1. Com. 1/37 Māyināṁ khalānāṁ dvaninā ayaṁ Rāmapālaḥ kṣamodhikāri sarvasammata tataśca devasya rājyamgrahisyaiti sucanayā saṇkitavipada pramāmasau hanisyatīti saṅikitavipadyena tasya bhuvobhartur-Mahīpālasya prabhutāya vahutarāya nirākṛti prayūktita śāṭhya prayogāt upāyavadha-cestayā tathā tvanākākārenapaune duıgate kaniṣṭhe brātari Rāmapāle rakṣitari.

2. 1/33.

3. BI., p. 280.

4. EI., II, p.198, Vs. 188.

northern Bengal by the army of a Vaṅgāla king also took place, in course of which the Buddhist teacher Karuṇāśrīmitra's house at Somapura-vihāra was set on fire and he was burnt to death.[1]

Rāmapāla succeeded Śūarpāla. Mr. A. K. Maitra[2] suggested that he passed these days in Aṅga with his maternal uncle Mathanadeva. It may be pointed out that an image inscription of the second year of Rāmapāla[3] has been found in Bihar. During these critical days he was always closeted in discussion with his ministers and his son Rājyapāla in order to arrive at a decision as to the course of action to be taken. It was perhaps settled that by any hasty action they might fare like Mahīpāla, and before any action to be taken, it would be wiser to win the confidence and active support of the Sāmantas. To this effect Rāmapāla now turned his whole attention and he met the important chiefs, implored their help and promised them reward of money and further extension of territory in case of victory. This produced the desired effect. The Sāmantas were satisfied with his behaviour and assurance. The right-hand man of Rāmapāla in the suppression of the Kaivarta revolt was Rāṣṭrakūṭa Mathanadvea who with his two sons, Kāhṇuradeva and Suvarṇadeva, and his nephew Śivarāja played an effective part in the battle. The commentary[4] informs us that Mathanadeva defeated the king of Pīṭhī and Magadha. In the Sarnatha inscription of Kumāradevī, queen of Gāhaḍavāla Govindacandra, it is said, "In the Gauḍa country there was a priceless warrior with quiver (kaṇḍapatika), this incomparable diadem of the Kṣatriyas, the Aṅga king Mahana,[5] the vener-

1. EI., XXI, pp.97-131. The Nālandā inscription of Vipilaśrīmitra has been assigned to the middle of the 12th century. Karuṇāśrimitra was removed by two generations of teachers from Vipulaśrīmitra.

2. A course of lecture delivered by Mr. A. K. Maitra in the Calcutta University on the fall of the Pāla empire published in a summary form by Dr. R. C. Majumdar, Mainavāṇi, 1828 B.S.

3. JASB, 1908, pp. 108-9

4. Rāmacarita 2/8. 5. The Prākṛta form of Mathana is Mahana.

able maternal uncle of kings. He conquered Devaraksita in war, maintained the glory of Rāmapāla, which rose in splendour because the obstruction by his foes was removed."[1] R. D. Banerjee[2] suggested that Devaraksita rose against the Pālas during the Kaivarta imbroglio but was subdued and then won over to the Pāla side by the marriage of his daughter Saṅkaradevī, mother or Kumāradevī.

In the commentary fourteen sāmantas are named, who took active part in the war against the Kaivarta chief Bhīma on the side of Rāmapāla. They are :—

(1). Bhīmayaśa, ruler Pīṭhī and Magadha, and described as 'Kānyakuvja-vājinīganṭhana-bhujaṅga'. Pīthī was the name of Bodh-Gaya and the neighbouring region.[3] If the above expression means any hostility to a Kānyakuvja king, he is to be identified with a Gāhaḍavāla king and not with Kalacuri Yaśaḥkarṇa as suggested by R. D. Banerjee.[4] Devarakṣita preceded Bhīmayaśa on the throne of Pīṭhī and his daughter was married to Govindacandra. Gāhaḍavāla Madanapāla's inscriptions are dated from 1104 to 1109 A. D., and in his Rahan grant[5] the victories over the Gauḍa elephants are said to have been achieved by his son Govindacandra. It may be that Rāmapāla after the Kaivarta war made an attempt to extend his sway in the west but was checked by the rising power of the Gāhaḍavālas. The eastward advance of the Gāhaḍavāla power during the period 1124-1146 A. D. is indicated by the Maner and Lar plates. Govindacandra's fight with the kings of Vaṅga and Gauḍa is alluded to in the Prākṛt-paiṅgalam, a work on Prākṛta metrical science.[6] Govindacandra's contemporaries were Rāmapāla, Kumārapāla, Gopāla III. Madanapāla and Vijayasena.

(2). Vīraguṇa of Koṭāṭavī, described as 'dakṣiṇa-siṁhasana-cakravartī'. Mr. N. N. Vasu identifies Koṭaṭaṭavī with Koṭa-deśa in

---

1. EI., IX. p. 320.
2. Bl., d. 226.
3. JBORS., IV, p. 273.
4. Bl., p. 284.
5. IA. XV 111, p. 46,
6. IHQ., xl,p, 564 ff.

Sarkar Kaṭaka of the Āin-Āi-kbari.[1] Vīraguṇa may be identified with Vīra of the Deopara praśasti, who was defeated by Vijayasena.

(3). Jayasiṁha, ruler of Daṇḍabhukti, who is said to have defeated the Utkala king Karṇakeśarī, who most probably belonged to the Keśarī dynasty but whose name has not been found anywhere else.[2]

(4). Vikramarāja, ruler of Bāla-Vallabhī, adjacent to Devagrāma. The location of Bāla-Vallabhī is uncertain. Mr. N. N. Vasu identifies Devagrāma with a village of that name, 5 miles east of Ranaghat in Nadia.[3] There are many villages of the name of Devagrāma. It may be noted that Bhaṭṭa Bhavadeva, a minister of Harivarman, is styled Bāla-Vallabhujaṅga,[4] and the original home of his family was Siddhala in the Birbhum district.

(5). Lakṣmīśūra dercribed as 'apāramandāra-madhusūdana and samasta-āṭavīka-sāmantacakra-cuḍāmaṇi'. Apāra-mandāra has been identified with the Mandāra hill in the Bhagalpur district[5]. It is to be noteed that he is called a Sāmanta of the forest region.

(6). Śūrapāla of Kujavaṭī. Its identification is uncertain.

(7). Rudraśikhara of Tailakampa, which is perhaps represented by its non-sanskritized form Telakupī[6] in the Manbhum district.

(8). Mayagalasiṁha of Ucchala which cannot be located.

(9). Pratāpasiṁha of Dhekkarīya, which is to be identified with modern Dhekur in the Burdwan district.

(10). Narasiṁhārjjūna of Kayaṁgal-maṇḍala which may be identified with Kankjol in the Rajmahal.

(11). Caṇḍārjjuna of Saṁkaṭagrāma. Its location is uncertain.

(12). Vijayarāja of Nidrāvala. Dr. H. C. Roychowdhury is

1. Rājanyakāṇḍa, v. 191.
2. DH., I, p. 412
3. Rājanyakāṇḍa, p. 198.
4. JASB., 1912, p. 341
5. IA, 1930, p. 244.
6. Cunningham, ASR., VII, p. 169.

inclined to identify this chief with Vijayasena of the Sena dynasty[1]. If this is to be accepted, Nidrāvala is to be located in Rāḍha where the Senas were originally settled.

(13). Dvorapavardhana of Kauśambī. R. D. Bannerjee[2] surmised that Dvorapavardhana had been written in place of Govardhana through the mistake of the copist and was inclined to identify him with the chief of that name defeated by Jātavarman of the Varman dynasty. Kausāmbī in the Puṇḍravardhanabhukti has been mentioned in the Belava plate and has been located in the Diamond Harbour sub-division.[3]

(14). Soma of Paduvana. Its location is uncertain.

The list of the sāmantas whose services were utilised by Rāmapāla and some of whose achievements have been described in the commentary gives an idea of the magnitude of the task that confronted him. Their support being won over, Ramapāla collected the threefold army, the cavalry, the infantry and the elephants. With arrangents thus complete, Rāmapāla began the campaign and asked the Rāṣṭrakūṭa prince Śivarāja to cross the Ganges with the vanguard and to assure the people that the property of the Brahmanas and religious endowments would not be interfered with in any way. True to the direction of Rāmpāla, Śivarāja kept himself informed of the property of the Brahmanas and the gods and expelled the front guards of Bhīma.[4] This was successful and thus the landing of the main army was made safe.

Rāmapāla at the head of the main army crossed the Ganges by a bridge of boats. Rājyapāla made all preparations for war and arranged the soldiers in customary arrays. The battle that ensued was one of the hottest that were fought in northern Bengal. Bhīma was captured on his elephant's back and kept under

1. IHQ., XIII, p. 358
2. BI., p. 277
3. SPP, 1339, B.S. pp. 80-81
4. We cannot accept the statement in the 'Rāmacarita' that Śivarāja delivered Varendra from the enemies. Then what was the necessity of the campaign of Rāmapāla at the head of the main army? It seems that Śivarāja made a cavalry raid and expelled the guards.

the charge of his son Vittapāla. His army broke up but his friend and general Hari collected the scattered army and made a desperate attack. Once more the battle was fierce. But the the Kaivarta army was finally routed.

Thus ended the Kaivarta revolt. Of late there has been much discussion as to its origin and nature. The occupation of Varendra by ousting the deep-seated Pāla power naturally rouses the suspicion that this revolution was organised on a large scale. Mr. A. K. Maitra[1] expressed the opinion that Divvoka, like Gopāla I, the founder of the Pāla power, was the chosen of the people. He went so far as to assert that he was elected king by the people and that the common people had a great share in determining the succession to the Pāla throne. The 'Rāmacarita' describes Rāmapāla as 'sarvasammata'[2] which he takes to mean "accepted by all", and from this Mr. Maitra concluded that Rāmapāla was the king-elect and Mahīpāla II claimed the throne by the law of primogeniture. This was the underlying cause of the Kaivarta revolution. On this assumption he further concluded that Varendra as a whole was against that Pālas and Rāmapāla forced the Pāla rule against the declared voice of the people. The mainstay of the Pāla power was the popular support. and this was lost for ever. His opinion that Divvoka was elected by the people has been supported by R. P. Chanda[3] and Sir J. N. Sarkar.[4] But the crucial point is that if this would have really been the case, why the people did not elect Rāmapāla. If Rāmapāla was the chosen of the people, why after the death of Mahī-

---

1. Lecture on the 'Fall of the Pāla empire' delivered by A. K. Maitra in the Calcutta University, a summary of which was published by Dr. R. C. Majumdar in the defunct Bengali journal 'Marmavāṇī, 1422 B. S.

2. Com. 'Rāmcaritra' 1/37. The word 'sarvasammata' actually occurs in connection with the reports of the evil-mongers and designing persons who reported Rāmpāla to be so to Mahīpāla. Whether it was really so cannot be ascertained.

3. Modern Review, 1935, p. 347

4. Ibid., 1936. April issue.

pāla II the Kaivarta chief occupied the throne ? This is the most important point which Mr. Maitra did not try to answer. Mahīpāla II was of suspicious nature and he deviated from the right course of action. His imprisonment of Śūrapāla and Rāmapāla can hardly be defended as a course of right judgment and was extremely impolitic because these two brothers would have stood by him in the impending danger. Divvoka has been described with the modest appellation 'bhṛtya'[1] which is perhaps to be taken in the sense of an officer of the Pālas. He was certainly not a Bachai Sako, as it is clear from the commentary that he enjoyed considerable power and was a man of much importance in the kingdom. Dr. N. K. Bhattasali[2] has drawn attention to certain passages in the commentary[3] which go to show that he began the action against Mahīpāla as a matter of duty with ulterior motives in his mind. When Mahīpāla II fought with Divvoka, the combined army of the 'sāmantas' was with the latter. It is therefore very very likely that the revolution at first broke out in favour of Rāmapāla because of Mahīpāla's unrighteous rule, or it was professed to be so, and and subsequently Divvoka fished in the troubled waters. As it often happens that a revolution breaks out with certain end in view but is exploited by ambitious and designing men for their personal ends, the Kaivarta chief made himself master of the situation and usurped the throne. Discussing the whole episode, Dr. R. C. Majumdar[4] rightly observes that to rise against the ruling dynasty must always be regarded as an act of rebellion. The occupation of northern Bengal by the Kaivartas should be properly described as a political and military 'coup d'etat'.

---

1. Com. 1/38. Kāntā kamaṇīyā divyāhvayena Divyanāmnā Divvokena māṁsabhujā lakṣmya aṁśaṁ bhuñjānena bhṛtyena uccaiḥ-darśakena uccaiḥ-mahatī daśā avasthā yasya atyucchritenetyartha dasyūṇā śatrunā tad-bhāvāpannātvāt avaśya-kartavyatayā āravdham karma vratam chadmani vratī.

2. Bhāratvarṣa, 1343 B.S., pp. 32-41

3. Com. 1/38. quoted above. 4. Bhāratvarṣa, 1342 B. S., Aṣāḍha issue

After the recovery of his fatherland, Rāmpāla bent himself to lay the foundation of the Pāla kingdom more deeply by wining the love and affection of all people. He built a new capital which has since been associated with his name,—Rāmāvatī[1] or Ramauti of the Muslim writers. He adorned this city with numerous Buddhist and Hindu images, the chief of which were Saura, Śaiva and Skānda. This must have produced profound impression on the people at large. True to the Pāla tradition, he established the famous Buddhist monastary of Jagaddala whose fame travelled far beyond the borders of Bengal. Besides, he built many temples and excavated canals and tanks.

Thus making the foundation of the Pāla power once more secure, Rāmapāla engaged his attention for glory abroad. Eastern Bengal seceded from the Pāla empire and a new independent power was established by the Varmans. The verse 44 (ch. III) states that a Varman king propitiated Rāmapāla by presenting him with his chariot and elephants. The Varman king referred to was probably Harivarman or Sāmalavarman, and thus eastern Bengal was once more brought within the Pāla sphere of influence. In course of his digvijaya Rāmapāla advanced as far as the sea-coast of Orissa[2] and reinstated the vanquised king of Utkala. Kāma-

---

1. Rāmāvatī was most probably included within the precints of Gauḍa. ASIR., 1923-24, p. 79

2. Mr. A. K Maitra takes 'bhavabhuṣana santati' used in this connection to refer to the Somavaṁśī kings of Orissa. Messrs. H. P, Shastri and R. D. Banerjee take it to refer to the Nāgavaṁśa. We are inclined to take the latter view because in verse 43 the word nāga actually occurs. It is not known who was the vanquished king reinstated by Rāmapāla. It may be mentioned that the Nāgavaṁśī kings ruled during the 11th century in the present Bastar state (EI., IX, pp. 161-64). Mr. N. G. Majumder conjcetures from the word nāgāntaka applied to his minister Bhaṭṭa Bhavadeva that the Nāgāvaṁśī king was defeated by Harivarma but was favoured by Rāmapāla (IB., p. 80).

rūpa was also conquered by one of his generals.[1] These are clear indications of the revival of the lost supremacy of the Pālas over eastern India. In his old age Rāmapāla entrusted the task of the government to his son Rājyapāla and retired from active political life. When at Mongyr, he received the sad news of the death of his maternal uncle Mathanadeva to whom he owed so much of his political achievement and he died by immersing himself in the holy waters of the Ganges,[2] and this is confirmed by the 'Sekh-śubhodayā.'[3]

Rāmapāla was the last great Pāla king and was undoubtedly one of the greatest diplomats and statesmen of his age. He realised from the very deginning that the task that confronted him was by no means an easy one. He came to the wise and sane decision that without the help and snpport of the sāmantas it would be very difficult, if not impossible, to recover Varendra. A rash and hasty policy would have met with the fatal result of Mahīpāla's march against the Kaivarta chief. What by persuasion and what by promise of rewards the support of the vassals was secured. This is the clearest proof of his sobriety of judgment and diplomacy. In the actual war also he showed the qualities of a great general and statesman. His conduct and policy in the ciritical days of his life, as it can be gleaned from the incidental references in the commentary, reveal the statesmanlike traits of his character. He had the genius to organise and to execute marvellously. Far from being revengeful of the enemies, the officers of the Kaivarta king were appointed to high posts, thus making them loyal and grateful servants of the kingdom. He was wide in his sympathy

1. Kāmarūpa king overthrown by Rāmapāla was, according to Pandit P. Bhattacaryya, Dharmapāla of Brahmapāla's dynasty. According to K. L. Barua, he might have been Jayapāla of the Silimpur inscription (See Intro. Kāmarūpaśāsanāvalī ; also Early History of Kāmarūpa, Ch. on the dynasty of Brahmapāla). It is not improbable that Rāmapāla sent a general to subjugate the rebellious chief, Iśvaraghoṣa who seems to have assumed an independent attitude during the Kaivarta revolt (see Ch. on Administration.)

2. Rāmacarita 4/8-18 3. S. K. Sen. Sekhśubhodayā, p. 46.

and tolerant in religious outlook. With him the sun of the Pāla power began to set down, never to rise again in splendour.

The Kaivarta rebellion had been quelled but the spirit of defiance was not extinguished. When the strong arm of Rāmapāla was not more, ambitious chiefs and rulers tried to raise their heads. During the reign of Kumārapāla, successor of Rāmapāla, two rebellions broke out. The Kamauli plate of Vaidyadeva describes vividly his naval battle in southern (anuttara-vaṅga) and the suppression of the revolt of Tiṁgyadeva of Kāmapūra. Vaidyadeva was at first a minister and general of Kumārapāla. The naval battle in southern Bengal most probably refers to a fight with a Varman king who tried to shake off the Pāla yoke established by Rāmapāla. No sooner had Vaidyadeva won this battle than the news of the revolt of Kāmarūpa reached him, and after a few days' rapid march he took Tiṁgyadeva by surprise. It was put down with a strong hand and a large number of people were slain and wounded. In the Kamauli plate Vaidyadeva assumed the imperial titles generally associated with an independent king. It seems that he asserted his independence at a later period. As his relation with Kumārapāla was very cordial (he is called a 'suhṛd and amātya'), he could not but mention his previous relation with the Pāla king whom he had served loyally. Nothing more is known of the reign of Kumārapāla except the exploits of Vaidyadeva whose personality overshadowed that of the king himself, and the 'Rāmacarita' dismisses his reign in one verse[1] only. Most probably he had a very short reign. It is likely that the invasion of Aṅga, Kaliṅga and Vaṅga by the Cālukya king Tribhuvanamalla Paramādideva, which is recorded in an inscription[2] of 1128 A. D., took place in his reign.

Kumārapāla was succeeded by his son Gopāla III. Very recently an image of Sadāśiva has been descovered in the Dinajpur district and there is a votive inscription on the pedestal, recording that it was installed by Purṣottamadeva in the 14th year

---

1. 4/11

2. Ep. Carn., XI. p. 68

of Gopāladeva.[1] Its characters are almost similar to those of the Deopara praśasti of Vijayasena, and the king Gopāladeva is to be identified with Gopāla III. This identification goes to disprove the old view[2] that he had a very short reign and died in his childhood. He seems to have ruled at least for 14 years. The 'Rāmacarita' dismisses his reign in one verse[3] from which it appears that his enemies had a hand in his death which was not perhaps natural. The Manda inscription, which is to be assigned for palæographical reasons to Gopāla III, is full of so many scribal mistakes that no meaning can be made out of it confidently.[3] It seems that this record also refers to his enemies and one person named Mijum (?) fought for or stood by him. It is to be noted that it is a posthumous record.

Gopāla III was succeeded by Madanpāla, the last known king of the Pāla dynasty. He was the son of Rāmapāla by his queen Madanadevī. In his accession he was assisted by Mahāmāṇḍalika Candra of Aṅga, son of Suvarṇacandra.[4] Sandhyākaranandī describes Madanapāla as king with a religious bent of mind and as a liberal-minded man. He is said to have uprooted one Govardhana. The leader of the Nāga army was his ally and with his help he seems to have crippled the fortune of Hari.[5] A victory is also claimed in his favour over Kaliṅga. But whatever success he had, it seems that northern Bengal passed in the hands of Vijayasena

1. I am thankful to Mr. N. G. Majumder, Superintendent of Archaeological Survey (Eastern Circle), for kindly allowing me to examine the inscription. For an account of the inscription, see the Amrita Bazar Partrika, dated May 14, 1937

2. BI., p. 311

3. 4/12. 'Api śatrughna-upāyad Gopālaḥ svaḥ jagāma tatsunuh Hantu kumbhīnasya-astanavaisya tasya sāmayikam-etat.

3. An attempt has been made to interpret this inscription by V. Vidyavinode. See SPP, 1319 B. S., pp. 153 ff. The reading and translation are highly conjectural. He reads 'sechyam' in the 3rd line and is of opinion that he gave up his life voluntarily. The word looks like 'sacya' and gives no meaning.

4. We agree with Dr. R. G. Basak in identifying Candra with the grandson of Mathanadeva. IHQ., V, p.85.

5. No commentary of the last part of the Rāmacarita has been discovered. We follow Mm. H. P. Shastri's interpretation.

during his reign. The Deopara praśasti states that the Sena king impetuously assailed the king of Gauḍa and also shows that at least southern Varendra was under him. The Manahali plate records grant of land by Madanapāla in the Puṇḍravardhanabhukti in his 8th regnal year. The Jayanagar image inscription goes to indicate that he ruled at least for 19 years in Bihar. Two other kings, Govindapāla and Palapāla, have been styled Gauḍeśvara,[1] but their relation with the Pāla dynasty is uncertain, and there is nothing to show that their authority extended over any part of Bengal, as all records alluding to their reign come from Magadha. Therefore it seems that Madanapāla was the last Pāla king of Bengal.

The Pālas were entangled in severe struggle with the Pratihāras and Rāṣṭrakūṭas from the very foundation of the empire. It seems that the struggle was keener and more long-drawn with the Pratihāras than with the latter. A close study of the Rāṣṭrakūṭa and Pāla records tends to show that the Pālas were politically or matrimonially allied with the Rāṣṭrakūṭas. It was held by some scholars that Dhruva Dhārāvarṣa undertook his campaign against Vatsarāja as an ally of Dharmapāla, but this is to be given up in view of the direct mention of his encounter with the Gauḍa king in the 14th verse of the Sanjan plates. The Rāṣṭrakūṭa help was perhaps sought by Dharmapāla when he was defeated by Nāgabhaṭa II. The 23rd verse of the same record, which describes the northern campaign of Govinda III and his victory over Nāgabhaṭa II, informs us that Dharmapāla and Cakrāyudha submitted to him of their own accord. The conclusion becomes more probable because Dharmapāla married Raṇṇādevī, daughter of a Rāṣṭrakūṭa prince named Parabala[2].

1. Pālas of Bengal, pl. XXVII; JBORS, 1923, pp. 588 ff; IC., II, pp. 579 ff, IHQ. XIII, pp. 359-60.

2. This Parabala has not been yet definitely identified. One Parabala is known from the Pathari Pillar inscription (EI., IX, p. 249). Kielhorn read the date as 917 V· S.—861 A. D. which in his opinion is clear. It is impossible to verify it from the facsimile. It is to be noted that Parabala's dated is dependent on that of Dharmapāla and not vice versa. Fleet expressed the opinion that Parabala is to be identified witk Govinda III, but no virūḍa of Govinda III as such is known. Mr. R. D. Banerji was of opinion that Parabala of the Pāthari inscription had a very long life and there is no difficulty in identifying him with Dharmapāla's father-in-law. (Bl., p.196.)

The sixth Pāla king Rājyapāla married Bhāgyadevī, daughter of a Rāṣṭrakūṭa prince named Tuṅga. The identification of this Rāṣṭrakūṭa prince is also far from being certain. Rājyapāla ruled during C. 810-985 A.D., and the Pāla power was passing through the most critical days at this period, as the Pratihāras under Mahendrapāla occupied northern Bihar and Bengal. The strenghening of the Pāla power by a matrimonial alliance can be presumed. What is more important to notice is that in every official record of the Pālas after Rājyapāla this matrimonial alliance has been very prominently referred to, while Dharmapāla's marriage with Raṇṇādevī is known from the Mongyr and Nālandā grants of Devapāla. Vigrahapāla I's marriage with the Kalacuri princess Lajjādevī is known only from the Bhagalpur grant of Nārāyaṇapāla. But Rājyapāla's marriage with Bhāgyadevī has been repeated in the genealogical account of the Pālas in every grant. It is quite probable that this marriage was of great political importance to the Pālas. Kielhorn suggested that Rājyapāla's father-in-law was Jagattuṅga, son of Kṛṣṇa II.[1] Jagattuṅga predeceased his son. III and did not reign.[2] It cannot be ascertained whether the northern campaign of Indra III and his signal victory over the Pratihāra emperor Mahīpāla had something to do in connection with this matrimonial alliance. But it seems certain that this death-blow to the Pratihāras offered a good opportunity to the Pālas for the recovery of the lost possessions. Every Rāṣṭrakūṭa campaign against the Pratihāras, whether undertaken for their own sake or otherwise, was indirectly of great political advantage to the Pālas.

If the northern campaigns of Govinda III and Indra III are somewhat doubtful as of direct help to the Pālas, the evidence of the Rāmacarita of Sandhyākaranandī is conclusive of the fact that the

---

1. IA., XLVIII, p. III. Mr. N. N. Vasu identified him with Kṛṣṅa II himself who had also the title Tuṅga (VJI, Rājanya Kāṇḍa, p. 128). Mr. R. D. Banerj remarks that he is perhaps to be a identified with Tuṅgadharmāvaloka whose inscription has been found at Boddh-Gaya (R. L. Mitra, Buddha Gaya, p. 195, pl. XL.)

2. Dr. Altekar, Op. Cit., p. 99,

Rastrakūṭa branch of Magadha rendered incalculable service to the cause of the Pālas at one of the most critical junctures of their fortunes. Vigrahapāla III married a sister of Mathanadeva who was the right-hand man of Rāmapāla in his suppression of the Kaivarta revolt. The vanguard of Ramapāla's army was led by Mathanadeva's nephew Mahāpratihāra Śivarāja and his own sons Mahāmāṇḍalika Kāhṇuradeva and Suvarṇadeva also took an important part in that war. Madanapāla, the last known Pāla king of northern Bengal, was assisted in his succession by the Rāṣṭrakūṭa prince Candradeva.[1]

It seems therefore that the Rāṣṭrakūṭa alliance was the corner-stone of the Pāla foreign policy and the Rāṣṭrakūṭas directly or indirectly rendered great service to the Pāla empire from almost its foundation to the last day of its existence. But this intimate matrimonial and political relations did not prevent them from undertaking campaigns against Bengal or claiming suzerainty over the Pālas. The statement of the Muslim traveller Sulaiman[2] that the Rāṣṭrakūṭas compelled "every prince, though master in his own house, to pay homage to themselves" seem to be quite appropriate. Nor did the Pālas, if they found a favourable opportunity, felt any scruples to invade the Rāṣṭrakuṭa kindom. The defeat of a Drāviḍa king by Devapāla, who from his mother's side had Rāṣṭrakuṭa blood in him, most probably refers to a Rastrakuta king.

After the end of the triangular struggle among the Pālas, Pratihāras and Rāṣṭrakūṭas, the new powers like the Kalacuris, Candellas, Cālukyas and Paramāras carried on raids almost on every opportune occasion. Certainly some of these raids were accompanied with loots and plunders. Political and military glory might have been one of the leading motives but the more material and economic motive was not also perhaps absent. Whoever might have been the victor, these incessant raids were a great strain on the treasury of the Pālas.

1. IHQ., V. p. 35 2. Elliot, History of India, Vol. I, p. 7

The constant and repeated foreign invasions were not the only scourge of the Pāla kingdom. It appears that the feudatories also took utmost advantage of the weakness of the central power to assume a defiant, if not almost independent, attitude. We know of two such cases in Magadha. Two records from Gaya[1] of the 15th year of Nayapāla introduce us to one Viśvāditya or Viśvarūpa,[2] son of Śūdraka and grandson of Paritoṣa. The family seems to have been devoted to religion and constructed temples and installed gods at Gaya. Nothing is known of its political status. Another Gaya inscription[3] of the 5th regnal year of Vigrahapāla III describes Śūdraka in vague terms and records that Viśvarūpa destroyed his enemies. It is clear that he was a contemporary of Nayapāla and Vigrahapāla III. In another Gaya record of Yakṣapāla (Viśvarūpa's son) Śūdraka is described as, "Śrī Śūdrakaḥ svayam-apūjad-indra-kalpa Gauḍeśvara nṛpati-lakṣaṇa-pūjayāyam." Dr. H. C. Ray[4] takes it to mean that the lord of Gauḍa paid homage to Śūdraka, while Dr. R. C. Majumder[5] is inclined to take the expression to mean that the lord of Gauḍa formally honoured Śūdraka by investing him as king with proper ceremony. Whatever may be the meaning, it is clear that during the time of Nayapāla and Vigrahapāla III, these pretensions were becoming higher and higher. To crown all, it is said at the end of the Gaya record of Yakṣapāla,[6] "Sūrya-candra māsau yāvat kṣauṇī sasāgara tāvat Śrī Yakṣapālasya rājantam bhuvi kīrttayaḥ" and there is no reference to any suzerain. It seems therefore that this family was assuming an attitude of independence in the Gaya region during or after the reign of Vigrahapāla III.

The Govindapur praśasti of the poet Gaṅgādhara of 1137-38 A. D. introduces us to two princes of the Māna family, namely

1. Gauḍalekhamālā, pp. 111 ff ; Pālas of Bengal, p. 78

2. They seem to be identical and it may be also possible that they were two brothers. Two records give two different names.

3. Pālas of Bengal, pp. 81-82   4. DH., I. p, 348

5. DUS., No I, Pt II, p. 135

6. Pālas of Bengal. p. 97

Magadharāja Varṇamāna and Rudramāna, who ruled towards the end of the 11th and the beginning of the 12th century A. D.. It is not known what was the attitude of these two princes towards the Pālas. We have already noted that Devarakṣita of the Cikkore family and ruler of Pīṭhī, who was subdued by Mathanadeva, might have tried to secede from the Pāla kingdom. It seems that at the time of the Kaivarta revolt the Pāla feudatories of Magadha were assuming a semi-independent attitude. The history of eastern and western Bengal which will be narrated in the next chapter also shows the same state of things. The verses 1/37 and 1/38 of the Rāmacarita indicate that Divvoka was an officer of the Pālas, and the Sāmanta-cakra at first sided with him.

Taking a broader view of the Pāla history, it appears that from the tenth century onwards the Pāla power was collapsing. The disruptive tendencies and disintegrating forces were kept in check for the time being by the vigour and energy of Mahīpāla I and Rāmapāla, who tried to revive the Pāla suzerainty in eastern India and gave it a longer lease of life. It began to crumble after the death of Rāmapāla and the task devolved on the Karṇāṭa chief Vijayasena to found a united kingdom all over Bengal by suppressing all the disintegrating forces, and the death-knell of the tottering Pāla kingdom was rung by him.

APPENDIX A

Pāla Chronology

There have been much heated discussions[1] on Pāla and Sena chronologies. We need not repeat all the arguments and

1. For Pāla and Sena chronologies, see. JBORS., 1928, pp.489-538; 1929, pp.642-50; IA., 1930, XLIX, pp. 942-50; JASB, 1921,pp. 112; IHQ, 1927, pp. 571-91; 1929, pp. 133-37.

counter-arguments. We have based our study of the Pāla history on the following chronology :—

	Kings.	Probable dates	Known reign-period
1.	Gopāla	5. 750 A.D.	....
2.	Dharmapāla	„ 776-810 A. D.	32 years.
3.	Devapāla	„ 810-850 „	39 „
4.	Vigrahapāla I or Surapāla I	„ 850-855 „	3 „
5.	Nārāyaṇapala	„ 855-910 „	54 „
6.	Rājyapala	„ 910-935 „	24 „
7.	Gopāla II	„ 935-970 „	35 (?)[1] „
8.	Vigrahapāla II	„ 970	....
9.	Mahipala I	„ 980-1030 „	48 „

The definitely known date is 1026 A.D. of the Sarnath inscription of the reign of Mahīpāla I who is to be identified with Mahīpāla mentioned in the Tirumalai inscription because the Cola invasion took place in c.1025 A.D. The synchronisms of Dharmapāla, Cakrāyudha, Rāṣṭrakūṭa Govinda III (793-814 A.D.) and Pratihāra Nagabhaṭa II (c. 807-33 A.D.) are established by the Sanjan plates of Amoghavarṣa, the Gwalior inscription of Bhoja and the Bhagalpur plate of Nārāyaṇapāla. There are reasons to believe from a comparison of the Radhanpur and Wani plates that Dharmapala and Cakrayudha submitted to Govinda III between 807 and 808 A.D. If we subtract the sum total 230 of all the known reign periods from 1026, we get 796.

But 796 cannot be taken as the date of accession of Dharmapāla because of the following uncertain factors. The date 1026 A. D. might not have been the last date of Mahīpāla I, and the unknown reign-periods of all monarchs (of Vigrahapāla II's

1. As regards Gopāla II's reign-period, he is said to have reigned 'cirataram', most probably in comparison with his father Rājyapāla's reign-period, which is 24 years. I agree with R. D. Banerjee in reading the date in the Maitreya Vyākaraṇa as 17 and not 57 or 11 as auggested by Mm. H. P. Shastri and Prof. Bhandarkar; see photograph and discussion, JBORS, 1928, pp. 489ff.

reign-period nothing is known) have not been taken into account. Taking 808 A. D. as the 32nd year of Dharmapāla's reign, we cannot push his acceesion before 776 A. D. This uncertain period cannot be very long (796-776 = 20 years). Taking all factors into casideration, it seems that Mahīpāla 1's last date is not very far from 1026 A. D.

The prodable reign-periods of other Pāla kings may be fixed in this way :—

10. Nayapāla	c. 1030-1045 A.D.	15 years
11. Vigrahapāla III	„ 1045-1072 „	26 „
12. Mahīpāla II	....	....
13. Śūrapāla II	....	....
14. Rāmapāla	c. 1080-1123 „	42 years.
15. Kumārapāla	....	....
16. Gopāla III	„ 1125-1139 „	14 years.
17. Madanapāla	„ 1139-1158 „	19 years.
? Govindapāla	„ 1162 „	....
? Palapāla	....	35 years.

Atīśa Dīpaṅkara went to Tibet during the reign of Nayapāla in c. 1038 A.D. Nayapāla and Vigrahapāla III were contemporaries of Kalacuri Karṇa (c.1040-70 A.D.). A Gaya inscription is dated in 1232 V.E., which is referred to as " Śrī Govindapāladeva-gata-rājya-caturdaśa-samvatsare", i-e., the 14th year having passed since the end of his reign. This places the end of his reign in 1162 A.D.. It is possible that Govindapāla and Madanapāla ruled contemporaneously in two parts of Magadha. It appears from the 'Rāmacarita' that Mahīpāla II, Śūrapāla II and Kumārapāla had very short reigns. It is quite possible that Śūrapāla II and Rāmapāla ruled contemporaneously with Kaivarta Divvoka and Bhīma in different parts of Bengal and Magadha. Of course it is true that after a certain period of his reign Rāmapāla ousted Bhīma from Varendra. Again, it is also possible that Vijayasena ruled contemporaneously with Rāmapāla, Gopāla III and Madanapāla.

CHAPTER V

Independent Dynasties in Vaṅga and Rāḍha

The history of south-eastern Bengal in the eighth century is almost dark. The unfinished Chittagong plate of Kāntideva does not throw much light on the political condition. From palaeographical considerations Kāntideva may be placed in the period 750-851[1] A. D.. Like the Kedarpur plate of Śrīcandra, it is a peculiar record in which the object of its issue has not been mentioned and goes to strengthen the view that the common (metrical) portion of copper plate grants made by the same king used to be inscribed previously, the formal grant being inscribed on the actual occasion. It was issued from Vardhamānapura which cannot be satisfactorily identified.[2] Kāntideva's father Dhanadatta and grandfather Bhadradatta becamc powerful by victories in battles. His title is Paramesvara and Mahārājadhirāja and the inscription comes to an abrupt cose by an address to the future kings of Harikela-maṇḍala.[3] It seems therefore that his power was confined to a small principality.

In one of his latest papers R. D. Banerjee expressed the opinion that eastern Bengal did not possibly form a part of the Pāla kingdom before the reign of Mahīpāla I. This remark seems to be correct inasmuch as there is no definite evidence of Pāla

1. Modern Review, 1922, p. 612.

2. Dr. R. G. Basak locates Vardhamānapura in Burdwan. This would make Kāntideva a king of western Bengal. But as he addresses the king's of Harikela-maṇḍa, it seems that he had some authority over Harikela which, in our present state of knowledge, should be located in eastern Bengal. Dr. N. K. Bhattasali conjectures that Vardhamānapura is identical with Vikrampura, but there is no evidence to support it. IHQ. 11, pp. 822-25.

3, For location, see Ante,

4. Ashutosh Silver Jubilee Volume, Orientalia. At. 111., p. 221.

authority over eastern Bengal in the 8th, 9th and 10th centuries. But some indirect references tend to show that Vaṅga was probably included within the kingdom of Dharmapāla and Devapāla. In the Gwalior praśasti[1] of Bhoja it is stated that Nāgabhaṭa defeated Cakrāyudha and the lord of Vaṅga who is to be identified with Dharmapāla. Alluding to the same incident in the Baroda plates[2] of Kakka it is said that the Pratihāra king (Nāgabhaṭa II) humbled Gauḍendra and Vaṅgapati by which perhaps the same person (Dharmapāla) was meant: But it must be admitted that the terms Gauḍa and Vaṅga have been somewhat loosely used in the contemporary Pratihāra and Rāṣṭrakūṭa records. The land granted by the Khalimpur grant was in Vyāgrataṭī-maṇḍala within the Puṇḍravardhana-bhukti, and Bālavarman, the governor of that maṇḍala, was the dūtaka of the Nālandā grant of Devapāla. Vyāgrataṭī has been identified with Vāgḍī (the delta of the Ganges and the Brahmaputra) on phonetic grounds[3] There is nothing definite to show the extension of the Pāla power over Vaṅgāla.

If the establishment of the Pāla suzerainty over Vaṅga is somewhat problematical, it is certain that during the earlier part of the tenth century Bengal was under an independent dynasty. The Bharella Naṭṭeśvara[4] image inscription acquaints us with a king named Layahacandra who is to be palæographically assigned to the beginning of the 10th century. His capital was at Karmamanta which has been identified with Bad-Kamta in the Tippera district. It is known from the Rampal, Kedarpur, Dhulla and Edilpur plates of Śrīcandra that a line of kings with their names ending in Candra ruled in eastern Bengal. The names of Purṇacandra, Suvarṇacandra and Trailokyacandra are known. Śrīcandra has been assigned to the 10th century and seems to have preceded Mahīpāla I.[5] The title Mahārājādhirāja has been applied to

1. El., XVIII. pp. 101 ff. 2. IV, XIII, p. 160.
3. Sir Ashutosh Silver Jublee Volume, Orientalia, pt. 1, pp. 423-24.
4. EI. XVII, p, 350.
5, Sir Ashutosh Silver Jubilee Volume, Orientalia, Pt. 111, pp.221ff,

Trailokycandra who had been at first a ruler of Harikela and extended his authority over Candradıvpa.[1] It is stated in the Rampal plate that the Candras were originally rulers of Rohitagiri. Messrs. R. D. Banerjee[2] and N. G. Majumdar[3] are inclined to to identify it with Rhotasgarh in the Shahabad district of Bihar. Dr. N. K. Bhattasali suggests its identification with the Lalmai Hills in Tippera, and Mr H. D. Mitra, with Rangamati in the Hill Tippera.[5] The existence of a line of Candra kings for 19 generations in Arakan[6] and the extension of Arakan power over Chittagong[7] in the 9th century go to support the eastern origin of the family of Śrīcandra. The gradual extension of the Candra power from Harikela to Candradvīpa and then to Vaṅga also strenghens the view of their eastern origin. Though no lineal connection can yet be established between Layahacandra, the family of Śrīcandra and the Arakan Candra dynasty, the probability of such a connection is strong.

The Baghaura image inscription goes to show that Samataṭa acknowledged the suzerainty of Mahīpāla I in his third regnal year. It is learnt from the Tirumulai inscription that sometime about 1025 A. D. the Cola army under a general of Rājendra Cola defeated Govindacandra of Vaṅgāladeśa. It is quite likely that Govindacandra belonged to the Candra family and it seems that the Candras were pushed eastward by Mahīpāla I in Vaṅgāla (their original land ?).

Another independent power was established in eastern Bengal

---

1. Mr. N. G. Majumdar takes Trailokyacandra as the king of Harikela which included Candradvīpa (IB, p. 3). This conclusion is based on the following passage.,—"Adhāro Harikela-rājakakuda-smitanāṁ-śriyaṁ yaścandropāde babhuva nṛpatir dvīpe dilīpopamaḥ." But to take Trailokyacnadra originally to be king of Harikela from which position he became king of Candradvīpa seems to us a better conclusion.

2. BI, p. 283 3. IB. p. 3 4. IHQ, III, p. 418

5. IHQ, II, pp. 313, 665 6. ASIR, 1929-27, pp. 146-48; IHQ, 1931, p. 87

7. Chittagong Gazetteer, p. 20

about the middle of the eleventh century. It is stated in the Belava plate of Bhojavrman that the Varmans originally belonged to Siṁhapura which has been identified by some scholars with Siṁhapura in Kaliṅga, and by R. D. Banerjee, with Siṁhapura of the Lakhamandala inscription in the Panjab, and by Dr. R. G. Basak, with Sīhapura in Rāḍha mentioned in the Mahāvaṁśa.[1] The real founder of the political fortunes of the Varman family was Jātavarman, a contemporary of Vigrahapāla III. He is said to have spread his paramount sovereignty by marrying Vīraśrī, daughter of (Kalacuri) Karṇa, by extending his dominion over Aṅga, by crippling the Kāmarūpa king, Divya and Govardhana. It is to be particularly noted that in the 8th verse[2] of the Belava plate where the military and political activities or Jātavarman are described, great stress has been first laid on his marriage with Vīraśrī, daughter of Karṇa, and it seems that this marriage has got something to do with his military conquests. Again, although no connected meaning can be made out of the broken Vajrayogini plate of Sāmalavarman, from the way in which the words Kalacuri and Mātṛvaṁśya occur it can be surmised that this marriage of Jātavarman was perhaps a great factor in determining the political fortunes of the Varman family. It may be therefore held that the Varmans came in the wake of Kalacuri Karṇa's invasions during the troubled period of the Kaivarta revolt or shortly before it.

The position of Harivarman in the chronology and genealogy of the Varmans was so long controversial, but the evidence of the broken Vajrayogini plate shows that he is to be placed between Jātavarman and Sāmalavarman. The recovery of the lost Samantasara plate of Harivarman enables us to verify the name of his father, which was read by Mr. N. N. Vasu as Jyotivarman. Its defaced condition prevents us from being definitely certain, as the

1. IB., p. 16. · Dr. D. C. Ganguli is also inclined to identify Siṁhapura with Sīhapura in Rāḍha, see IHQ, XI-1, pp. 605ff. also X111, pp. 158ff.

2. This begins the description of Jātvarman's political conquests :— "pariṇayan-Karṇasya-Vīraśriyaṁ-yoṅgāsu-prathayani-paribhanani-stāṁ-Kāmarūpa-śriyaṁ..."

letters in question are very indistinct, but it seems that the name is to be read as Jātavarman[1]. In the Nagpur prasasti[2] of the Paramāra kings it is stated that Lakṣmadeva (1086-1094 A. D.) first proceeded to Hari's quarters and entered the town of the lord of Gauḍa. Hari's quarters have been generally taken to mean east, but it may refer to the kingdom of Harivarman. The 'Aṣṭasāhasrika-Prājñapāramitā' was copied in his 19th year, and a commentary on 'Kāla-cakra-yāna' was written in the 23rd year of Harivarmadeva[3]. He had a long reign and probably ruled contemporaneously with Rāmapāla. From the Bhuvanesvara praśasti of his minister Bhaṭṭa Bhavadeva and from the Vajrayogini plate it appears that he had a son who distinguished himself in battles, but it is not clear whether this son actually ruled. It is important to notice that there is no mention of Harivarman and his son in the Belava plate in which Jātavarman seems to have been succeeded by his son Sāmalavarman. The foundation of the Varman power did not go unchallenged by the Pālas. The presentation of an elephant and the chariot by a Varman king of the east and the victorious naval battle of Vaidyadeva in southern Bengal indicate that the Varmans were occasionally compelled to acknowledge the Pāla suzerainty[4], though they assumed imperial titles in their own records and were ready to cast off the yoke at every opportune moment. The last known Varman king is Sāmalavarman's son Bhojavarman by Trailokyasundarī, the daughter of the Paramāra king Jagaddeva. The Varmans were most probably ousted from Vikrampura by Vijayasena.

The recently published Irda plate of the Kamboja king Nayapāladeva raises many important and interesting problems. It

1. I am thankful to Dr. N. K. Bhattasali, Curator of the Dacca Museum, for kindly allowing me to examine the plate. Dr. Bhattasali also agrees with me in reading the name. See Bharatvarsa, 1344 B. S., Phalgun issue.

2. EI, 11, p. 193, v. 38.

3. SPP., 1327 B.S. Pl.2, No. 3. Mm. H. P. Shastri read the date as 39 but it seems to be 32.

4. See Ante.

introduces us to Kamboja-vaṁsa-tilaka Rājyapāla and to his two sons Nārāyaṇapāla and Nayapāla by queen Bhāgyadevī. The grant was issued from the capital (rājadhanī) Priyaṅgu, and the land donated was situated in Daṇḍabhukti-maṇḍala within the Vardhamāna-bhukti. The Tirumalai inscription mentions Dandabhukti after Oḍḍa-viṣaya and Kosala-naḍu and before Dakṣiṇa-Raḍha. As it was within Vardhamāna-bhukti, late Mr. R. D. Banerjee's[1] opinion that Daṇḍabhukti is roughly represented by Midnapore and Balasore districts seems to be to the mark.

Palæographically Nayapāladeva is to be assigned to the tenth century. The names of the princes of the Irda plate end in Pāla, and moreover, Rājyapala (of the Pāla dynasty), father of Gopala II, married Bhāgyadevī which is the name of the mother of Kamboja Nayapāladeva. It is therefore tempting to hold that this family was a branch family of the Pālas. Mr. N. G. Majumdar,[2] who first held this proposition 'quite unlikely', writes in a recent note[3] that it is 'very likely'. Again, it may be pointed out that Devapala, the 3rd Pāla king, had a son of the name of Rājyapala who was the crown prince and dūtaka at the time of his issuing of the Mongyr plate, and we have already referred to the theory of a palace revolution after the death of Devapala[4]. The acceptance of the view that the princes of the Irda plate belong to a branch family of the Pala dynasty would support the theory of late Dr. Hoernle,[5] who long ago held that after Nārāyaṇapāla (of the Pāla dynasty) two rival lines of Pāla kings were ruling in two parts of Bengal owing to internal dissensions.

But there are serious objections against this view which should not be overlooked. The princes of the Irda plate belonged to the Kamboja-vaṁśa (v. 6). The Pālas are nowhere described as

1. Pālas of Bengal, pp. 71, 89 ; BI, p. 248.
2. EI, XXII, p. 152.
3. Modern Review, 1937, September issue, pp. 323-24
4. See Ante. Devapāla's reign
5. IA, XIV, pp. 165 ff.

Kambojas. The coincidences of the names of Rājyapāla and Bhāgvadevī may be accidental. If two Rājyapālas are to be identified, it is to be accepted that Gopāla II had two brothers, namely Nārāyaṇapāla and Nayapāla, who subscribed to the Brahmanical faith. At the present state of our knowledge it seems better to take the prince of the Kamboja family of the Irda plate as belonging to a separate line and the assumption of imperial titles by Rājyapāla and Nayapāla indicates that they were independent kings. The Kamboja king who has been styled Gauḍapati in the Dinajpur pillar inscription and whose occupation of northern Bengal has been perhaps described in Banagar grant of Mahīpāla I as "pitryaṁ rājayaṁ-anadhikṛta" most probably belonged to this family. The king Dharmapāla of Daṇḍabhukti mentioned in the Tirumalai inscription was possibly another ruler of this family.

The question how this family came into power in extreme south-western Bengal cannot be satisfactorily solved. During the reign of Aśoka the Kambojas along with the Yonas were in the north-western frontier of India.[1] The same position is given to the Kambojas and Yavanas in the Mahābhārata, and the Kamboja country was famous for its good breed of horses.[2] The same thing has been mentioned in the Mongyr grant of Devapāla where it is said that his horses met their old mates in Kamboja in course of his military campaigns. There was also a Kambojadeśa in eastern India[3] which has been indentified with Lushai tracts between Bengal and Burma. There is yet no clue to connect this ruling Kamboja family with Kamboja countries in western or eastern India.

The Tirumalai inscription records that the Cola army after killing Dharmapāla of Daṇḍabhukti, defeated Raṇaśūra of Dakṣiṇa-

1. Bhandarkar, Aśoka, p. 32.

2. JRAS, 1912, p. 256 ; Arthaśāstra, II, 30. For detailed description of the Kambojas see Dr B. C. Law, 'Some Kṣatriya tribes of Ancient India', pp. 230-51,

3. DH, I, pp. 308-9 ; EI XXII, p. 158.

Rāḍha, Govindacandra of Vaṅgāladesa and Mahīpāla of Uttara-Rāḍha. The controversy[1] that has been raised whether this Tāmil record or the Trivalangadu plates give the correct route of the Cola army is to be closed after the definite location of Daṇḍabhukti from the evidence of the Irda plate. The Trivalangadu plates state that the defeat of Raṇaśūra took place before the discomfiture of Dharmapāla, and this cannot be accepted in view of the geographical position of Daṇḍabhukti and Dakṣiṇa-Rāḍha. Prof. Nilkanta Shastri[2] correctly observes that the Tāmil 'praśasti' (Tirumalai) which was recorded almost immediately after the campaign must be accepted as more authentic, and he continues, "The language of the Tāmil inscriptions appears to suggest, *what seems otherwise*, that Mahīpāla had a sort of supremacy over the other chiefs named in this context and that the overthrow of Dharmapāla, Raṇaśūra and Govindacandra led to the final struggle in which Mahīpāla was captured." We have got no knowledge of Tāmil and what he says from the point of the language of this record we are not in a position to judge ; but by 'what seems otherwise' he refers to R. D. Banerjee's opinion that Bengal was divided into many independent principalities at the time of the Cola invasion. We think that this view still holds good and should not be changed until some other stronger proof can be adduced to replace it. The other view would mean that Mahīpāla I was the king of almost the whole of Bengal and Bihar in their present geographical denomination, as the Baghaura and Imadpur image inscriptions go to show.

Raṇaśūra of Dakṣiṇa-Rāḍha raises the question of the existence of the Śūra dynasty of which so much is heard in genealogical books and traditions, but very little is known of them from reliable documents. The first member is said to have been Adiśūra who is one of the central figures of the social history of Bengal. We have tried to show elsewhere[3] that Ādiśūra of the Kulaśāstras

1. JRAS, 1935, pp. 655·66, pp. 59-79.
2. The Colas, pp. 251.52.
3. See Chapter IX, Brahmana Immigrations in Bengal.

may be identified with Magadhādhiraja Adisiṁha of the Dudhpani rock inscription of the 8th century A. D. The genealogical books preserve a tradition that the Brahmanical Suras were forced to take shelter in Raḍha after the establishment of the Buddhist Pāla power.[1] The names of Bhūśūra, Mādhavasura, Adityasura, Yāmini. sura, Varendrasura, Pradyumṇasura, Anusura and Bhānuśūra are known from the Kulagranthas. The genealogy of the Varmans and Senas as given in them have proved to be false and unreliable. It is not therefore safe to construct the dynastic history of the Suras and not even their genealogy, relying on their accounts. Occasionally the names of Śūra princes are found in inscriptions and contemporary literature. A pillar from Rajaona bears an inscription[2] in the 7th-8th century characters with the word 'Raṇa-śūrasya'. Lakṣmisura of the Rāmacarita was the ruler of Apāramandāra. Vijayasena married Vilāsadevī who has been described as Śūrakulambodhi. All these would point to the existence of a Sura family, though nothing is known definitely of the extent of their territory or political status. The evidence of the Tirumulại inscription and the Ramacarita would indicate that they raised their heads during the rule of weak Pāla kings but were forced to accept the position of sāmantas when there was a strong Pāla king.

We have seen that the kingdoms of some of the sāmantas who fought for Rāmapāla may be located in Rāḍha and there cannot be any doubt about the location of Jayasiṁha of Daṇḍabhukti. The samantacakra (the whole body of feudatories) who fought on his side may be regarded as hereditary feudatories of the Pālas in normal circumstances. At the time of the out-break of the Kaivarta revolt, the sāmanta-cakra was against Mahīpāla II,[3] and it was due to the resourcefulness of Rāmapāla that they were persuaded to make common cause with him.

1. VJI, Rājanya Kaṇḍa, p. 121.
2. Cunningham, ASR III, pl. XLV.
3. Ramacartia, 1/31 ; 1/29,

Taking all facts into consideration, it must be said that it is too hazardous to conclude that either Vaṅga and Rāḍha were included within the Pāla kingdom or they were separate political entities. In the 10th century when the Pāla power was at its lowest ebb, both in eastern and western Bengal we find the existence of two independent kingdoms. There is no definite evidence to prove the establishment of Pāla power in Vaṅga before Mahīpāla I and also in Rāḍha. With the accession of Mahīpāla I there was an attempt to extend the Pāla power over eastern Bengal, if not over western Bengal also, as the evidence of the Bāghaura image inscription and the Tirumalai inscription tends to show. During the Kaivarta imbroglio the Varmans founded a kingdom in eastern Bengal. But again Rāmapāla tried to establish Pāla suzerainty over the Varmans. If there was no permanent and direct authority of the Pālas over Vaṅga and Rāḍha, there were occasional attempts to bring them under their sphere of influence. But it is also clear that the Pāla power was more firmly rooted in northern Bengal and Bihar than in Vaṅga and Rāḍha. All records pointing to their authority excepting the Baghaura inscription have been found in Magadha and Varendra. The rise of the Candras, Varmans, Kambojas and Senas (who were at first settled in Rāḍha) makes it emphatically clear. There was an invasion of Varenda by a Vaṅgāla king, and it seems that a Kamboja king ousted Vigrahapāla II from his throne. Vaṅga and Rāḍha were ready to set at naught the Pāla yoke at every opportune moment and to utilise the weakness of the Pāla kings.

CHAPTER VI

The Sena Dynasty

The Senas originally belonged to the Karṇāṭa country. It is stated in the Deopara praśasti and Madhainagar grant that the remote ancestor of the Senas was the Deccan king Vīrasena. Mr. R. Chakravarti[1] is inclined to identify him with Vīrasena of the south, mentioned in the Sahyādri Khaṇḍa of the Skandapurāṇa. Mr. A.K. Maitra was of opinion that he is to be identified with Vīrasena, father of king Nala of the Mahābhārata.[2] Dr. R C. Majumdar[3] draws attention to a line of Jaina teachers (whose names end with Sena) of the Dharwar district which was the heart of the Karnāṭa country—

Kumārasena	....
Vīrasena	C.850-903 A. D.
Kanakasena	....
Ajitasena	C. 950-975 A. D.
Brahmasena	....
Āryasena	C. 1000-1045 A. D.
Mahāsena	....

There is no definite evidence to connect the Senas of Bengal with the line of these Jaina teachers, and it is difficult to believe that all the Senas of Karṇāṭa were Jainas.

R. D. Banerjee[4] held that the ancestors of the Senas came to

1. Gauḍera Itihāsa, p. 156.
2. In various parts of India kings of the name of Vīrasena are to be found. In the Harṣacrita there are references to two Vīrasenas—one is the king of Kaliṅga and another of the Sauvīras. In the Vallālacarita it is said that Vīrasena descended from the epic hero Karṇa and came to Gauḍa from Aṅga.
3. Transactions and Proceedings of the Oriental Conference, 1922, p. 343.
4. BI., p. 251 ; Prabāsī, 1913 B. S., pp. 396 ff.

Bengal in the train of the Cola invasion. In the Deopara praśasti it is said that Sāmantasena, grandfather of Vijayasena, "singly slaughtered the wicked robbers of the wealth of Karṇāṭa, overrun by hostile tribes" (v. 8). The relation between the Karṇaṭas and the Colas was far from being friendly. In order to solve the difficulties involved in this suggestion he presumed that after the defeat of the Cālukya king Jayasiṁha II by Rājendra Cola some Karṇāṭa soldiers took service in the Cola army and accompanied it in the Cola expedition in Bengal. The enemy against whom Sāmantasena fought was Mahīpāla I of the Pāla dynasty whom R. D., Banerjee identified with Mahīpāla of the drama 'Caṇḍakauśikam' by Kṣemīśvara. Mr. J. M. Roy[1] supported this view by pointing out that in the 5th verses of the Sunderban, Anulia and Tarpandighi grants of Lakṣmaṇasena the city of Kāñcī has been referred to as the ornament of southern India. Dhoyī in his 'Pavana-dūtam' gives a glowing picture of Kāñchī. Recent discussions[2] on 'Mahīpāla of Caṇḍakauśikam' have shown that his identification with the Pāla king cannot be maintained, and in all reasonableness he is to be identified with the Pratihāra king Mahīpāla. The Cola army was not defeated by Mahīpāla I, as the evidence of the Tirumalai inscription is definite on that point. There is nothing to show that Mahīpāla I of the Pāla dynasty came into conflict with the Karṇāṭas.

R. P. Chanda[3] drew attention to the 3rd verse of the Naihati plate where it is said that of the lunar family (the Senas belonged to the lunar race) many kings ruled in Rāḍha and in that family was born Sāmantasena. Owing to the apparent contradiction in the statements in the Deopara and Naihati inscriptions he presumed that Rāḍha was under the suzerainty of the Cālukyas and the predecessors of the Senas governed this remote possession. Mr Chanda was of opinion that the origin of the Senas is to be

1. Dhākāra Itihāsa, p. 309.

2. Journal of Oriental Research, Madras, VI, pp. 191 ff ; IC, II p. 354, 797 ; IHQ, XIII, p. 149.

3. Gauḍarājamālā, p. 46-7.

connected with the exploits of the Cālukya king Vikramāditya VI. Sāmantasena was engaged in fighting the enemies of Karṇāṭa in Rāḍha. We think that too much importance should not be attached to the 3rd verse of the Naihati plate of Vallālasena in all its details. It is admitted by all that before Vallālasena the Senas were settled in Bengal at least for three generations. The court panegyrist could then easily compose a verse by proclaiming that many princes of the family of his patron adorned Rāḍha. It appears from the description of the heroic activities of Sāmantasena that they took place in Karṇāṭa. He is said to have carried his victorious arms as far as the Adam's bridge and punished the spoilers of the fortunes of the Karṇāṭa country and in his old age retired on the banks of the Ganges.[1] While we are thus inclined to differ with Mr. Chanda in regarding Sāmantasena as the first settler of the Sena family in Rāḍha, the probability of his coming in the train of a Cālukya invasion seems to be strong. We have already referred to the Cālukya invasions of Bengal by Someśvara I, Someśvara II and Vikramāditya VI. Towards the close of the 11th century we find Nānyadeva,[2] admittedly another Karṇāṭa chief, ruling in Mithilā and Nepāla. The proud way of styling themselves Karṇāṭa-Kṣatriyas by the Senas in their own records and the marriage of Vallālasena with a Cālukya princess point to connect the establishment of the Sena power in Bengal with the exploits of a Karṇāṭa king, be he Someśvara I or Vikramāditva VI.

The Senas claim descent from the lunar race, and it is said that Sāmantasena belonged to the head-garland of the clans of Brahma-Kṣatriyas (Brahma-Kṣatiryanāṁ Kulaśirodāma). Kielhorn translated the phrase "Brahma-Kṣatriyas" as "the class of the Brahmana and the Kṣatriyas."[3] Prof. Bhandarkar[4] takes this

1. Deopara praśasti. vs., 1-9 2. IHQ, 1931. pp. 681ff.

3. The term Brahmakṣatra has been used in this sense in the Rāmāyaṇa (Bālakaṇḍa, 13, 7 ; Kiṣkindhyākāṇḍa, 39, 17). But this has been used in the genealogical accounts of the Bhāgavata (9 skandha, 22 adhyāya, 44 st.) and in the Viṣṇupurāṇa (4th Aṁśa) to mean a person born of a Brahmana and Kṣatriya parentage.

4. JASB, 1909, p, 186

expression to refer to a family having priestly and martial energy and says that the Brahma-Kṣatriyas were originally Brahmana classes of new tribes who afterwards turned Kṣatriyas, before their final merging into the Hindu society. In western India a caste called Brahmakṣatri still exists, and as the Senas came from Karṇāṭa, it is quite likely that they became known as Brahmakṣatriyas when they began to weild political and military power.

Hemantasena was the son of Sāmantasena, and in the Deopara praśasti the title Mahārājñī has been applied to his wife Yaśodevī. In the Barrackpore plate the title of Hemantasena is Mahārājādhirāja. It is very likely that Hemantasena had some pretension to royal dignity.

The real founder of the political fortunes of the Senas in Bengal was his son Vijayasena. His Barrackpore plate is dated in the 62nd regnal year. The recent attempt to fix the Sena chronology[1] on astronomical grounds also shows that Vijayasena like his centemporary, Coḍagaṅga of Kaliṅga, had an unusually long reign. Therefore the suggestion to identify the sāmantarāja Vijayarāja of Nidrāvala of the Rāmacarita cannot be set aside for chronological difficulties. A pillar with the figure of the goddess Manasā with an inscription, "Rājena Śrī-Vijayase," has been found at Paikore in the Birbhum district. This 'Vijayase' is generally identified with Vijayasena. The Senas were at first settled in Rāḍha and this inscription indicates to locate their original territory in the Birbhum district. Paikore is almost near to the bank of the Ganges, where it meets the Padmā—a place of great strategic value perhaps to Rāmapāla in his war against the Kaivartas and also to Vijayasena in his war against the Gauḍa king. It seems that the 17th, 18th and 19th verses of the Deopara praśasti in a veiled but clever manner refer to the part played by Vijayasena in helping Rāmapāla to recover Varendra and this established his future claim to the throne of Gauḍa, when there arose a dispute regarding it. The poet Umāpatidhara was an adept in

1. IC, IV, p 227

playing with words and it is difficult to comprehend clearly what he actually drove at. In the 17th verse Vijayasena is compared with Rāma and Arjuna and his arms to theirs. In the 18th verse 'divyaḥ bhuva' has been used, recalling 'divya-viṣaya' of the Rāmacarita. The 19th verse has been translated thus[1]: "By him who gave away land in heaven to his rival princes and accepted (from them) the earth in return, the sword-blade marked the writing in the blood of heroes was made to serve the purpose of document, as it were, in anticipation, otherwise how could earth come to be enjoyed by him when there arose disputes regarding her and presenting his drawn sword the host of his opponents would admit defeat." If it be true that Vijayasena helped Rāmapāla against the Kaivartas, there was no question of rivalry with the Pālas at that time, but at a later period when Vijayasena was aspiring after the Gauḍa kingdom, the Pāla king was certainly his rival. This is perhaps what is meant by giving land to a 'pratipakṣa' (rival) king which most probably refers to a Pāla king. There is no doubt that there arose a dispute for the throne of Gauḍa in which the sword and might of Vijayasena decided the issue.

In the next verse is given a list of the chiefs and kings with whom the Sena king came into conflict and all of whom were probably aspirants after the Pāla throne. The first king referred to is Nānya who is to be identified with Nānyadeva of Mithilā, who ascended the throne in 1097 A.D.. A commentary on Bharata's Nāṭyaśāstra written by king Nānyadeva has come to light,[2] and in addition to the high-sounding titles he is said to have broken the powers of Gauḍa and Vaṅga kings. Both Vijayasena and Nānyadeva were Karnatic in origin. It may be that they at first followed a concerted action. But the Deopara inscription shows that they came into conflict in which the Sena

1. We follow Mr. N. G. Majumdar's translation of the verse. Attention was first drawn to this by Mr N. N. Vasu, VJI. Rājanya Kāṇḍa, pp. 302-3.

2. Quarterly Journal of the Andhra Historical Research Society, 1926, Oct. pp. 55-63, ; IHQ. 1931, pp. 681 ff.

king claimed victory. The other chiefs defeated by Vijayasena were Vīra, Vardhana and Rāghava. It has been suggested that Vīra and Vardhana are to be identified with Vīraguṇa and Govardhana of the Rāmacarita.[1] Rāghava is to be identified with the Kaliṅga king of that name, son of Coḍagaṅga. Coḍagaṅga's rule lasted from c. 1076 to 1147 A. D., and his son Rāghava's from c. 1156-60 A. D., In the Kendulapata[2] plates of Narasiṁha it is said that Coḍagaṅga levied tributes from the lands bordering on the Ganges and forced the ruler of the Mandāra to flee. It may be that Vijayasena warded off the Kaliṅga invasion under Rāghava's leadership. In the Deopara 'praśasti' it is further said that the Sena king attacked the lord of Gauḍa and drove away the Kāmarūpa king. The king of Gauḍa has been generally identified with Madanapāla. Some scholars are inclined to think that the Kāmarūpa king refers to Rāyārideva, and this has perhaps been alluded to in the Assam plates of Vallabhadeva. The 22nd verse records that Vijayasena sent a navy against the combination of the western powers (pāścātya-cakra) against him. This might have been meant against the Pālas who seem to have sought refuge in Magadha after the occupation of Varendra by the Seṇa king and rallied once more their strength to fight. Most probably when all the chiefs were fighting among themselves, the Kalacuri king Pṛthivīdeva II of Ratanpur made a raid on Lādaha (Rādha ?) and Gauḍa, as it is stated in the Akatara stone inscription that his feudatory Vallabharāja overran these two countries. Both of them were living in 1141 A. D.[3] The eastward advance of the Gāhaḍavāla power during the period 1124-1146 A. D., which is proved by the Maner and Lar plates, probably took place, when all the rival chiefs were fighting among themselves.

It seems that there was a general scramble for power during the rule of the weak successors of Rāmapāla among some of the

1. IA, 1920, pp. 175 ff,

2. JASB, 1896, pt. I. p. 239.

3. Dr. Hiralal, Inscriptions of C. P. and Berrar, p. 109.

feudatories of the Pāla kingdom and the neighbouring kings. The political condition of Bengal was extremely favourable for the foundation of a new power, and in the struggle that followed Vijayasena came out successful. His matrimonial alliance with the Śūra family might have raised his political and social status in the estimation of the contemporary people. The Barrackpore plate was issued from Vikrampura in his 62nd year, in which the chief queen Vilāsadevī performed the 'tulā-puruṣa' ceremony. It is therefore clear that he must have ousted the Varmans from Vikrampura by that time. The Deopara inscription shows that southern Varendra was under him.[1]

Vijayasena was the real founder of the Sena power in Bengal. It seems that since his early life he was a successful soldier and general, and that was a great asset in his adventurous career. Hero of many battle-fields, he succeeded in foiling the attempts of all other aspirants and took the utmost advantage of the declining and tottering Pāla power. He was lavish in his gifts to the Brahmanas and performed many sacrifices. He excavated many tanks and built a magnificent temple of Pradyumneśvara which was the wonder and admiration of his time

Vijayasena was succeeded by his son Vallālasena in 1159. A.D.. In his Naihati plate no military achievement excepting some vague statements has been ascribed to him. In the Madhainagar grant of his son it is said that Lakṣmanasena, when a crown prince, seized suddenly the fortune of the Gauḍa king, made war on Kaliṅga and Kāśī. It seems that these campaigns took place during the reign of Vallālasena. It is important to notice that Vijayasena and Vallālasena did not assume the title of Gauḍeśvara in their own records, though it has been attributed to them in the grants of their successors. If Gauḍeśvara Govindapāla and Palapāla, whose rule

1. The view that Vijayasena became the king of the whole of Varendra rests on a passage of Dānasāgara but the reading is not free from doubts. Some scholars read it as "Tadā Vijayasena prādurāsīdvarendra". while others read "narendra" in place of "varendra". See Dhākāra Itihāsa, p. 313.

in all probadility was confined to some part of Magadha, are to be regarded as kings of the Pāla dynasty, they did not give up their claim to the throne of Gauḍa and might have held some portion of northern Bengal under them. Most probably the war of Viajayasena was not decisive and Vallālasena had to fight with the successor of Madanapāla. The Vallālacarita[1] also records that the war with the Pālas was going on at the time of Vallālasena. Owing to the financial stringency caused by this long-drawn war Vallālasena wanted to borrow money from the great banker Vallabhānanda of the Suvarṇavaṇik community. It is further said that the banker was the father-in-law of the Magadha king and was siding with the Pālas. In our opinion, this is to be credited with some historicity.

Of all the kings of anciect period Vallālasena is the best known in every rank and grade of the Hindu society of Bengal as the founder of the institution of Kulinism. We have discussed the whole topic elsewhere in details and have come to the conclusion that the volumes of evidence are now overwhelming in favour of the view that some re-organisation of the Hindu society was made in the Sena period and the start in that direction was given by Vallālasena in Rāḍha among the Brahmanās, although he cannot be called the founder of modern Kulinism with all its parapharnelia in the strict sense of the term. If he is the idol of those who were favoured with Kaulinya rank, it appears that at a later period those who were adversely affected by it tried to blacken the character of the monarch in order to lower him in the estimation of the comtemporary people and posterity. The Vallālacarita by tne Suvarṇavaniks and another book of the same name by the Yogis[2] were composed with that avowed object, and the true purport of other flimsy stories associated with the name of Vallālasena seems to be that. His connection with a low caste girl, a consequent domestic quarrel with Lakṣmaṇasena and the division of the Vaidya society

1. Eng. Trans. by Mm. H. P. Shastri, pp. 15, 90.
2. Vallālacarita published by Haris Candra Kaviratna.

into Vallālī (the followers of Vallālasena) and Lakṣmaṇī (the followers of Lakṣmaṇasana) and stories like these seem to be proagandist in nature,[1] and it is dificult to say how much truth there is underlying them.

Lakṣmaṇasena ascended the throne in 1178 A. D. His military exploits, when a crown prince, as described in the Madhainagara grant, have been discussed. It is said in the same record that he crippled Kaliṅga and Kāmarūpa It is known from the Madanapara grant of his son Viśvarūpasena that he erected pillars of victory in Puri, Benares and Prāyāga. It appears therefore that Lakṣmaṇasena made another expedition against Kaliṅga and Gāhaḍavāla power. His contemporaries on the Kaliṅga throne were Rājarāja II and Anaṅgabhīma II, both sons of Coḍagaṅga. The name of the contemporary Kāmarūpa king is not known. The Gāhaḍavāla king was Jayacandra whose inscriptions[2] have been found at Benares and Kanouj ranging from 1170 to 1188 A. D., and who was defeated and killed by Sahabuddin in 1194 A .D. Pavanadūtam narrates his march of universal conquest as far south as the Malaya hills, "roughly the southern part of the Western Ghats." It has been pertinently pointed out the it may refer to his invasion of Kaliṅga.[3] From the evidence of the Madanapara grant and Dhovī's book it may be inferred that Lakṣmaṇasena undertook a war of digvijaya, though it must be admitted that the poet's love of exaggeration "served the double purpose of eulogising his patron and finding a most suitable abode for the heroine of his poem." It seems that the Sena power reached its high water-mark during his reign and the kingdom was expanding in the west, which probably necessitated the formation of a new bhukti, namely, Kaṅkagrāma-bhukti, comprising the Santal-paraganas.[4]

Lakṣmaṇasena was the last great Hindu king of Bengal. His name and fame spead far and wide. The Muslim historian Minhaj-

1. B. Sengupta, Vaidya Jātīra, Itihāsa, pt. 1, pp. 166-180.
2. DH. I, p. 541
3. C. Chakravarti, Pavanadūtam, Introduction.
4. EI. XX1, pp. 211ff.

uddin[1] says that he was a 'great Rai' and 'most respected in Hindusthan.' He further records that trustworthy persons have related to this effect, "from his hand never did any tyranny proceed ; and whosoever preferred a request to him for anything, other than one lak he did not bestow, after the manner of Kutub-ud-din......the least gift he used to bestow was a lak of Kauris. The Almighty mitigate his punishment (in hell) !" But the king, to whose power, charity and just government Minhaj pays such glowing tributes, suffered a severe reverse during the closing years of his reign. There are differences of opinion[2] as to the actual date of the raid of Nadia by Mahammad ibn Bakht-yar, and we shall not be very wrong if we place it in c. 1200 A. D.. As regards the story of the raid, the very nature of Minhaj's sources of information makes us very cautious, and every statement in that conncetion requires critical scrutiny. It is also clear that when Minhaj wrote his account of the expedition in 641 A. D., there were many rumours and gossips about Lakṣmaṇasena which the historian heard from his informants in Lakṣmaṇāvatī. His reporters seem to have been two brothers, Nizam-ud-din and Samsum-ud-din by name, who served under Bakht-yar. It is natural that they should exaggerate the part played by them and their master. How far reliable are their reports can be better judged by narrating some of their stories. It is said that Lakṣmaṇasena was born after the death of Vallālasena. As the time of his birth approached, the sooth-sayers said that the was an ominous time and if the child would see the light of the sun two hours later, he would be a famous king. So the queen's feet were tied up and the child was born

1. Tabaqat-i-Nasiri, Eng. Trans. by Raverty. The following account is based on Minaj's account, pp. 552-559

2. Blochman placed it in 1197-8 A. D. ; E. Thomas in 1202·3 A. D. ; and Stewart in 1203-4 A. D. The definite information is that Bakt-yar entered Kutub-ud-din's service in 590 A. H, and after his sack of Nadia and establishment of headquarters at Lakṣmaṇāvatı started for his Tibetan expedition in 601 A. H., and also saw Kutub-ud-din at Mahoba in 599 A. H. with presents from Bengal spoils.

after two hours. That Lakṣmaṇasena was born after the death of Vallālasena is opposed to the plain testimony of the Madhainagar plate. Again, the sooth-sayers told Lakṣmaṇasena that the invasion of the Yavanas would soon happen and it would be better to abandon Nadia. Most of the officers and men fled and sent their property and families to other places. It is quite likely that the fall of one kingdom of northern India after another might have caused some panic among the general people. But the whole thing has been ascribed to the sooth-sayers. If there be any truth in this report, it must be said that Lakṣmaṇasena himself did not abandon Nadia but was determined to stay there. The statement that at the time of the raid he had been on the throne for a period of eighty years is opposed to all other contemporary evidence like Adbhutasāgara, Dānasāgara and Ṣaduktikarṇāmṛta. This perhaps indicates his actual age rather than his reign-period. It is also likely that the reporters confused the beginning of his reign with the starting-point of the Lakṣmaṇasena Era in 1119-20 A. D., and this is in complete agreement with the view that the raid took place in 1199-1200 A.D..[2]

Minhaj gives the following account of the raid : "Bakt-yar caused a force to be prepared, pressed on from Behar, and suddenly appeared before the city of Nudiah." The march was so swift and rapid that only seventeen of his horsemen could keep pace with him, who entered the gate unsuspectingly and were taken to be dealers in horse by the gate-keepers. Entering the inner palace, he surprised the inmates and began slaughter. The king was at his dining table and took a boat by the back door of his palace. "When the whole army arrived and the city round about had been taken possession of, he there took up his quarters ; and Rai got away towards Sankwat and Bang and there the period of his reign shortly afterwards came to a termination.........After Bakt-yar possessed himself of that territory he left the city of Nudiah in desolation and the place which is now Lakhnwati he made the seat of government."

1. IHQ, V, pp. 133-5 2. See Appendix C.

A controversy has been raised whether Nadia was the capital of the Senas. Whether the capital or not, it is clear from Minhaj that it was a 'seat of government' of Lakṣmaṇasena, and there is nothing improbable in the fact that like Vikramapura and Lakṣmaṇāvatī, Nadia was another headquarter of the Senas. The evidence to identify Vijayapura, a city founded by Vijayasena, with Nudiah of Minhaj is stronger than that to identify it with the place of that name, near the findspot of the Deopara praśasti in the Rajshahi district, because 'Pavanadūtam' places it in Suhmadeśa on the other side of the Ganges.[1]

The above account of the sack and raid of Nadia seems to be true in broad outline, though there might be some exaggeration in matters of details, and it does not reflect much credit on the administration of Lakṣmaṇasena, as the Muslim army could come from Bihar to Bengal unnoticed and unopposed. It apears that it was a surprise attack and every one was unprepared for it and bewildered and puzzled by its suddenness. Judged by its results, the raid of the daring Muslim general was eminently successful. The Sena power collapsed in western and northern Bengal and Minhaj does not mention of any effective opposition in his march to Lakṣmaṇavatī and Devīkot.

According to the Āin-i-Ākbari,[2] Lakhan Sen was succeeded by his son Madhu Sen who ruled for 10 years. Saduktikarṇāmṛta refers to a verse of Mādhavasena. Madhu Sen's rule is known only from Abul Fazal whose account of the Hindu kings cannot be always relied upon, if it is not corroborated from other evidence.[3] Two sons of Lakṣmaṇasena, Viṣvarūpasena and Keśavasena, who ruled after him, are known from their own records[4] and the known periods of their reigns are 17 years.

1. C. Chakravartti. Pavanadūtam, Intro. p. 8

2. Vol. II. p. 146

3. According to Mr. N. N. Vasu one copper-plate of Mādhava Sena has been found in the Almora district and the reference given is 'Kumaon' by Atkinson, p. 519. But as I cannot verify this, nothing can be said definitely on this point.

4. IB, No. XIII, XIV, XV.

It is therefore almost certain that for the first quarter of the 13th century these two Sena kings could hold themselves against Muslim aggression. Both of them assumed the proud title of Gauḍeśvara and the epithet "Garga.Yavanānvaya-pralaya-kāla-rudra" has been applied to them. This does not seem to be an empty boast and both the brothers boast that they were dread to the Yavanas and it seems that they successfully repulsed some Muslim invasions.

The author of the Tabaqat-i-Nasiri did not directly record any invasion of east Bengal by the Muslim governors and rulers of Laknauti, but that there were several such attempts is clear from some incidental references by Minhaj. It is therefore quite possible that there had been some other attempts to conquer Bang, which were not recorded at all. Giyasuddin was the independent ruler of Lakṣmṇāvatī (1211-1226 A. D.). The rulers of Jajnagar, Tirhut, Kāmarūpa and Bang[1] paid tribute to him. Just before the end of his reign, he is said to have invaded Kāmarūpa and Vaṅga. Natural conclusion seems to be that there was previously an invasion against these two countries, and because they refused to pay tribute to the Muslim ruler, another expedition was undertaken against them. It is clear from the account of Minhaj that before Giyasuddin could achieve anything substantial, he had to return on account of the usurpation of Lakṣmṇāvatī by Nasiruddin. Next reference to the invasion of east Bengal is made in connection with the rule of Malik Safuddin who sent some elephants to the court of Delhi which were captured in Bang[2] (1231-33 A. D.). It is not known who was the ruling Sena king at this time. Abul Fazal mentions a king of the name of Sūrasena or Sadāsena. Two princes of the Sena dynasty, Sūryasena and Puruṣottamasena, are known from the Sahitya Parisat plate of Viśvarūpasena, and it is quite probable that Sūrasena of Abul Fazal is Sūryasena of this plate. Another invasion of east Bengal

1. Tabaqat-i-Nasiri, pp. 587-588
2. Ibid., p. 782

took place in the reign of Ijjuddin Balban[1] in or about 1258 A. D. Minhaj finished his account in 1259 A. D. and makes the statement that at that time the descendants of Lakṣmaṇasena were ruling in eastern Bengal.[2]

Another Hindu king is known from the Adavadi plate[3] of Daśarathadeva and Danujamādhava was his virūda. He may be identified with Rājā Danujah of Zia-ud-din Barni,[4] who describes him as king of Sonargaon. According to the genealogical book of Harimiśra, he flourished after the Sena rule.[5] When Delhi Sultan Giyasuddin Balban came to supress the rebellion of the Bengal governor Tughril Khan, an agreement was reached between the Delhi Sultan and this Hindu king of Sonargaon to the effect that the latter would prevent the escape of Tughril Khan by water. The Muslim occupation of eastern Bengal must have been completed by the close of the !3th century.[6]

It cannot be properly ascertained whether the extreme eastern districts like Noakhali and Chittagong were included in the Pāla and Sena kingdoms. No evidence has yet been discovered to prove the extension of the Sena power in the Chittagong division. The Mainamati plate[7] speaks of the existence of an independent kingdom in Paṭṭikerā which is a pargana in modern Tippera. The name of the king is Harikāladeva whose virūda is Raṇavaṅkamalla and he came to the throne in in 1203-4 A. D. If he was the first king of this family and this principality was included in the Sena kingdom, it seems that with the fall of the Senas in Gauḍa an independent kingdom arose in eastern Bengal. Even within the lifetime of Lakṣmaṇasena a Pāla family from Ayodhyā settled in Khāḍi (in the Sunderbans), and it seems from the Sunderban

1. Ibid., pp, 769-70
2. Ibid., pp. 558. 715
3. IB., p. 181
4. Elliot, History of India vol, III. p. 116
5. Bhāratvarṣa, 1332, B. S. pp. 78-81
6. BI. vol. II. pp. 93 14
7. IHQ. IX. p. 282

plate[1] of Dommonapāla that this king set at naught. the Sena authority in that locality and assumed an attitude of independence by 1196 A. D. Another Hindu kingdom was founded about this time. It is known from the Chittagong plate of Dāmodara[2] who was ruling in 1243 A. D.. His earliest known ancestor is Puruṣottoma whose son was Madhusūdana. The title nṛpa occurs before his name and it may be that the rise of the family to political power began from him. His son was Vasudeva whose son Dāmodara assumed the proud title "sakala-bhūpati-cakravartī." Nothing more is known of these kingdoms.

The conquest of north-western Bengal by the Muslims and the maintenance of independence by eastern Bengal in spite of the repeated attempts of the Muslims to conquer it suggest one important conclusion. A sudden cavalry raid was sufficient to break the power of the Sena kings in north-western Bengal and the whole of it passed into Muslim hands within a short time. But the physical features of eastern Bengal prevented such an eventuality. It is the country of big rivers and hence cavalry was practically useless. Here for a permanent conquest the naval power was the most important factor. A raid might have been carried on in a certain part but it could not produce a lasting effect. The seeking of the help of Danujamādhava by Sultan Giyasuddin Balban to prevent the escape of the rebellious governor Tughril Khan by boat clearly illustrates the weakness of the power in eastern Bengal—a power strong in every other respect excepting the navy. This also accounts for the reason why the descendants of Lakṣmaṇasena fought the Muslims from east Bengal and why this part of the country could resist Muslim attacks for about a century, while the great kingdoms of northern India succumbed to Muslim attacks quickly. Before the final conquest of eastern Bengal, the Muslims must have realised the difficulty and perhaps built a navy equal to the occasion.

1. IHQ., X, p, 321 ; IC, I, p 679,

2. IB., No. XVII.

Appendix B

Our study of the Sena history is based on the following chronology :—

	Probable	Known reign-perioiod
Sāmantasena	....	....
Hemantasena	....	....
Vijayasena	c. 1097-1159 A. D.	62 years.
Vallālalsena	1159-1178 A. D.	19 years.
Lakṣmaṇsena	c. 1178-1205 A. D.	27 years.
Keśavasena	....	3 years.
Viśvarūpasena	....	14 years.

This chronology satisfies (1) the statement in Dānasāgara that it was finished by Vallālasena in 1091 S. E., (2) the date 1082 S. E. referred to in some Mss. of Adbhūtasāgara as the initial date of Vallālasena's reign, and (3) the date 1127 S. E. as the 27th year (Ras-aikaviṁśābde)[1] of Lakṣmaṇasena's reign mentioned in Sadukti-karṇāmṛta. This also satisfies the contemporaneity of Vijayasena and Nānyadeva of Mithilā (c. 1097-1150 A. D.) and Rāghava of Kaliṅga (c. 1156 A. D.) and also the astronomical data.[2] This is also in accord with the evidence of the Tabaqati-i-Nasiri that Lakṣmaṇasena was defeated by Bakht-yar between 1193 and 1205 A. D..

Appendix C

The Lakṣmaṇasena Era.

The origin of the Lakṣmaṇasena Era abbreviated as La Sam is a matter of controversy among scholars. That it was counted at first from 1119-20 (October to October) is perhaps to be accepted after what Mr. K. P. Jayaswal has written on the subject.[3] Kielhorn verified six dates of La Sam and came to the

1. IHQ. III, p. 188.
2. EI., Vol.XXI, pp. 211 ff.
3. JBORS., XX, p. 20.

conclusion that they work out satisfactorily, if the initial year was the Kārtikādi Sudi I of the expired Śaka year 1041, with the Āmanta scheme of lunar fortnight = the 7th October, A. D. 1119, and it is supported by a statement of Abul Fazl in the Ākbarnāmā.[1] But the initial year of La Sam, as it is still used in the almanacs of Mithilā, falls on the 30th January, A. D. 1108.. Mr. P. N. Misra verifiied 12 dates and came to the conclusion that 4 dates work out satisfactorily with Kielhorn's or Mithiiā almanac epochs, while the remaining dates work out satisfactorily with the latter.[2] Mr. Jayaswal says that up to a certain period the dating was on the basis of the era commencing in 1119-20 A. D., but after the Muslim conquest of Tirhut the Fasli Era, a lunar reckoning, was promulgated at the time of Akbar. La Sam received from that time a lunar (instead of the earlier luni-solar) calculation and hence the difference in the initial year of the earlier dates and of the later dates. Mr. Jayaswal quotes a passage from a MS. in the possession of Pandit Ganga Nath Misra, according to which a fixed figure is deducted from the current year to obtain La Sam, as well as fixed figures are deducted to obtain Śaka and Vikrama years.

If the initial date of La Sam is thus settled, its origin is far from being so. Discussing the subject, Dr. H. C. Roy Chowdhury writes that its origin is to be sought in the Sena dynasty of Piṭhī and not in the Sena dynasty of Bengal, because it was never used by the Senas of Bengal and its earliest use was confined to Bihar where there is epigraphic evidence of the existence of a line of Sena kings who actually used the era.[3] There are two epigraphs of Aśokavalla known as Bodh-Gaya inscriptions[4] and another of Jayasena found at Janibigha,[5] a place close to Bodh-Gaya, and the dates of these three epigraphs are expressed as follows :—

I. Śrīmal-Lakhvana (Kṣmaṇa) Senasya-atīta-rājye, S. 51.

1. IA., 1890, p. 1. 2. JASB., 1926, p. 373.
3. Sir Asutosh Jubilee Volume, Orientalia, pt. 2. p. 1.
4. Cunningham, Mahābodhi, p. 78. pl. XXVII A ; and JASB., V, p. 951, pl. XXX.
5. JBORS., IV, p. 273.

II. Śrīmal-Lakṣmaṇasenadevapādānāṁ-atīta-rājye, S. 74.

III. Lakṣmaṇasenasya-atīta-rājya, S. 83.

The uniform manner of the expression of these three dates in the records of two kings of Pīṭhī shows that they refer clearly to the post-regnal year of a king or an era. Calculating these dates according to La Sam, Dr. Roy Chowdhury says that the king whose reign was a thing of the past in the year 51 (1170 A. D.) cannot be identified with Lakṣmaṇasena of Bengal who ruled in the last quarter of the twelfth century. Therefore he concludes, 'If the founder of Lakṣmaṇasena Era was not identical with Lakṣmaṇsena of Bengal, he must have been the founder of the Sena dynasty of Pīṭhī.' But Dr. Roy Chowdhury does not mention any king of Pīṭhī of the name of Lakṣmaṇsena.

So far as we know, Tārānātha speaks of two Lavasenas.[1] Granting that Tārānātha's chronology and genealogy of the kings of Magadha and Bengal are faulty, it is to be noticed that Lavasena, the predecessor of Budhasena, Hāritasena, and Pratītasena, is contemporaneous with the Muslim invasion of Bihar and Bengal, and Tārānātha places him after the Senas of Bengal. If it is to be accepted that this Lavasena was king of Pīṭhī and was the founder of La Sam in 1119 A. D., the recording of the epigraphs of the time of Jayasena (one of the Sena kings of Pīṭhī) in the year 83 of this era and also of Aśokavalla in the years 51 and 73 shows that Pīṭhī was in the possession of these kings from 1119 A. D. to the close of the twelfth century. As regards the correct location of Pīṭhī, Mr. H. Panday who edited the Janibigha inscription writes that 'our record proves that the sites of the village Janibigha and also Bodh-Gaya were included in the country called Pīṭhī. As such it appears to have been the name given to the southern portion of Magadha at least about this time, probably on account of its association with Vajrāsana.'[2]

The history of Pīṭhī in the 11th and 12th centuries is known from contemporary records. It is known from the Saranath inscrip-

1. IA., 1875, p. 366.

2. JBQRS., 1918, p. 273.

tion of Kumāradevī[1] that Pīṭhī was ruled by Vallabaharāja and his son Devarakṣita of the Chikkore family about the middle of the 11th century. Devarakṣita was defeated by Mathanadeva, maternal uncle of Rāmapāla. The chief of Pīṭhī who helped Rāmapāla in his Kaivarta war was Bhīmayaśa. The Gaya stone inscription of Govindapāla[2] is dated in the 12th V. E. = 1175 A.D., that year being the "gatarājya caturddaśa samvatsara" of Govindapāla. The affix Pāla, the Buddhist title Paramasaugata and the title Gauḍeśvara raise a strong presumption that he belonged to the Pāla dynasty. Whether Govindapāla was a king of the Pāla dynasty or not, the Gaya stone inscription clearly proves that he ruled in Gaya and in its vicinities about the middle of the twelfth century. R. D. Banerjee assumes[3] with a tolerable degree of certainty that Govindapāla ruled a portion, probably the eastern one, of Magadha. The Jayanagar Image inscription of Palapāla[4] also goes to show that some portion of Magadha was under the rule of this king. The known period of his reign is 35 years and he should be placed before Govindapāla or more probably after him. The evidence of the Rāmacarita, Gaya stone inscription and the Jayanagar inscription tends to show that Magadha was in the 11th and 12th centuries under the possession of the Pālas or under the kings whose names end in Pālas. The Senas of Pīṭhī could not possibly rule centemporaneously in the same locality with the Pālas. In all reasonableness, therefore, the Senas of Pīṭhī should be placed towards the very close of the 12th century or after that. This is in complete agreement with what we know from Tārānātha, according to whom Lavasena, the predecessor of Budhasena, Hāritasena, and Pratītasena, is contemporaneous with the Muslim invasion of Bihar and the Tibetan historian placed him after the Senas of Bengal. Or, even if it be granted that the Senas of Pīṭhī ruled in the 12th century from 1119 A. D., it must be admitted that

1. EI., IX, pp, 324-27.
2. The Pālas of Bengal, pl. XXVIII.
3. Ibid,, p. 109.
4. JBORS., XIV. pp. 489 ff.

they were local rulers, as the Gaya inscription of 1175 A. D. shows the control of Govindapāla over Pīṭhī.

Four inscriptions of Aśokavalla have come to light, and R. D. Banerjee has shown that Aśokavallas of the four epigraphs are identical.[1] The inscription in the walls of the Sūrya temple near Viṣṇupāda at Gaya is dated in the year 1813 of the Nirvāṇa Era. Fleet has shown that this date agrees well with Wednesday, first October, A.D. 1270.[2] It has been pointed out by Dr. R. C. Majumdar that there are reasons to believe that Aśokavalla flourished about 1270 A. D., and naturally the dates in the Bodh-Gaya inscriptions (and also in Janibigha inscription) would be taken as counted from the cessation of the reign of Lakṣmaṇasena, that event itself being placed towards the end of the twelfth century, and 'atīta rājya' 51 may easily be taken to mean that 50 or 51 years had elapsed since 'atītarājya' or the cessation of the reign.[3] It is quite natural that the Hindus or Buddhists were unwilling to refer to the 'pravardhamāna-vijaya-rājya' of the Muslims who were alien in culture and newcomers and who of late destroyed their temples or monasteries. Therefore the records of this time were dated by referring to the expired years of an Indian king.

Now the question is who is Lakṣmaṇasena from the cessation of whose reign or fall these records were dated ? Is he the famous Lakṣmaṇasena of Bengal or Lavasena of Tārānātha, predecessor of Budhasena ?

The existence of Lavasna rests on the sole authority of Tārānātha. It is not known where he actually ruled and what was his relation with Budhasena. An era is generally associated with the name of a great king. Traditions from different sources associate this era with the Sena dynasty of Bengal. According to Tāranātha,[4] it was counted from the time of Hemantasena, and Abul Fazl[5] associates it with Lakṣmaṇasena. That he was a great king and

1. JASB., 1913, pp. 271 ff.
2. JRAS., 1909, pp, 323 ff.
3. JASB, 1221, p. 13.
4. JASB., 1935, p, 48.
5. IA., 1890, p. 1.

that his fame spread far and wide are evident from his own records and from the testimony of Minhaj who says that Rai Laksmania was a great Rai. An MS. of the Viṣṇu Purāṇa written by Pakṣadhara Miśra is dated in the past year 345 of the king Lakṣmaṇsena of Gauḍa[1]. So far as we know, the Senas ot Pīṭhī were never called kings of Gauḍa and perhaps they cannot be called so.

If this era is to be associated with a Sena king of Bengal, it is better to do so with the king whose name and whose stamp of personality it perhaps bears. It cannot be maintained that Lakṣmaṇasena of Bengal started a new era in 1119 A.D.,[2] commemorating his accession, because the evidence of Dānasāgara, Adbhūtasāgara, Saduktikarṇamṛta, and Tabaqati-Nasiri is conclusive on this point. No record dated distinctly in La Sam (as opposed to atītārājye, vinaṣṭa-rājye, etc.) can be placed in the twelfth century. The earliest known document dated in this era is the colophon of an MS. belonging to the Darbar Library of Nepal and the date is La Sam 91 Caitra Vādi Gurau A.D., i.e, 1310. Is it then improbable that this era became current after the death of Lakṣmaṇasena? We have got at least one instance of an era of this period which was associated with the name of a king after his death. The Vallālī San or Parganāti San was current in Bengal even less than two hundred years ago. After a careful examination of all available data Dr. N. K. Bhattasali[3] has come to the conclusion that it began on the 28th September, A.D. 1202. It is significant that in two records this era is clearly called Vallālī San. In any case, Vallālasena's rule cannot be pushed so late as 1202 A.D., Vallālasena has

1. JASB., 1926, p. 373. Referred to by Mr. P, N. Misra.

2. R. D. Banerjee (JASB, 1913, pp. 271 ff.) contended that the Dacca Candi Image inscription was dated in La Sam. Mr. N. G. Majumdar who also maintained that Lakṣmaṇasena started this era (IA., 1919, p. 171) admited that "it is by no means the only conclusion deducible from the expression Śrimal-Lakṣmaṇasenadevasya Samvat 3. It can also mean simply in the 3rd regnal year of the king without necessarily having any reference to the era started by him."

3. IA., 1923, pp. 314ff.

a unique place in the social history of Bengal and the popular imagination has perhaps associated this era with his name which in all probability marks the fall or termination of Lakṣmaṇasena's rule. Lakṣmaṇasena was undoubtedly one of the last great Hindu kings of northern India and the Senas of Bengal had important political relations with Bihar. It is not unfair to infer that the people of Bihar dated their records by associating them with a great Hindu king with whom they had some connection. The erection of pillars of victory at Kāśī and Allahabad suggests that Lakṣmaṇasena had some hold over Bihar too. They did not find it difficult to make the year 1119 A.D. the initial year of this era. This may be the date when the Senas under Vijayasena for the first time came into conflict with Nānyadeva of Mithilā or more probably the date of the birth of Lakṣmaṇasena. Minhaj says that Lakṣmaṇasena was in his eightieth year at the time of Baktyar's invasion of Bengal. Lakṣmaṇasena did not possibly rule for 80 years but might have been 80 years old at that time.

Appendix D

Some Doubtful Invasions of Bengal

It is a well-known fact that the composers of royal praśastis described the conquests and achievments of their royal patrons in glowing and very exaggerated terms. Some inscriptions record invasions af Aṅga, Vaṅga and Kaliṅga by some petty kings who, it seems, could not have undertaken any expedition to these distant countries on their own accounts, nor does it seem that they accompanied any powerful king in his victorious expedition. Therefore it is natural that doubts should be expressed about these exaggerated descriptions of the court-poets. Our doubts are further confirmed by the fact that the statement of the conquest of Aṅga, Vaṅga and Kaliṅga was sometimes used as a poetic ornamentation. Thus it is claimed in the inscriptions of the Vijayanagara king Kṛṣṇarāya that the rulers of Aṅga, Vaṅga and Kaliṅga waited upon Vijayanagara kings.[1] It needs hardly be said that it was parctically impossible for a Vijayanagara king to hold any sway over Aṅga, Vaṅga and Kaliṅga in the fifteenth and sixteenth centuries. Again, it is stated in the Chitrogadh[2] Stone inscription dated in V.S. 1485 that the king Mokala of Mewaḍ subdued the Aṅgas, Kāmarūpas and Vaṅgas. These should be regarded as vague and general statements.

The Pithapuram Pillar inscription[3] of Pṛthivīśvara dated in S. E. 1082 records that Malla I of Dhandapura, son of Kīrtivarman II, subdued the Gaṅgas Kaliṅgas, Vaṅgas and Magadhas. The rulers of this family were chiefs of Velanāḍu. The fifth descendant of Malla I, Kulyavarman II, was a contemporary of the Eastern Cālukya king Vikramādiya (1015-22 A. D.), and Malla may be roughly assigned to the first half of the 10th century A.D.. He might have accompanied a Rāṣṭrakūṭa monarch. Otherwise the subjection of these countries by this chief seems to be a hollow statement.

The Eastern Cālukya king Kulottuṅga (c. 1070-86 A. D.) is said to have invaded about 45 countries[4] among which the names of Vaṅga and Vaṅgālas also appear. The Kalacuri king Vijjana of Kalyāṇa pretended to conquer Pāṇḍya, Cola and Vaṅga.[5] Again, his son Saṅkāmadeva's exploits are said to have extended over Gauḍa, Turuṣkas, Siṁhala, Cola, Magadha and Malaya. One of his known date is 1186 A. D., that year being the fifth year of his reign.[6] It is said that Udayarāja, son of Soccharāja, conquered

1. EI., XII, p. 132 ; XIV, p 170
2. Ibid, II, p. 439
3. Ibid IV, p. 32
4. IA., IX, pp. 33ff.
5, IA., IV, p. 275
6. Ibid, V, p. 45

Cola, Gauḍa and Karṇāṭa.[1] He belonged to the Bhinmal Paramāra branch and is to be placed before 1161[2] A.D.. Kalacurya Bhillama (one of whose inscriptions is dated in 1189 A. D.) is said to have been "a severe pain in the head of the Mālavas, a thunderbolt to that mountain Varālas, a lion to the tall elephants of Kaliṅgas, the roar of a cloud to the flocks of those swans of Gurjaras, Colas, Gauḍas and Pāñcalas, Kāla to the brilliant kings of Aṅgas, Vaṅgas and Nepālas."[3] It is not known from any other source that in the last half of the 12th century any king of Kuntala was so powerful as to defeat all these kings. Curiously enough, in the inscription of his son Jaitugi no victory is ascribed to the father, but Jaitugi himself is said to have conquered the Gurjaras, Pāṇḍyas, Colas, Lāṭas, Gauḍas, and some of his officers are said to have invaded Mālavas, Kaliṅgas, Turuṣkas and Nepālas.[4] All these exaggerated statements of both the father and the son cannot be taken as historical facts. Two more kings of Kuntala, Bijjala and his son Soma (the former is described as the founder of the Kalacurya kingdom), are said to have raided the Colas, Nepālas, Kaliṅgas, Pāñcālas and Gurjaras and to have received the homage of the Gauḍas, Pāṇdyās, Malayalas and Varālas.[5] It is asserted in the Godag inscription[6] of Vīra-Vallava II, dated in 1114 S. E., that this Hoysala king frightened the Aṅgas, Kaliṅgas, Vaṅgas. Magadhas, Colas, Malayas, Pāṅdyas, Keralas and Gurjaras. In the Ekamantha inscription,[7] dated in 1172 S. E., Gaṇapatideva claims to have defeated Siṁhana (a Yādava king), kings of Kaliṅga, Lāṭa and Gauḍa. It is stated in the Mamadpur inscription[8] of Kanhara,

1. Bhandarkar's List No. 312
2. Dr. D. C. Ganguly, History of Paramāra Dynasty. p. 347
3. EI., XV, p, 33
4. Ibid. V. p. 31
5. EI., V. p. 257 ; XV, p. 317
6. Ibid, VI, p. 92
7. IA., XXI, p. 197
8. EI., XIX, p. 21

dated in 1177 S. E., that his grandfather Simhana overcame the Gurjaras, Magadha and Gauḍas.

In the absence of any corroborative evidence these bold and and wide claims should be dismissed as baseless. It is quite possible that some of these chiefs might have accompanied their overlords and gained some victories which in their records are claimed as their own achievements. But it is also true that some of them are purely hollow statements.

CHAPTER VII

Administrative System

Central Government

The form of government was monarchical. The king was the apex of the whole system and had the usual imperial titles, 'Parameśvara,' 'Paramabhaṭṭāraka' and 'Mahārājādhirāja'. In the Edilpur grant of Keśavasena Aśvapati, Gajapati, Narapati[1] are also the titles of the king in addition to the usual ones. "Royalty is limited to the descendants of one family", observes merchant Sulaiman, "and never goes to another." This remark appears to be quite correct in view of the almost continuous rule of the Pālas for about four centuries and of the Senas for about one century. Force was the only factor by which a dynasty was ousted, as the Pālas were. Election was not unknown but very uncommon. A king was elected only in extraordinary circumstances. Gopala I, the founder of the Pāla dynasty, was elected king to escape from anarchy (mātsyanyāyaṃ-apahituṁ). The Rājataraṅgiṇī refers to the election of Yaśakara by the Brāhmaṇas after 939 A. D.. Kalhaṇa's remark on this election that to take such a course (to elect a king) is tantamount to lunacy is instructive.[2] The inscription of Ratanpāla records the election of Brahmapāla in the neighbouring kingdom of Kāmarūpa.[3] Gopāla's election by the 'prakṛtis'

---

1. In the Gāhaḍavāla records the kings are given the appellations of Aśvapati, Narapati, Gajapati, Giripati and Triśaṅkapati, These terms, according to Dr. R. S. Tripathi, signify lords of various classes of feudatories, but the first three may denote three branches of army (IHQ 1933. p. 121). According to Si-yu-ki, however, when there is no paramount monarch, the southern, northern and eastern parts of Jambudvīpa (India) are respectively supposed to be ruled over by four sovereigns called Gajapati, Chatrapati, Aśvapati and and Narapati (Beal's Translation Vol. I, p. 13, note)

2. BK. V, 456 ff 3. JASB, 1898, p. 99

has generally been taken as an election by the poeple.[1] But 'prakṛti' is a technical political term meaning principal officers. The Śukranīti gives a list of ten 'prakṛtis' consisting of the chaplain, the minister, the judge and so on.[2] In the Rājataraṅginī a group of seven officials who elected Jalauka, son and successor of Aśoka, is called 'prakṛtis.'[3] The election of Yaśakara was made by the Brāhmaṇas. It is improbable that there was a general election in the 8th century. We are, therefore, inclined to take the view that Gopāla was placed on the throne by the officers of state.

It cannot be definitely stated what happened in the case of the succession of a minor to the throne. Either a regent or a council of regency was perhaps set up. It is also quite possible that the great officers carried on the of the government in the name of the minor king.

The Queen-Consort's position was vegy high. She figures third in the list of the officers and feudatories. Kauṭilya also placed her in the first grade of officers with Mantrin and Purohita, drawing 48,000 paṇas from the state treasury. The actual political influence exercised by the Queen-Consort is not known, but it seems that as the chief queen her influence was considerable. In the Arthaśāstra the Queen Mother also gets 48,000 paṇas. What her position was is not known. Vilāsadevī, the Śūra princess and mother of Vallālasena, performed a religious ceremony and lands were granted to the sacrificial priest as dakṣiṇā.[4]

Yuvarāja—The heir-apparent was perhaps selected during the lifetime of the ruling king. Tribhuvanapāla and Rājyapāla were heir-apparents of Dharmapāla and Devapāla. Most probably these

---

1. Gauḍalekhamālā p. 19 fn. 2 ; Bānglāra Itihāsa, p. 151

2. Śukra. Book II, 196-70

Samāstaṁ purodhā lakṣaṇaṁ yam taducyate purodāśca pratinidhiḥ pradhānaḥ sacivastathā mantrī prāḍvivākaśca paṇḍita sumantrakaḥ amātya dūta ityetā ṛājṇa prakṛtayo dasaḥ

3. Rājataraṇginī, Bk. I, 118.20.

5, Naihati plate.

two princes predeceased their fathers. It is certain that the crown-princes had important functions in the government. The above-mentioned princes are referred to as the dūtakas of the Khālimpur and Monghyr grants. It is known from the Rāmacarita that Rāmapāla was closeted in discussions with his son Rājyapāla[1] who was entrusted with the task of government in the old age of the king.[2] Lakṣmaṇasena, when a crown prince, invaded Gauḍa and Kaliṅga, and defeated the king of Kāśī.[3] It has been suggested that Rājaputras of the land grants were most probably not the princes of the blood royal but the ordinary Rajput soldiers, holding fiefs from the kings in return for their military service.[4] Rājaputra figures after Rājñī and Rāṇaka and before Rājāmātya, Mahāpurohita and Mahāsenāpati. It is, therefore, reasonable to take Rājaputra to be princes, if not the crown princes. Princes sometimes enjoyed land. Kumāra Sūryasena and Puruṣottamasena enjoyed land which was granted by them on ceremonial occasions (on birth-day and on the occasion of Uttarāyaṇasaṁkramaṇa) but these grants were confirmed by a royal charter.[5]

The status of another officer may be discussed here. Kumārāmātya and Māhākumārāmātya figure in the list of officers but their position is not very high. Literally the word means the minister of princes. In the Gupta period Kumārāmātyas were the governors of Koṭivarṣaviṣaya. The Basarh seals refer to various classes of Kumārāmātyas. Mr. R. D. Banerjee divides them into four classes according to their ranks[6] : (1) ordinary, (2) equal in rank to princes of the royal blood (Yuvarājapādiya), (3) equal in rank to the crown prince (Śrī-Yuvarājabhaṭṭāraka-pādiya), (4) equal in rank to his Majesty (Paramabhaṭṭāraka-pādiya). The position and

1. BK. 1, 421
2. BK. 4, 1
3. Madhainagar plate.
4. JDL. XVI, p. 30. Our records do not favour the interpretation offered by Dr. Vogel as 'noble man.' See, Chamba, p. 122
5. Sahitya Parisat plate of Viśvarūpasena.
6. The Age of Imperial Guptas, Ch. on Administration.

status of Kumārāmātya and Mahākumārāmātya cannot be determined in the Pāla period, as nothing particular is known of them from the records. The term Mahākumārāmātya suggests that there might have been different classes of Kumārāmātyas.

Rājāmātya—Most probably he was 'Mantrin' (the prime minister) of the Arthaśāstra or Sarvadarśin of the Śukranīti. Among the officials proper he figures first, and it goes to signify that next to the king he was the most important personage in the government. The ancient writers on political science recognised the supreme importance of ministers and enjoin that they should be very carefully selected. Two great ministerial families who served the Pālas are known from their own records. They were learned men as well as men of great ability and capacity. It is claimed in the Badal Pillar inscription that Garga made Dharmapāla, lord of the east, master of all quarters. His son Darbhapāṇi by his wisdom and diplomacy made Devapāla lord of the earth from the Vindhyās to the Himālayas. This talented minister was held in high respect by the king. Darbhapāṇi's son, Someśvara, was dear to the king. By the wise counsel of Kedārmiśra, Someśvara's son, Devapāla uprooted the Utkalas, shattered the pride of the Huṇas and crushed the power of the Drāviḍas and the Gurjjaras. Guravamiśra, builder of the Badal Pillar, was the minister of Nārāyaṇapāla and 'dūtaka' of the Bhāgalpur grant. He was eloquent in speech, proficient in Āgamas, Tantras, astrology and in the Vedas and a fighter in the assembly as well as in the field. The Kamauli plates of Vaidyadeva introduce us to another line of hereditary ministers whose services to the Pālas were of great value. Yogadeva was the minister of Vigrahapāla III and his son Bodhideva was the counsellor of Rāmapāla. But the most successful and ablest minister of the family was Bodhideva's son Vaidyadeva. He was dear to Kumārapāla as his own life. He put down a rebellion in southern Bengal by winning a naval victory and by rapid marches surprised Tiṁgyadeva who raised the standard of revolt in Kāmarūpa. This record clearly shows that ministers were sometimes capable generals too. Perhaps as a reward for his service he was appointed ruler of Kāmarūpa. Or, it may be that Vaidyadeva asserted his independence after the death of Kumārapāla. In any case his titles, Parameśvara Paramabhaṭṭāraka and Mahārājādhirāja in his own record indicate his pretension to royal dignity.

In the Kamauli plate it is said that Yogadeva came to office through heredity. The Badal praśasti and the Kamauli plates would go to indicate that during the time of the Pālas hereditary ministers were preferred. While speaking of the hereditary mona rchy prevalent in India, the merchant Sulaiman writes, "The same is the case with families of wazirs, kazis and other high officers. They are all hereditary and never changed or altered." It seems that the principle of heredity was followed in the selection of the high officers of state.

The Edilpur grant of Keśavasena and the Madanpara grant of Viśvarūpasena are at first passed by the clerk of the Mahāsāndhivigrahika who was the minister of peace and war. They are then endrosed by the clerk of the Mahāmahattaka and finally approved by the clerk of his Majesty. Mr. N. G. Majumdar translates 'Mahāmattaka' as Prime Minister.[1] It seems that grants passed from the office of the Sāndhivigrahika were to be endorsed by the office of the Mahāmahattaka This goes to show that the Prime Minister had some pre-eminence over the Sāndhivigrahika who was also a minister and high officer.

Mahāpurohita—He is not mentioned in the Pāla grants, and it may be suggested that this office did not exist under the Buddhist Pālas. In the Ṛgvedic time the Purohita used to advise the king in all religious matters. In the Maurya and Gupta periods Dharmamahāmātyas and Vinayasthitisthāpakas were ministers of morals. The Kalacuris had Dharmapradhāna in addition to Mahāpurohita.[2] It cannot be exactly determined what was the function of the Mahāpurohita under the Senas. Undoubtedly his poisition

1. IB. p. 131
2. JASB. XXXI. p. 116 ; Kumbhi plates of Vijayasiṁha I,

was very high as his rank in the list of officers is next to Rājāmātya. In the Arthaśastra the sacrificial priest, the spiritual preceptor and the Purohita were to get 48,000 paṇas. Rājapaṇdita,[1] Rājaguru[2] and Śāntivārika[3] were granted lands on many occasions in the Sena period. The Mahāpurohita might have superintended royal religious establishments. Whether he had some pre-eminence over other religious officers of the king cannot be ascertained.

Mahādharmādhyakṣa—He was the chief justice. This post was held by very learned men. The famous scholar Halāyudha was Dharmādhyaṣka of Lakṣmaṇasena. Paṇḍita Gonandana was the Dharmādhikāra of Vaidyadeva at whose request the Kamauli grant was made.

Mahāsāndhivigrahika—Minister in charge of war and peace, corresponding to the Foreign Secretary of modern times. The dūtaka of the Sena grants was generally this officer. A verse in the Mitākṣarā on Yājñavalkya states that Sāndhivigrahika should be the drafter of the copper plate charters, and this rule was followed by the Senas, as the grants were first issued from his office. This responsible office was sometimes held by learned and capable men. Famous Bhaṭṭa Bhavadeva of the Bhuvanesvara praśasti was the Sāndhivigrahika of Harivarmadeva of Eastern Bengal and his grandfather Ādideva held this post of another un-named king of Vaṅga. Nārāyaṇadatta held this post under Lakṣmaṇasena and was dūtaka of four grants of his reign.

Mahāsenāpati – Commander-in-chief. In the Arthaśāstra he is a first-grade officer. As the head of the army his influence was

1. In the Sahitya Parisat Plate of Viśvarūpasena there is a reference to a Rājapaṇḍita named Maheśvara. Most probably he was a court Paṅḍita. In the Śukranīti Paṇḍita is the minister of morality and religion.

2. Murāri was the Rājaguru of Vaidyadeva and his son Manoratha composed the Kamauli grant.

3. Sāntivārika is known from the Rampal and Dhulla plate of Śrīcandra and the Sunderban plate of Lakṣmaṇasena. Mr. N. G. Majumdar suggests that he may be the priest in charge of propitiatory rites. Śāntyagārika was perhaps the priest in charge of the room where propitiatory rites are performed.

4. BK.I. 319-20

very great. According to Kāmandaka[1], the following should be the qualifications for this office. He is to be healthy, enduring, self-confident, amiable, generous, respected, energetic, heroic, valorous, of noble family, native of the land and of commanding personality. He is to be an expert in the use of four-fold forces. "He should be familiar with the movement of informants and reconnoiterers, skilful and competent to manage the whole force, read the minds of others including those of animals, know the routes to march through, not be dismayed by the lack of food, or drink, or by inclement weather, who can sow dissensions among the enemy's army, who is capable of protecting his camp and is equal to the occasion and who takes to work regardless of consequences but with full hopes of fruition of his labours."

Mahāmudrādhikṛta, Antaraṅga-Vṛhaduparika and Mahākṣ-paṭalika. These three officers are mentioned always jointly, and it seems that they are connected with finances and revenue administration. Kauṭilya's Mudrādhyakṣa is the superintendent of passports and a minor officer. Dr. R. G. Basak takes him to be the keeper of Royal Seal[2]. But the reasonable view seems to be to take Mahāmudrādhikṛta as the officer in charge of Treasury and Currency. His functions might have been like those of the Sannidhātā of the Arthaśāstra[3]

There is much misconception about the term Antaraṅga-Vṛhaduparika. Dr. R. G. Basak[4] translates it as "Chief-Privy councillor", and Dr. N. K. Bhattasali as "of the intimate class of servants.[5] It has been suggested by some[6] that he should be taken as the royal physician because in Śivadāsa's commentary on

1. Ch. XVIII. 26-42.
2. EI. XII, p. 37.
3. Arthaśāstra Book II. 4. EI. XII, p. 37.
5. Ibid. Vol. XVIII, p. 76ff
6. JDL. XVI. p. 33 ; IC. Vol. 1. p, 684 ; Again, some have suggested that antaraṅgavṛhaduparika is the head of spies, see chapter on administration. Dhākāra Itihāsa.

Cakrapāṇidatta the word antaraṅga has been used in a technical sense to signify the royal physician. But this explanation does not seem to be appropriate in view of the fact that this officer figures between Mahāmudrādhikṛta and Mahākṣapaṭalika, who are undoubtedly two officers of the finance department. In the Gugrahati plate of Samācāradeva[1] Antaraṅga-uparika and Suvarṇavīthyādhikṛta Jīvadatta was the governor of Varākamaṇḍala. It is highly improbable that a physician should hold the office of a governor. Dr. Bhattasali translates 'suvarṇavīthyādhikṛta' as the master of the bullion market but suggests that the real title may have been master of the Mint or Treasury. This unmistakably shows his connection with the revenue administration. Equally unacceptable is the suggestion of Mr. G. P. Sarkar that by the term antaraṅga-vṛhaduparika two officers are meant because it is the epithet of Jīvadatta in the Gugrahati plate. But it is most likely, as it has been suggested by the same writer, that Vṛhaduparika must be some higher official who perhaps used to superintend the subordinate uparikas who are, according to Bühler's explanation on uparikara, fiscal officers.[2] Now what does the word 'antaraṅga' signify ? Antaraṅga literally means 'intimate,' 'dear', 'of one's own.' It may be suggested that this officer was also in charge of crown land and property. Thus this officer seems to have double functions, viz., to superintend the work of the subordinate uparikas and to look after crown property. His work may be equated to that of Samāhartā of the Arthaśāstra.

Mahākṣapaṭalika was the head of ths Record office. Mr. Monahan[3] interprets the word akṣapaṭala both as an accountant's office and a general record room and this seems to be correct in view of the fact that in the description of his duties in the

---

1. E1. XV111, p. 76

2. IA. 1878. p. 66. Additional Vallabhi grants, "Upari, usually spelt upri, is a Maratha revenue term which denotes a temporary holder who cultivates land in a village, where he does not reside".

3. BK. II. Sec. 6. Early History of Bengal—Monahan.

Arthaśāstra he was also an accountant general of the state.[1] The Belava plate of Bhojavarman was finally approved by Mahākṣapaṭalika.

Mahāpratihāra – He was the great chamberlain. In the Mahābhārata he is one of the 18 tīrthas and in the Arthaśāstra his name occurs in the second grade of officers along with Samāhartā and Sannidhātā. He is sometimes mentioned in our records along with military officers and it may indicate that he was also regarded as a military officer. The feudatories and high administrative officers were sometimes honoured with this title. In the Gunaighar grant of 508 A.D. of Vainyagupta the dūtaka of the grant had the title Mahāpratihāra in addition to three other titles.[2] The Rāṣṭrakūṭa prince Śivarāja who led the vanguard of Rāmapāla's army in the Kaivarta war had this title.[3] It may be that there were honorary *aid de camps* of the king (like Mahārājā of Kashmir and some other native rulers of India).

Two other high officers seem to have been associated with the central administration – Mahāsarvādhikṛta and Mahākartākṛtika, though their functions are not known. That Mahāsarvādhikṛta was an important officer is evident from the fact that he is mentioned[4] in the Rampal plate of Śrīcandra between Mahākṣapaṭalika and Mahāpratīhāra and in the Ramganj plate of Iśvaraghoṣa between Mahākṣapaṭalika and Mahāsenāpati. According to Dr. Monier-Williams, this word has been used in the Rājataraṅgiṇī in the sense of general superintendent. He may be the superintendent of public works or superintendent of the state mines and other state industries. Mahākartākṛtika figures in the Mongyr plate of Devapāla after Amātya and in the Bhagalpur grant of Nārāyaṇapāla after Mahāpratīhāra. The meaning of the term cannot be made out, but

---

1. Bk. II, 7.
2. IHQ. 1930. p. 40.
3. Rāmacarita. Bk. I. 47.
4. Gupta Ins. Vakataka plates, p. 237. EI., XIV, p. 36 2.1.30. This officer is mentioned in these two grants also.

it may be that he was an officer of Mahāsarvādhikṛta's type. Another high officer, Pīṭhikāvitta, figures after Mahāpurohita and before Mahādharmādhyakṣa in the Belava plate. The meaning of the term is not known. The author of the Ḍhākāra Itihāsa says that Pīṭhikā means the main part of an image and takes him to be a sculptor.[1] But it can hardly be accepted that a sculptor should occupy such a high position. Pīṭha means a religious student's seat, office, a royal seal. As he is mentioned after Mahāpurohita, he may be taken to be a religious officer.

The most important question as to who constituted the council of ministers is not easy to answer. The fact that in the Sunderban plate of Ḍommaṇapāla the expression 'saptasaciva' has been used perhaps indicates that the ministers were seven in number in the Sena period in normal circumstances. The Sena inscriptions are uniform in describing the list of officers and therefore it may be inferred that seven high officers proper who figure first in the list formed the ministry. In normal circumstances the ministry then seems to have consisted of Rājāmātya, Mahāpurohita, Mahādharmādhyakṣa, Mahāsāndhivigrahika, Mahāsenāpati, Mahāmudrādhikṛta and Antaraṅgavṛhaduparika. The evidence of the Rāmacarita is conclusive of the fact that on important and urgent matters the ministers were consulted. It is said that Rāmapāla was always closeted with the ministers in deciding the course of action to be taken against the revolting Kaivarta chief.[2]

Another important point may be discussed here. All the officers mentioned above have the affix 'mahā' attached to their designation, and therefore the question may be raised whether they had under-secretaries under them like modern Under-Secretary for Foreign affairs and Under-Secretary of State for India, etc. It is certain that these high officers had separate departments and offices of their own, as we have most of the Sena grants passed

---

1. Dhākāra Itihāsa by J. M. Roy. p. 489.
2. Rāmacarita 1/42.

and endorsed by the clerks of Mahāsāndhivigrahika, of Mahāmahattaka and of the Majesty. The Belava plate was issued from the office of Mahākṣapaṭalika. Nārāyaṇadatta, who was the dūtaka of the four grants of Lakṣmaṇasena, had the designation of Sāndhivigrahika, while those grants were issued from the office of Mahāsāndhivigrahika. It may be then reasonably inferred that Mahāsāndhivigrahika had at least one Sāndhivigrahika under him. The same may hold good of other high officers who have 'mahā' affixed to their official designation.

Ambassadors and Messengers

The mention of four classes of ambassadors and messengers in the Pāla records indicates that there were perhaps different ranks and gradations. Kauṭilya gives different names to the envoys according to their rank and the work entrusted to them was in accordance with their status. In the Arthaśāstra the first in rank enjoyed the status of a minister and is called Niśriṣṭārthaḥ. Then next comes Parimitartha who has the same qualifications less by one quarter and is an agent entrusted with a definite mission. The last one is Sāsanaharaḥ who has the same qualification less by one-half and is a conveyer of royal writs. It must be observed that the envoys of the Arthaśāstra have to do much of the spying work in the country where he was sent. The envoys of the different ranks of the Arthaśāstra can very well be compared with the regular order of rank and precedence of envoys established by the congress of Vienna in 1815 :—

(a) Ambassadors—represented the person and dignity of their sovereigns as well as their affairs.

(b) Envoys, Ministers Plenipotentiary and others accredited to sovereigns.

(c) *Charge's d' Affairs*, accredited not to sovereigns, but to Ministers of Foreign Affairs.

It cannot be definitely said whether there was a regular gradation of envoys in the Pāla period but the mention of four classes suggests so.

(1) Dūta---He was perhaps highest in rank and represented the sovereign in foreign courts.

(2) Khola---The term cannot be properly explained. In the dictionaries we have one meaning. (Khola--Gamyarthe vikalpe). As he is mentioned always along with Dūta, it is very likely that his function was also that of an envoy.

(3) Gamāgamika—He was perhaps the messenger from the central court to the provinces or districts and *vice versa*.

(4) Abhittaramāna – As the name denotes, he was the carrier of urgent messages.

Besides these, Dūtapraiṣaṇika figures as an officer. He was probably the officer in charge of the messengers, under whose direction they were sent in different parts.

The Pālas and Senas had important political relations with the neighbouring kings. The Nālandā grant of Devapāla proves that there was regular intercourse between the Pāla empire and Indonesia. It is known that Bālaputradeva of Suvarṇadvīpa, a famous king of the Śailendra dynasty, asked through an ambassador (dūtakamukhena) for a grant of four villages for the maintenance of a Buddhist monastery from the Pāla king and the dūtaka of the royal grant of this land was Bālavarman, governor of Vyāghrataṭīmaṇḍala, who has been described as the right hand man of Devavapāla (dakṣiṇahasta iva). This probably tends to show that when the transaction was between two independent monarchs a distinguished officer, conversant with court formalities and etiquette, was the messenger.

Territorial divisions and their administration

The largest territorial division of the Pāla and Sena kingdoms was Bhukti. In the glorious days of the Pālas, their empire extended as far as Kanouj in the west and it seems that Tīrabhukti (Bhagalpur grant) and Śrīnagarabhukti (Mongyr and Nālandā grants) were under the direct administration of the Pālas. Other known Bhuktis of the Pāla and Sena kingdoms are Pauṇḍravardhanabhukti, Vardhamānabhukti and Kaṅkagrāmabhukti. The last one seems to have been formed in the reign of Lakṣmaṇasena probably in view of his conquests in the direction of Bihar. All Bhuktis were not equal in area. Pauṇḍrvardhanabhukti was perhaps the largest and compared with it Vardhamānabhukti and Kaṅkagrāmabhukti were much smaller.

Bhuktis were divided into Maṇḍalas and Viṣayas. The relation between Maṇḍala and Viṣaya is not known. In majority of the grants Maṇḍala is a sub-division of a Viṣaya. But in the Khalimpur inscription Mahāntaprakāśaviṣaya is a subdivision of the Vyāghrataṭīmaṇḍala. This discrepancy may be explained by the assumption that the term Maṇḍala was given to well-known divisions of the country. Uttara-Rāḍha is a well-known division of Rāḍhā and in the Naihati plate of Vallālasena it is called a Maṇḍala. Our assumption is further strengthened by the fact that we have a class of feudatories with the title Mahāmāṇḍalika. In the land grant of Mahāmāṇḍalika Iśvaraghoṣa there is no mention of any Bhukti in the description of the land granted and Piyokamaṇḍala is the highest division of which Gallitipyakviṣaya is a subdivision. In the Sena grants Varendra, Uttara-Rāḍha, Vyāgrataṭī, Vaṅga have been mentioned as a part of the Bhukti; Viṣaya is conspicuous by its absence but in the list of officers Viṣayapati is invariably present. It would seem therefore that bigger Maṇḍalas like Vyāgrataṭī, Uttara-Rāḍha denote well-known parts of the kingdom and these bigger Maṇḍalas were perhaps the highest administrative section, next to Bhukti. But ordinarily (as is the case in most of the Pāla grants) Maṇḍalas were subdivisions of the Viṣayas.

Smaller Maṇḍalas were divided into Khaṇḍalas and Vīthīs whose relation is not known. Vīthī was divided into Khaṭikā which was again subdivied into Vṛtta. Caturaka formed the next subdivision which was composed of Grāmas. In the Nālandā grant of Devapāla Grāmas were included into Naya. The lowest subdivision was Pāṭaka. It is not to be supposed that all these territorial divisions were uniform in every locality. The minute divisons like Khaṭikā, Vṛtta, Caturaka are found in some of the Sena grants and Naya as a subdivision is mentioned only in the Nālandā grant of Devapāla,

The Bhuktipatis were governors of Bhuktis or provinces. In the Pāla records Bhuktipati does not figure in the list of officers but there is a high officer designated Rājasthānīya-uparika. Uparika-Mahārāja was the title of the governor of Pauṇḍravardhanabhukti during the Gupta period.[1] The Rājasthānīya-uparikas were perhaps provincial governors representing the crown. As it has already been suggested that the term Uparika is connected with revenue administration, it is quite prodable that one of the main duties of the governor was the collection of revenues. But they must have other administrative duties also. The relation of the Bhuktipati with the governor of bigger Maṇḍalas is not known. Bālavarman, officer in charge of Vyāghrataṭīmaṇḍala, and described as the right hand a man of Devapāla and a man of great military renown, was perhaps appointed by the emperor himself. In the sixth century the governors of Varākamaṇḍala in East Bengal meditated on the feet of his Majesty and no mention of Bhukti or Bhuktipati is found in them.[2] It is also to be noted that in the Faridpur plates the officers in charge of Varākamaṇḍala had also sometimes the designation of Uparika which indicates their connection with revenue administration. In the Gugrahati plate (Faridpur grant D) it is specially mentioned that the Viṣayapati Pavitraka was approved of by Jīvadatta, governor of Varākamaṇḍala.

Nothing particular is known of the district officers or Viṣayapatis. They figure as minor officers in the Pāla and Sena records. The Damodarpur plates and the Faridpur grants supply sufficient information about the district government and administration that were prevalent in Bengal in the Gupta and post-Gupta period. Viṣayapatis were probably appointed by the Bhuktipati and the sanction of the central government was perhaps required. In the Damodarpur plates Nos. 1, 2, 5, the Viṣayapatis meditate on the feet of the Bhuktipatis but in the Baigram plate[3] Kulavṛddhi,

---

1. EI. XV, pp, 130 ff.
2. Faridpur grants, IA. 1910, pp. 193. ff.
3. EI., XXI, p. 78

the district officer, meditates on the feet of his Majesty and the same is the case in the Vappaghoṣavaṭa grant of the time of Jayanāga. In the Damodarpur plates the Viṣayapatis had the title of Kumārāmātya or Tat-niyuktaks. The title Sāmanta in the Vappaghoṣavaṭa grant probably indicates that the Viṣayapatis were sometimes men of military renown or, that feudatories were also appointed as district officers. They might have been responsible for the revenues and good government of the districts under them.

The headquarters of the districts were in towns. In important cities or districts like Koṭivarṣa or Puṇḍravardhana the district officer was helped by a board consisting of Nagaraśreṣthī, Svārthavāha, Prathama-kulika and Prathama-kāyastha, i.e. the guild-president, the leading merchant, the leading banker[1] and the leading scribe. There is considerable disagreement among scholars about the functions of this board which constituted the Adhisṭhānādhikaraṇa. Dr. Ghoshal has rightly pointed out the Act IX of the Mṛchchakaṭikā, describing the famous trial scene, referring to the king's judges (called Adhikaraṇikas and Adhikaraṇabhojakas) who were assisted by the guild-president and the scribe.[2] It is to be conceded then that in important district headquarters justice was administered with the help of a board in which the important interests of those days were represented. Though this board has been mentioned in the land records, its relation with other branches of administration (excepting judicial) cannot be definitely established from the data at our hand. It is important to notice here that the existence of this board has not been referred to in the Dhanaidaha, Baigram plates and Damodarpur No. 4 and not also in the Faridpur plates. It is, therefore, permissible to hold that such a board existed only in important cities or districts. However, its existence in Koṭivarṣa and Puṇḍravardhana points to organised life among the commercial and industrial classes of those days. How could there be a Prathama-kulika

2. Dr. R. G. Basak translates Kulika as artisan (following Bhānuji Dīkṣita)

2. *Hindu Revenue system*, pp. 202-3. Various other views held by different scholars are discussed there.

and Prathama-kāyastha without an organized following or how could the community be represented without an organization ? The answer to these questions affirms this. That their position and influence was felt in the society is proved by their relation with the government. The four representatives came to hold their position either by their leading position or by election.

In the Dhanaidaha plate and the Damodarpur plate No. 3 the application from the intending purchaser is received by Grāmika, Aṣṭakulādhikaraṇa[1], Kuṭumbin[2] and named and unnamed Brahmanas. In other grants of the Gupta perid in northern Bengal the district officer and the office of the district headquarters receive the application. In the Damodarpur plates Nos. 3 and 5 the Prakṛtis (subjects) and Kuṭumbins are informed of the transaction. In the Vaigram plate the Kuṭumbins along with the Brahmanas and Samavyavahārins are informed. In the Faridpur grants the application for purchase was received and land was disposed of by the district office and the Prakṛtis headed by eighteen leading men of the district (in Grant A) and in other three grants by the district office headed by the named chief scribe[3] and leading men of the district, as well as Vyāpārins or Vyavahārins.[4]

It is difficult to say what were the fuctions of the Mahattaras

---

1. Some scholars like to explain the term Aṣṭakulādhikaraṇa as meaning one in charge of supervision of eight families. In Manu (VII. 118-19) and the Mahābhārata (xii. 6816-8) the lord of one village would enjoy one Kula of land and the lord of ten villages 5 Kulas and so on. In the Gupta period Aṣṭakulādhikaraṇa might have been a village officer higher in rank than Grāmika and enjoyed 8 Kulas of land.

2. Dr. R. G. Basak translated Kuṭumbins as householders, and Dr. Ghoshal as heads of families.

3. Dr. Ghoshal equates the office of Jyeṣṭhakāyastha with that of Sheristadar of a modern district. *Hindu Revenue system.* p. 204, fn 2 ; cf Mahākāyastha of the Ramganj plote.

4. Vyāpārins and Vyavahārins are officers carrying on affairs of the state in connection with land grants. Ibid. p. 205. fn. 2.

or leading men[1] referred to in the Dāmodarpur plates and in the Faridpur plates. Dr. Ghosal's suggestion[2] to identify the Viṣaya-mahattaras of the Faridpur plates with the Vyāpārins and Vyāvahārins of the same plates B.C.D. cannot be accepted, as in these plates the Mahattaras have been mentioned in addition to Vyapārins and Vyavahārins. Most probably the Mahattaras were men of position in the locality. Their representative capacity is perhaps to be understood from the Grant A, in which Prakṛtis (people) headed by eighteen leading men of the district have been alluded to. It cannot be ascertained whether they were elected representatives of the people or chosen by the government because of their eminent position in the locality. It is further known from the copper plates of the Gupta period and the Faridpur plates that before the actual sale was made, the record-keepers (pustapālas) would make all necessary enquiries to the titles to the lands concerned and would sever the land according to the standard measure of 8×9 reeds then prevalent. The Paharpur plate[3] specifically refers to a board of record-keepers headed by Divākaranandī. In some cases the Brāhmaṇas, leading men and heads of families were informed of the transaction possibly to raise objections, if there would have been any.

The above facts unmistakably point to high administrative efficiency of the local governments in the Gupta and post-Gupta period. Nothing is known of the existence of Adhiṣṭhānādhikaraṇa and the procedures of the sale of waste land in the Pāla and Sena periods. Both progress and retrogression are possible in the political system. But it must be observed that the Gupta plates hitherto discovered in Bengal (excepting the Gunaighar plate[4]) and the

1. We accept Mr. Pargiter's interpretation of Mahattara as men of position ; leading men ; Ill A. 1900, p. 123, ff. Dr. Bhattasali suggests that Viṣaya-mahattara is to be taken in the sense of Mahattaras in charge of affairs. But "leading men of the district" seems to be a better interpretation. See EI. XVIII, p. 76.

2. *Hindu Revenue system*, p. 205.

3. EI. XX, p. 59.

4. IHQ. 1930, p. 40.

Faridpur plates record transaction between the state and the private persons who purchased lands for donating them for some meritorious purpose. The surviving seal-legends of the Viṣayādhikaraṇa go to show that the highest authority concerned were the district officers. The Pāla and Sena grants are royal bequests and to them are attached the seals of their Majesties themselves. The Viṣayapatis figure only as minor officials and it is hardly to be expected that the details of the district government are to be found in them. The Gunaighar plate of Vainyagupta, dated in 508 A.D., which records the grant of land to a Buddhist vihāra by the Emperor himself at the request of a dependent chief like that of the Khalimpur plate of Dharmapāla, does not refer to the local officials connected with the execution of the land grants. The same is the case with the Vappaghoṣavāṭa grant of Jayanāga, Tippera grant of Lokanātha and the Asrafpur plates.

While emphasising the silence of the grants of our period on the detailed local administration, it must be noted that in the Pāla records Grāmika, Grāmapati, Dāśagrāmika, Mahattaras and others appear as local officials.

Grāmika or Grāmapati—He is the village headman. His office must have been of considerable responsibility. Most probably he was responsible for the collection of royal dues of the village under his care. In the Arthaśātra and Yājñavalkya he had got police functions, to keep the village free from thieves. He might have tried minor cases too.

Dāśagrāmika---Officer in charge of ten villages, perhaps corresponding to Aṣṭakulādhikaraṇa. He was perhaps to supervise the work of the Grāmikas under him.

Mahattara---In the Khalimpur plate we find both Mahāmahattaras and Mahattaras which go to show that there was some gradation of these officials or semi-officials. In addition to what has already been said of them, it is noted here that in the contemporary Rāṣṭrakūṭa kingdom in Mahārāṣṭra and southern Guzrat the

Mahattaras constituted village assemblies[1] which looked after and managed the public works of the villages. We have no evidence to show the existence of any village council in Bengal. But it may be presumed that they must have held very important position in the localities.

Lekhaka—He is mentioned only in the Ramganj plate. According to Śukra,[2] his duty was to keep accounts of income and expenditure, to receive and dispose of goods after making entries in the registers and to carry on correspondence. In the Cola records it was he who wrote the orders of the village assembly.[3]

Tadā-yuktas and Viniyuktas—Dr. Altekar takes Yuktas or Niyuktas and Upa-niyuktas as officers in charge of the clerical work connected with the village administration.[4] If this interpretation be correct, Tadā-yuktas and Vini-yuktas of the Pāla grants and Ramganj plate should be taken to be clerical officers attached to various offices. They have been generally mentioned after Viṣayapatis and Uparikas.

Besides these, we have Kṣetrapa, Kṣetrapāla, Prāntapāla, Tarika, Tarapati and various other unspecified officers who were more or less connected with the local government. Their duties and functions will be discussed in connection with the departments with which they were directly concerned.

Town administration and guild organisation

Our records give absolutely no information as to how the administration of towns was carried on. Towns there must have been many. Rāmāvatī, Mudgagiri were the headquarters of the Pālas, and Vikrampura of the Candras, Varmans and Senas. The headquarters of the feudatory kings, Bhuktipatis and Viṣayapatis must have had some special arrangements. Nor do we know

1. Dr. Altekar : Rāṣṭrakūṭas and their times. p. 205.
2. Śukra. II, 348.
3. SII. II. Ukkal. No. 10
4. Dr. Altekar, Op. cit. p, 197.

anything definitely about the communal organisations like guilds of merchants, of artisans, etc., though they had important corporate functions in the Rāṣṭrakūṭa empire[1] and the Gurjjra-Pratihāra and Gāhaḍavāla kingdoms of Kanouj.[2] In the Deopara inscription of Vijayasena the scribe Śūlapāṇi has been described as 'Varendra-śilpī-goṣṭhī-cuḍāmaṇi' and it has been suggested that 'śilpī-goṣṭhī' may be taken to refer to the guild of Varendra artists. But it is hazardous to draw any inference from this expression of whose interpretation we cannot be sure.[3]

Revenue and Expenditure

Great importance was laid on finances by the writers on ancient Indian polity and it is also clear from the fact that three high officers, Mahāmudrādhikṛta, Antraṅga-Vṛhaduparika and Mahākṣapaṭalika who were connected with the finance department, served the central government. In the Pāla records Mahāmudrādhikṛta and Antaraṅga-Vṛhaduparika are conspicuous by their absence but we have got another high officer Mahākartākṛta wh might have been connected with the revenue administration.

The sources of revenue may be classified under the following heads :—

(1) Regular Taxes.

(2) Occasional Taxes and Exactions.

(3) Fines.

(4) Income from government properties.

(5) Tribute from feudatories.

Regular Taxes

In the Pāla grants the regular taxes mentioned by name are—(a) Bhāga, (b) Bhoga, (c) Kara, (d) Hiraṇya.

(a) Bhāga means the usual grain-share of the king. In the

1. Dr. Altekar, Op. Cit, pp. 210, 202.
2. IHQ. 1933, p. 121.
3. Mr. N. G. Majumdar, IB. p. 45; he takes goṣṭhī in the sense of 'host', 'multitude'.

Kalimpur plate of Dharmapāla an officer named Ṣaṣṭhādhikṛta is mentioned, who was most probably in charge of the sixth part of royal grain-share and it seems that the grain-share was levied at the old rate of the sixth part of the produce as recommended in the Arthaśāstra and Smṛtis.

(b) Bhoga means "the periodical supplies of fruits, firewood, flowers and the like, which the villagers had to furnish to the king." It is interesting to note that in the land grants it is specially said that the donee is to have the privilege of the enjoyment of madhuka, mango, jackfruit, betelnut and coconut trees. This goes to show that the king had some share from their income. This is further confirmed by the fact that in the Sahitya Parisat grant of Viśvarūpasena the income derived from the betel-leaf plantations is to be enjoyed by the donee.

(c) Kara means tax in general. In the Arthaśāstra it has been used to mean three kinds of taxes : (i) periodical tax over and above the king's customary grain-share, (2) emergency tax, (3) tax upon merchant's profits. Kara in our period may include taxes not specified in the grants which the people had to pay to the government.

(d) Hiraṇya has been explained generally to mean gold. It is always mentioned with Bhāgabhogakara. We are inclined to accept the meaning proposed by Dr. Ghoshal that it refers to king's share of certain crops paid in cash[1].

Land revenue was assessed in cash in the Sena period and every grant specifically mentions the income derived from the lands donated in terms of current coins. The incidence of actual taxation cannot be precisely determined at the present state of our knowledge, although the Sena grants describe in minute details the lands granted. The relation between Bhu-pāṭaka, Droṇa, Ādhakā, Unmāna,[2] and Kāka, is not known and also between Purāṇa and

1. Dr. Ghoshal, Hindu Revenue System. p. 61.

2. In the Sunderban plate of Lakṣmaṇasena it is said that according to the standard of 32 cubits – 1 unmāna, and 1 cubit – 12 aṅgulas.

Kapardaka-purāṇa, nor have we any idea about the approximate value of Kapardaka-purāṇa. But the reference in the Govindapura plate of Lakṣmaṇasena that each Droṇa yielded 15 Purāṇas proves that "standard rates of land assessment were known in this period." It is also clear from the Sahitya Parisat grant that lands having the same area in the same locality were not of equal value as income from them varied and it is quite probable that tax on agricultural land also varied according to its quality and also income from it.

The Gupta plates and the Faridpur plates refer to standard measurement of land, aṣṭaka-navaka-nalāblyam i.e. 8 × 9 reeds. In the Pāla grants no reference is made to any standard of measurement. It must be noted that the seven Pāla plates that have hitherto come to light record the grant of at least a full village with well-defined boundaries. It cannot, therefore, be concluded that there was no fixed standard of measurement as the occasion perhaps did not arise. The grants of the Candras and the Varmans who flourished in the 10th and 11th centuries respectively in East Bengal "specify the areas of lands granted in terms of the current land measure." The Sena grants clearly show that the standard units of length were not uniform in every locality but different systems of measarement in different parts. Four kinds of measurement are known from the Sena grants—(1) Samataṭīyanala[2] (2) Vṛṣabhaśankaranala[3] (3) the Nala current in Varendrī[4] and (4) the Nala of 56 cubits.[5]

(e) Uparikara – Dr. Altekar suggests that Uparikara is identical

1. Prof. D. R. Bhandarkar suggests that Kapardakapurana is "Purāṇa which is shaped like a Kapardaka or cowrie.......It is a Rūpa class of coinage", "A Purāṇa must contain 52 ratis of silver'. Carmaichael Leclures, p,39-4 10.

2. The Barrackpore grant of Vijayasena.

3. The Naihati plate of Vallālasena and the Anulia plate of Lakṣmaṇasena. The standard was perehaps named after the name of Vijayasena who had got Vṛsabaṣaṇkara as his virūda.

4. The Tarpandighi plate of Lakśmaṇasena.

5. The Govindapur plate of the same king,

with Bhogakara.[1] We are inclined to accept the meaning proposed by Dr. Ghoshal that it means the tax paid by temporary tenants[2], as in the Bhagalpur grant Soparikara is one of the privileges of the donee in addition to the enjoyment of Bhāgabhogakra.

(f) Cauroddharaṅa – In all land grants one of the privileges of the donee is Cauroddharaṇa. Mr. N. G. Majumdar takes it to mean "with police protection", while Dr. Ghoshal takes it to mean "with the exemption from the police tax". It is quite likely that there might have been a general police-tax like modern Caukidari. Other regular taxes are not mentioned in the grants but some of them can be somewhat ascertained from the list of officers and their functions. The mention of Śaulkika and Gaulmika indicates that tolls and customs duties were important sources of revenues. Śulka in the Arthaśāstra stands for duties levied upon articles imported into the city, port dues, duty upon the sale of liquors, customs collected by the ferryman, and boundary officers, duty upon mining products, duty upon imported salt, duty upon animals intended for slaughter. The Tezpur Rock inscription of 829-30 A. D. refers to a legal dispute in Kāmarūpa involving a toll-collcetor.[3] Tarapati and Tarika are ferry-men and this perhaps indicates the prevalence of ferry-duties in the Pāla period. Probably the government regulated ferries either by state or private boats but it is clear that Tarapati and Tarika are royal officers.[4] In the Manahali grant Śaunika[5] or the superintendent of slaughter house is a royal officer and the Prāntapāla of the Mongyr plate of Devapāla may be compared with the Antapāla of the Arthaśāstra who is to levy transit duties.[6] Haṭṭapati or the superintendent of markets is a royal officer mentioned in the Ramganj plate of Iśvarghoṣa and it is stated in

1. Dr. Altekar, Rāṣṭrakūṭas and their times, p. 216.
2. Dr. Ghoshal, Op. Cit. p. 210.
3. JBORS. 1917. p. 508ff.
4. In Manu a scale of ferry dues from different classes of goods and persons is given. Bk. VIII, 404-6.
5. Śuna means slaughter-house. 'Māṁsa vikretari,' Hemacandra.
6. Arthaśāstra, Bk. II, 1.

the Khalimpur plate that income from the markets in the donated land would be enjoyed by the donee.

Gaulmika most probably means overseer or superintendent of forests.[1]

Besides these, mention must be made of the superintendents of cows, buffaloes, goats, sheep, etc. and other unspecified Adhyakṣas of the land grants who may be compared with the various superintendents of the Arthaśāstra.[2]

(2) Occasional taxes and exactions.

(a) Acaṭṭabhaṭṭapraveśa – This expression occurs in all grants and means that the lands granted should not be entered by Caṭṭas and Bhaṭṭas. Caṭṭas and Bhaṭṭas were regular and irregular military and police forces. When they were on march or encamped, the people of the locality had probably to supply their demands and other necessary things.

(b) Apahṛtasarbapīḍā—The lands were granted "with immunity from all burdens." It has generally been taken to refer to forced labour. But it seems Sarbapiḍā has been used in very wide sense and may include many interference by the state, forced labour being one of them. It may also mean dues leviable at the time of the halt or departure of royal officers,[3] customary presents to the king or high officers on some ceremonial occasions and emergency taxes of the state mentioned in the Mahābhārata[4] and the Arthaśāstra[5] and Śukranīti.[6] Attention may be invited to the list of oppressors mentioned in four grants of the neighbouring province of Kāmarūpa. In the grant of Bālavarman (c. 990 A. D.)

1. EI. IV, 258. fn9 and Fleet CII, p. 52. n4. In the Arthaśāstra Gulmadeya means dues paid to the army or police stations. Dr. R. G. Basak takes Gaulmika to be an officer in charge of a Gulma squadron.

2. Artha, Bk. II describes the functions of various superintendents.

3. A. Yādava grant ; IA. VIX, p. 819. Tandontottam plates SII, Vol II, p. 531.

4. Mahā, XII. 87.

5. Artha. V. 2.

6. Śukra, IV. 2, 10.

the list of oppressors consist of the queen, the royal favourites, the eunuchs, the persons pasturing elephants and mooring boats, the officers tracking thieves as well as officers charged with the Uparikara tax and with the Utkheta import. They are repeated in the two grants of Ratnapāla (c. 1010 A. D.) and one grant of Indrapāla (c. 1060 A. D.).

(c) Piṇḍaka—It is mentioned only in the Khalimpur plate. Kielhorn identified it with Bhāgabhogakara and Dr. Ghoshal is of opinion that it probably stands for Hiraṇya. In our opinion it is the same as the Piṇḍakara of the Arthaśāstra which, according to the commentator Bhaṭṭa, means taxes livied upon whole villages.

(d) Ratnatrayasambhoga—It is mentioned only in the Manahali plate of Madanapāla. It is quite likely, as Dr. Ghoshal suggests, that it was probably a contribution from the villages for the support of the Buddhist faith. The Pālas were devout Buddhists and great builders. It may be that a tax was lived for the maintenance and upkeep of big Buddhist establishments. But the meaning of the term is far from benig certain and it cannot be maintained that it was a general and regular tax, as it occurs only in one grant.

(3) Fines.

Sahyadaśāparādha—This expression shows that fines were levied for offences. The traditional ten offences are—(a) three offences of the body, theft, murder and adultery, (b) four offences of speech, harsh, untruthful, libellous and pointless words, and (c) three offences of mind, coveting other's property, thinking of worng and devotion to what is not true. Most probably in our period it stands for judicial fines in general. Donees of the grants enjoyed the income from the fines.[1] It seems, therefore, that justice was also a source of revenue.

1. We cannot accept the opinion of Dr. Ghoshal that the expression Sahyadaśāparādha confers upon the donee the right to be exempted from the ordinary penalties for the commission of some of the traditional offences, Hindu Revenue System, p. 220.

(4) Income from Government properties, crown lands and other rights of the state on land and water.

It cannot be stated with certainty whether the state had its own lands at this period because no instance of crown land is known. But the possibility is strongly there that the state might have owned some land which had lapsed as heirless property, confiscated properties, lands purchased for state purpose or waste lands brought under cultivation by the government. As regards the general question whether the state claimed to be the proprietor of cultivable land, Dr. Altekar's remarks on this point are applicable in the case of Pāla and Sena grants. "The numerous copper plate grants, giving villages to temples and Brahmaṇas, assign to the donees the government right to the taxes derived from the land and other sources ; there is not a single case where the proprietory right in the entire land under cultivation in any village has been transferred to the donee. The plate uses a long series of expressions specifying the right accruing to the donees, but not a single expression is used in any of our grants, suggesting that the donees acquired the proprietory rights in the cultivable lands in the village. Even the right of ejection is nowhere mentioned. It is therefore clear that in our period the state did not claim the ownership of the entire soil of the realm."[1] The fact that Viśvarūpasena should find it necessary to give only detached pieces of cultivable land situated in the different corners of different villages shows that the state was not, and did not claim to be, proprietor of the entire realm. In this grant (the Sahitya Parisat plate of Viśvarupasena) there are actual cases of previous purchase when land, and not the revenue rights, was assigned to the donees.

Although the proprietorship of cultivable land was not claimed, the state in addition to the taxes and privileges mentioned above probably conceded the following additional rights to the donee. We quote them from the Rampal grant of Śrīcandradeva who ruled in the 10th century in East Bengal. They are Satala, Soddeśa, Sāmrap-

1. Dr, Altekar, Op. Cit.

anasa, Saguvākanārikela, Salavaṇa, Sajalasthala, Sagarttoṣara. They are more or less same in all grants. Salavaṇa is only met with in this grant. The Mongyr grant has in addition to them Satriṇa, and Samatsya, the Barrackpur grant of Vijayasena has Sabana and the Naihati grant has Sabhāṭaviṭapa. Messers R. D. Banerjee,[1] R. G. Basak[2] and N. G. Majumdar have taken Satala and Soddeśa to mean land with bottom and surface, i.e., the with the underground right and the surface right. Messrs G. P. Sarkar[3] and K. M. Gupta[4] take them to mean low and high land. Sāmrapanasa-saguvāka-nārikela means with mango, jackfruit, betelnut and coconut trees. Sajalasthala means with land and water. According to Mr. G. P. Sarkar,[5] Jala included tanks, wells, lakes, etc., while Sthala probably included various gardens. Sagarttoṣara means with pits and barren land. Salavaṇa means with salt. Satṛṇa and Samatsya mean with grass and fishes, Sabana with forests and Sabhāṭaviṭapa with forests and branches.

Now the question is whether the state claimed some rights over the land and things mentioned above. No definite answer is possible because the above expressions can be taken to be the descriptions of the land granted. But against this view it may be pointed out that in the Arthaśāstra mines, fisheries, salt were state monopolies. In the Gupta period the state was the owner of the waste land.[6] The most interesting evidencee in this connection comes from the Gāhaḍavāla inscription in which Gokara, Jalakara, Lavaṇakara in addition to the refernce of state monopoly of mines are taxes that are to be paid to the donees.[7] With this

1. El. XV, p. 259.
2. Ibid, XII, p. 35.
3. JDL. XVI. p. 43.
4. IA. XLI, p. 74.
5. See above,
6. EI. XV, p. 139 ; Dr. Ghoshal. Op. cit, p. 206.
7. IA. XV ; EI. IX, No 11 ; Ibid, VIII, No. 14 D ; Ibid, X No. 23 ; Ibid. XIII. No. 20 ; Ibid, XI, p, 24 ; also Tandonotolam plate of Vinayandīvikramavarman, SII. II., p. 531-2.

specific mention of these taxes in the Gāhaḍavāla records we are rather inclined to accept the view that the state claimed certain rights over the land and things referred to above and these rights were alienated to the donees. Of course, it is not easy to understand what right the state claimed over the pits, but it must be said that these land grants are title-deeds and therefore legal documents in a sense and as such the description in them should be very wide and general, covering every possible right the state could claim and was prepared to concede to the person in whose favour they were drawn up. Still more difficult it is to explain the significance of another expression 'tṛṇaputi gocaraparyants.' It occurs generally after the description of the boundaries but in the Naihati plate of Vallālasena it occurs among the privileges conferred on the donee. In the Mongyr plate we have Saṭṛṇa. Two interpretations are possible—(1) the lands with boundaries thus defined up to the pasturage, grass, puti plants and grazing ground for cattle, or (2) with the right conceded to the donee over these things. In the Arthaśāstra one of the duties of the superintendent of pastures was to set up pasture lands in troublesome tracts intervening between the village.[1] In the Pāla records Kṣetrapāla and Kṣetrapa whose functions may be compared with those of the superintendent of pasture of the Arthaśāstra are two royal officers. In the Rāṣṭrakūṭa records the right to utilise grass, fuel, etc. growing on the waste land was transferred to the donee.[2] It is quite likely that the state derived some income from the pasture lands.

(5) Tributes from Feudatories

Our information about this source of revenue is wanting. But it is almost certain that the vassal kings paid some tributes to the imperial government in the normal circumstances. It is stated in the Khalimpur plate of Dharmapāla that kings of northern India

1. Artha, 11 34.
2. Dr. Altekar, Op. Cit. p. 241.

who were most probably dependent kings made many presents to the emperor.

Expenditure

No information is available from the land grants regarding the expenditure of the state. The author of the Arthaśāstra supplies a list of 18 specified items of expenditure. Besides, gifts to Brahmanas, relief to the poor, the sick and the destitute and pensions to the dependents of dead public servants are also recommended. Śukra's list of expenditure on specified items is interesting for our purpose, as he was a medieval writer.[1] The state expenditure should be in the following scale :—$\frac{1}{8}$th of the revenue for the army, $\frac{1}{12}$th for gifts, $\frac{1}{12}$th for principal officers, $\frac{1}{12}$th for heads of departments, $\frac{1}{12}$th for king's personal expenditure and $\frac{1}{6}$th to be deposited in the treasury. The Pālas and Senas had to maintain huge armies and the constant wars must have been a great strain on their finances. Educational and religious establishments and other public works associated with the names of the Pāla and Sena kings also cost the treasury. Both the Pālas and Senas granted many plots of lands to the Brahmanas and forother meritorious purposes.

The Military

Very few things regarding the army department are known from the inscriptions. The following officers and their functions, as can be suggested from their names, will give some idea about the organisation of the army.

The highest officer of the army department was Mahāsenāpati or commander-in-chief who was, as we have already stated, one of the members of the ministry,

Mahāpādamulika—He is mentioned in the Ramganj plate of Iśvaraghoṣa after Mahāsenāpati. The technical meaning is not known. In the Arthaśāstra Pādika is a military officer and Mūla

1. Sukra. 1. p. 315-6,

means hereditary troops.[1] It can be therefore suggested that he was in charge of infantry or hereditary troops.

Mahābhogapati or Mahābhogika—Dr. R. G. Basak takes him to be the chief groom but does not cite any authority. He is always mentioned along with the army officers. Bhoga is the technical name of a particular kind of array of soldiers in the Arthaśāstra.[2] Therefore he can be taken to be a military officer.

Mahātantrādhikṛta—He is also mentioned with the army officers in the Ramganj plate. In Monier Williams's dictionary one meaning of the word Tantra is an army. He may also be taken to be an army officer.

Mahavyūhapati—Officer in charge of arrays.

Mahādaṇḍanāyaka—In the Arthaśāstra Nāyaka is a military officer. "Caturaṇga valādhyakṣa senānī daṇḍanāyaka"—Hemacandra. Some scholars have taken him to be a judicial officer. According to Mr. R. D. Banerjee, he is the chief criminal judge.

Nāvādhyakṣa—Mentioned in the Pāla grants. He was probably the head of the navy.

Mahāsāmanta—He was perhaps the head of the Sāmantas (feudatories) but is a regular officer in some of the Pāla grants. He probably enjoyed high military rank.

Mahāpīlupati—Officer in charge of the elephants.

Mahāgaṇastha – According to Amara, 27 elephants, 27 chariots 81 horses, and 135 foot-soldiers constitute one Gaṇa. The officer in charge of a Gaṇa was called Gaṇastha. 1 chariot, 1 elephant, 3 horses, and 5 foot soldiers was called a Paṭṭi. 3 Paṭṭis formed one Senāmukha and 3 Senāmukhas one Gulma and 3 Gulmas one Gaṇa.

Koṭṭapati---Officer in charge of forts.

Prāntapāla---Mentioned in the Pāla grants. He is the officer

---

1. For every ten members of each of the constituents of the army, there must be one commadder called Pādika ; ten Pādikas under a Senāpati ; ten Senāpatis under a Nāyaka. Artha. X. 6.

2. Wings and front, capable to turn against an enemy, is a snake-like army (Bhoga). Artha XI. 6.

in charge of forntier fortresses. Vṛhadhanuṣka—the chief archer (Rāmganj plate).

Besides these, we have Nauvala - hastyāśva—vyāpṛtaka—officers in charge of the navy, elephants and horses. The Pālas and Senas were constantly at war with their neighbours and the Pālas were the rival of the Pratihāras of Kanouj and the Rāṣṭrakūṭas of Mālkhed for the overlordship of Northern India. The army must have received the utmost attention of the monarchs because it was the mainstay of their power and prestige. It is also clear from the account of the Muslim writers[1] that the Pālas maintained huge armies. The merchant Sulaiman observes that "the king of Rahma (Bengal) had great strength in troops, elephants and horses. His troops are more numerous than those of the Balhara (the Rāṣṭrakūṭs) and the king of Jurz (Gurjjaras). It is told that the Barua king of Kanouj (the Gūrjjara-Pratiharas) keeps four armies in the four quarters. Each of these numbers 7 to 9 lakhs of men. Coming to the details of the army of Rahma the same writer says, "When he goes out to battle, he is follwed by about 50,000 elephants. There are from ten to fifteen thousand men in his army who are employed in fuelling and washing clothes. Sulaiman's account seems to be based on exaggerated report. In Ibn Khurdan's account the number of the elephants is 5,000. In the Arthaśāstra the army consisted of four classes of soldiers—(1) Maula, (hereditary), (2) Bṛtaka (mercenary), (3) Śrenī (corporation) and (4) Aṭavī (wild tribes). In

1. The following observations of the Muslim writers go to show the identification of the Pāla king (or kingdom) with Rahmi. The kingdom of Rahmi "extends both along the sea and the continent. It is frequently at war with Balhara (the Rāṣṭrakūṭa king and the Gurz (Gurjjaras) on whose kingdoms it borders. It is bounded by an inland kingdom called Kamrun (Kāmarūpa.)" "There is a stuff made in this country which is not found elsewhere so fine and delicate that a dress made of it may pass through a signet ring. It is made of cotton". This of course refers to famous muslin, As all these descriptions agree well with the Pāla kingdom, we have got no hesitation in identifying Rahma with the Pāla kingdom. For the account of Muslim writers, see Elliot, History of India, 1. p. 5, 25, 36.

the period under review it seems that the army also consisted of four classes of soldiers. The office of Mahāpādamulika suggests the existence of Maulabala. It is interesting to note that in the list of soldiers from many countries Gauḍas also figure in the Pāla grants and it is quite possible that Gauḍa forces were Maulabala. It is clear from the Pāla inscriptions that the Pālas recruited soldiers from many countries. In all grants soldiers of Mālava, Khaśa, Hūṇa, Kulika, Karṇāta, Lāṭa are referred to. The Nālandā grant of Devapāla adds the name of Oḍra and the Manahali plate Coḍa. It seems, therefore, that the Pālas had to depend mainly on mercenary soldiers who were recruited from every possiple quarter. In this period the feudatories supplied soldiers to the suzerain. Rāmapāla was assisted a great deal by the forces and resources of the Sāmantas in his suppression of the Kaivarta revolt. The same monarch in order to secure the help of the feudatories allied himself with the Sāmantas of the forest regions.[1]

The Muslim writers and the epigraphic records all refer to the elephants, horses and infantry and this is also corroborated by the evidence of the Rāmacarita. Rāmapāla prepared for his expedition with these threefold forces.[2] Thus it seems that of the traditional caturaṅga forces the chariots were abandoned.[3] According to the testimony of the Muslim writers, the Rāṣṭrakūṭas possessed the best infantry because their seat of the government was in the mountains and the Gurjjara-Pratihāras had the finest cavalry. But the elephant forces of the Pālas were the largest. The Pālas counted a great deal in their wars on the elephants.' So much so they depended on this force that Al-Masudi remarks that Rahma (the Pāla king) takes field only in winter, because elephants

1. Rāmacarita 1/43.

2. Ibid 1/45.

3. The formidable array of the mighty elephants, horses and chariots of Dharmapāla have been mentioned in the Gwalior Praśasti of Bhoja, (EI, XVIII p, 101). But much stress cannot be laid on it, as the composers of praśastis described army from traditional military phraseology.

cannot endure thirst and can only go in cold season. The mighty elephants of Bengal were a dread to foreign powers. It is stated in the Bargaon grant of the Kāmarūpa king Ratnapāla that the walls of the impregnable fort built by him are so strong that they would give fever to the heads of the untameable elephants of the Gauḍa king.[1] This is an eloquent testimony to the strength of the elephant forces of Bengal.

Cavalry was not neglected. The Pālas and Senas had to undertake military campaigns in foreign countries and the former was at constant struggle with the Pratihāras who were strong in cavalry. Bengal had no good breed of horses. Horses were imported from foreign countries. It is said in the Mongyr plate of Devapāla that the horses met their old mates in the Kamboja country. Kamboja was reputed for the finest breed in ancient times.[2]

The actual methods of warfare are not known but the existence of the offices of Mahāvyūhapati and Mahābhogika would go to indicate that soldiers were arranged in different arrays as would suit the circumstances. It is also clear from the statement of Al-Masudi that the army had a large number of camp-followers, though the approximate number 15,000 given by him seems to be considerably exaggerated. Innocent lives and property of the gods and Brahmanas were honoured. It is important to notice that the Rāṣṭrakūṭa prince Śivarāja who led the vanguard of Rāmapāla's army enquired about particular villages and Viṣayas in order to ensure the safety of the properties of the temples and Brahmanas.

Navy

Bengal is the country of big rivers and has an extensive seaboard. A mercantile navy was indispensable for commerce and trade in different parts of the country and with coastal countries. It is evident from the evidence recorded by Fa-hien, Yuan Chwang

---

1. JASB, LXVII, p. 115-18.
2 Artha. II. 30.

and the Nālandā plate of Devapāla that there was regular intercourse with the Far Eastern countries. Writing about 912 A.D., Ibn Khurdan remarks that between Rahmi and other kingdoms communication is kept by ships. Ship's mast and harbours are referred to in the Faridpur grants of Dharmāditya.

The navy was not only necessary for commerce and trade but it was also extremely useful both for defence and offence in Bengal. The Bengal kings always maintained a fleet. The camp of victory at Krīpura in the Gunaighar inscription of Vainyagupta, dated in 508 A. D., is described as full of ships, elephants and horses. The Haraha inscription of the Maukhari king Īśānavarman[1] refers to the Gauḍa people as 'Samudrāśrāyān'. Attention may be invited to the story of colonisation of Ceylon by prince Vijaya of Vaṅga which must have taken place[2] before the time of Aśoka and to Kālidāsa's remarks[3] on the nautical resources of Bengal. The importance of Nāvādhyakṣa and nau-vala-vyāpṛtaka needs hardly to be emphasised. In every Pāla grant the royal fleet is first mentioned in the description of the camp of victory. The royal camp at Pāṭaliputra is thus described in the Khalimpur plate : "Sakhalu Bhāgirathī-patha-pravattamāna nānāvidha-nauvāṭaka-sampādita-setubandha-nihita-śaila-śikhara-śreṇī-vibhramata". The Kamauli plate records a naval victory won by Kumārapāla's minister and general Vaidyadeva. It is known from the Deopara plate of Vijayasena that he sent a flect to meet the pāścātyacakra. A sudden cavalry raid proved disastrous for the Senas who were ousted from western and northern Bengal within a very short time but perhaps for their navy the descendants of Lakṣmaṇasena could maintain themselves in east Bengal for a long time. Nothing illustrates more forcibly the supreme necessity of a fleet in Eastern

1. EI, vol. XIV. 117.

2. Early Seamen of India, Asutosh Jubilee Volume, Orientalia, Pt. 2. p. 105

3. Raghuvaṁsa IV. 36

Bengal than the fact that the Delhi Sultan Balban in his expedition in 1183 A. D. against the rebellious governor, Tughril Khaṇ, had to seek the assistance of Danuja Rāja of Sonargaon in order to prevent his escape by boat.[1]

Defences

The Jayaskandhāvāra or the camp of victory from which the royal grants were issued seems to have been well-protected and strongly fortified. Mudgagiri (modern Mongyr) was perhaps the strategic point, where the Pālas concentrated their forces to check the Pratihāra advance, because it is the Jasyaskandhāvāra in three Pāla grants.[2] Pāṭaliputra is the camp of victory in the Khalimpur plate and Vilāsapura was at the time of Mahīpāla. Madanapāla issued his grant from Rāmāvatī, the city built by his father Rāmapāla. The Sena grants upto the time of Lakṣmaṇasena were issued from Vfkramapura and during the the time of Keśavasena the camp of victory was at Phalgugrāma, probably somewhere in Eastern Bengal.

It seems that the Senas had their administrative headquarters at three strategic points. The Pāla power was set at naught twice in East Bengal—first by the Candras and then by the Varmans and Vikrampura was the capital of both these powers. The Senas by establishing their headquarters at Vikramapura removed that danger. A strong and well-fortified Gauḍa or Laknauti was extremely useful to check any foreign invader from the west, advancing along the banks of the Ganges through the Rajmahal hills as the advance and occupation of northern Bengal by the Pratihāras would show it. Again, it would have been advantageous with headquarters at Nudiah (Navadwip ?) to oppose any foreign power advancing through southern Bihar and Birbhum as the Paikore inscription of the Cedi Karṇa would indicate it. This would also serve the purpose of checking any invasion through Orissa and Midnapore.

1. Elliot, vol. III p. 196.

2. This is also corroborated by the evidence of the Jodhpur inscription of Pratihāra Bauka which records a Pratihāra victory at Mudgagiri over the Gauḍa king.

Besides, forts were constructed at strategic points both for external and internal defence. The provincial governors and district officers must have some garrisons under them for maintaining peace and tranquility of the realm.

Military Secretariat

In the Ramganj plate of Iśvaraghoṣa Mahāvalādhikaraṇika is an important officer. The name itself would go to suggest that he was in charge of the military secretariat. This indicates in a way that every important department had a different secretariat of its own. Mahāvalakoṣṭhika is also an officer of the military department in the same inscription. He may be taken to be the officer-in-charge of the armoury. One of the clay seals of the Gupta period discovered by Bloch at Basrah in Tīrabhukti refers to Raṇabhāṇḍāgārādhikaraṇa.[1] Dr. Ghosal takes it to mean the office of Treasure of the War Department and remarks that this slight hint is sufficient to show that in the provinces (and almost certainly in the centeral government as well) the deparlment of the military finance was separated from that of civil finance. This conclusion can hardly be accepted as the interpretation of the word 'Raṇabhāṇḍāgārādhikaraṇa' as the office of armoury keeper or the commissariat seems to be more probable.

Police Department

It has already been stated that there was probably a police-tax for maintaining the police force. Caurodharaṇika and Daṇḍapāśika figure in almost all grants and seem to be high police officers. Though the function of Caurodharaṇika cannot be precisely assertained, he was in all probability in charge of all criminal matters under his jurisdiction. Daṇḍika, Daṇḍapāṅi or Daṇḍapāṇika also seem to be police officers.

The functions of Grāmika, Dāśagrāmika, Kṣetrapa have been discussed elsewhere. In addition to their duties already observed, it may be noted here that they might have policing duties also. In the Arthaśāstra the Vivitabhārtā, guardian of pasture land, is to examine *inter alia* the passports of those lurking on out of the way tracts, to make the lower forest region safe from thieves, to ensure security against thieves, to escort caravans and to protect cattle.[1] The village headman is to compensate the caravan for theft or removal of their goods at night within the village limits, the superintendent of pastures is to be liable for their loss within the village boundary, while the officer charged with the arrest of thieves in other cases. If the loss of merchandise occurs in such parts of the country as are not provided even with such security, the people in the boundaries of the place shall contribute to make up the loss. If there are no people in the boundaries, the people of 5 or 10 villages in the neighbourhood shall make up the loss.[2] Dr. Altekar draws attention to a 12th century inscription of Rajputana which embodies an agreement on the part of the townsmen of a city that they would be responsible for any thefts that might occur in their town. The king of the place had made arrangements about the watch and ward of the place.[3]

It will not be out of place here to discuss the position and function of another officer variously designated, Dauḥsādhanika, Duḥsādhyasādhanika, Dauḥsādhyasādhanika. He always figures before Cauraddharaṇikā. That he was an important officer is clear from the fact that the epithet 'mahā' is affixed to him. Dr. R. G. Basak takes him either to be a porter or superintendent of villages. It is not known what is the technical meaning of the term. The literal meaning is that one who is entrusted with difficult undertakings. We would rather suggest that he was the superintendent of spies whose functions and importance in the work of the government have been so much emphasised by the author of the Arthaśāstra. He might have been connected with many departments but certainly very intimately with the police department.

1. Artha. II. 34.

2. Ibid. IV. 13. The liability of the three officers, the guardian of the pasture land, village headman and Cauarajjuka is repeated in Yājñavalkya. II. 271.

3. El. XI, p. 40.

It is quite probable that the police officers mentioned above were under provincial governors, district officers and officers in-charge of cities.

Besides these, mention may be made here of some of the officers who are body-guards and the like of the kings, chiefs and officials.

Antaḥpratihāra—probably guard of the inner palace.

Ābhyantarika—probably a class of royal servants of the harem.

Vāsagārika—probably in charge of the royal palaces.

Śirorakṣika—probably a class of body-guards.

Khaṇḍagrāha—It is probably the same as Khaṇḍaraka of the Chamba inscriptions, which, according to Dr. Vogel, means a class of body-guards carring swords.

Aṅgarakṣas – body-guards.

Ārohakas – royal guards on horse.

Judicial Department

Very few facts regarding this important branch of administration are known. Some judicial officers no doubt figure in the inscriptions but their duties and functions are not precisely known. Mahādharmādhyakṣa or the chief judge was at the central government. The king with some selected officials might have tried important cases. The provincial governors and district officers might have some judicial functions.

Mahādaṇḍanāyaka—He may be taken either to be an army officer or a judicial officer.

Dāśaparādhika—The officer who tried cases connected with traditional offences. He is mentioned only in the Khalimpur plate.

Pramātṛ[1]—The dictionary meaning is proving, evidence,

1. Dr. Beni Prasad takes Pramātṛs to be surveyors and measurers but does not cite any authority. State in Ancient India, p. 299. In the Madhuban plate of Harṣavardhana the Pramātṛs are mentioned after Dausādhanikas and the dūtaka mahāsāmanta, mahārāja Skandagupta has also the title pramātṛ EI, Vol. I, No, II.

who or what is proof or authority. He may be taken to be a judicial officer.

Aṅgikaraṇika—The officer in charge of oath. He was, therefore a judicial officer and has been mentioned only in the Ramganj plate.

Daṇḍika, Daṇḍaśakti, Daṇḍapāṇika, Daṇḍapāśika—we have suggested that they were probably police officers. Daṇḍa means punishment and therefore can equally be taken to be judicial officers.

Miscellaneous officers

The functions of the following officers cannot be explained either etymologically or technically : Ekasaraka, Autthitāsanika. Ṭhakura, Mahākaṭuka, Śāntakika. All of them figure in the Ramganj plate In the same record Karmakāra is mentioned as a royal officer. Most probably he is a state artisan. Ekapātra occurs in the Sunderban plate of Ḍommaṇapāla.

Feudatories

Most of the ancient Indian empires had feudatory rulers under the central government. The Pāla and Sena kingdoms were no exception to this general feature. Some parts were under the direct administration of the imperial government and some parts under subordinate chiefs. In almost all grants the following personages enjoying royal or semi-royal status are mentioned-

Rājan—Vassal kings.

Rājanyaka—One having the status of a Rājā.

Rāṇaka—He figures after the royal consort. According to Dr. Basak, Rāṇakas were a class of subordinate chiefs.

The most curious fact is that these three royal personages are also mentioned in the Rāmganj plate of Mahāsāmantādhipati Ḍommana pāla, who were, as it appears from their titles, mere feudatory rulers. This can of course be explained by the assumption that feudatory rulers had got subordinate chiefs under them and that they had pretension to semi-indepedent position or royal status in the extraordinary political circumstance.[1] The list of officers in these two grants goes to show that the government of the feudatories was replica of the imperial system.

The Gunaighar grant of Vainyagupta shows that the vassal princes sometimes accepted office under the central authority. The frontier king Mahārāja Vijayasena, dūtaka of the grant, was officer in charge of the elephants and had three high-sounding titles In the commentary of the Rāmacarita the vassal rulers are called Sāmantas. In the Vappaghoṣavaṭa grant of Jayanāga a Sāmanta was in charge of a Viṣaya. It cannot be definitely stated whether Raṇaśūra of Dakṣiṇa-Rāḍha, Dharmapāla of Daṇḍabhukti. Govindacandra of Vaṅgāladeśa were feudatories under Mahīpāla I. They might have fought against the Cola[2] emperor either on their own account or for Mahīpāla I. It is clear from the Baghaura image inscription of

1. Mr. R. D. Banerjee suggested that palæographically Iśvaraghoṣa should be placed before Vijayasena and Vallālasena (Banglārā Itihāsa, p. 330,). Mr. N. G. Majumdar remarks that the characters of the Ramganj plate represent a variety of northen alphabets which is evidently earlier than those used in the Sena grants and akin to those found in the copper-plates of the later Pālas, e. g. the Bangar grant of Mahīpāla I and the Amgachi grant of Vigrahapāla IB, p. 149), Mr. N. N. vasu has rightly pointed out that Dhekkarī, from where the grant was issued, is to be located in the Goalpara district of Assam and the river Joṭoda, according to the Kālikāpurāṇa, flowed through Kāmarūpa. The characters of the Ramganj plate have close resemblance with those of the Puspabhadra plate of Dharmapāla who flourished towards the close of the eleventh century A. D.. Iṣvaraghoṣa was most probably a feudatory ruler on the north-eastern frontier of the Pāla empire and issued his grant during the troublesome days of the Kaivarta revolt. This is in a way strengthened by the fact that after the suppression of the Kaivarta rebellion Rāmapāla sent a general to conquer Kāmarūpa (Rāmacarita, 3/47). Ḍommanapāḷa granted his charter in 1196 A. D. i. e., just on the eve of the Muslim conquest when the central government perhaps became weak. The fact that these two chiefs were bold enough to issue their grants without any referece to the paramount power perhaps indicates that their attitude was defiant to the imperial power.

2. Trimulai Rock inscription of Rājendracola EI, IX, p. 229.

the 3rd year of Mahīpāla I[1] that his sovereignty was acknowledged in East Bengal. Daṇḍabhuki and Dakṣiṇa-Rāḍha appear to be small principalities. All these suggest that the chiefs of these places must have had an overlord, though there is no evidence to prove Mahīpāla's authority over them. The existence of the subordinate chiefs is definitely proved by the evidence of the Rāmacarita and the commentator gives a list of 14 such rulers who helped Rāmapāla in the recovery of Varendra from the Kaivartas.

The Pāla kings like Dharmapāla and Devapāla conquered many kingdoms of north-western India. The policy adopted towards a conquered country seems to be what was advocated by Manu. The conqueror should not annex the enemy's state but should appoint a near relative of the former ruler as his own nominee on the throne. The contemporary Muslim writer Sulaiman writes, "When a king subdues a neighbouing state in India, he places over it a man belonging to the family of the fallen prince, who carries on the government in the name of the conqueror. The inhabitants would not suffer it to be otherwise." If the identification of Indrāyudha of the Jaina Harivaṁśa with Indrarāja of the Bhāgalpur grant be correct. the placing of Cakrāyadha on the throne of Kanouj by Dharmapāla perhaps points to that fact.

The control exercised by the paramount power varied according to circumstances. If the central government was strong, the subordinate rulers paid customary obedience to the imperial court. Most probably fiscal dues were regularly sent to the imperial exchequer. Nothing particular is known of the relation between the imperial power and the feudatories. The Agnipurāṇa enjoins the following duties on the part of the feudatories which may be taken to be the relation in normal circumstances. "In times of war the feudatories must be at the beck and call of the sovereign. They should mark out the sovereign's friends from his foes. They should rally supporters to king's banners and

1. E1. XV11, p. 353.

collect troops for him. They should apease the public feeling for him. They must help him with their resources."[1]

The Chatsu inscription of Bālāditya records the services of a line of feudatory rulers to the Pratihāra empire.[2] Sulaiman observes that the ambassador from the imperial court was received with great respect in the Rāṣṭrakūṭa empire and the ambassadors like modern Political Agents in Native States exercised general powers of superintendence. The same practice might have been in vogue in Bengal.

But when the imperial power was weak, the feudatories tried to assume semi-independent attitude. Nothing illustrates more clearly the changed attitude of the Sāmantas of the Pāla empire than that Rāmapāla had to secure their service after a great deal of persuasion. In ordinary circumstances it is to be expected that they would stand by the dispossessed prince in the critical period of the Kaivarta rebellion. Rāmapāla had to meet personally the principal Sāmantas[3] and implore their assistance which he secured with the promise of further increase of territory and reward of money.[4] If the arms and resources of the vassals were a strength to the imperial power, they were also a source of weakness. Rebellions and risings due to general discontent or weakness of the central government would be generally under the banner of a feudatory chief. Most probably the ambitious Kaivarta chief Divvoka was a subordinate chief of the Pālas, who, taking advantage of the misgovernment of Mahīpāla II and consequent general discontent, raised the standard of revolt and ousted the Pālas from Varendra for a considerable time. The powers and prestige of powerful chiefs were sometimes a challenge to the imperial power.

1. Agni Purāṇa, Ed. Manmatha Dutt CCXLI, 16-28.
2. EI, XII, p. 11.
3. Rāmacarita, 1/43.
4. Ibid, 1/45.

Errata

Page						
Page	II	fn 5	read	Division	for	Divition
„	III	fn 4	„	of	„	oi
„	IV	line 18	„	the	„	thea
„	VII	„ 30	„	Araṇyaka	„	Araṇyak
„	7	line	insert	,	after	'Purāṇa
„	8	fn 4	read	has been	for	is
„	14	line 6	insert	,	after	bhaṭṭāraka
„	17	line 14	„	.	for	
„	22	fn I	read	after	„	aftcr
„	23	line I	insert	,	after	vow
„	28	line 7	read	than	for	then
	„	„ 15	„	Jātakhaḍga	„	Jātakhāḍga
„	37	„ 22	„	themselves	„	themselve
„	38	„ 12	„	Nārāyaṇapāla	„	Nārāyāṇapala
„	39	„ 15	„	necessarily	„	necssarily
„	41	„ 12	insert		for	,
„	46	„ 21	„	"	before	elder
„	47	„ 13	read	dūtāka	for	dātāka
„	48	„ 9	„	Vākpāla	„	Vakpāla
„	„	„ 18	„	Rājyapāla	„	Rajyapāla
„	„	„ 30	insert		after	thereon
„	52	„ 12	read	anadhikṛta	for	anaduikṛta
„	58	„ 20	„	achievements	„	achicyemants
„	60	line 6	read	of	for	or
„	60	„ 27	insert	for	for	(after Gapāla

Errata

Page 61	line 12	read	III) Bāla-vallabhi-bhujaṅga	for Vāla-Vallabhujaṅga
,, 65	,, 2	,,	winning	for wining
,, 68	,, 18	,,	Madanapāla	,, Madanpala
,, 70	,, 10	insert	Indra	after son
,, 84	,, 17	read	dynasty	for family
,, 87	,, 14	read	Kāñci	,, Kāṅci
,, ,,	,, 16	,,	,,	,, ,,
,, 92	,, 8	,,	is	,, Is
,, 93	,, 14	,,	ancient	,, anciect
,, ,,	,, 27	,,	the	,, tne
,, 95	,, 16	,,	A. H.	,, A. D.
,, 106	,, 26	insert	.	after A. D.
,, 109	,, 22	,,	,	after Vaṅgas
,, 112	,, 13	,,	work	before of
,, 115	,, 3	,,	,	after Parameśvara
,, 116	,, 2	,,	Arthaśāstra	for Arthaṣastra
,, ,,	,, 22	read	under	for of
,, 118	fn 2	insert	,	after village
,, 125	line 12	read	Taḍā-niyuktakas	for Tatiniyuktas
,, 126	,, 12	,,	period	for perid
,, 151	,, 20	insert		after correct

the early history of eastern india

(From the Earliest Times to the Muslim Conquest)

Vol. II.

PROMODE LAL PAUL

Forwarded by :
Dr. R.C. MAJUMDAR

SHARADA

Sharada Prakashan
DELHI-110052
1990

TO

Dr. RABINDRA NATH TAGORE

With Profound Respect and Admiration.

বাংলার মাটি, বাংলার জল
বাংলার বায়ু, বাংলার ফল
পুণ্য হউক, পুণ্য হউক
পুণ্য হউক, হে ভগবান্।

—রবীন্দ্রনাথ।

A NOTE

The publication of this Second Volume completes the Early History of Bengal by Prof. P. L. Paul, M.A. It goes as the third number of the Indian History Series of the Indian Research Institute publications. It is expected that it will throw a flood of light on the obscure corners of the social, religious and cultural history of Ancient Bengal. It deals with dry topics in a lucid style and new materials have been digested and marshalled with accuracy and artistic skill. Properly speaking this being the first attempt of its kind, we expect it will stimulate further and more elaborate researches. Unfortunately, inspite of best efforts few discrepancies in diacritical marks and misprints have crept in, and they will be rectified in the next edition.

We earnestly hope that the scholars and lay readers alike will offer it the welcome it deserves.

Janmāṣṭamī Day.
Dated the 26th August, 1940.
THE INDIAN REASEARCH INSTITUTE,
Calcutta.

SATIS CHANDRA SEAL.

Author's Preface

This is the first attempt to write the social, religious and cultural history of ancient Bengal on a comprehensive scale. I have spared no pains to make it thorough and exhaustive so far as materials at present permit.

I have endeavoured my best to interpret the history of ancient Bengal in all its phases. I shall consider my labour worth while if these two volumes help others to go deeper into the subject.

In the publication of this volume I must express my thankfulness to my friends and colleagues Profs. G. S. Ghar M. A. and P. R. Burua M. A. for going through the proofs and to Prof. K. C. Chakravarty M. A. and Mr. Chittaranjan Das B. A. for preparing the Index. My best thanks are due to Mr. Satis Chandra Seal M.A., B.L, Secretary of the Indian Research Institute, for publishing these two volumes under the auspices of the Institute.

5th June, 1940 P. L. Paul

Contents

Author's Preface

Chapter VIII — Literature, Learned Men and Centres of Learning 1-30

Chapter IX — Social Condition 31-61

Chapter X — Religious Condition 65-89

Chapter XI — Religious Condition (continued) 90-115

Chapter XII — Art and Architecture 116-128

APPENDICES

Appendix E — Authorities 61-62

Appendix F — Different gāiñs 62-64

Appendix G — Coinage 129-132

Appendix H — The Gauḍas and Gauḍa 133-136

List of Abbreviations

ASI	Archæological Survey of India (Cunningham)
ASIR	Archæological Survey of India, Reports
BI	Banglara Itihasa
BD. Icon.	Buddhist Iconography
BS.	Bengali San.
CHI	Cambridge History of India
CII	Corpus Inscriptionun Indica
DH	Dynastic History of Northern India
DM	Dacca Museum
DMC	Catalogue of the Dacca Museum
DMS	Dacca University Studies
EHI	Early History of India
EI	Epigraphia Indica
ESMS	Eastern School of Mediaeval Sculptures
GOS	Gaekwad Oriental Series
IA	Indian Antiquary
IB	Inscriptions of Bengal
IHQ	Indian Historical Quaterly
IM	Indian Museum.
JASB	Journal of the Royal Asiatic Society of Bengal
JBORS	Journal of the Bihar and Orissa Research Society
JBTS	Journal of the Buddhistic Society
JDL	Journal of the Department of Letters

JIH	Journal of Indian History
JRAS	Journal of the Royal Asiatic Society
MASB	Memoirs of the Asiatic Society of Bengal
PHAI	Political History of Ancient India
SBE	Sacred Books of the East
SII	Southern Indian Inscriptions
SPP	Sahitya Parisat Patrika
VJI	Vangera Jatiya Itihasa
VRS	Varendra Research Society
VRSC	Varendra Research Society Catalogue
VRSM	Varendra Research Society Museum
VRSR	Varendra Research Society Reports
VSPC	Vangiya Sahitya Parisat Catalogue
VSPM	Vangiya Sahitya Parisat Museum.

THE EARLY HISTORY OF BENGAL

CHAPTER VIII

Literature, Learned Men and Centres of Learing

The task of writing the literary history of a particular province is in one way more difficult than that of ancient India as a whole. The question of settling the chronology is common to both. But as many authors are silent on their place of origin, it is sometimes hardly possible to arrive at any satisfactory conclusion on that point. It is not unoften that in order to determine the nativity of an author, we have to rely on his cognomen, the popularity of his work in a certain locality and the provenance of the manuscripts. It is to be admitted by all that in the absence of some other stronger proof the claim of a particular locality or country on the above grounds rests on a very weak foundation. The fact being so, 'provincialism' is sometimes at work now-a-days in claiming the honour of adding many great writers of the ancient period to the native province of some modern writers. Kālidāsa has been claimed by many provinces[1] and the so-called 'internal evidence' has not helped much and on the very same ground a claim has been put forward for the Bengali origin of Viśākhadatta.[2] The *Vaidika* Brahmanas of Bengal regard Murāri, the author of *Anargha-Rāghava,* as one of their kinsmen, but this cannot be substantiated in any way.

Grammar—The science of grammar was cultivated assiduously. Candragomin, founder of the Cāndra school of grammar, seems to have belonged to Bengal. There were two other Candragomins. One was a logician and another appears to have been a Tāntrika scholar. These three Candragomins have been confused by Tārānātha[3] and by the

1. ABI, X111, pp. 235 ff. 2. JABS, 1930, pp. 240 ff,
3. Tārānātha, pp. 148 ff, 159 ff.

author of *Pag-Sam-jon-zang.*[1] The grammarian Candragomin has been assigned to the period between 450-660 A.D.[2] and was a contemporary of Candrakīrti. There can be no doubt about the fact that he was the earliest, for the other two flourished in the 10th. century A.D.[3] It is definite that the grammarian Candragomin hailed from eastern India and he has been connected by a story with Varendra and Candradvīpa in Tibetan books. Later, the other two were also confused with him. He followed Pāṇini in many respects but he omitted Pāṇinian rules about Vedic grammar in order to make his work free from the "traditional Brahmanical element". The really original contributions of Candragomin amount to about 35 *sūtras*[4] and these have been borrowed by *Kāśikā* without acknowledgement. Most probably his work was popular with the Buddhists and it is still used in Tibet and in a modified form in Ceylon[5]. It was very popular in Java also[6].

It has been said that the Buddhist grammarian Jinendrabodhi, the author of *Kāśikā-vivaraṇa-pañjikā* or *Nyāsa,* may be looked upon as a native of Bengal or one who had lived and worked long in that province[7]. The utmost that can be said in the present state of our knowledge is that his work was extensively used and some commentaries were written on it in Bengal. Govardhana, Dāmodarasena and Indumitra are three grammarians who seem to have flourished in Bengal in the eleventh century[8]. Govardhana's *Uṇādivṛtti* is known only from quotations, and Dāmodarasena is the author of *Upādhyāya-sarvasva.* Indumitra is known by his *Anu-nyāsa,* a commentary on *Nyāsa.* It has been suggested that Maitreya Rakṣita, the author of *Tantrapradīpa* and *Dhātupradīpa,* was a northern Bengali Brahmana but nothing can be said in support of this

---

1. S. C. Das, Pag-Sam-jon-zang, pp. 95, 139
2. Belvalkar, Systems of Sanskrit Grammar, p. 35.
3. S. C. Vidyabhusana, History of Indian Logic, pp, 333 336
4. Belvalkar, op. cit., pp. 59-60. 5. Ibid.
6. Journal of Greater India Society, Vol. III pp. 108 ff.
7. Sir Asutosh Silver Jubilee Volume, III, p. t. I pp. 194-197,
8. Ibid.

conjecture[1]. Puruṣottamadeva flourished in the 12th century and in his *Bhāṣāvṛtti* he depended on *Kāśikā* and *Nyāsa*. He was a Buddhist and excluded the texts appertaining to the Vedas. He simplified difficult grammatical rules in such a way as would make them easy to be understood by preliminary students of the subject, and his quotations and illustrations are to the point. Besides this great work, he is credited with the authorship of *Lalita-paribhāṣā, Jñānapāka-samuccaya, Uṇādivṛtti* and a commentary on *Mahābhāṣya*[2]. Śarṇadeva, another Buddhist grammarian, was the author of Durghaṭavṛtti. He was a younger contemporary of Puruṣottamadeva from whom he quoted extensively and was patronised by Lakṣmaṇasena[3].

Lexicography–Side by side with grammar, the science of lexicography was cultivated with equal zeal. The earliest writer seems to have been *Vandyaghāṭīya* Rāḍhīya Brahmana, Sarvānanda. He finished his *Ṭīkāsarvasva,* a commentary on *Amarakoṣa* in1159 A.D.[4]. Puruṣottamadeva's fame does not rest only on his grammatical works; as a lexicographer he is equally famous. His *Trikāṇḍaśeṣa* is not a commentary but a supplement to *Amarakoṣa*. It adds the words that had come into use since Amara's time. Many new names of Buddha, Avalokiteśvara, Tāntrika gods and goddesses are to be found in it, which were not perhaps known to Amara[5]. He was not satisfied with writing a supplementary book but also wrote a separate book called *Hāralīlā*. It consists of 278 *Ślokas* and in it are to be found words that were obsolete or were not in common use in his time. In the opinion of Mm. H. P. Sastri[6] his chief title to greatness lies in the fact that he is said to have composed a separate lexicon on spelling. Spelling in Bengal was greatly influenced by *Prākṛta* and many words were capable of two spellings and double meanings. He laid stress on this aspect and his work was an example

1. Mr. D. C. Bhattacharyya wants us to believe that the name was Rakṣita Maitreya, and as Maitreya was the surname of a gāiṅ of northern Bengali Brahmanas he was a Vārendra. But it is in the least crnvincing. Ibid.
2. Ibid. 3. Ibid.
4. Published by Ganapati Shastri, Madras 1911, 1917
5. SPP, 1339, B. S. P. I. 6. Ibid.

of accuracy and preciseness in spelling. Another Buddhist, Maheśvara[1] wrote a book on spelling in 1111 A.D.

Gauḍī-rīti—*Gauḍī-rīti* was one of the principal styles of poetic composition, the other important one being *Vaidarbhī*[2]. *Gauḍī* derived its name from the place of its origin and Daṇḍin calls it *paurastya,* i.e. eastern, and therefore there can be no doubt about the fact that it had its origin in Bengal. Bāṇabhaṭṭa informs us that the people of different places followed different poetic devices and the Gauḍas are fond of the display of bombastic words[3]. Bhāmaha (7th-8th cent.) distinguishes betwteen Vaidharbha and Gauḍa *Kāvyas,* though he does not use the term *rīti*[4]. He refers to the opinions of previous writers according to which there are differences of manner and treatment but he does not attach much importance to the difference[5]. In Daṇḍin's time (8th-9th) the difference was very wide and marked[6]. In Daṇḍin seems to be very severe in his condemnation of *Gauḍī* which is "loose, more often cumbrous and bombastic, is vitiated by an inordinate craze for verbal juggles and alliteration and casts to the winds clarity of expression and all sense of proportion and welcomes verbosity, pedantry and hyperbole[7]". But it is also clear from Daṇḍin that the Gauḍas laid great stress on *ojas*[8] and attempted at *arthavyakti*[9] i.e., explicitness of meaning. Vāmana (9th A.D.), who follows Daṇḍin, admits that *Gauḍī* has two *guṇas, ojas* and *kānti,* but is wanting in *mādhurya* and *saukumārya* (tenderness) and is full of harsh-sounding words. Rudraṭa (9th) says that in *Gauḍī* compounds are formed by as many words

1. Ibid. 2. The minor two are Pāncālī and Lāṭī
3. Harṣacarita Sl. 7
4. S. K. De, History of Sanskrit Poetics II pp. 100 ff; we follow the dates of the writers on rītis as determined by Dr. De. 5. 1, 31-35.
6. Jacobi holds that the Vaidarbhī style which came into existence in the third century A. D. was a reaction against the older and more ornate Gauḍī (Mahārāṣṭrī pp XVI): Dr. Nobel also holds that the Gauḍī was earlier (Foundations of Indian Poetics, Ch. VI). But Dr. S. K. De maintains that Gauḍī is a sign of further develop ment or decadence (History of Sanskrit Poetics, II, p. 116 n).
7. IHQ. III, pp. 377-78. 8. 1, 80. 9. 1, 75

as possible. Rājaśekhara (10th) takes the *rītis* as forms of speech without further explaining them, and Mammaṭa considers them repetition of the same consonants. Thus the *rītis* lost their importance as given by Daṇḍin[1].

It is not to be supposed that Gauḍī was used only in the land of its origin or eastern India. The Mandasor inscription of Yaśodharman, Haraha inscription of Īśānavarman and Nālandā inscription of the time of Yaśovarman were written in this style. Bhavabhūti, Bhaṭṭa-Nārāyaṇa, Murāri, Kṣemīśvara, Sandhyākaranandī and Śrīharṣa followed this style, and therefore it seems that different authors chose their style according to their convenience and predilections. The poetry portions of the Nidhanpur plates of Bhāskaravarman and of the Tippera plate of Lokanātha and of the Pāla and Sena inscriptions were written in this style which was evidently suited for *praśastis.*

Medical literature--In ancient India importance of the medical science was realised, as *Āyurveda* or the Science of Longevity was called an *Upa-Veda.* Yuan Chwang tells us that great stress was laid on it in the Nālandā monastery[2]. The *Tāntrikas* were expected to have minute knowledge of human anatomy and physiognomy, as they tried to control the senses by regulating breathing and by some process of physical exercises. Mādhavakara, author of *Rug-viniścaya,* or *Nidāna,* which enjoyed all India popularity and was translated into Arabic for the Caliphs of Bagdad in the latter half of the 8th century, has been claimed to be a Bengalee on the grounds that (a) his cognomen was " Kara ", (b) his book was extensively used in Bengal and (c) many Bengali words occur in another of his works, *Paryāya-ratnamālā*[3]. But it has been questioned in the absence of stronger proofs[4]. We are, however, on surer grounds in case of Cakrapāṇidatta. He came of a celebrated family of physicians. His father Nārāyaṇa was the superintendent of the culiniary department of the Pāla king, Nayapāla, and seems to be identical with the author of *Ratnamālā,* a medical vocabulary, and with Nārāyaṇa

1. Dr. Nobel, Foundations of Indian Poetry pp. 124-5
2. Beal, Records. pp. 77-79 ; Life, p. 112
3. IC, III, pp. 153-156 4. Ibid, I, pp. 273-4

Kavirāja who has been quoted in the *Saduktikarṇāmṛta*[1]. Cakrapāṇi's brother Bhānu has been called an *antaraṅga* which means a physician of a high family[2]. Cakrapāṇi was a prolific medical writer. His famous work, *Cakradatta,* was written on the model of a previous work, *Siddha-Yoga* of Vṛnda, and was meant for medical practitioners. It was very ably commented on by Sivadāsasena of the Pabna district in the 16th century. His *Dravya-guṇa-Saṁgraha* is a glossary of medical drugs and *Śabda-candrikā* is a vocabulary of vegetables and mineral substances. Besides, Cakrapāṇi is credited with the authorship of the *Bhānumatī* and *Āyurveda-dīpikā* which were meant to elucidate the *saṁhitās* of Suśruta and Caraka[3].

We know of another family of celebrated physicians who served in many courts. Bhadreśvara was the physician of Rāmapāla. His grandfather, Devagaṇa, served in that capacity to Govindacandra who may be identified with the king of that name known from the Tirumalai inscription. Sureśvara, son of Bhadreśvara, was the important man of this family and was the physician of Bhīmapāla, described as *Pādīśvara*[4] (lord of Pādī) who cannot be satisfactorily identified. He composed a dictionary on medical botany, called *Śabdapradīpa,* and another work on medical use of iron, called *Loha-paddhati.* Another medical writer called Gadādhara-vaidya in the *Saduktikarṇāmṛta* may be identified with Gadādhara, a commentator of Suśruta[5]. Vaṅgasena, the reputed author of *Cikitsā-sāra-saṁgraha,* was born in the house of Gadādhara and was an inhabitant of *Kāñjikā*[6]. According to Hœrnle[7], his work was a compilation from different medical writers, although he himself declares at the end that his work is a new recension of a previous one, named *Agastya-Saṁhitā.* Hemādri in his commentary on *Aṣṭāṅga-hṛdaya* of Vāgbhaṭa II quotes extensively from Vaṅgasena who can therefore be

1. For the first time suggested by Mr. N. N. Dasgupta, IC, III, p. 156
2. IC, I. p. 684 3. IC, III, pp. 156-58
4. Eggeling, Catalogue of Sanskrit Mss in the India office Library, 1896, Pt. V, pp. 294-5. 5. IC, III, pp. 157 ff,
6. Ibid.; also, IV, p. 109. 7. JASB, 1891, p. 183.

placed in the 12th-13th century[1]. The commentaries of Aruṇadatta, Vijayarakṣita, Niścalakara and Śrīkaṇṭha gained great popularity in Bengal but it is not certain whether they were Bengalees[2].

An interesting work on the taming and treatment of elephants has been ascribed to one Pālakāpya, son of the sage Lomaśa. It is written in *Sūtra* style and Mm. H. P. Shastri assigned it to a period before the Christian Era[3], and it was composed where "the Brahmaputra flows and the Himalaya is in the north". Strictly speaking, it was written in Assam. The Pāla kings were strong in elephants and they were a great dread to the other contemporary dynasties. It is therefore quite likely that the science of taming and treating elephants was cultivated in Bengal.

Astronomy—The astronomer Mallikārjuna Sūri hailed from Vaṅga and flourished in the 12th century. He wrote a commentary on *Śiṣyadhī-mahātantra* by Lallācārya and no other commentary on this is known. He also seems to be the earliest commentator on *Sūryasiddhānta*. He was of the *Kaundinya gotra* but his name *Sūri* and proficiency in astronomy suggest that his family might originally have been Jaina. It is to be noted that he invokes Viṣṇu and Gaṇeśa in his works and his grand-father was an *ācārya*. (SPP, 1340 pp. 83 ff.).

Philosophy—Various branches of philosophy were cultivated. Acording to Sureśvarācārya[4], the Vedantic work *Gauḍapāda-kārikā* embodied the view of the Gauḍas. It is admitted by all that it is a very old work[5]. Udayanācārya refers to a Gauḍa *Mīmāṁsaka* and his commentator Varadarāja says that it refers to *Pañjikā-kāra*. Therefore Śalikanātha, author of *Pañjikā*, seems to have been a Bengalee[6]. Śrīdharadāsa, author of *Nyāya-kandalī*, hailed from Bhūriśreṣṭhī (in the Hoogly district) in Rāḍha and composed his work in 913 S.E. under the patronage of a local *Kāyastha* chief, Pāṇḍudāsa by name. In his *Nyāyakandalī* there is reference to Śalikanātha and also there are re-

1. IC, III, pp. 585 ff.
2. Ibid, III, pp. 159-160 ; also IV, p. 275.
3. JBORS, 1919, pp. 307 ff.
4. Naiṣkarṇya-siddhi, IV, 41-44
5. IA, 1929, pp. 203-4 ; Belvalkar and Ranade, Hist. of Ind Philosophy, II, p. 963.
6. IA, 1929, p. 202.

ferences to two of his own works, *Advayasiddhi* and *Tattva-bodha-saṁgraha-ṭīkā,* none of which is known from any other source. The *Nyāyakandalī* was much used outside Bengal and commented on by non-Bengalee authors[1]. The *Tautātita-matatilaka* of Bhaṭṭa Bhavadeva, minister of Harivarmadeva, was a gloss on Kumārila Bhaṭṭa's *Tantravārtika.* Halāyuddha, a judge of Lakṣmaṇasena s court, wrote a work on *Mīmāṁsā,* called *Mīmāṁsā-sarvasva,* which is a running commentary on the *sūtras* of Jaiminī[2]. It has been argued by some writers[3] that Śrīharṣa enjoyed the patronage of Vijayasena in the early part of his career, but in his philosophical work *Khaṇḍana-Khaṇḍa-Khādya* (in which he criticises the main schools of Indian philosophy) he says that he was honoured by a Kāṅyakuvja king. Therefore this work does not seem to be a production of Bengal.

Smṛti and ritualistic literature—The first Smṛti-writer of note is Bhaṭṭa Bhavadeva. His *Karmānuṣṭhāna-paddhati,* also known as *Daśakarma-paddhati,* gives detailed description of the purifying ceremonies of marriage and domestic ceremonies to be performed by the Brahmanas in accordance with the *Chāndogya* schools of the Sāmaveda. This work is very important for the *Rāḍhīya* and *Vārendra* Brahmanas, most of whom belong to the *Kauthuma-śākhā* of the Sāmaveda. His *Prāyaścitta-nirūpaṇa* deals with sins and modes of their expiation. Murder of men, women and animals is called great crimes. Other crimes are the taking of forbidden food and drink, thefts, sexual intercourse with forbidden persons, forbidden marriages, sale of forbidden goods and contact with untouchables[4]. Govindarāja, son of Mādhava Bhaṭṭa, wrote a commentary on *Manusaṁhitā* and the manuscript was copied in 1145 A.D. It seems to be a "comprehensive compilation of domestic and social regulations for the Brahmanas of Bengal."[5]

Traditionally Jīmūtavāhana is known as *amātya* and *prāḍviveka* of Vijayasena[6]. He is styled in the colophons *Paribhādrīya Mahāmahopādhyāya* or *Paribhādra-kulāvadhūta.* Paribhadra is the Pari *gāiñ* of the *Rāḍhīya* Brahmanas. Mr. M. Chakravarti[7] draws

1. IC, IV, p. 276.
2. JASB, 1915, p. 328.
3. IC, II, pp. 576 ff. See infra.
4. JASB, 1912, pp. 335 ff.
5. JBORB, V, p. 173.
6. Dhākāra Itihāsa, II, p. 334.
7. JASB, 1915, p. 321.

attention to the fact that in his *Kāla-viveka* Rāḍha is mentioned along with Ujjayinī and suuggests that he was referring to his homeland. The same scholar after a detailed examination of all literary references has come to the conclusion that Jīmūtavāhana is to be placed in the beginning of the 12th century. His *Kāla-viveka* deals with appropriate months and seasons for religious duties and festivals. The *Dharmasūtras, Purāṇas* and Brahmagupta and Varāhamihira are cited as authorities. The *Vyavahāra-mātṛkā* deals with legal procedure in the court of justice and the nature of evidence. It is interesting to note that oral evidence, written documents, possession, and inference constitute various kinds of evidence, while trials by ordeals have no place in this book. "Like the *Kāla-viveka,* it is full of quotations, some six hundred in number." This fact alone shows Jīmūtavāhana's wide study and learning. His chief title to fame rests on the *Dāya-bhāga* which is the leading authority of the Bengal school of law and still determines the succession and inheritance of the Hindus of Bengal. "The *Dāya-bhāga* enunciates considerably advanced ideas of law on inheritance and partition, and displays an acute intelligence, a wide grasp of the subject and a skill in marshalling authorities in favour of its view."

Aniruddha-bhaṭṭa was the preceptor of Vallālasena and composed two works on rituals, namely, *Śuddhi-viveka* and *Hāralatā*[1]. It was at his instance that *Dānasāgara* was compiled by his royal disciple, which deals with various kinds of gifts and ceremonies connected therewith. The composition of the *Adbhutasāgara* is also ascribed to Vallālasena and it deals with omens and portents.

Halāyudha, a judge of Lakṣmaṇasena, was a prolific writer on *Smṛti.* His father Dhanañjaya was also a judge and he himself was at first a *rāja-paṇḍita, mahāmātra* and finally a *dharmādhikāra.* In some of the introductory verses and final colophons he styles himself '*āvasathika*'. If *āvasathika* is a mistake for *āvallika,* he may be identified with *āvallika paṇḍita* Halāyudha of the Vātsya *gotra,* one of the donees of the Sāhitya Pariṣat plate of Viśvarūpasena[2]. His mother belonged to the *Gochasaṇḍi Kula* (identifiable with *Gocaṇḍi*

1. JASB, 1906, p. 158.
2. The suggestion that āvasathika is a mistake for āvantika is unwarranted. IC, I, pp. 502-6.

gāiñ of the *Vārendra* Brahmanas of the *Bharadvāja gotra).* It may be that his father was also a *Vārendra*[1]. Of all his works, *Brāhmaṇa Sarvasva* is the best known. It deals with the daily rites and periodical *ācāras* of the Brahmanas. He has explained the rites and ceremonies of the Brahmanas in the light of the *Mantra-bhāṣya* of Uvaṭa and the *Gṛhya-mantra-bhāsya* of Guṇaviṣṇu. This work was meant for the Brahmanas of the *Vājasaneyī Kāṇvaśākhā.* Besides, he is credited with the authorship of the *Vaiṣṇava-sarvasva, Śaiva-sarvasva* and *Paṇḍita-sarvasva*. His two elder brothers, Paśupati and Īśāna, also composed several books. In the *Daśakarma-paddhati,* Paśupati is called *Rājapaṇḍita* and it deals with the ten domestic ceremonies according to the *Śukla-Yajurveda.* Paśupati also wrote *Śrāddha-kṛtya-paddhati* and *Pāka-yajña-paddhati. Īśāna* is said to have written a book on rites relating to the *āhnika* of the Brahmanas, called *Dvij-āhnika-paddhati*[2].

Kāvya—Tradition connects Bhaṭṭa-Nārāyaṇa, the author of *Veṇīsaṁhāra,* with Ādiśūra, but this is not corroborated from any other source. Mention may be made here of one Bhaṭṭa Nārāyaṇa of Uttara-Rāḍha, belonging to the *Vātsya gotra.* His son emigrated to Orissa where he figures as a donee of a grant of the eighth century[3]. But it is to be noted that Bhaṭṭa Nārāyaṇa connected with Ādiśūra was of the *Śāṇḍilya gotra.*

A strong case has been made for regarding Abhinanda, the author of *Rāmacarita,* as a writer who enjoyed the patronage of a Pāla prince named Hāravarṣa belonging to the family of Vikramaśīla[4]. As Vikramaśīla was another name of Dharmapāla, the suggestion of identifying Hāravarṣa with Devapāla is reasonable, though this is not corroborated from any other source. Abhinanda who enjoyed an all India fame and has been compared with Kālidāsa[5] must have produced a work of high poetic merit like *Rāmacarita.* But it must be noted that most of the verses attributed to Abhinanda in the anthologies cannot be traced in *Rāmacarita* and only a few are traceable[6]. Either Abhinanda composed other works or some other verses which

1. Ibid. 2. JASB, 1906, pp. 158A. 3. EI, XXIII, p. 74,
4. Introduction, Rāmacarita published in GOS.
5. Ibid. 6. Ibid.

are not yet known, or there was another Abhinanda. It is also to be noted that in the anthologies Abhinanda is occasionally called *Gauḍābhinanda*. The father of the author of *Rāmacarita* was Śatānanda, and it is a significant fact that some verses have been attributed to one Śatānanda in *Sadukti-karṇāmṛta,* and they either precede or follow those attributed to Abhinanda. It is his father's name that enables us to distinguish him from another Abhinanda, son of Jayantabhaṭṭa, and the author of *Kādambarī-kathā-sāra and Yagavāsiṣṭha-śāra.* The family of the latter originally belonged to Gauḍa but migrated to, and settled, in Kāśmīra six generations earlier[1]. His grandfather Śaktivarman was the minister of Lalitāditya Muktāpīḍa and his father Jayantabhaṭṭa was the author of *Nyāyamañjarī.* The author of *Rāmcarita* and the author of *Kādambarīkathā-sāra* belonged to the same time. *Rāmacarita* fulfils all the tests of a *Mahākāvya* and is written in the *Vaidarbhī-rīti.* It seems that Abhinanda ended his work with the 36th canto, and three other cantos have been added later.

Sandhyākaranandin's *Rāmacarita*[2] is a unique historical work. It is written in double *en tendre.* In one way it gives the story of the recovery of Sītā by Rāma and in another way it narrates the story of the recovery of Varendra by Rāmapāla from the Kaivarta chief Bhīma. Most of the words used are capable of two meanings and the author has been called " not only a poet but also a linguist." It is very difficult to understand the verses without the commentary which only comes upto the first canto and 36 verses of the second.

The Sena period has been called the *Augustan Age* of Sanskrit literature in Bengal[3]. The Sena kings lavishly patronised the scholars, and in *Saduktikarṇāmṛta* many verses are attributed to Lakṣmaṇasena, Keśavasena, Viśvarūpasena and Mādhavasena; and Vallālasena himself was a reputed author. The Sena court resembled Dhārā under Paramāra Bhoja and ancient Ujjayinī. The outburst of Brahmanical learning made itself felt in two directions—in ritualistic works and in the production of *Kāvyas.* Śrīharṣa, the author of *Naiṣadhīya,* is said to have enjoyed at first the patronage of Vijayasena. It has been suggested that this book has got some covert allu-

1. Ibid. 2. Published in MASB, III, pt. I
3. JASB, 1906, p. 157.

sion in it to the Sena dynasty[1]. It deals with the story of Nala and Damayantī, and Nala is described as the son of Vīrasena. It is known from the Sena inscriptions that Vīrasena of Puranic celebrity was the remote ancestor of the Senas. It may be noted in this connection that the Sarnath inscription of Kumāradevī, queen of Jayacandra, was composed by Śrī-Kunda, a friend of the king of Vaṅga. In *Khaṇḍana-khaṇḍ-khādya* it is said that he was honoured by the Kānyakubja king Jayacandra. In the above inscription Śrī-kunda has been decsribed as a " lion to attack the crowds of the elephant like heretics, and as a Rohaṇa mountain of the flashing jewels of poetical composition[2]". If this has any reference to the above philosophical work and to *Naiṣadhiya,* Śrī-Kunda may be identified with Śrī-Harṣa, though this does not prove his Bengali origin.

Umāpatidhara, the composer of the Deopara *praśasti* of Vijayasena, is quoted extensively in *Saduktikarṇāmṛta* and hundred verses have been attributed to him[3]. Referring to himself, the poet says that "his understanding has been purified by the study of words and their meanings" and this is amply proved even from this *praśasti.* Jayadeva is said to have criticised his fellow-poets of Lakṣmaṇasena's court thus[4]—"Umāpati is verbose in style, but devoid of sweet words. Śaraṇa has the merit of composing poems within a short time but his verses are very difficult to be understood. Govardhana is expert in erotic compositions. Dhoyī could remember what he heard but is vain." In *Saduktikarṇāmṛta* many verses have been quoted under Śaraṇadeva and Cirantana-śaraṇa all of whom according to Mr. M. Chakravarti,[5] refer to the same man. The poet Śaraṇa has been identified with the grammarian of the same name[6]. Ācārya Govardhana is known by his *Āryā-saptaśatī* which is full of erotic sentiment.

---

1. IC, II, 578-9. 2. EI. IX, pp. 323 ff,
3. JASB, 1906, p. 159 ff.
4. Then he praises himself with the remark that Jayadeva alone possesses all the merits of a good poet. I think this verse about his fellow poets and himself is a later interpolation, though it brings into prominence the characteristics of the five poets.
5. JASB, 1906. pp. 173 ff.
6. S. C. Chakravārty, Intro. Durghaṭavṛtti, p. 7.

Pavanadūtam of Dhoyī is a *dūta kāvya* and has been written in imitation of *Meghadūta* from which expressions have been sometimes borrowed. In spite of this, he exhibits a good deal of poetic skill. He wrote in an elegant and easy-going language and his descriptions are sometimes "vivid, lifelike and full of pathos.[1]" Of all the authors of Bengal Jayadeva is the best known. He was born at Kendubilva in the modern Birbhum district. His *Gīta-govinda* is one of the most popular books ever written in Sanskrit language. It is very sacred to the Vaiṣṇavas. There are very few hearts from which its sweet melody does not get response, and Jayadeva is known as the nightingale of Sanskrit poets.

Besides these, there are many authors like Udayana, Yogeśvara, Bālabhadra, Madhu *(dharmādhikāra)*, Vetāla, Vyāsa (Kavirāja) whose verses in praise of the king of Gauḍa or Vaṭudāsa, (the father of the anthologist) have been quoted in *Saduktikarṇāmṛta*[2] They were either poets of Bengal or connected with the Gauḍa court. This anthology deserves more than a passing notice. The work was finished in 1205 A.D.. Vaṭudāsa is called a *mahāsāmanta-cūḍāmaṇi* and a friend of Lakṣmaṇasena, and Śrī-dharadāsa was a *mahāmāṇḍalika*. The work contains the names of more than 450 authors and " bears ample testimony to his taste and industry..... the authors have been fairly selected and sorted under different subjects; and they bespeak a fairly wide culture with formation of libraries[3]".

The above account, incomplete as it is, is sufficient to indicate the extent and nature of the Brahmanical culture in various branches. Rājaśekhara in his *Kāvyamīmāṁsā*[4] twice refers to the extreme popularity of Sanskrit in Gauḍa. From the foreign accounts and epigraphic records we can trace the following centres of learning in different parts of Bengal.

In Rāḍha—Fa-hein speaks of Tāmralipti as an important centre of learning. There he lived two years in copying manuscripts. Yuan Chwang was very much impressed by the love of learning of

1. C. Chakravarti, Pavanadūtam, Intro., p. 12.
2. Published by H. D. Sharma ; see also JASB, 1906, pp. 157 ff,
3. Ibid., p. 175. 4. Pp. 31, 51.

five capital towns of Bengal that he visited. It-sing learnt the *Brahma* language and science of grammar at Tāmralipti and describes in detail the organisation and working of Bhā-rā-hā monastery there. It is thus clear that Tāmralipti was an important centre of learning in the Gupta and post–Gupta periods.

Bhuriśreṣṭha where *Nyāyakandalī* of Śrīdharācārya was composed was in Dakṣiṇa-Rāḍha and it is identified with the Bhursut *parganā* in the Hoogly district. It seems to have been a famous seat of learning. Kṛṣṇa Miśra in his *Prabodha-candrodaya* (it was dramatised in the court of the Candella king Kīrtivarman c. 1065 A.D.) caricatured the pride of Gauḍa philosophers thus, "Gauḍa kingdom is the best; in that the town of Rāḍha is above all comparison; the residence of Bhuriśreṣṭhaka is excellent; there my father is best[1]." It is known from an inscription[2] in the temple at Mandhata in the Central Provinces that Halāyudha, an emigrant from Navagrāma in Dakṣiṇa-Rāḍha, composed 64 verses of that record, dated in 1130 V.E. There exists a village named Navagrāma in the *parganā* of Bhursut[3].

Siddhala, home of Bhaṭṭa Bhavadeva, is in the Birbhum district, and in the Bhuvanesvar *praśasti* an account of his seven ancestors has been given. The village itself has been described as an ornament of Uttara-Rāḍha and a pride of Āryāvarta. All his ancestors were learned men. His seventh ascendant was the recipient of a *śāsana* of the village Hastinībhaṭṭa from a Gauḍa king, and his grandfather Ādideva was a minister of a Vaṅga king and he himself a *Sāndhivigrahika* of Harivarmadeva. His extant works have already been noted. In the panegyric he is described as 'omniscient'. "Having seen the other shore of the sea of *Siddhānta, Tantra* and

---

1. Prabodha-candrodaya, Canto II.
2. Hiralal, Inscriptions of C. P. and Berar., p. 84.
3. IC, I, p. 503. Mr. J. C. Ghose refers the date to the Śaka era but without any reason. He is also inclined to regard the three donees of the Mandhata plates of Devapāla and Jayavarman, dated in 1260-61 A. D. as emigrants from Bengal. One of them was an emigrant from Navagrāma, another from Tarkāri and the other from Ghataushari. It is not unlikely that a batch of Bengal Brahmaṇas emigrated to C. P. after the fall of Nadia.

Gaṇita, producing world-wide wonder in *Phala-Saṁhitās,* the maker and proclaimer of a new *Horāśāstra,* he became manifest as another Varāha (v.21). In the paths of *Dharma-śāstra,* by composing good treatises he blended old productions. By good glosses elucidating the *Dharmagāthās* of sages, he wiped away doubt on points of legal acts (v.22). In *Mīmāṁsā* he composed, following the sayings of Bhaṭṭa, a guide in which thousands of maxims etc., etc. . . . ." (v.23).

In Varendra–The Garuḍa pillar inscription introduces us to a *Śāṇḍilya* family of hereditary ministers of the Pālas. Their political activity has already been noted but their learning also finds a conspicuous mention in this record. Darbhapāṇi was a master of four *vidyās* (most probably the four Vedas) and so also his son Kedārmiśra. Gurava Miśra, minister of Nārāyaṇapāla, was proficient in many subjects, viz., in *Āgamas* (sacred lore), *Jyotiṣa* (astronomy) and in Vedas. He semes to have composed a book on *Śrutis* (v.24). He was a keen fighter in assembly as well as in the battle-field. The Silimpur *praśasti*[1] of Prahāsa supplies us with the information of the existence of a learned *Bharadvāja* family and of some villages and localities where Brahmanical learning and rites were in a flourishing condition. The family originally lived in Tarkāri within the limits of Śrāvasti[2] and migrated to Bālagrāma in Varendra in the Puṇḍra country and again to an adjacent village named Śiyāmbaka. All these places were abodes of learned Brahmanas and Vedic rites and homas were zealously performed. Palæographically Prahāsa may be assigned to the eleventh century and his grandfather Taponidhi attained perfection in the doctrines of Kumārila Bhaṭṭa. His father Kārtikeya was proficient in *Mīmāṁsā, Śrutis* and *Smṛtis.* Prahāsa himself was learned in logic, *Tantras,* and *Dharmaśāstras.* The king Jayapāla of Kāmarūpa tried to induce him to emigrate to that country with the promise of a gift of 900 gold coins and a grant of land yielding an annual income of 1000 coins. This offer was refused. He set up an image of Varāha and absorbed himself in pious and charitable activities. In his old age he retired on the bank of the Ganges.

---

1. EI, XIII, p. 283.
For location see supra.

BUDDHIST LITERATURE

Mm. H. P. Shastri[1] classified the literature of the Pāla period under four headings—(1) Sanskrit Brahmanic, (2) Sanskrit Buddhist (3) Vernacular Brahmanic[2] and (4) Vernacular Buddhist Literature. Though we cannot strictly follow this classification, it has got the merit of bringing into prominence the huge mass of Buddhist literature that was produced in the Pāla period. The later Buddhist literature has not yet been adequately studied, and we are not in possession of all the materials. Sometimes discoveries of some important books are announced from Nepal libraries. Many of the books are preserved in the *Bstan-hgyur* some of whose originals seem to have been lost. In studying this vast literature scientifically, there are various difficulties, some of which cannot be at present solved.

The later Buddhist literature is generally *Tantric* in character. Five important centres of Tantrikism were Kāmakhyā, Śrīhaṭṭa, Pūrṇagiri, Uḍḍīyāna and Zāhore. The first two are well-known places, and it is to be mentioned that Śrīhaṭṭa or Sylhet, though at present included in Assam, is linguistically and culturally a part of Bengal. Purṇagiri cannot be located. The last two localities are frequently mentioned as important centres of Buddhist Tantrikism and there is considerable disagreement among scholars about the location of Uḍḍīyāna and Zāhore. Uḍḍīyāna[3] has been sought to be located in in Swat valley, Kasgarh, Orissa, on the north-east fringe of Bengal and in the Chittagong region ; and Zāhore[4] has been identified with Mandi in the Panjab, Lahore, Jessore, Sabhar in Dacca and Sahore in Rāḍha. It is difficult to accept any one of these suggestions in the absence of definite evidence. Apart from the consideration that the stronghold of Tantrik Buddhism was in eastern India, the sug-

1. JBORS, V, p. 171.

2. Mm. H. P. Shastri could not mention any book of this class, though he asserted that there was such a class of literature. Ibid.

3. IHQ, VI, pp. 576ff ; Dr. M. Bhattacharyya, Sādhadāmāitā (GOS) intro. pp. xxxii-xxxix ; IHO, XI, p. 142.

4. Le Nepa, II, p. 177 ; Francke, Antiquities of Indian Tibet, II, p. 87 sādhanā-mālā, Intro., pp. XVXVII-XXXVIII ; IHQ, XI p. 144

gestion to locate Uḍḍīyāna in Bengal gains additional support from the simple fact that while Lui-pāda, Sarahā, Advaya-vajra and Tailaka-pāda have been described as of Uḍḍīyāna, they have been again called natives of Bangala[1] (Vaṅgāla ?). Again, Śāntarakṣita has been described as a scion of the royal family of Zahore. But according to the *Pag-sam-jon-zang,* he was born in Bangala.[2] This can be satisfied by locating Uḍḍiyāna and Zāhore in Bengal or by the supposition that there were two sets of Tantric scholars bearing the above names—a contention not easily to be conceded without strong proof. Another difficulty that confronts us is the settling of the chronology of the authors. Information on this point comes from Tārānātha, Bu-ston and the *Pag-sam-jon-zang* whose chronologies and genealogies are admittedly faulty and inaccurate, and therefore these Tibetan authorities cannot be much relied on. In order to fix the time of the Tantric authors attempt should rather be made from some definite known dates, say from Śāntarakṣita and disciples (*guru-paramparās)* as preserved by the Bstan--hgyur and the *Pag-sam-jon-zang* are to be utilised with the caution[3] that, "the mystics still believe that the *Siddhas* do not die..........such alleged relation only speaks of a spiritual connection and not of any historical one." The confusion of their chronology is worse confounded by the fact that many scholars of different periods bear the same name. There were at least three Candragomins,[4] three Nāgārjunas,[5] two Lui-pās[6] and two Śāntidevas.[7] I have got no doubt about the fact that there are many such cases of confusion in the Tibetan accounts. The apparent inconsistency and confusion in the Tibetan books cannot be solved until and unless the separate identity of different

1. IHQ. XI pp. 141-3
2. Ibid. pp. 142-43.
3. Sādhanamālā Intro. p. xl xli Dr. P. C. Bagchi, Kaulajṇāna-nirṇaya. Intro. pp. 25 26
4. History of Indian Logic pp. 333 336
5. Sādhanamālā, Intro., p. XIV ; JASB, 1930, pp. 142 ff
6. Lui-pā who has been identified with Matsyendranātha cannot be the same person to whom Sāntarakṣita refers; former seems to have flourished in the 10th century, while the latter in the 8th.
7. Śāntideva, the author of the Śikṣā-Samuccaya, (whose latest possi ble date is the 8th century) cannot be identified with Śāntideva, disciple of Dīpaṅkara Śrījṇāna of the 11th century

scholars of different periods can be definitely established. This perhaps explains also why a great many books have been attributed to a single author in the *Bstan-hgyur*. The numbers come sometimes to thirty or even to forty, and it may be that they are not the productions of one author. But it must also be said that we need not be surprised by these numbers, for twenty works of Advayavajra, when published,[1] contain only about sixty pages.

The earliest known Buddhist author seems to be the grammarian Candragomin. *Śiṣya-lekhā-dharma,* an epistle in *Kāvya* style, which has been addressed to the pupils, propounding Buddhist doctrines, is also attributed to him.[2]

Śīlabhadra, the preceptor of Yuan Chwang, was a scion of the Brahmanical royal family of Samataṭa. He enjoys a unique position in the Buddhist world as one of the celebrated heads of the Nālandā University. He was a disciple of Dharmapāla and is said to have defeated a learned Brahman from southern India in a discussion and the local king (most probably of Magadha) was so much satisfied with his victory that he made an offer of a city to Śīlabhadra which he reluctantly accepted, as it was opposed to the spirit of the Holy Master's teaching. He made a religious offering of the city and built a monastery there. The Chinese pilgrim and disciple pays eloquent tribute to his learning and liberality and says that he wrote several treatises.[3] "He rose to be eminent for his principles and subtleties and his fame extended to foreign countries." A work entitled *Ārya-Buddha-bhūmi-vyākhyā,* preserved in the *Bstan-hgyur,* has been attributed to one Śīlabhadra.

Sarahā is said to have belonged to Uḍḍiyāna[4] but according to *Pag-sam-jon-zang,* he hailed from Bangala.[5] He was also known as Sarahabhadra and Rāhulabhadra and was one of the earliest *Tāntrika*

1. GOS, No. XL. Edited by Mm. H. P. Shastri.
2. Nariman, Lit. Hist. of Sans. Buddhism, p. 100.
3. Watters, II, pp. 105, 109.
4. Cordier, II, p. 375.
5. Index, p. cxxi.

Buddhist scholars. He was equally learned in Brahmanical and Buddhist lore and has been assigned to the seventh century.[1] In the *Bstan-hgyur* twenty-one books are attributed to him.

Śabarīpa or Śabarīśvara came of a Śabara (huntsmen) tribe in Bangala and was a disciple of the Tantrika Nāgārjuna. He has been assigned to the seventh century and a *Sādhana* of Kurukullā in *Sādhanamālā* is attributed to him.[2] Some of his vernacular songs are known.[3]

Lui-pāda, according to the *Pag-sam-jon-zang*,[4] hailed from Uḍḍiyāna but in the *Bstan-hgyur* it is mentioned that he belonged to Bangala.[5] He came of the fisherman caste. He is said to have been the first *Siddhācārya* and has been assigned to the seventh century.[6] In the *Bstan-hgyur* five works on Tantrika Buddhism are attributed to him. Some of his vernacular songs have been published.[7]

Nāgabodhi was born in Varendra and was the disciple of Nāgārjuna who has been assigned to the 7th century.[7] The authorship of thirteen works is ascribed to him in the *Bstan-hgyur*.

The *Pag-sam-jon-zang*[9] states that Śāntarakṣita was a contemporary of Gopāla I and Dharmapāla and was a scion of the royal family of Zahore and a native of Bangala. He was a *paṇḍita of* the Nālandā University and was invited by the Tibetan king Khrisron-den-tsan to visit Tibet. He established the first Buddhist monastery Sam-ye in 749 A.D. and stayed there for 13 years and died in 762 A.D.. Śāntarakṣita is one of the greatest Buddhist scholars. His literary fame mainly rests on his monumental work

---

1. Sādhanamālā, Intro., p. xliv. 2. Idid , p. xlvi.
3. Published by Mm, H. P. Shastri in the Bauddha-Gāna-o-Dohā.
4. Index, p. cxv. 5. Cordier, II, p. 33.
6. Sādhanamālā, Intro., p. xlvii.
7. Bauddha-Gāna-o-Dohā.
8. Sādhanamālā, Intro., p. xiv.
9. Index, p. xcix, p. 112 ; Mr. S. C. Das, the famous Tibetan scholar, wrote that he was a native of Gauḍa. See JBTS, I, pt. II, p. 10.

called *Tattva-saṁgraha.*[1] It is an exposition of the *Mahāyāna* and refutation of other systems of Indian philosophy. He quotes from no less than sixty previous authors, the hollowness of whose arguments is exposed in this book. A learned commentary on *Tattva-saṁgraha* was written by his own disciple, Kamalaśīla. Besides, Śāntarakṣita is said to have written eight books.[2]

Haribhadra flourished during the reign of Dharmapāla at whose request he is said to have written a commentary on *Aṣṭa-sahasra-Prajñā-pāramitā* in order to work out a compromise between *Śūnyavāda* and *Vijñanavāda* of Nāgārjuna and Maitreyanātha.[3] Kāyastha Ṭaṅkadāsa was the chief *lekhaka* of Dharmapāla.[4] He wrote a commentary called *Suviśada-sampuṭa*[5] on *Hevajra-tantra.*

Various legends have grown around the name of Matsyendra-nātha, also known as Mīnanātha and Mīnapāda. It is really difficult to know the truth about this man who occupies a foremost place among both the Buddhist and Hindu *Tāntrikas.* He was the *guru* of Gorakṣanātha and is much revered by the Nātha sect all over northern India. Most probably he was a fisherman by caste and was born in Candradvīpa. He preached his doctrine in Kāmarūpa. Dr. P. C. Bagchi after a careful examination of all the available legendary accounts is inclined to place him in the beginning of the 10th century A.D. and accepts the identification of Matseyndranātha with Lui-pā.[6] His *Kaulajñāna-nirṇaya* deals with the *Kaula* doctrine of the Śaiva Tāntrikas but shows his acquintance with Buddhist Tāntrika doctrines.

Ācārya Jetāri came of a Brahmana family. He was a teacher of Dīpaṅkara and may be assigned to the last part of the 10th century. His father Garbhapāda served the local king of Varendra, Sanātana by name. Jetāri is said to have been expelled by his kinsmen and consequently entered the Buddhist order. Three books on

---

1. Published in GOS, No. XXX.
2. Ibid., Intro., p., Hist. of Ind. Logic, pp. 323 ff.
3. JBORS, V, p. 177. 4. Spp, 1318, p. 254.
5. Cordier, II, p. 67.
6. See the learned Introduction by Dr. P. C. Bagchi to Kaulajnāna-nirnaya, published in the Calcutta Sanskrit Series, No. III.

logic called *Hetu-tattvopadeśa, Dharmādharma-viniścaya* and *Bālāvatāra-tarka* are attributed to him in the *Bstan-hgyur*.[1]

Tailika-pāda or Tilopā was a contemporary of Mahīpāla. In the *Bstan-hgyur* he is described as of Uḍḍiyāna,[2] while the *Pag-sam-jon-zang*[3] records that he was originally a Brahmana of Chittagong and lived in the Paṇḍita Vihāra there. Several books on Tāntrika Buddhism are attributed to him.

According to Tārānātha, Avadūtapāda Advayavajra was a contemporary of Mahīpāla I, and Dīpaṅkara. Fifty-three works have been attributed to him. Twenty of them have been published under the heading *Advayavajra-saṁgraha*.[4]

Jñānaśrī Mitra was born in Gauḍa. He was a gate-keeper of the Vikramaśīlā monastery during the time of Dīpaṅkara's visit to Tibet and he is said to have owed a great deal to Jñānaśrī.[5] He was at first a follower of the *Śrāvaka* school but later accepted *Mahāyāna*. Three works, entitled *Kāryakāraṇa-bhāva-siddhi* (on logic), *Tantra-mūla-vṛtti* (a *Tāntrika* Buddhist work) and *Vṛtti-mālā-stuti* (on metre) are attributed to him.

Dīpaṅkara Śrījñāna Atīśa is a great name in later Buddhist history and in Tibet he occupies a place, second only to Buddha himself. His biography is known from a Tibetan source.[6] He was born in 980 A.D. in the royal family of Vikramaṇipura in Bangala. He was the son of Kalyāṇaśrī and Prabhāvatī, and his original name was Candragarbha. He learnt five minor sciences from Jetāri and *piṭakas* of the *Mahāyāna* doctrine, *Mādhyamika* and *Yogācāra* metaphysics from Rāhulagupta. At the age of thirty-one he became a full-fledged *bhikṣu* and spent 12 years in Suvarṇadvīpa in studying under Dharmakīrti. His vast learning won for him the exalted position of the high priest of Vikramaśīlā. He mediated the hostilities between king Karṇa and Nayapāla. In course of the description of a

1. For short notices of these books, see Hist. of Ind. Logic, p. 337.
2. Cordier, II, p. 79.
3. Index, p. xli.
4. GOS, No. XL.
5. Hist. Ind. Logic. p. 387.
6. JBTS. I, p. 9 ff.

convocation at Vikramaśilā, the Tibetan envoy who was deputed to escort him says, "When all the rows of seats were filled up, there came lord Atīśa, the *Venerable of Venerables,* in all his glory at whose sight the eyes felt no satiety. His graceful appearance and smiling face struck every one of the assembly. From his waist hung down a bundle of keys. The Indians, Nepalese and Tibetans all looked at him and looked upon him for a countryman of their own. There was brightness mixed with simplicity of expression on his face, which acted as a magic-spell upon those who beheld him."[1] After repeated invitations he went to Tibet to reform the Buddhist church there. He died in 1053 A.D. at the age of seventy-three. Twenty of his works are known in the *Bstan-hgyur.* Besides, with the help of some *lotsavas* (Paṇḍitas) he translated many Sanskrit books, more than hundred of which are mentioned in the *Bstan-hgyur.*

Ratnākara Śāntideva, also known as Bubhukṣu, was a gate keeper of the Vikramaśīlā monastery. Tārānātha says that he was a disciple of Dīpaṅkara and was a native of Zāhore in Bangala. He composed a *sādhana.*[2] He went to Ceylon to preach Buddhist doctrine. A work on prosody, called *Chando-Ratnākara,* is attributed to him. Two works on logic *Vijñapti-mātrā-siddhi* and *Antar-vyāpti,* are also known[3] and some of his vernacular songs have been published.

Prajñāvarman hailed from Kāva in Bhoṅgala (Vaṅgāla)[4] and was contemporary of Dānaśīla who flourished during the reign of Nayapāla. Prajñāvarman is known as a translator of Sanskrit books in Tibetan. He composed two works on Tāntrika Buddhism and a commentary on *Udāna-varga.*

Besides the above-mentioned authors and writers, there must have been many other Bengali scholars. In the above account only those have been included, about whom there is some definite evidence to show that they belonged to some part of Bengal. Some of the

---

1. JASB, 1891, pt. I, pp. 46-53.
2. No. 78. of Sādhnamālā, Intro., y. cxi.
3. Htst. of Ind. Logic. pp. 342-3.
4. Rockhill, Udānavarga, Intro., p. XII,

scholars whom we know only as teachers of the monasteries of Nālandā, Vikramaśīlā, Jagaddala, Paṇḍita Vihāra and Vikramapurī Vihāra must have hailed from Bengal but the fact is that nothing is known of their nativity.

Vernacular Buddhist Literature – Mm. H. P. Shastri published the mystic vernacular songs of 34 authors[1] and he regarded all of them as Bengalees because he noticed use of some obsolete and peculiar Bengali words in them. These mystic songs were composed by *Mahāsiddhas* who are said to have performed great miracles. There are various legends connected with their lives current in Nepal and Tibet, and it is difficult to know their real life-stories. The songs show that they were teachers of Buddhist *Sahaja* cult and seem to have some connection with the Śaiva *Nātha-panthīs*. Matsyendranātha, Gorakṣanātha and Jālandharipā are claimed by both the sects and held in great reverence. It is also clear that the *Siddhas* practised esoteric doctrines and *yoga*. Attempts have been made sometimes to explain abstruse philosophy in a popular way through these songs.

The distinguished linguist Dr. S. K. Chatterjee[2] notices distinctive Bengali traits of speech in the *dohās* of 20 writers Lui-pā (2 poems), Kukkurī (2), Virūpa or Birūwā (1), Gu(ṇ)ḍari (1), Cāṭila (1), Bhusuka (8), Kāmali or Kambalāmabara (1), Ḍombī (1), Śānti (2), Mahittā or Mahīdhara (1), Bijjila or Vīṇā-pāda (1), Śabara (2), Aja or Āryadeva (1), Dheṇḍhana (1), Dārika (1), Bhāde or Bhādrapāda (1), Tāḍaka (1), Kaṅkaṇa (1), Jaya-nandī (1), Guñjarī (1). The only exceptions are the *dohās* of Saraha (4) and Kānha (12) which are written in *Apabhraṁśa* dialect. Judging from the language, he expresses the opinion that these authors should be assigned to the period between 950-1200 A.D. and finds great influence of Western Śaurasenī *Apabhraṁśa,* "the most cultivated literary language" of that period on these songs, and he further says that their language seems to be

---

1. Bauddha-Gāna-o-Dohā, Intro.
2. Origin and Development of the Bengali Language, I. pp. 119-23, 117.

based on a West Bengali dialect. The same scholar[1] admits that in the 8th-11th centuries Bengali, Maithilī and Oriyā characteristics were probably in "formative fluid" and only in the 14th century they were fully developed. Though there is difference of opinion about the date of these *dohās,* it is generally admitted that they cannot be posterior to 1200 A.D.. It is therefore reasonable to hold that in the period of these *Āścarya-caryā-caya*[2] the distinctive features of Oriyā, Bengali and Maithilī were not fully developed from their common parent Magadhan *Apabhraṁśa.* There is nothing to show that all the authors were Bengalees. These songs were meant for the people at large and were very popular in eastern India. Most probably they belonged to different parts of eastern India, if not to other parts of northern India.

Budhist Universities–The account of the Buddhist scholars remains unfinished without the description of the Buddhist Vihāras in which they congregated for higher studies.

Nālandā–The first and foremost one was the famous Nālandā University. It came into prominence as a seat of learning from the time of Kumāragupta I, and since then many other kings bestowed their favours on it. The royal patrons mentioned by Yuan Chwang were Śakrāditya, Budhaguptarāja, Tathāgatagupta, Bālādityarāja, Vajra and Harṣavardhana or Śīlāditya. The Nālandā inscription of the time of Yaśovarman of Kanouj records that his minister's son, Mālaḍa by name, made various offerings to the monks of this Vihāra.

With the establishment of the Pāla power over Magadha the Buddhist Pāla kings played an important part in the growth of the University of Nālandā. A copper plate of Dharmapāla has been found in course of excavations but the object of this grant cannot be ascertained because of its defaced condition.[1] The two inscriptions of the time of Devapāla throw a flood of light on the importance of this international seat of learning. The Nālandā grant of his 39th regnal year records that king Bālaputradeva of Suvarṇa-

1. Ibid, p. 97. 2. IHQ, 1930, p. 169.
After the publication of this note, these songs should be better denoted by this term and not 'Cārryyācaryyaviniscaya.

1. ASIR, 1926-27, pp. 138-39.

dvīpa and Yavadvīpa (Sumatra and Java) was "attracted by the manifold excellences of Nālandā" and built a monastery[1] there, which was the abode of the assembly of monks of various good qualities and was white with series of stucco and lofty buildings." This king requested Devapāla to grant five villages for the offerings, oblations, shelter, garments of the assembly of monks. This proves beyond doubt that it was a far-famed seat of learning and its fame was not confined within the borders of India. The Gosarawa inscription or Vīradeva *praśasti* supplies also some interesting information. Vīradeva, a native of modern Jalalabad, after visiting Kaniṣka-vihāra at Puṣpapura and meeting the monks of his own country at Yaśovarmapura (which perhaps could not satisfy his thirst for knowledge) was attracted by Nālandā. His vast erudition won for him the admiration of Devapāla[2] and the exalted position of the head of the great University. Many images were installed there during his regime and it seems that he added some structures to the establishments. A votive *stūpa* was built in the reign of Mahīndrapāla[3] who is most probably to be identified with the Pratihāra king Mahendrapāla. An image of Vāgīśvarī was covered with golden leaves in the reign of Gopāla II.[4] In the sixth year of Mahīpāla I the *Aṣṭa-sāhasrikā-Prajñā-pāramitā* was copied by one Kalyāṇamitra.[5] In the 11th year of his reign a temple was rebuilt by one Bālāditya, a jyāviṣa of Tiladhaka (modern Telera) who had emigrated from Kauśāmbī.[6] In the fourth year of Rāmapāla's reign the *Aṣṭa-sāhasrikā-Prajñā-pāramitā* was copied[7] and the same book was copied there in the 4th year of Govindapāla.[8] All these show that the Pālas exercised control over the University of Nālandā upto their last days.

1. The remains of the monastery of Bālaputradeva form one of the levels of Monastery No. 1, Kurashi, Guide to Nālandā, p. 4.
2. It is not clear whether he was appointed by Devapāla or elected by the assembly of the monks.
3. ASIR, 1925-6, p. 86 ; EI, VIII, App., p. 118, Note 2.
4. JASB, NS, IV, p. 105.
5. Bendall, Cat. of Bd. San. Ms. in the Camb. U. Library, p. 101.
6. JASB, IV, p. 106.
7. Cat. Sans. Mss. in the Bodelian Library, p. 250.
8. JRAS, NS, VIII, p. 3.

Vikramaśīlā—The other important monastery of which some interesting details are known from the Tibetan accounts is that of Vikramaśīla.[1] As regards its origin various legends have been narrated in Tibetan books, but it seems that it was founded by Dharmapāla who bore the title Vikramaśīla, and as such it is sometimes called *"Śrīmad-Vikramaśīla-deva-vihāra."*[2] Opinions of scholars are divided as to the site of this famous monastery. It has been sought to be identified with Silas near Baragaon,[3] with Patharghata[4] and Keur.[5] All that is definitely known from the Tibetan account is that it was situated on a precipitous hill in Bihar on the right bank of the Ganges. "Patharghata" says Mr. N. L. De, "is about six miles to the north of Colgong, 24 miles to the east of Bhagalpur and 28 to the east of Campanagar; while "Keur is in direct line with Nālandā and Odantapurī and within 15 miles of Nālandā, and its close similarity with Nālandā remains, amply satisfies every known detail of Vikramaśīlā." Dharmapāla provided it with four establishments and 27 monks were accommodated in each of them. Provisions were also made for the maintenance of resident monks and pilgrims. In his time the head of the vihāra was Buddha-jñāna-pāda. In Nayapāla's time the central hall had six gates which opened six colleges. Each college had one hundred students and eight professors. There was an encircling wall around the whole establishment. The portraits of Nāgārjuna and Atīśa Dīpaṅkara adorned the main entrance and the subjects on which great stress was laid were grammar, theology and philosophy. But the most important subject that was taught here and which gained high recognition was Tāntrikism. Vikramaśīlā's fame rests mainly on producing great *Tāntrika* scholars and it seems that because of this it outshone Nālandā in importance. Distinguished scholars like Jetāri of Varendra and Ratnavajra of Kāśmīra received the diploma of "paṇḍita" from the kings themselves.[6] It may be men-

1. S. C. Das, Indian Pandits in the Land of Snow, pp. 10-11.
2. R. L. Mitra, Nepalese Bd. Literature, p. 229 ; Bhāratī, B. S., 1315, p. 2, JRAS, 1910, pp. 150-51 ; GOS, Rāmacarita, Intro., p. xxii.
3. Cunningham, ASR, VIII, p. 75.
4. JASB, V, p. 7 ; Samaddar, Glories of Magadha, p. 157.
5. JBORS, XV, p. 276.
6. Hist. Ind. Logic, p. 520.

tioned in this connection that the titles of the Buddhist scholars were generally *Ācārya, Mahācārya, Upādhyāya, Mahopādhyāya, Paṇḍita, Mahāpaṇḍita and Bhikṣu.*

When Dīpaṅkara was the head, there were 108 professors and each of the six gates had a gate-keeper. Only erudite scholars were appointed gate-keepers. Students seeking admission were put to a test before one of the gate-keepers who, I think, should be better called Heads of the Departments as in modern Universities. A board consisting of eminent professors supervised the affairs of the University and issued instructions to the professors. Disciplinary action against a monk was only taken on consulting the whole congregation of the monks. The life and character of Dīpaṅkara, so vividly described by the Tibetan envoy Nag-tsho, shows the regard for truth and the high sense of duty of the monks of Vikramaśīlā.

In Bengal proper there were many monasteries. Nothing in partciular is known of the monastery of Ācārya-Śāntideva to which Vainyagupta granted land in 508 A.D. for providing perfumes, flowers, lights and incense and also garments, food, beds, seats and medicines for the sick. The vihāra of Ācārya Jitasena is also mentioned in this record. It is recorded by Yuan Chwang[1] that in his time there were at least two famous colleges. In the Po-chi-po *saṅghārāma* which has been identified by Cunningham with Bhasu Vihāra, four miles to the west of Mahāsthāna,[2] there lived 700 *Mahāyāna* priests and many renowned priests from eastern India also dwelt there. Its courts were lighty and roomy; its towers and pavilions were very lofty. In the Raktaviti *saṅghārāma* at Karṇasuvarṇa congregated all the most disitinguished men of the kingdom, who strove to promote each other's advancement by exhortation and to perfect their character. Its halls were lighty and spacious and the storeyed towers were lofty. The monastery of the revered teacher Saṅghamitra to which Devakhaḍga granted land for the longevity of his son Rājarājabhaṭa seems to have been an important institution, although nothing is known about it. It is also to be mentioned that we have

1. Watters, II, pp. 184-191 ; Beal, Records, II, pp. 195-202.
2. ASR, XV, pp. 104-7.

reference in the second Asrafpur plate to four others *(vihāra-vihārikā-catuṣṭaya).*

We are rather fortunate in having a vivid account of the Bhā-rā-hā monastery at Tāmralipti from I-tsing.[1] The residents did not themselves cultivate lands of the monasteries but the tenants did it for them. The priests received only 1/3 of the vegetables. "Thus they live their just life, avoiding worldly affairs, and free from the faults of destroying lives by ploughing and watering fields." Every morning the managing priest examined the water of the well in order to see if there was any insect or animate being in it. Every business was done with the assent of the assembly of the monks There was no head. If any priest did anything according to his own will in disregard of the decision of the assembly, he was expelled from the monastery as he behaved like a householder. The nuns wishing to visit the priests were to inform the assembly of their purpose of visit. The priest were to go to nuns' apartments after making an inquiry. When the nuns walked outside the monastery, they walked in a company of two and when they went to any layman's house, they were to go in a company of four. When women visited the monastery, they did not go to the apartments of priests but talked in the corridor. Monastic rules and rites were explained on the four *Uposatha* days of every month to the assembly of the monks. A junior monk had to leave the monastery because of playing trick on a tenant's wife, although it was not considered an offence. The pilgrim observes that Rāhulamitra of excellent character, who had never spoken with any woman face to face except his mother and sister, was the model of all monks and was the most honoured priest in the eastern districts of India. Learned monks who had mastered the *piṭakas* were provided with the best rooms and servants. If they delivered daily lectures, they were relieved of the usual duties of an ordinary priest. On account of the priests' mutual confession, their faults were prevented before their growth and as a rule they submitted to laws. The rites of Nālandā,[2] we are told, were still stricter and hence its great fame and greater number of students.

---

1. Takakasu, Ch. X, pp. 62-65.
2. Ably discussed by Sankalia, University of Nālandā, Ch. II, pt. II; Ch. VIII.

Somapurī Mahāvihāra—Although nothing definite is known from literary source regarding the site of this great monastery, the evidence is now overwhelming for its identification with the Paharpur temple.[1] A clay seal found in course of excavations at Paharpur supplies the information that the Vihāra was founded by Dharmapāla.[2] Tārānātha[3] and the author of the *Pag-sam-jon-zang*[4] attribute its foundation to Devapāla, and this perhaps indicates that he added some structures[5] which were begun by his father. About the middle of the 12th century a Buddhist monk, Vipulaśrīmitra by name, built a shrine of Tārā, and this temple has been identified with that of the same goddess, exposed at Satyapira Bhita[6] at Paharpur. The Nālandā inscription of Vipulaśrīmitra further informs that Karuṇāśrīmitra died at Somapura when his house was set on fire by an army of a Vaṅgāla king. Karuṇāśrīmitra was removed from him by two generations of teachers, namely Maitrīśrīmitra and Asokaśrīmitra. Besides the building of the shrine of Tārā, all other pious activities of Vipulaśrīmitra have been enumerated in this record. On a festival day he offered a casket to the temple of Khasarpaṇa for the *Prajñāpāramitā* manuscript, installed four images at its alms-houses at Choyandaka, installed an image of Dīpaṅkara Buddha at Harṣapura and offered a gold ornament for the decoration of an image of Buddha at Somapura. It is known from a Bodh-Gaya inscription[7] that a *Mahāyāna* monk named Vīryendrabodhi who hailed from Samataṭa and was a resident of the Somapura-vihāra installed a Buddha image near the Mahābodhi temple (in *c.* the tenth century). Other celebrated scholars connected with this monastery were *Mahāpaṇḍita* Bodhibhadra[8] and Advaya-

1. VRS, Monograph No. 5, p. 27.
2. ASIR, 1626-7, p. 149 ; 1227-21, pp. 105-6.
3. IA, IV, p. 366,
4. Index, p. cxxx,
5. A colophon of Atīśa Dipaṅkara's Ratna-Karaṇodghaṭa ascribes the foundation of the Vikramaśīlā-vihāra to Devapāla who most probably, as Mr. N. N. Dasgupta suggests, added some structures to both the monasteries started by his father, see IC. 1, p. 229
6. EI, XXI, p. 101.
7. SPP, 1823, B. S., p. 70,
8. Cordier, II, pp. 98, 250.

vajra.[1] Atīśa passed some time in it in translating the *Madhyamaka-Ratna-Pradīpa*.[2]

Jagaddala-vihāra—This last great Buddhist monastery was built by Rāmapāla at the confluence of the Ganges and the Karatoyā. Its renowned alumni were Bibhūticandra, Dānaśīla, Mokṣakaragupta, Śubhakaragupta and Dharmākara.[3] The works composed by its *paṇḍitas* are grossly Tāntrik in character and generally deal with Piśācas, owls Nāgas, Yokṣas etc., and their *sādhanās*.[4] One special feature of Jagaddala-vihāra was that many *lotsavas* (Tibetan scholars) thronged here and translated many Sanskrit books in Tibetan.

Other minor Vihāras—The existence of Vikramapurī-vihāra is known from the *Bstan-hgyur* but nothing definitely is known about its origin.[5] Kumāracandra belonged to this monastery. The existence of the Traikuṭaka-vihāra in Baṅgāla is known from *Pag-sam-jon-zang*,[6] and it was here that Haribhadra wrote his commentary on *Aṣṭa-sāhasrikā-Prajñāpāramitā*. The same book refers to the Paṇḍita-vihāra in Chittagong where flourished Tailikapāda.[7] The Suvarṇa-vihāra was in Nadia.[8] The Kanaka-stūpa-vihāra[9] was situted in Paṭṭikarā, easily identifiable with the Paṭikera *paraganā* of the Tippera district. From the Mainamati plate of Raṇavaṅkamalla Harikāladeva, dated in 1141 S.E., it is further known that there was a *vihāra* in that locality and it was dedicated to the goddess *Durgottarā*, a form of Tārā. Chittagong is the only place where a Buddhist community still thrives and traces of Buddhism can be found in many localities.[10]

---

1. Ibid, pp. 116, 120 ; III, p. 5.
2. Ibid, III, p. 299.
3. IC, I, p. 232.
4. Sankalia, University of Nālandā, p. 189
5. Mr. N. N. Dasgupta suggests that it owed its origin to Dharmapāla. Bhāratvarṣa, 1341 B. S., pp. 962-970 ; IC, I, p. 230.
6. Index pp. xciv, xli ; MASB, III, No. I, p. 5.
7. Index, p, lxii ; JASB, 1898, p. 24.
8. SPP, 1321, B. S, p. 205.
9. IHQ, Ix, pp. 282 ff.
10. IHQ, 1932, pp. 332 ff.

CHAPTER IX

SOCIAL CONDITION

Brahmana Immigrations—The genealogical books of the Bengali *ghaṭakas* (match-makers) form a class of literature by themselves and it is a separate *śāstra* by its special importance like the *Śrutis* and *Smṛtis*. There is an extensive literature on the subject, variously called *Kulaśāstras, Kulagranthas* or *Kulapañjikās*. The main object of the genealogical books is to keep a correct record of the lineal descendants of important families, their branches and sub-branches with their social impurities and indignities in order to enable to gauge their social rank and status. The list of the ascendants of a family is necessary on some ceremonial occasions and they are supremely useful in forming matrimonial relationship, as connection of a pure family with a lower one will degrade the former also. Generally the lists coming from different sources agree with one another. But it is very difficult to handle these books for historical purposes. None of them has proved to be old and most of them are based on current traditions, sometimes orally transmitted from generation to generation. But what diminishes their historical value is that they are 'propagandist' in the extreme sense of the term. The *Rāḍhīya* and *Vārendra* Brahmanas assert that they are the pure descendants of the five immigrants alleged to have been imported by king Ādiśūra. The contention of their books is that the original Brahmanas of Bengal lost their purity and competence in performing religious rites and rituals correctly and hence the importation of five pure Brahmanas at the instance of Ādiśūra. The *Pāścātya Vaidikas* declare that the *Rāḍhīyas* and *Vārendras* were incapable of understanding the proper meaning of the Vedic *mantras*, and so king Sāmalavarman had to invite some *Vaidika* Brahmanas from the western provinces because of their profound knowledge in Vedic lore and rites. Not to speak of the important sections like the *Rāḍhīyas, Vārendras* and *Vaidikas*, every genealogist or protagonist tries to prove the purity and superiority of those whose cause he espouses. In course of the development of Kulinism with all its intricacies and complexities there arose a class of professional *ghaṭakas* who may properly be regarded as heralds. There are instances of their tampering with the *Kulapañjikās* with not very disinterested or good motives. What is most instructive and interesting in this connection is that even most of the modern writers on the subject (though they profess to be critical and scientific) suffer from this defect. Few would give out the social stigma, if there were any, on their own families and by distorting truths by every possible means they would prove their purity and superiority. Above all, it must be borne in mind that the desire to associate oneself with a celebrated man or family or to claim a high pedigree is more or less inherent in human nature. In spite of these defects, it may be said that the traditions may contain some historical truths underlying them. In the *Kulaśāstras* are to be found the social organisations and reorganisations in various ranks and grades that were made by great social reformers to meet the needs of the changing circumstances from time to time, and some of them still hold good in case of the majority of the Hindu society of Bengal. They offer us a glimpse into the Hindu society during the Muslim rule which it is impossible to have from any other source.

Scholars with a scientific bent of mind have generally expressed grave doubts on the *Kulaśāstras* as reliable sources of evidence. Thus Messrs. R. D. Banerjee[1] and R. P. Chanda[2] who have discussed the historicity of Ādiśūra at great length have ultimately come to the conclusion that so long as his name is not to be found in some other more reliable recrods, it is futile to determine his place in history. But both of them conceded the historical existence of a king of that name because of the unanimity of all traditions from different *Kulapañjikās*. The introduction of *Kulinism* by Vallālasena has also been doubted by this school of wirters because of the absence of its mention in the Sena grants.

---

1. BI, 2nd and 3rd Appendices
2. Sāhitya, 1321 B S, p 751

The opposite school is led by Mr. N. N. Vasu[1] and the native orthodox school of writers[2] who are ready to accept the evidence of the *Kulapañjikās* in toto. They write generally from the social standpoint. Excepting Mr. N. N. Vasu, none of them seems to be well acquainted with the archæological materials for history, and naturally the accounts of these books are given prominence and preference. But it does not seem that the 'scientific school' of writers have gone deep into this class of literature from the standpoint of social history. Most of the books are in MSS. and adequate study of the subject has not been made. A critical study of the subject is worth attempting

It must be made clear that the accounts of the royal genealogies in *Kulagranthas* are faulty and inaccurate, and their composers were not so much concerned with political history. Sāmalavarman is spelt as Śyāmalavarman and Vijayasena has been made his father. They were written long after the Sena period, and their authors do not seem to have based their accounts on accurate history. Only echoes of some historical truths are sometimes heard, when Vallālasena is connected with the Śūra dynasty through his mother's side and the date 1079 A.D. is mentioned as the time of Sāmalavarman. Their importance lies in the fact that they give a picture of the Hindu society which cannot be found elsewhere.

The *Kulatattvārṇava*[3] (about the genuineness of which we have grave doubts)[4] states that a king named Śūdraka imported *Sārasvata* Brahmanas in Vaṅga in order to perform a *putreṣṭi* sacrifice, but this lacks corroboration from any other book. All books agree in stating that king Ādiśūra brought five Brahmanas

1. His ten volumes on Castes and Sects of Bengal (in Bengali) called Vaṅger Jātīya Itihāsa.
2. For names of authors, see Appendix E.
3. Vs. 10-20.
4. See my remarks on this book in Winternitz commemoration volume.

5

from Kanouj or Kolāñca. In most of the books[1] the names of the five Brahmanas are Kṣitīśa of the *Sāṇḍilya gotra,* Vītarāga of the *Kāśyapa gotra,* Sudhānidhi of *Vātsya gotra,* Medhātithi of the *Bharadvāja gotra,* and Sambhari of the *Sābarṇa gotra.* The story of their migration is as follows :—Ādiśūra was the lord of Pañca-Gauḍas and vanquished many kings of different parts of India. He had a rival in Vīrasiṁha who is described in some books[2] as king of Kanouj and in others, of Kāśī. This king was not subdued by ordinary warfare. Therefore seven hundred armed Brahmanas of Bengal were sent on cows' back by Ādīśūra to fight with him. There could not be any fighting without killing the cows and Brahmanas, which, as a pious and religious-minded man, Vīrasiṁha could not do. Thus he was compelled to send five pure *Sāgnika* Brahmans to Ādiśūra in whom Bengal was lacking. The *Kulatattvārṇava* supports this story but adds that Ādiśūra needed these Brahmanas for the performance of a *putreṣṭi* sacrifice. The *Vārendra Kula-pañjikā*[3] supplies the information that Ādiśūra brought the Brahmanas from Kanouj for fulfilling the wishes of his wife Candramukhī, the daughter of the Kanauj king Candraketu, who wanted to perform a *vrata* by pure Brahmanas.

The dates of the migration of the five Brahmanas in differnet books fall within the period between the eighth and the eleventh centuries. The earliest is 654 S.E:=732 A.D., and it is mentioned in many books.[4] The dates S.E., 954, S.E., 994 S.E. and 999 S.E. are

1. There is some discrepancy in the names of the five immigrants. According to the Vārendra Kulapanjikā, Bhaṭṭa Nārāyaṇa, Dakṣa, Chāndaḍa, Harṣa and Vedagarbha are the original settlers. Mr. N. N. Vasu cites a book in which Bhaṭṭa Nārāyaṇa, Suṣeṇa, Dharādhara, Gautama and Parāśara are the original settlers but are called the sons of Kṣitiśa, Vītarāga, Sudhānidhi, Medhātithi and Sambhari. We therefore take this list (which is found in Rāḍhiya books) as more trustworthy and reliable. (VJI, I,p. 102).

2. VJI, I, pp. 73-82, see different versions of the story.

3. Ibid.

4. IHQ, XI, pp. 73-74, Appendix F.

also met with.[1] It is definite that Ādiśūra was not responsible for the migrations of the Brahmanas on all these dates which fall within three centuries. Either these dates are wrong or they record the time of migrations of different batches of Brahmanas. It is also interesting to note that at the time of Vallālasena there was the 13th generation of the *Bharadvājas* and *Sābarṇas,* the 12th of the *Śāṇḍilyas* and *Vātsyas* and the 8th of the *Kāśyapas* in Rāḍha; and in Varendra there was the 14th of the *Śāṇḍilyas,* the 15th of the *Kāśyapas,* the 13th of the *Bharadvājas* and *Sābarṇas* and the 4th of the *Vātsyas* of the descendants of the five immigrants.[2] All the difficulties can be solved by the natural presumption that the Brahmanas came to settle from time to time, and every migration has been associated with the name of Ādiśūra (whose zeal and effort were perhaps the cause of one) in the *Kulaśāstras* which were composed long after that event. It may be that all dates have not been remembered. It is not to be believed on the authority of the *Kulaśāstras* that there had been no Brahmanas of the above five *gotras* before the alleged migration through the efforts of Ādiśūra. The evidence of the Faridpur plate (No. 3), the Vappagoshavata plate of the time of Jayanāga and the Nidhanpur plates is conclusive on the point, as they mention many Brahmanas of the five *gotras.* This may explain in a way why the ancestors of *Sābarṇa* Bhatta Bhavadeva and *Bharadvāja* Prahāsa of the Silimpur inscription and Śāṇḍliya Guravamiśra have not been described as immigrants from outside, as their families had been settled in Bengal from very remote times.

There has been much discussion on the vexed question of Ādiśūra, and previous writers could not offer any satisfactory solution of the problem. The present writer drew attention to a hitherto unnoticed king, *Magadhādhirāja* Ādisiṁha of the Dudhpani Rock inscription, who may be identified with Ādiśūra[3] of the *Kulaśāstras* with some degree of plausibility. There is no difference in the meaing of the names, the words 'śūra' and 'siṁha' being used in the sense

1. See Appendix F.
2. VJI. I.
3. IHQ. XI, p. 70.

of hero. Palæographically the record has been assigned by Kielhorn to the eighth century. The earliest date 732 A.D. of the migration has been mentioned in the majority of the books so far known. The king Ādisiṁha is to be placed after the Later Guptas and before the extension of the Pāla power over Magadha. There could not have been any room for *Magadhādhirāja* Ādisiṁha when these two dynasties were ruling there. There is nothing improbable in the fact that a king of Magadha had some portion of Gauḍa under him. Gauḍa and Magadha were on many occasions politically united. The unnamed king of Gauḍa who was defeated and killed by Yaśovarman of Kanauj in the first half of the eighth century has been described by Vākpati as *Magadanātha* also. It is mentioned in the *Kulaśāstras* that the five Brahmana immigrants were granted the villages of Pañcakoṭi in Manbhum, Vaṭagrāma in Burdwan, Harikoṭi in Midnapore, Kāmakoṭi in Birbhum and Kaṅkagrāma not far from Bāṇakuṇḍa.[1] After the discovery of the Saktipur grant of Lakṣmaṇasena[2] the last mentioned village can be identfiied with some degree of certainty, and it seems that it is represented by Kāgrāma in the Kandi sub-division of Murshidabad.[3] It is also to be mentioned that Bārakuṇḍa, a locality in P. S. Suri, may be identified with Bāṇakuṇḍa near Kaṅkagrāma of the *Kulapañjikās*.

Most of the books record that the five immigrants came from Kanouj or Kolāñca. Only one Vārendra *Kulapañjikā*[4] states that they migrated from different places—the *Śāṇḍilyâ* family from Jambucatvara, the *Vātsya* from Tāḍita, the *Bharadvāja* from Audumbara, the *Sābarṇa* from Madra and the *Kāśyapa* from Kolañca. The fact that in this account there are the names of three important places like Audambara, Madra and Kolāñca gives it some degree of credibility, though Jambucatvara and Tāḍita cannot be located. There are many epigraphic evidences of the fact that many Brahmana emi-

1. VJI., I, pp. 109-111.
2. EI., XXI, p. 214.
3. SPP, 1340 B.S., pp. 78.
4. VJI, I, p. 102.

grants from Tarkāri[1] (variantly called Tarkkāri, Tarkkārikā), Kroḍāñja[2] or Kroḍāñca or Kulāñca (easily identifiable with Kolāñca of the *Kulaśāstras)* and from Madhyadeśa figure as donees of royal grants of different provinces. Let us first take the case of Tarkāri. It is recorded in the Silimpur *praśasti* of Prahāsa that his ancestors (a Bharadvāja family) originally lived in Tarkāri within Śrāvastī-*janapada* from where they migrated to Bālagrāma and Śiyāmvaka which have been described as ornaments of Varendra. In two inscriptions[3] it has been definitely stated that Tarkāri was in Madhyadeśa, and it deserves particular notice that in one of the Baudh plates of Raṇabhañjadeva of the year 50 Tarkāri has been specifically mentioned to have been in Śrāvastīdeśa.[4] In the Ajayagar inscription[5] Tarkārikā has been called the chief abode of the *Śrīvāstava* Kāyasthas who are still now an important section of the Kāyasthas of the United Provinces. All these point to the fact that there was a Tarkāri within far-famed Śrāvastī in the Gonda district of U.P. Brahmana emigrants[6] from Śrāvastī-*maṇḍala, bhukti* and *viṣaya* figure as donees in the Mahāśivagupta Yayāti's Patna plates, the Katak plates of Mahāśivagupta II, the Sonpur plate of Someśvaradeva, the Madhuvan plate of Harṣavardhana, the Dighwa-Dubhali plate of Mahendrapāla and the Lucknow Museum plate of Kīrtipāla. The donee of the Bangarh grant of Mahīpāla I has been described as an emigrant from Hastipāda. The donees of two grants from Orissa[7] also hailed from a village of that name, and in one of them it is mentioned that Hastipāda was in Madhyadeśa. The donees of the Irda plate of the Kamboja king Nayapāla and the Jajilpara grant of Gopāla II have been described as emigrants from Kunṭīra and Muktāvastu which cannot be located at present. The ascendants of the donees of the Belāva plate of Bhojavarman and the Barrackpore plate of Vijayasena have been described as *Madhya-*

1. SPP., 1341 B. S., pp. 25 ff; see also IA., 1931, pp. 14 ff; XLVIII, p. 208.
2. IC., II, pp. 386 ff.
3. IA., XLVIII p. 280.
4. IHQ, x, pp. 477.
5. N. N. Vasu, Kāyastha Varṇa-Nirṇaya, p. 72
6. SPP., 1341 B. S., pp. 25 ff.
7. Ibid.

deśa-vinirgata. There are at least seven charters[1] which record land grants to Brahmana emigrants from Kroḍāñja, the location of which is not yet certain ; but it is to be observed that the tradition as preserved in the *Kulaśāstras* unanimously associates it with Kanauj i.e., in Madhyadeśa.

It is almost certain that there was a Śrāvastī in northern Bengal, the existence of which is perhaps indicated by a *śloka*[2] in the *Matsya* and *Kurma Purāṇas* and is proved by the evidence of the two inscriptions of the Kāmarūpa kings Dharmapāla and Indrapāla and the Vaigrāma plate. Its location in Bogra and Dinajpur Districts is also certain.[3] It is also quite possible, as has been suggested by some scholars, that there was a Kolāñca[4] within the locality of Śrāvastī in Bengal (which has been identified with Kulāñca in the Bogra district[5]). It is to be noticed that this Śrāvastī and Kulāñca were not far removed from the city of Gauḍa in northern Bengal. Long ago Cunningham[6] pointed out that there was a Gauḍa in the Gonda district, and the *Rāmāyaṇa* and *Vāyupurāṇa* also mention a Gauḍa in Uttarakośala.[7] It seems that northern Bengal had very important relations with Śrāvastīdeśa, so far as the migrations of the Brahmanas were concerned. The far-famed Śrāvastī was not only a centre of Buddhism, Jainism and Ājivikism but also a strong-hold of the Brahmanical religions, as it has been shown by Dr. B. C. Law[8] even from the stray references in the early

1. IC, II, pp. 386 ff.
2. EI, XIII, p. 290.
3. Kāmarūpa-śāsanāvalī p. 137 ; EI, XXIII, p. 108 ; IC, II, p. 386 ff. The Assam inscriptions refer to Sāvathi and one of them mentions a place called Vagirāma in it, the identity of which is established by the Vaigram plate.
4. Ibid.
5. Ibid.
6. ASI, I, p. 327 ; IX, pp. 151-152.
7. EI., XIII, p. 290 ; IHQ, XIII, p. 162.
8. Mr. B. C. Law, Śrāvasti in Ancient Indian Literature, p. 26,

Buddhist literatures. According to Baudhāyana[1] and Vaśīṣṭha[2] it was in Madhyadeśa that the practice and tradition of the Āryas or *śiṣṭas* (cultured men) prevailed and the customs of this place were regarded with special veneration. According to Manu,[3] Madhyadeśa is the country which lies between Himavat and the Vindhya, to the west of Prayāga and to the east of Vinaśana, where the Sarasvatī disappears. It was here that the Brahmanical rituals and social institutions like the caste were developed and elaborated and hence it became "the model country for all ages" and for all *Āryāvarta.*[4] Viewed in this light, the tradition of the *Kulaśāstras* seems to reflect some truth and the migration of the Brahmanas from Madhyadeśa and the honour shown to them are historically intelligible, if not a necessity of the Hindu society of ancient Bengal.

Bengal is not the only province where in epigraphic records the Brahmanas, significantly described as *Madhyadeśa-vinirgata,* have been honoured with grants of land and other endowments. The instances of the Brahmanas who emigrated from Śrāvastī *-bhukti, maṇḍala* and *viṣaya* have already been noted. In the neighbouring province of Orissa there are about six or seven epigraphs[5] and there is no doubt that such cases can be easily multiplied from the inscriptions of other provinces.

As regards the incident of the migration, there is nothing improbable in the tradition that a king brought some Brahmanas from upper India in course of an expedition. An instance exactly of this nature may be cited. It is known from a southern India inscription,[6] that Biṭṭiga of the *Hārita gotra,* a minister of the Hoysala king Narasiṁha I, descended from one of the fifty chief Brahmanas whom Gaṅga kings brought from the *agrahāra* of Ahichatra in the north when he had gone there in course of a

---

1. SBE., XIV, 143-4, 147.
2. Ibid, 1-3.
3. Ibid, XXV, 33 ; IHQ., IV, pp. 84 ff.
4. Mr. N. K. Dutta, Aryanisation of India, pp. 89-91
5. SPP., 1341 B. S., pp. 25 ff.
6. Ep. Carn. IV Intro., p. 21.

victorious expedition. The allegation that there were no pure Brahmanas in Bengal is perhaps to be understood with references to the manner and way[1] in which tribes or parts of eastern India have been mentioned in the *Aitareya Brāhmaṇa, Aitareya Āraṇyaka* and by Baudhāyana. In the later Vedic period Bengal was inhabited by non-Aryan and nomadic tribes and peoples, and orthodox writers like Baudhāyana did not deem it a proper place for Aryan habitation. There is no denying the fact that Bengal received her stock of Aryan population later than the Upper Gangetic countries. In discussing the Brahmana immigrations, the early spread of two manifestly non-Brahmanical religions—Jainism and Buddhism—and their gaining strong foot-holds should also be taken into consideration. There seems to be much truth in the broad generalisation of Prof. Bhandarkar[2] that Bengal was first *Śramanised* and then *Brahmanised.*

But definite evidence regarding the active propagation of the Brahmanical religion and a vigorous movement for *Brahmanisation* of the country we have in the Gupta period, and in this connection the testimony of the five Damodarpur plates[3] is very significant. The objects of the purchase of land as stated in these plates were as follows :—for the purpose of conducting *agnihotra* rites by a Brahmana (N.I), for conducting the daily sacrifices of a Brahmana (N.2), for settling some prominent Brahmanas (No.3), for erection of temples of two Brahmanical gods.(N. 4), and to make some repairs in a temple by an inhabitant of Ayodhyā (No. 5). The Dhanaidaha and Vaigram plates also had almost similar objects in view. All these transactions were made within the confines of the Puṇḍravardhana-*bhukti* and in most cases in the Koṭivarṣa-*viṣaya* in the Dinajpur district. These plates bear ample testimony to the fact that during the rule of the staunch Brahmanical Gupta emperors Brahmanical influence was being spread in northern Bengal by the Brahmanas themselves, by local officers and chiefs (No. 3)

1. See *Ante*
2. ABI, XII, pp. 111 ff.
3. EI, XV, p. 113. The same fact is to be noticed in the Faridpur plates (IA 1910, pp 193 ff)

and even by outsiders who were deeply interested in this faith (No.5). The Nidhanpur plates[1] also go to show how almost in the same period Bhutivarman, great-great-grandfather of Bhāskaravarman, was inviting Brahmanas from western provinces by conferring rent-free land in Sylhet. It has been shown by Dr. N. K. Bhattasali that the land granted by these plates is to be located in Panchakhanda in the Sylhet district.[2] The plates are also very important in so far as they preserve the names of more than 200 Brahmanas with their *gotras* and the Vedas they studied. The Tippera grant[3] of Lokanātha is extremely interesting as it reveals the process and way in which a jungly (and presumably non-Brahmanical) tract was brought under the influence of the Brahmanical religion. It is stated therein that in the *viṣaya* of Suvaṅga (not yet located but most probably in the Tippera district) "in the forest region, having no distinction of natural or artificial boundary, having a thick network of bush and creeper, where deer, buffaloes, boars, tigers, serpents etc., enjoy according to their will all pleasures of home life" a Brahmana *Sāmanta* Pradoṣaśarman built a temple of Anantanārāyaṇa and prayed to his chief Lokanātha for some land for the maintenance of the daily worship of the god. This plate also records the names of more than 100 Brahmanaṣ but not their *gotras* and Vedas.

The Brahmanas mentioned in the Nidhanpur and Tippera plates deserve more than a passing notice. It has been pointed out by Mr. J. C. Ghose[4] and Prof. Bhandarkar[5] that they were *Nāgara Brahmanas* who emigrated from western provinces. The issues involved in the latter's illuminating paper on the *Nāgara Brahmanas and the Kāyasthas of Bengal* are various and many, but it is perhaps to be conceded that Vādanagar or Ānandapura, Ahichatra and Sapādalakṣma were important centres of the *Nāgara Brahmanas,* from where they migrated in course of time to different parts of India. What is more important for our purpose is that, similar to the tradi-

1. Ibid, XIX, p. 115, 245.
2. JASB., 1935, p 419.
3. EI., xv, p. 301.
4. IHQ., 19[illegible], p. 60.
5. IA., 1932, pp. 41, 91.

tion of the importation of five Brahmanas from Madhyadeśa by Ādiśura, there is a strong tradition among the Sāmpradāyika Brahmanas in Sylhet[1] that five of their ancestors were imported from Mithilā by a king named Ādi Dharmaphā in 641 A.D.. The influence of the former tradition on the latter is perhaps easily traceable, but the date agrees fairly well with the time of Bhāskaravarman and Lokanātha. If there be any truth underlying the tradition current among the *Sāmpradāyikas* in Sylhet, the most interesting point is that those who claim to be their descendants have entirely forgotten the real identity of their forefathers.[2] Mention may also be made of the existence of the Lāṭa Brahmanas in Bengal who were placed in charge of the temple of Nanna-Nārāyaṇa built by *Mahāsāmantādhipati* Nārāyaṇavarman during the reign of Dharmapāla.[3]

Another significant fact is also worthy of special notice in this connection. While in the Gupta and post-Gupta periods private persons or officials and semi-officials in their personal capacities made gifts of lands to the Brahmanas or temples, the Pāla and Sena kings conferred lands of their own accord out of the traditional royal policy, as outlined in the *Arthaśātras* that the king should reward the pious and learned men of the country or because of some services done to the kings or queens. Therefore it is quite reasonable to take the pro-Brahmanical activties of the Gupta and post-Gupta periods as active steps for Brahmanisation of the country.

In the story of the migration of five Brahmanas it is also obvious that there is a propaganda to discredit and lower the original Brahmanas of Bengal. The sendnig of a Brahmana army on cow's back is an absurd thing and it needs no comment. In their zeal to prove their own purity and superiority the *Rāḍhīya* and *Vārendra* writers forget that this would reflect discredit on the king whose religious fervour was at the root of the immigration of their

1. IHQ., 1931, p. 716.

2. Dr. K. M. Gupta suspects that Sāmpradāyika is a modern literary infiltration of the long forgotten significant term Sapādalakṣa.

3. Prof. Bhandarkar is of opinion that these Lāṭa Brahmans were also Nāgara Brahmanas.

five illustrious predecessors. It is said that there were seven hundred Brahmanas in Bengal before that event and hence they were called *Sapta-śatī*. Again, it has been suggested that the word *'Sātsatī'* is the vernacular from of *Sārasvata* but has been again sanskritised into *Sapta-śatī*. Acceptance of this view means that the original Brahmanas were all *Sārasvatas*, but it has no basis to support it excepting the *Kulutattvārṇava*. The *Goṣṭhikathā* sarcastically remarks that their knowledge of the Vedas was very poor and were engaged by the Śūdras as priests. The *Sapta-satīs* in Rāḍha had at least seven *gotras*,[1] while those in Varendra had five.[2] The *Sapta-śatīs* had *gāiñs* like the *Rāḍhīyas* and *Vārendras* and the number amounted to about forty.[3]

In the Pāla and Sena grants there are many Brahmanas who, judged by their *gotras*,[4] are to be regarded in all reasonableness as Sapta-śatīs. Their learning in the *śāstras* is evident from their their description in the grants. They sometimes performed sacrifices and were readers of moral texts and religious books. Mention may be made of a *Kauśika gotra* Brahmana who migrated from Puṇḍravardhana to the Rāṣṭrakūṭa kingdom in the ninth century.[5] The charge of impurity and ignorance of the *śāstras* laid against the *Sapta-śatīs* is, therefore, altogether unjustified and must be regarded as merely a propaganda. But the most important fact is that this persistent prapaganda has met with complete success. Few Brahmanas will give out the fact that they are really *Sapta-śatīis* and in the Census of 1931 only nineteen persons were returned as *Sapta-śatīs*.

---

1. VJI, I, p. 88. They are Śaunaka, Gautama, Kaundanya, Parāśara, Vaśiṣṭha, Hārita and Kautsa. Śāṇḍilya and Ālambāna are also mentioned by N. N. Vasu for which he cites no authority.

2. Ibid., p. 89.

3. See Appendix F.

4. The donee of the Banagrh grant of Mahīpāla I was of the Parāśara gotra and followed the Vājasenya-śākhā of the Yajur Veda; of the Manahali plate is of Kautsa-gotra of the Kauthuma-śākha of the Sāmaveda; of the Amgachi plate is of the Kauśikā of Yajurveda; of the Madhainagara grant of the Kauśika-gotra and Paippaladā śakhā of the Atharvaveda; of the Sunderban plate is of Gārgya-gotra and of Aśvalāyana-śākhā of the Ṛgveda.

5. IA, xxxi, p. 220.

A careful investigation into the *gotras* and *gāiñs* will undoubtedly reveal the existence of a greater number of them who are concealing their identity in order to escape the social stigma and odium due to this propaganda. Some have managed to merge themselves in the *Rāḍhīya, Vārendra* and *Vaidika* societies and it is impossible to discern them. This explains why the number of the descendants of the *Sapta-śatīs* or seven hundred men has been returned as nineteen only, while those of the five Brahmana immigrants of the time of Ādiśūra have reached such a big figure as 351,136 in course of 1000 to 1200 years. The *Kulaśāstras* bear testimony to the fact that the *Sapta-śatīs* entered the *Vārendra* and *Rāḍīya* societies not in inconsiderable numbers. What is more interesting is that at a subsequent period three other *gotras*, viz. *Parāśara, Vaśiṣṭha* and *Gautama*, were added to the original five of the *Rāḍhīyas*. A modern Brahmana author confesses that besides these eight *gotras*, three others, *Ghṛtakauśika, Kaundanya* and *Ālamyāna*, are also met with in the *Rāḍhīya* society.[1]

Rāḍhīyas and Vārendra—There is a veritable wordy warfare between the *Rāḍhīyas* and *Vārendras* for the claim of regarding the five immigrants as their own countrymen. *Śāṇḍilya* Nārāyaṇa, *Vātsya* Dharādhara, *Kāśyapa* Suṣeṇa, *Bharadvāja* Gautama and *Śābarṇa* Parāśara whom most of the *Kulapañjikās* claim to be the earliest ancestors of the *Vārendras* appear to be the sons of the five predecessors of the *Rāḍhīyas*. It is quite possible that some of the sons of the Brahmana immigrants migrated to northern Bengal. This is quite in agreement with our location of the five villages granted by Ādiśūra in Rāḍha. But the *Rāḍhiya* and *Vārendra* quarrel does not end there. The *Vārendras* accuse the *Rāḍhīyas* of *Sapta-śatī* contamination and declare that they are the sons of the five immigrants by their *Sapta-śatī* wives. The *Rāḍhīyas* countercharge their *Vārendra* brethren with the same blemish.[2] But the

---

1. K. P. Bhattacharyya, Rāḍhīya-kulattatva, pp. 124–126.

2. For the charges and counter-charges see Sambandha-Nirṇaya by L. Vidyanidhi (pp. 617-634). After refuting the charges of the Vārendras, the author himself counter-charges them. The author, it needs be mentioned, was a Rāḍhīya.

plain truth is that both the groups got *Sapta-śatī* contact from very early times. But as the *Vārendras* seem to be a sectionally conscious community and as the *Rāḍhīyas* excel them in number, the *Sapta-śatī* contact was perhaps more in case of the *Rāḍhīyas.*

The descendants of the five immigrants in Rāḍha came to be known as *Rāḍhīyas* and those in Varendra as *Vārendras.* Their emergence as two separate endogamous groups was not perhaps sudden and various causes might have contributed to this. There are few instances of *Rāḍhīya* and *Vārendra* inter-marriages in the *Kula-śāstras* even at a late period,[1] but the geographical situation, political condition and difficult communications of that period did not promote such marriages. In course of time different social customs and usages grew up in two parts of Bengal and from that point of view such marriages were not perhaps liked also. Kulinism, the foundation of which is ascribed to Vallālasena by both the sections, has different history and developments in the two localities. It is difficult to say when these two sections had got separate denominations in spite of their common ancestry. Rāḍha as the name of western Bengal is mentioned in ancient books like Jaina *Ācārаṅga Sūtra,* while the name Varendra is not known before the tenth century.[2] The existence of the *Rāḍhīyas* and *Vārendras* as two separate sections is definitely known for the first time from the *Brāhmaṇa-sarvasva*[3] of Halayudha, who was the chief judge of Lakṣmaṇasena. He takes both these groups severely to task for their ignorance of the proper meaning of the Vedic *mantras,* and from his description it seems clear that the *Rāḍhīyas* and *Vārendras* as two separate sections were quite well-known in his time.

It may not be out of place here to note that there is no section or class of Brahmanas who are known by the territorial name of eastern Bengal, though a section of the *Kāyasthas* is called *Vaṅgaja.* Again, it would be a mistake to think that there were no Brahmanas in eastern Bengal, as the tesitmony of the four Faridpur plates, Nidhanpur and Tippera grants is conclusive on that point. In this connection it may be mentioned that the Cheedivlasa plates

---

1. Ibid, p. 720 ; Appendix C, p. 204.
2. See Introduction.
3. T.C. Vidyananda's edition, pp. 9-10.

of the Gaṅga king Devendravarman, son of Bhupendravarman, record grants of land to *Vaṅgaja* Brahmanas who have been described as "eager in performing sacrifices and studying Vedas, well-versed in Vedas and Vedāṅgas, and practising Dharmas as described in *Śrūtis* and *Smṛtis*"[1] It seems that the early Brahmana inhabitants managed to get into the *Rāḍhīya, Vārendra* and *Vaidika* societies of eastern Bengal and their real identity cannot be traced at all. But it is also true that many Brahmanas from western and northern Bengal migrated to eastern Bengal. The Kewar image inscription[2] records the migration of a *Vārendra Śāṇḍilya* family and from palæographical considerations this is to be assigned to the 12-13th century A.D. The Adavadi plate of Daśarathadeva refers to the settlement of a batch of Rāḍhīya Brahmanas in Vikramapura. After the occupation of western and northern Bengal by the Muslims eastern Bengal remained under the Hindu kings for about a century more[3] and it can be easily understood that with the fall of the Hindu political power in Gauḍa many Brahmanas migrated to the neighbouring Hindu kingdoms. What is important for our purpose is that in eastern Bengal, which was not their early home, the *Rāḍhīyas* and *Vārendras* could establish their superiority and the earlier Brahmanical population was absorbed in their societies.

It is stated in some *Kulapañjikās* that Bhūśūra, son of Ādiśūra, was compelled to take shelter in Rāḍha owing to the rise of the Pāla power. His son Khitiśūra is said to have granted 56 villages to the 56 descendants of the five immigrants in Rāḍha.[3] It deserves special mention that it is by the names of these villages or *gāiñs* that the Brahmanas at a later period became known. The surnames *Chatterjee, Mukherjee, Maitra, Bhaduri,* etc. are derived from the names of these villages. It is to be noted that even in the Pāla grants some of these 56 *gāiñs* have been mentioned in course of

1. Jour. Andhra. Hist. Res. Soc. II, p. 149.
2. EI. XVII, p. 355.
3. IHQ., XII, pp. 81-83.
4. VGI., I, pp. 115-127. The location of Mr. N. N. Vasu is not always correct and in some cases has proved to be wrong.

the introduction of the Brahmana donees. The donee Khodulaśarman of the Amgachi plate is described as *Matsavāsa-Vinirgata*, and and Matsyāsī is a well-known *gāiñ* of the *Kaṣṭa śrotriya Vārendra Śāṇḍilyas.*[1] The donee Vaṭeśvarasvāmī of the Manahali plate is described as *Campahīṭṭīya Campahīṭṭī vāstavya.*[2] Campatī is a well-known *gāiñ* of the *Vārendra* Śāṇḍilyas. It is known from the Bhuvanesvara *praśasti* of Bhaṭṭa Bhavadeva that his mother belonged to a *Bandyaghāṭī* family which is an important *gāiñ* of *Rāḍhīyas.* Important is in this connection the evidence of the Adavadi plate of the 13th century in which all the Brahmana donees have been particularly introduced by their respective *gāiñs*, and all of them correspond to those named in the *Kulagranthas.*[3] Dharāśūra, another Śūra king, is said to have classified these 56 *gāiñs* into two divisions. Twenty-two were raised to the status of *Kulācala* and the remaining thirty-four became *sat-śrotriya.* It is not known on what basis this classification was made. If there be any truth underlying this, Vallālasena seems to have at least one precedent. Those who had got matrimonial connection with the *Kulācalas* commanded greater respect and honour, and inter-marriages between the two classes were not restricted.

The history of the *Vārendras* prcatically begins from Vallālasena and the *Kulaśāstras* are absolutely silent about them for the period intervening between Ādiśūra and Vallālasena. The reason is not far to seek. Northern Bengal was under the Buddhist Pālas for about four centuries with very few short breaks. No doubt the Pālas were tolerant towards other religions. But to promote the welfare of a religion by actively associating with it is one thing and to be tolerant towards a religion is another. Their granting of lands to Brahmanas can be explained by the fact that they were following the traditional policy of rewarding the learned and the pious.

---

1. Y.C. Chakravarty, Kulaśāstra-dīpikā, p. 84, 85, 260.

2. He was of the Kautsa gotra but Champatī is a gāiñ of the Śāṇḍilays. His pravaras were Śāṇḍilya, Asita and Devala. The last two are also the pravaras of the Śāṇḍilya gotra. It is not unlikely that this Kautsa family, having the pravaras of the Śāṇḍilyas and living in Champati, became Śāṇḍilya.

3. Bhāratvarṣa 1332 B, S., pp. 78-81. Appendix F.

The assurances in the Mongyr and Amgachi plates that Dharmapāla and Vigrahapāla III preserved the four *varṇas* in their proper order are indications of their official policy towards the Brahmanical society. As protectors of the body politic, it was their duty to see that no one should deviate from the rules of the *Śāstras* and social orders. The building of new monasteries, reconstructions of old ones and huge expenditure on Buddhist establishments clearly indicate where their active sympathies lay. The *Kulaśāstras* on one or two occasions[1] refer to the gift of lands by the Pāla kings but otherwise they do not make the slightest reference to them. Strictly speaking from the point of view of the *Kulaśāstras* which were mainly concerned with the Brahmanical society, the Pāla period was a social and religious *interregnum* of which it is better not to take any cognisance at all.

Another fact also needs special emphasis. If our identification of Ādisiṁha with Ādiśūra be accepted, the Śūras seem to have originally belonged to Magadha. Sāmalavarman at whose instance the *Vaidikas* are reported to have migrated belonged to the Varman dynasty whose original seat of power was at Siṁhapura which seems to have been outside Bengal. Again, Vallālasena of the Sena dynasty who is credited with the foundation of *Kulinism* was Karnatic in origin. All the dynasties, which, according to the *Kulaśāstras,* took vigorous steps and measures in spreading the Brahmanical religion, seem to have come from outside. It appears, therefore, clear that these outside dynasties which seized political power played an important role in the Brahmanisation of Bengal. Apart from the migrations of some Brahmanas, it may be surmised that in the royal entourage and retinue from their native country that necessarily settled with the establishment of such political dynasties, there were in all probability many Brahmanical elements (lkie their domestic priests and the like) whose influence was not perhaps inconsiderable.

Vallālasena and Kulinism in Rāḍha—It is well to mention in the beginning that on the subject of the organisation of the Brahmanical society on the basis of *Kulinism* evidences come from two

1. Adigāñi Ojhā, son of Bhaṭṭa Nārāyaṇa, is said to have received a village from Dharmapāla. It is said in some books that the Śūras fought with the Pālas.

interested parties. Those who are placed in privileged position and are consequently supporters of the system speak of some well-recognised principles on which the different grades of social standing were created. The other party or parties which are placed in an unfavourable position have fabricated stories by distorting facts which go to discredit the whole system. The fact being so, it is difficult to judge what propagandist account comes from which of these parties, because both these ponits of view have been jumbled together and the account of the *Kulapañjikās* is confused. But something is so avowedly pro-*Kulinstic* and something so manifestly anti-*Kulinstic* that their significance or motive behind them is clear to every intelligent reader.

The *Rāḍhīya Kula-mañjarī*[1] states that Vallālasena through the grace of a goddess whom he worshipped for full one year with severe austerities was in a position to understand properly the nine essential virtues that are the tests of a good and pure *kula*. They are (1) *ācāra,* ceremonial purity; (2) *vinaya,* discipline; (3) *vidyā,* learning; (4) *pratiṣṭhā,* reputation for purity; (5) *niṣṭhā,* piety; (6) *tīrtha-darśana,* zeal in pilgrimages; (7) *āvṛtti,* observance of marriages with men and women of equal rank; (8) *tapaḥ,* ascetic self-devotion; (9) *dāna,* liberality. The Sena king is said to have examined the qualifications of 750 *Rāḍhīya* Brahmanas of his time on the basis of these principles to determine their social status. Of the twenty-two *Kulācala gāiñs* of the time of Dharāśūra only eight stood all the nine tests and were raised to the status of the *mukhya kulīna* (highest in status). In the remaining fourteen all the nine qualifications were missing and became *gauṇa-kulīna* (inferior *kulīna).* On a further examination of the eight *gāiñs* selected for the highest rank, only nineteen men strictly fulfilled all the requirements and they were the recipients of the highest honour. Further, Vallālasena is said to have attempted to classify the thirty-four *śrotriya gāiñs* of Dharāśūra into two divisions, *Śuddha* and *Kaṣṭha,* according to their respective qualifications. But this was opposed by them. The *Kula-Mañjarī* gives a very graphic account of the meeting in which a party of the *śrotriyas* headed by Vikartana protested against this and left the kingdom. They questioned the royal prerogative

1. VJI., I, pp. 146-52

to judge the qualifications or disqualifications of a Brahmana. "Every Brahmana is born pure *par excellence* and no earthly deed can make him impure. This is the divine dispensation. Like fire the utterer of the Gāyatrī *mantra* is the purifier of everything." They challenged the king to cite any precedent for his proposed *Kulinism*. Indignant at this insolent conduct, the king is said to have left the meeting with the remark, "you must be satisfied with the rank of the *śrotriyas*."

The anti-party gives the following account: Vallālasena invited the Brahmanas to a meeting on a certain day to decide the question of *Kulinism*. Some came at 8-30 A.M., some at 11 A.M. and some at 1-30 P.M.. The daily duties and observances of a strict Brahmana take a long time and the presumption was that those who came earlier did not strictly observe their daily dutiies. Those who came last were regarded by the king as pure and stricttly religious and were recipients of *Kulinism*. The next batch were made *gauṇa* and the early-comers *śrotriyas*. Contrary to the well-recognised principles mentioned above, the obvious motive behind this account is to show that *Kulinism* was based on nothing else than the royal whims. So far as we know, the earliest reference to these stories is to be met with in the *Vallālacarita*,[1] a book which has been handled and rehandled many times by or for interested people like the Suvarṇavaṇikas and the Yogīs. This book, according to the confession of the interpolators, was not finally redacted before 1510 A.D., and there are sufficient reasons to disbelieve even this confession, because the sources from which the Mss. were procured are not above suspicion. But there are evidences to show that this sort of anti-propaganda was counteracted by the supporters and advocates *Kulinism* by counter-propaganda of equal nature. The section of the *śrotriyas* who revolted against the imposition of the artificial distinction settled in an intermediate tract between Midnapore and Orissa and were called *Madhyaśreṇī*, but they were called by their opposite party *Madyadoṣī*, i.e., guilty of drunkenness. This propaganda and counter-propaganda have made the confused story

1. H. P. Shastri, Vallālacarita and Eng. Trans. by him; and also Vallālacarita by Sasibhusan Bhattacharyya.

of the development of *Kulinism* worse confounded. But the very fact that one party credits Vallālasena with the organisation of the Brahmanical society on the above basis–and this still governs the higher grades of the Hindu society of Bengal even now-a-days–and that the other party without denying the fundamentals want to discredit the system itself is somewhat clear proof of the fact that some sort of social reorganisation was attempted by Vallālasena, though it is difficult to determine its nature and extent because of the different and diverse colours it has received at the hands of different writers, parties and also in popular imagination in subsequent periods.

Circumstantial evidence also goes to indicate that some social reorganisation was necessary in the Sena period. The Buddhist Pālas were ousted by the Senas, who came from the *Karnāṭa* country and were *Brahmakṣtriyas,* i.e., originally Brahmanas who became Kṣatriyas afterwards by wielding the sceptre instead of teaching the scripture. It is natural that the royal power under them should be used for the welfare and promotion of the Brahmanical religion and society. The fact that during the long period of the Pāla rule, only seven charters recording land grants to the Brahmanas have come to light, while during the single reign of Lakṣmaṇasena no less than seven grants for the same purpose were at least issued, is perhaps a clear indication of the rising tide of the Brahmanical religion. The accession of the Brahma-Kṣatriya Senas certainly gave a fresh impetus to the Brahmanical religion whose star was perhaps already in the ascendant. It has been emphasised by late Mm. H. P. Shastri[1] that it was during the Sena period that many Buddhists were converted to the Hindu religion, and that for these new converts and adherents some castes and subcastes of Bengal were organised or reorganised and even new ones were formed.

There are positive evidences of somewhat definite character which go to affirm that the Senas were deeply interested in the reorganisation of the Hindu society. The Senas were preceded in eastern Bengal by the Varmans who also seem to have espoused the cause of Brahmanism to a great degree. The *Pāścātya Vaidikas* associate

1. H. P. Shastri's Introduction to Modern Buddhism in Orissa by N. N. Vasu, pp. 14-28.

their migration with Sāmalavarman, and Bhaṭṭa Bhavadeva, the Brahmana minister of Harivarman, seems to have typified the spirit of assertive Hinduism over decadent Buddhism and other 'heretical' religions.[1] His *Tautātimata-ṭīkā,* a gloss on Kumāril's *Tantra-vārtikā,* and well-known *smṛti* works, *Karmānusṭhāna-paddhati,* and *Prāyaścitya-prakaraṇa* are perhaps indicative of the forces employed to fight Buddhism and of the steps taken to make new converts, to regain the faltering ones and to purify the impure. Doubtless, ministers like Garga, Darbhapāṇi, Kedāramiśra, Gurava-miśra, Jogadeva, Bodhideva and scholars like Prahāsa and Śrīdhara-dāsa, the author of *Nyāya-kandalī,* kindled Brahmanical learning and religion in all their lustre and glory during the Pāla period. But when the king of a dynasty which boasts of their zeal in the propagation of the Vedic religion to counteract the preaching of the naked ascetics[2] is styled *Dharmavijayī*[3] (applied to Harivarman) and chooses a man like Bhṭṭa Bhavadeva as his minister, it must be taken to have a special significance. It is now an admitted fact that in the Sena period there had been a renaissance of Sanskrit learning and literature. In that renaissance, it is to be specially noticed, there were a great number of *Smṛti* books, dealing with *āhṇika* (daily rites), *Saṁskāra* (periodical rites), *śuddhi* or *aśuca* (purification), *prāyaścitta* (expiations) *śraddhā* (funerals), *kṛtya* (festivals), *pūjā* (worship), *pratiṣṭhā* (consecration), *dāna* (gifts) and *kāla* (appropriate time). To refer to the *Kāla-viveka, Dāyabhāga, Vyavahāra-mātṛkā* of Jīmūtavāhana and the *Brāhmaṇa-sarvasva, Dvija-nayana, Śrāddhā-paddhati-ṭīkā* is to name only a few of them. The works of Anirud-dha Bhaṭṭa, Īśāna and Paśupati also should be taken into considera-tion in this connection. From the middle of the eleventh to the close of the twelfth century all these writers wrote on Brahmanical rites and observances, having the *Śrūtis* and *Smṛtis* as their authority. It seems that these psuedo-*smṛti* books were composed with a view to suit the changed social and religious condition of Bengal and the

---

1. Bhuvanesvar praśasti, v. 20.

2. Belava plate, v. 5.

3. Bhuvanesvar praśasti, v. 16.

growing needs of the Hindu society. What is more important to bear in mind is that all these writers were connected with the court and were liberally patronised and highly honoured. The Sena kings were not content with patronising only. Two encyclopædic works, namely the *Dānasāgara* and the *Adbhutasāgara,* are attributed to Vallālasena. He died before the completion of the latter work which was finished by his son. It is thus clear that the Sena kings and their court actively associated themselves with the propagation of the Brahmanical rituals and observances for which so many works were composed. These evidences read along with the strong tradition in the *Kulaśāstras* make it almost plain that some steps were taken to organise the Hindu society in the Sena period.

Some scholars have summarily discussed the question of social organisation by the Senas by asserting that the foundation of *Kulinism* attributed to Vallālasena cannot be credited with historicity, because there is not the slightest reference to it in the Sena grants. Deeper social and religious forces that were at work in Bengal in the twelfth century were not taken into consideration by this class of writers. But still more significant is the silence of the pseudo-*smṛti* books written by men like Halāyudha who were intimately connected with the Sena court. But this silence cannot be taken as an irreconcilable bar to the acceptance of the view that Vallālasena selected nineteen persons out of the twenty-two *gāiñs* of Dharāśūra. If that be true, there seems to have been at least one precedent for his action and there was continuity in determining the social status. It was perhaps no deviation or any departure from old rules and customs. It did not appear to be such a revolutionary or a very important measure to the contemporaries as would merit reference in the land grants in which generally the politictal and military achievements of the kings are given prominence. Nor is it to be believed that it was universally accepted by the Hindu society all at once that it would find a place in the *smṛti* books which have got the sanction of centuries behind them. When the Government of India with the advantages of modern communication and propaganda and with its elaborate administrative machinery cannot enforce all the provisions of a

1. BI, See two Appendices on the Śūras.

moderate bill like the Sarda Act for the prevention of child marriages, it is hardly to be expected that a royal decree (if that was really the case) enforcing *Kulinism* which makes some socially higher than others, was accepted by all in the twelfth century. Such a measure must have taken a long time even for recognition, not to speak of acceptance. When people from other religions were entering into the Hindu fold and the Brahmanas themselves were contaminated to a certain extent by extraneous influences, Vallālasena and Lakṣmaṇasena perhaps selected some pure and religious-minded Brahmanas who would serve as models to others by their conduct and conviction. It has been observed rightly[1] that "It is interesting to trace in Vallālaesna's inquiry the survival or reassertion of the principle as recognised in ancient tiimes. that the Brahmanhood depends not merely on birth, but also upon personal endowments. It is a question of virtue, not a question of descent. Vallālasena, of course, could not go so far as this. The time had long passed when a Kṣatriya could transform himself into a Brahmana by a penance or self-denial. But the Sena monarch sought to affirm the ancient principle, so far as was then possible, by testing the qualifications of each *Rāḍhīya* family for the priestly office and classifying them, in order of their virtue, according to the results of the examination." Vallālasena was not perhaps conscious of the fact that he was taking a step which had in it the seeds of such far-reaching importance and consequence as the complicated and elaborate system that aorse out of it had. *Kulinism* in the Muslim period underwent such radical and startling changes through extraordinay circumstances as its authors could not even dream of. Strictly speaking, Vallālasena cannot be called the founder of later day *Kulinism* though he seems to have made some beginning in that direction. The word *Kulīna* was not unknown in ancient literature and signified men of good social standing because of their learning and high heredity. In the above-mentioned nine qualifications the word *āvṛti,* which in the *Kulaśāstras* means "marriage within equal ranks" contained the germ of later day *Kulinism.* It became the back-bone of the whole system and was carried to an unhappy climax. But in Vallālasena's

---

1. Risley. Tribes and Castes of Bengal. Vol. I, p. 145.

time it was one of the nine qualifications. He is said to have instructed his son to take particular and special notice of it and to judge the rank of the Brahmanas with reference to it only. The *Kulīnas* must marry their girls to *Kulīnas* only and not to any one of inferior status but they themselves could marry girls of their immediate lower rank. When the *paryāya* has been fixed with reference to *āvṛtti*, *aṁśa* was to be determined, which was divided into three grades. The best is *ārti* which is gained by a man who marries his daughter to a man belonging to his father's generation. When married to one of his own generation, he gains *madhyāṁśa* and the lowest comes when married to a man of his son's generation. The generation (*paryāya*) is to be counted from the five illustrious immigrants of the time of Ādiśūra. The nine disqualifications by which *Kula* is lost are—(1) miserliness, (2) aversion to ascetic self-devotion, (3) addiction to sensual pleasure, (4) greediness, (5) illiteracy, (6) extinction of the family, (7) offering of *piṇḍa* of a living man, (8) adultery and (9) to live a bachelor. It is reported that these instructions he left for Lakṣmaṇasena for his guidance in tackling the question of *Kulinism*. It is difficult to say how far this is true but we have the incontestable and incontrovertible evidence of the *Mahāvaṁsa* of Dhruvānanda Miśra that Lakṣmaṇasena made two examinations (called *Samīkaraṇa*) for judging the status of the Kulīnas. After his first examination seven men were declared to be of equal rank and in the second fourteen others were added to the list. Of these twenty-one, seventeen were the same persons as were recipients of *Kaulinya* honour from his father and the other four were the sons of the two deceased *Kuliīnas*.[1] It is also to be noted that in the *Mahāvaṁśa* the division of *aṁśa* which a *Kulīna* shared has been mentioned.

---

1. We are not prepared to accept the remarks in the Kulamañjarī that Lakṣmaṇasena made a further sub-divisions of ārti. and madhyāṁśa into 15 sub-divisions (see VJI, I. pp 182-4). No other book refers to this. He is said to have introduced five kinds of paribarta, viz., ādāna, pradāna, kuśa-tyāga, yoga and vara. Most of the Kulaśāstras are silent over it and there is no doubt that Kusa-tyāga was introduced at a later period.

It has been recently suggested by some scholars[1] that the real cause behind this movement was political rather than social and religious. Those who were recipients of *Kaulinya* rank were royal favourites who helped the establishment of the Sena rule and on whom the Senas could rely for support in future. Mention must be made here of Vijayasena's marriage with a princess of the Śūra dynasty. If the *Kulaśāstras* are to be believed, the Śūras were the champions of the Brahmanical religion. The matrimonial alliance of the Śūras and Senas might have some political importance. There are instances in the history of many countries that after a period of political religious and social upheavals the new kings and rulers try to create a new social order plaint to them. *Legione de Honours* of Napoleon, the champion of Liberty, Equality and Fraternity, is an instance in point. But it is difficult to say how much Vallālasena was actuated by political consideration in offering the *Kaulinya* rank to some Brahmanas. Incidental reference from *Vallālacarita* go to indicate that the political considerations might have weighed with him in degrading the status of the *Suvarṇavaṇikas* and the *Kaivartas*. The banker Vallabhānanda, the leader of the *Suvarṇavaṇika* community, refused to offer a loan to the Sena king except on certain conditions and was suspected of helping the Pāla king of Magadha with whom the Senas were at war. His community also incurred the jealously of the Brahmanas by wearing the sacred thread and by their enviable personal beauty. Vallālasena in alliance with the Brahmanas found an opportunity to degrade the mercantile community to the status of the Śūdras by a royal proclamation. The *Vaṇikas* retaliated by the prohibition of slave trading in Gauda, which seems to have been their monopoly. The *Kaivartas* were employed in domestic service and were made a clean caste by a royal order and their headman Maheśa was raised to the rank of a *mahāmāṇḍalika*. There is no doubt about the fact

1. K. P. Bhattacharyya. Rāḍhīya-Kula-tatva, p. 93; Dr. N. K. Bhattasali has gone so far as to assert that Vallālasena adopted the policy of divide and rule in order to secure his own position against possible dangers, Bhāratvarṣa, 1343 B. S., Asadha issue, under the heading Kaivartarāja Divya; also Census of India, V, Pt. I, pp. 527-28.

that the Senas were at war with the Pālas for a considerable period and that the *Vaṇikas* might have sided with the Buddhist Pālas. In the latter part of the eleventh century the Pālas were ousted from Varendra by the Kaivarta chiefs Divvoka and Bhīma, and the raising of the social status of the *Kaivartas,* when the Pāla-Sena war was not over, might have some political significance. The story of the degradation of the *Yogīs* is also interesting. The royal Brahmana priest is said to have been insulted by a *Yogī* Buddhist priest in charge of the Mahasthana religious establishment and this provoked Vallālasena's wrath on the community and hence their degradation. Judging the question from every possible sources, it seems that causes behind the social reorganisation by Vallālasena were various and it is not unlikely that contemporary political events influenced this to a certain extent.

The *Kulaśāstras* confess that the genealogies of the Brahmana families had not been properly preserved before the time of Vallālasena and this perhaps explains some of the discrepancies regarding the number of the generations of the five immigrants of the time of *Ādiśūra.* It is also not unlikely that the details regarding their migration became very dim and faint and that those *gotras* from which some Brahmanas received the *Kaulinya* rank have been associated with the name of Ādīśūra. But henceforward the genealogies are more or less correct. Great attention and care was given to preserve them, as the *Kulīna* families formed the social aristocracy of the Brahmanical society. This necessitated the rise of a professional class namely the *ghaṭakas* or match-makers, who should be properly called the *heralds.*

Vārendra Kulinism—It is said that at the time of Vallālasena there were 350 descendants of the five Brahmana immigrants brought at the instance of Ādiśūra, and the Sena king sent sixty of them to Tibet, sixty to Rabhāṅga, forty to Utkala, fifty to Magadha and forty to Mauḍāṅga.[1] It is difficult to say how much truth is there in this statement. Of the remaining 100, eight received *Kaulinya* rank, and eight *siddha-śrotriyas.*[2] Nothing more of the acti-

1. VJI. II, Varendra Brāhmana Vivraṇa, p. 21.
2. Idid., pp. 21-25.

vity of Vallālasena with regard to the handling of the rank of the *Vārendra* Brahmanas is reported in the *Kulagranthas*. The hero of *Vārendra Kulinism* is the famous *ghaṭaka* Udayanācārya who seems to have belonged to the 14th-15th century, and his rules and regulations do not fall within the scope of this book.

The *Pāścātya Vaidikas* – The special trait of a *Vaidika* Brahmana is that he is said to be very learned in the Vedas. The *Bhavabhūmi-vārtā* by Rāghavendra Kaviśekhara[1] which is said to have been written in 1581 S.E. is the only book which states that Gaṅgāgati Miśra was the earliest *Pāścātya Vaidika* to come to Bengal from Karṇāvatī on the bank of the Sarasvatī during the reign of king Harivarman. But it is to be noted that this book became known only after the discovery of the Samantasara plate of Harivarmadeva. It is also said in that book that Gaṅgāgati Miśra induced Yaśodhara Miśra to migrate to Kotalipara (in the Faridpur district) through the offer of his daughter. All other *Pāścātya Vaidika* books are unanimous in declaring that their ancestors came on the invitation of Śyāmalavarman in 1079 A.D.. The story[2] that has been made much of is the fall of a vulture on the royal palace which was taken to be nothing but a foreboding of a coming evil. There was no competent Brahmana to perform the requisite ceremony for the prevention of this evil. At the suggestion of the queen (whose name is given in some books as Sudakṣiṇā[3] and in others as Suśīlā[4]) the king requested his father-in-law Nīlakaṇṭha, king of Kāśi (in one book[5] the name is Jayacandra), to send a competent priest for that purpose. This priestly hero is *Saunaka* Yaśodhara Miśra who along with four other Brahmanas came to Bengal in 1001 S.E.. Again, it is also said that Yaśodhara was presented to Śyāmalavarman by his father-in-law on the occasion of his marriage.[6] The four other Brahmanas[7] of the *Śāṇḍilya,*

1. VJI, II, Vaidika Brāhmaṇa-Vivaraṇa. Intro.
2. For different versions of the story, Ibid, pp. 25-38.
3. Ibid., p. 13 16.
4. Ibid., p. 18.
5. Ibid., p. 18.
6. Ibid., p. 16.
7. There is no agreement regarding their names and gotras, Ibid, p. 41

Vaśiṣṭha, Sābarṇa and *Bharadvāja gotras* were induced by Yaśodhara Miśra to settle in Bengal in 1067 S.E.[1]

The time of their migration mentioned in the *Kulagranthas* is in agreement with the Varman chronology. As regards their allegation that there were no competent Brahmanas to perform a ceremony, it is difficult to believe that all the Brahmanas of Bengal lost their aptitude in their profession in the 11th century. It is corroborated in one way only from the *Brāhmaṇa-sarvasva* of Halāyudha that the *Rāḍhīyas* and *Vārendras* were not acquiting themselves very creditably in that aspect.[2]

Kaulinya system in the Vaidika society is entirely of another kind but it does not fall within the scope of this work.

Other Castes—The *Bṛhaddharma Purāṇa,* the internal evidence of which suggests that it was written in Rāḍha not long after the Muslim conquest,[3] deals with the origin of the so-called thirty-six castes of Bengal. It was perhaps in the mind of the author to give an account of them but in fact, he named about forty castes and divided them into three grades in accordance with the prevalent notion of his time.[4]

(1) *Uttama-Saṅkaras* (best mixed castes) who engaged Śrotriya Brahmanas as their priests. They are (1) *Karaṇa* (expert in civil service and in writing), (2) *Ambaṣṭha* (expert in medical science), (3) *Ugra* (warriors), (4) *Māgadha* (originally Kṣatriyas but now bards), (5) Gandha-Vaṇikas (trader in spices), (6) *Kaṁsa-Vaṇikas*

1. Ibid., 39

2. Halāyudha observes, "the Utkalas, Pāścātyas and others only read the Vedas, while the Rāḍhīyas and the Vārendras without reading by means of Karma-mīmāṁsā discuss only the nature of sacrificial rites in connection with the Vedas. But there can be no (proper) knowledge of the Mantras froming the soul of the Vedas.........In this way the Rāḍhīyas and Vāendras merely create improper conduct." T. C. Vidyananda's edition, pp. 9-10 ; see also JASB, 1915, p. 211.

3. Bhāratvarṣa, 1337 B. S., Pt. II, pp. 673 ff.

4. Bṛhaddharma Purāṇa, Vangabāsī edition.

(braziers), (7) *Śaṅkha-Vaṇikas* (shell-dressers), (8) *Kumbhakāras* (potters), (9) *Tantuvāyas* (weavers), (10) *Karmakāras* (blacksmiths), (11) *Gopas* (milkmen), (12) *Dāsas* (Cāsī-Kaivartas), (13) *Rājputas* (fighters), (14) *Nāpitas* (barbers), (15) *Modakas* (sweet-meat-makers), (16) *Varajīvīs* (growers of betel-leaves), (17) *Sūtas* (bards and reciters), (18) *Mālākāras* (gardeners), (19) *Tāmbulī* (seller of betel-leaves), (20) *Tailikas* (traders in oil).

(II). *Madhyama Saṅkaras*–mixed castes of intermediate status, (21) *Takṣa* (wood-cutters), (22) *Rajakas* (washerman), (23) *Svarṇakāras* (goldsmiths, (24) *Suvarṇa-vaṇikas* (traders in gold), (25) *Ābhīras* (milk-men), (26) *Tailakāras* (oil-pressers), (27) Dhī-*varas* (fisherman), (28) *Śauṇḍika* (wine-sellers), (29) *Naṭas* (dancers and musicians), (30) *Śavakas,* (31) *Jālikas* fishermen).

(III). *Antyajas* or outcastes–(32) *Gṛhīs,* (33) *Kudavas,* (34) *Caṇḍālas,* (35) *Badura,* (36) *Carmakāra,* (37) *Ghaṭṭajīvīs,* (38) *Dolā-vāhīs,* (39) *Malla.*

Besides, the author speaks of the *Śakadvīpī* or Devala Brahmanas from whom the *Gaṇakas* originated, and of the Mleccha tribes (non-Aryans) like *Pulindas, Kakkasas, Khaśas, Yavanas, Sauhmas, Kambojas, Śabaras* and *Kharas.*

The account of the origin of these castes is as it should be expected from an *upa-Purāṇa.* The wicked demon king Veṇa compelled men and women of different castes to procreate children. When the *Uttama-Saṅkaras* were born, he compelled them to procreate the rest. Sins and crimes were very common because of the confusion of castes and the *Ṛṣis* effected Veṇa's death through super-natural power, and the pious and good Pṛthu was created to restore order. With his help the Brahmanas fixed the proper duties and occupations of each caste. The criticism that it is an artificial systematisation composed long after the origin of castes, which is generally laid against Manu's theory, equally holds good in case of this account. The above-mentioned castes or peoples can be divided into three classes–professional, functional and ethnic or tribal. There cannot be any doubt about the fact that in a professional and functional caste there were peoples of many castes and the author of a *Smṛti* or *Purāna* could not otherwise explain this state of things excepting referring to fictitious mixed breeding. These castes are doubtless of mixed origin, as peoples of many castes followed one profession or were engaged in a single occupation and then formed a caste. The words *Varṇa-saṅkara* and *Jāti-saṅkara* are important, as in case of the professional and functional castes there has been really confusion of *Varṇas* and *Jātis* in a single caste.

Appendix E.

Authorities.

The genealogical list of the *Mukherjees, Banerjees,*[1] and *Boses*[2] have been published. Two important *Kārikās* dealing with *Kulinism* are attributed to Harimiśra and Eḍumiśra who are said to have flourished during the reign of Danujamādhavadeva. Their works have not yet come to light, but later writers have occasionally quoted many passages from their works. The most important work on the subject discovered so far is that of the *Mahāvaṁśa* of Dhruvānanda Miśra who composed his work in 1407 S.E.=1485 A.D.. It deals with the *Samīkaraṇas* of the *Rāḍhīya Kulīnas* from the time of Lakṣmaṇasena. The *Rāḍhīyas* have *Rāḍhīya-Kula-Mañjarī,* while the *Vārendras* have *Vārendra-Kulapañjikā.* Mr. N. N. Vasu quotes extensively from the *Kulārṇava* of Vācaṣpati Miśra but I do not know whether this work has yet been published. Maheśa Miśra's *Rāḍhīya Nirodosa-Kula-Panjikā* is also an important work. Nula Pañcānan's *Goṣṭhi-Kathā* offers a scathing criticism on the whole system. Many witty couplets on the subject transmitted in oral tradition are attributed to him. It must be noted that none

---

1. Mukha-Vaṁśa and Bandhya-Vaṁśa published by Mr. L. M. Mukherjee.

2. Basu-Vaṁśa by B. Roy Chowdhury ; Mr. J. N. Kumar has published in his Vaṁśa-Paricaya the genealogies of many important families.

of these works excepting the *Mahāvaṁśa* has been properly edited. The Dacca University has got in its collection about twenty Mss. of various descriptions. Few of them are complete by themselves, and of some only four or five leaves remain. Mr. N. N. Vasu refers to and quotes from many books collected by him from various sources. It is reported that they amount to about 200. Mr. Vasu's voluminous works on *Castes and Sects of Bengal (Vaṅgera Jātīya Itihāsa)* in ten volumes are mainly based on them. But his works are to be utilised with caution. *Gauḍe-Brāhmana* by M. Majumdar and *Sambhandha-Nirṇaya* by L. Vidyanidhi are also important from one point of view. It is well-known that interested parties have tampered with the *Kulaśāstras.* Cases have occured that with the discovery of an inscription or an important book the genealogical list of a royal dynasty or of the author, quite in keeping with their evidence, has suddenly sprung into existence. The genealogy of the Nandī family after the publication of the Mahasthana inscription[1] and of Sandhyākaranandī, the author of the *Rāmacarita,* are instances to the point. The older books like *Gauḍe Brāhmaṇa* and *Sambandha-Nirṇaya* supply us what were really the current traditions in the 19th century. Historical researches have made considerable progress since their publication. An interested and clever person can now fabricate a story or tamper with a *Kulapañjikā* but that was not easy in the previous century. Further references to other books or authors have been cited in the footnotes.

Appendix F.

1. Forty-two *gāiñs* of the *Saptaśatīs.*

Śagāi, Surāi, Nālsī, Yagāi, Hāsāi, Kalāi, Dhāi, Bānsi, Bānturī, Dhānsī, Kātānī, Kuśala, Ujjvala, Kāśyapa-Kāñjārī, Bātari, Pitāri, Nātāri, Beru Bāgrāi, Ulluka, Jhajhjhara, Mulluk, Pharphara, Kunduka, Kerala, Cercaru, Bālthubi, Paṁsika, Dighala Bhādaḍī, Bhaṭṭaśālī, Karañja, Tāi, Āditva, Kāmadeva, Koyāḍī, Nagaḍī, Digaḍī, Hāmasecāi, Kauṇḍinya, Bāpāri, Bārgrāi and Belāḍī.

1. JASB, N. S., XVIII, p. 439.

These forty-two are mentioned by Mr. N. N. Vasu. Mr. L. Vidyanidhi speaks of forty *gāiñs* excepting very few most of them agree. According to Vācaspati Miśra, there were only twenty-eight *gāiñs* of the *Saptaśatīs*.

2. Fifty-six *gāiñs* of the *Rāḍhīyas*. Some add Purba, Cautkhaṇḍī and Dīghal, thus making fifty-nine *gāiñs*.

Śāṇḍilyas (16) – Bandya, Gaḍgaḍ, Keśarakoṇā, Kusumakali, Parihāi, Kulabhī, Ghoṣāla, Sejagā, Māsacaṭaka, Bāḍala, Basuyāḍī, Kadala, Kuśārī, Kuliśa or Kulkuli, Ākāśa, Dīrghaṭī.

Kāśyapas (16) – Guḍa, Ambula, Bhuri, Tailabhāṭī, Pītamuṇḍī, Caṭṭa, Palsai, Haḍa, Poḍari, Pāladhi, Koyari, Pākrāsī, Simlai, Pushali of Pushilal, Bhaṭṭa, Mula.

Bharadvājas (4)–Mukhaṭī, Diṇḍisāñi, Sāhuḍiyān, Rāyī.

Sābarṇas (12)–Gāṅgulī, Kundalala, Siddhala, Dāyī, Nandī, Bāli, Śihari, Puṅgśika, Saṇḍeśvarī, Pāli, Ghaṇṭeśvarī, Nāñadī.

Vātsyas (8)–Mahintā, Ghoṣāla, Simbalāla, Bāpuli, Pippalāi, Putituṇḍa, Kāñjilāla, Kānjiāḍi.

3. The following *gāiñs* were made *Kulīnas* –

Mukhya Kulīnas (8)–Bandya, Caṭṭa, Mukhaṭī, Ghoṣāla, Putituṇḍa, Gānguli, Kāñjilāla, Kundalala.

Gauṇa Kulīnas (14)–Rāyī, Guḍa, Mahintā, Kulabhī, Cautkhaṇḍī, Pippalai, Gaḍagaḍī, Ghaṇṭśvarī, Keśarakoṇā, Diṁsāi, Parihala, Haḍa, Pītamuṇḍī, Dīrghaṭī.

The rest are *Śrotriyas*.

4. The following *gāiñs* are mentioned in the Advadi plate of Daunjamādhavadeva :– Diṇḍī Gāñi, Pāli gāñi, Seu gāñi, Māsacaṭaka, Mula, Sehandāi, Puti, Mahantiyāḍa, Karañja gāñi.

5. Hundred gāiñs of the *Vārendras* –

Vātsayas (24)–Sānnyāla, Bhīmkalī, Bhaṭṭaśālī, Kāmkali, Kuḍamuḍī, Bhāriyāla, Lakṣa, Jāmrukhī, Simli, Dhosāli, Tanuri, Vatsagrāmī, Deuli, Nidrāli, Kukkuṭī, Bodhagrāmī, Śrutobaṭī, Akṣagrāmī, Śāhari, Ḳaligrāmī, Kalihal, Pauṇḍrakalī, Kālindī, Chaturbandī.

Bharadvājas (24)–Bhādaḍa, Lāḍulī, Jhāmal, Jhampatī, Āturthī, Rāi, Ratnāvalī, Uccharakhī, Gocchasī, Bāla, Śakāṭi, Simbi, Bahal, Sariyāla, Kṣetragrāmī, Dadhiyāla, Puti, Kācchṭī, Nandīgrāmī, Gogrāmī, Nikhaṭī, Pippalī, Śrīṅga, Khorjar, Goswalambi.

Sābarṇas (20)—Sṁgdiyaḍa, Pākaḍī, Dadhi, Śriṅgi, Medadi, Undhuḍi, Dhundhuri, Tatoyar, Setu, Naigrāmī, Nedhuḍī, Kapāli, Tutturi, Pañcabaṭī, Nikaḍi, Samudra, Ketugrāmī, Jaśogrāmī Sitalī.

Kāśyapas (18)—Maitra, Bhāduḍī, Karañja, Bālayaṣṭhī, Modhāgrāmī, Balahāri, Moyāli, Kiral, Bījikuñja, Saragrāmī, Katigrāmī, Saragrāmī, Madhyagrāmī, Maṭhagrāmī, Gaṅgagrāmī, Belagrāmī, Chamagrāmī, Aśukoṭi.

Śāṇḍilyas (14)—Rudrabāgchi, Lāhiḍī, Sadhubāgchi, Campaṭī, Nandanabāsī, Kāmendra, Sihari, Taḍoyālabisī, Matsyāsī, Champa, Suvarṇa, Toṭaka, Puṣaṇa, Beluri.

6. The following *gāiṅs* were made *Kulīnas* by Vallālasena.

Lāhiḍī, Bāgchi, Bhāduḍī, Maitra, Sānnyāla.

Bhādaḍa became *Kulīna* for the sake of metre. The *gāiñ* of another man cannot be stated precisely.

Siddhya Śrotriyas—Karañja, Nandanabāśī, Bhaṭṭaśālī, Lāḍulī, Campaṭī, Jhampaṭī, Āturthī, Kalihal.

Sādhya Śrotriyas—Uccharakalī, Jāmrukhī, Ratnāvalī Sihari, Rāi, Goswalambi, Biśī, Khorjarḍ.

The rest are *Kaṣṭa Śrotriyas*.

7. The different dates of the migration of the five Brahmanas through the instrumentality of Ādiśūra :—

The *Vārendra Kulapañjikā* places it in *vedakalaṅkaṣaṭavimite* i.e., in 654 S.E.; Vācaspati Miśra *vedabāṇāṅgaśake* i.e., in 654 S.E.; and the *Kularṇava* in *vedabāṇahīmésāke*. The *Kulatattvārṇava* place it in 675 S.E.; the *Vallālacarita* in 954 S.E. .

CHAPTER X

RELIGIOUS CONDITION

Jainism—The districts of Manbhum, Singhbhum, Birbhum and Burdwan derive their names from Mahāvīra or Vardhamāna.[1] Of the 24 Jaina *tīrthaṅkaras* no less than 20 attained *Nirvāṇa* on the Sametśikhara *(Samādhi-śikhara)* in the Paresnath Hill in the Hazaribagh district. It is narrated in the *Āyāraṅga Sutta*[2] that Mahāvīra had to undergo much suffering and hardship in Vajjabhūmi and Subbhabhūmi in Rāḍha. It was difficult to travel in the country and the natives treated the ascetics very cruelly. They incited dogs to bite them and the ascetics had to carry bamboo staves to keep off the dogs. It seems, therefore, that western Bengal felt the tide of the rise of Jainism at the time of Mahāvīra.

The *Vṛhatkathākoṣa* of Harisṣena, written in 931 A.D., records that the famous Jaina pontiff Bhadrabāhu, the preceptor of the Maurya emperor Candragupta, was the son of a Brahmana of Devakoṭa in the Puṇḍravardhana country. One day when Bhadrabāhu was at play with other children at Devakoṭa Govardhana, the fourth *Śrutakevalī,* happened to see him and perceived that the boy was destined to be the next *Śrutakevalī.* He took charge of him with his father's consent, and the boy afterwards succeeded him as the great Jaina pontiff. Whatever may be the truth underlying the story of killing 18,000 people in Puṇḍravardhana for the crime of a *Nirgrantha in the Divyāvadāna,* it tends to show that there were many Jainas in northern Bengal in the 3rd century B.C.

---

1. IHQ., IV, p. 44 ; SPP, 1322, p. 5 ; JBORS., 1927, p. 90.

2. SBE., XXII, pp. 85-5. That Puṇḍravardhana was a Jaina centre at the time of Buddha is corroborated by the story of Sumagadhā, daughter of Anāthapiṇḍaka (Sumāgadhāvadāna in the Bodhi Sattvāvadāna-Kalpalatā, Bengali translation by S. C. Das. pp. ,68-779).

Aṅga and Magadha are the eastern countries that occur in the list of *Solaśa-mahājanapadas* of the *Aṅguttara-nikāya.* The 15th chapter of the Jaina *Bhagavatī Sutta* also gives a list of sixteen countries, and the occurrence of the names of Aṅga, Vaṅga and Lāḍha (Rāḍha) in it shows that the Jainas had more acquaintance with Bengal than the Buddhists in an early period. The *Kalpasūtra* mentions four *śākhās* of the *Godāsagana* of the Jaina monks as Tāmalittyā, Koḍivarṣiyā, Poṁdavardhaniyā and (Dāsī) Khabbaḍiyā.[1] Tāmralipti, Koṭivarṣa and Puṇḍravardhana are in Midnapore, Dinajpur and Bogra districts respectively, and Khabbaḍiya has been identified with the principality of Kharvāṭa in western Bengal. The Jaina *Upāṅgas,* redacted in *c.* 454 A.C. but preserving earlier traditions, include Tāmalitta and Vaṅga among Aryan lands, as opposed to Milikka (=Mleccha or barbarian) peoples like Śaka, Yavana[2] etc. All these literary references go to show unmistakably that there had been considerable proselytising activity by the Jainas since the days of Mahāvīra, and Jainism had got strongholds almost in every part of Bengal. If the maltreatment of the ascetics narrated in the *Āyāraṅga Sutta* is to be believed, the Jainas seem to have met with much opposition from the natives. But the spread of the religion over the whole country shows that they were ultimately successful in their mission.

Though we do not know of any royal patron like Candragupta Maurya of Khāravela after the Christian era, Jainism did not lose much ground in Eastern India, as it is generally believed. A Mathurā inscription[3] records the erection of a Jaina image in the year 62 of an unspecified era (=140 A.D.?) at the request of a Jaina monk of Rārā (Rāḍha?). The Paharpur plate of 159 G.E.[4] records the gift of some land by a Brahmana couple for the maintenance of worship with sandal, incense, flowers for the *arhats* at the *vihāra* of Vaṭ-Gohāli. This *vihāra* was presided over by the disciples of the disciples of the *Nirgrantha* preceptor Guhanandin, belonging to the *Pañcastūpa* section of Benares. The evidence of the Paharpur

---

1. SBE., XXII, p. 288, also Kalpasūtra by Jacobi, p. 79; for the location of Khabbadiyā or Kharvāṭa see IHQ., VIII, pp. 529-30.

2. IA., 1891, pp. 374 ff.

3. JASB., V, p. 239.

4. EI., XX, 639.

plate, read along with the account of Yuan Chwang, testifies to the fact that Puṇḍravardhana, as a great Jaina centre, maintained its position at least up to the first half of the seventh century A.D.

Yuan Chwang's observations on the religious condition of India are, no doubt, of great importance for the proper understanding of the relative position of the important religions of the time. But it must be noted that in his account the details about all other religions excepting Buddhism are lacking and that he speaks of the *Nirgranthas* rather incidentally and summarily. The fact being so, the Buddhist pilgrim was constrained to remark that in Vaiśalī, Puṇḍravardhana, Samataṭa and Kaliṅga—all in Eastern India—the *Nirgranthas* were numerous. It is, therefore, clear that in these regions the Jainas had the largest number of adherents in the seventh century. The Chinese traveller does not refer to the *Nirgranthas* of the other localities specifically, but when he says that other religions live in pell-mell, it is to be understood that Jainas were included in them. His silence cannot be taken to mean that there were no Jainas in other parts of Eastern India. Thus in his description of Rājagṛha no mention is made of the Jainas, but he found many *Nirgranthas* near a tope *(stūpa)* on the Vipula mountain on the spot where Budha once preached. 'Many *Digambaras* now lodge here and practise austerities incessantly ; they turn round the sun, watching it from its rising to its setting.'[1] Rājagṛha, famous both in Buddhist and Jaina literature, is still a place of pilgrimage to the Jainas. A considerable number of Jaina images lie scattered in or about this place.[2]

We are quite in the dark about the state of this religion in Bengal after the seventh century. Its history, disappearance or absorption by another religion, is wrapt in complete obscurity. The fate of two other rival religions or sects is interesting and instructive in this connection. Whatever might have been the relation between Mahāvīra and Makhaliputta Gosāla at first, it is admitted by all

---

1. Watters on Yuan Chwang, Vol. II, p. 154.
2. ASIR., 1925.26, pp. 146 ff,

that as founders and champions[1] of two rival religions, their relation at a later period was far from being friendly, if not one of bitter rivalry and heinous propaganda against each other. The Jainas refer to Gosāla and his followers not in very honourable terms. If the *Bhagavatī* account of Gosāla and Mahāvīra is to be believed, they lived together for six years in Paṇitabhūmi, which was, according to some Jaina commentators, in Vajjabhūmi, one of the divisions of Rāḍha.[2] Mahāvīra in course of his wanderings in Rāḍha found ascetics carrying bamboo staves in their hands, who, in accordance with Pāṇini's description of *maskarin,* are to be identified with the Ājīvika ascetics and were also active in propagating their religion in western Bengal in the 6th century B.C. Maurya kings like Aśoka, Daśaratha and prince Vītaśoka sometimes patronised the Ājīvikas. The Nāgārjuni and Barabar caves[1] go to show that the Ājīvikas had got a fair number of followers in Eastern India in the 3rd century B.C.[3]

The *Bhagavatī* refers to a king of Mahāpauma of Puṇḍa, a patron of the Ājīvikas. Puṇḍa is said to be at the foot of the Viñjhā mountains and Mahāpauma's capital is described as having hundred gates.[4] The very name Puṇḍa suggests that it was most probably Puṇḍra. Whatever may be the truth underlying the episode that Aśoka put to death 18,000 Ājīvikas in Puṇḍravardhana for the crime of a *Nirgrantha,* it unmistakably shows that it was also a centre of the Ājīvikas. But the most important point in this episode is that the Ājīvikas were mistaken for the *Nirgranthas,* and there are other

1. For relation with Mahāvīra and Gosāla, see Ch. on Jāinism in CHI and also the excellent paper on the Ajīvikas in JDL, II, by Dr. B.M. Barua.

2. Ibid., p. 57, SBE., XXII, p. 264, Note. 4, It is a to be noted that other Jaina books have Paiśācabhūmi instead of Panitabhūmi. (See Mr. U. D. Barodia's History and Literature of Jainism.)

3. JBORS., XII, p. 53.

4. Dr. Barua identifies Puṇḍa with Pāṭaliputra because Mahāpauma's capital is described with hundred gates p. 67; cf. Megasthenes, description of Pāṭaliputra.

passages in the *Divyāvadāna*[1] in which the Ājīvikas have been confounded with the Jainas. We are, therefore, inclined to accept Dr. B. M. Barua's opinion that at the time of the composition of the *Divyāvadāna* 'the meaning of the confounding of the Ājīvikas with the Jainas is that the two sects living side by side at Puṇḍravardhana differed so slightly from each other, whether in their views or in their outward appearances, that it was difficult for a Buddhist observer to draw any sharp distinction between them.' In Southern India the Ājīvikas were regarded by the Jaina authors as a sect of the Buddhist *bhikṣus*.[2] It is quite natural to think that there were many Ājīvikas whom Yuan Chwang also confounded with the Jainas or at his time they became identical with the Jainas to all intents purposes and lived completely absorbed in Jainism, as the followers of Devadatta were living absorbed in Buddhism at Karṇasuvarṇa, only retaining their individuality in the matter of taking food. Broadly speaking, the differences between the Ājīvikas and the Jainas were not very fundamental. Amalgamation was perhaps possible when the initial bitterness was over and it was also possibly necessary in view of the vigorous activity of other rival religions in the field. Devadatta, the veritable Satan of the Buddhist *Jātakas*, was the founder of a sect, differing only in very minor points from Buddha[3] but it was, according to the testimony of Yuan Chwang, living within the bosom of Buddhism in the seventh century, and to a non-Buddhist it was then nothing but Buddhism, pure and simple. Although proofs are still lacking, it may be surmised that Jainism was at a later period absorbed by Buddhism and by the different sects of the Brahmanical religion. The Paharpur monastery which seems originally to have been a Jaina establishment was at a later period converted into a Brahmanical one and finally into a Buddhist *Vihāra*, the famous Somapura-*vihāra* of northern Bengal. Mallikārjuna Sūri, the cele-brated writer on astrology, who flourished in Vaṅga in the 12th

3. Dr. Barua, Op. Cit. P. 65.

4. IA., 1912, pp. 88ff.

1. Isan Ghose's Bengali translation of the Jātakas, Vol 1. Appendix, pp.214-6 ; 1A., 1923, p. 267 ; 1924, p. 125,

tury A.D., seeems to have been a Jaina,[1] but in his books he pays homage to the Hindu gods Gaṇapati, Viṣṇu and Kṛṣṇa.

Nothing is known of the existence of Jainism after Yuan Chwang's account excepting a few images of Jaina *tīrthaṅkaras*. The Jaina images are not so rare in Bengal, as has been observed by late Mr. R. D. Banerjee[2] who could number four of them only. The exploration of a certain part of the Sunderbans by Mr. K. D. Mitra has brought to light no less than ten Jaina images.[3] The fact that so many Jaina images have been found in one part of the Sunderbans, read along with the evidence of the Barrackpore plate of Vijayasena.[4] tends to lead to the conclusion that north-western Sunderbans were also included in the old principality of Samataṭa where Yuan Chwang saw the preponderance of the *Nirgranthas*. A careful investigation in the districts of Birbhum and Bankura, where occasional finds of Jaina images are reported[5] and which fall within the region which Mr. R. D. Banerjee calls the 'Jaina zone of influence,'[6] may add to the known numbers of the sculptural remains of the Jainas in Bengal. Of about twenty-five images so far discovered only one belongs to the *Śvetāmbaras*. This would go to indicate that the *Śvetāmbaras* had a very small following and that the *Digambaras* had a greater number of adherents. The images of *Ṛṣabhanātha, Ādinātha, Neminātha, Śāntināthā* and *Pārśvanātha* have been found, those of the last being more popular. The image of Ṛṣabhanātha in the VRSM. from

---

1. The very name ending in-Sūri suggests that he was a Jaina. The Jainas and the Ajīvikas were famous for their proficiency in Astrology, Beal, II. p. 168; also see Dr. Barua's paper and Mr. P. C. Sen's paper, Vicitrā, 1340 B. S., pp, 659 ff. Dr. B Dutta takes Mallikārjuna Sūri to be a Hindu because of his paying homage to Hindu god. SPP, 1340 B. S., p. 83,

2. ESMS., p. 144.

3. VRSR, 1921-29, 1930-31, Antiqnties of Khari and antiquities of North-Western Sunderbans.

4. IHQ.. XII, p. 67.

5. ASIR., 1921-22, pl. XXIXD. Bīrbhūma-vivaraṇa, p. 188; another Jaina image in Saptagrāma, JASB., 1909, pp. 237, 245.

6. R. D. Banerjee, Op. Cit.

7. VRSR., Op. Cit., 1928-29.

Surhor in Dinajpur[1] is interesting from the iconographical point of view and deserves more than a passing notice. The central figure with the perfect meditative pose, the oval nimbus over the head, the attendants with fly-whisks, the flying couples of Vidyādharas with garlands, the umbrella between 4 pairs of hands, indication of celestial offerings, resembles in many respects a seated Buddha image of the Pāla period. The perfect nudity of the figure, the bull, the emblem of Ṛṣabhanātha, and the presence of 23 *tīrthaṅkaras* who have come as if to pay their homage on the occasion of the installation of this remarkable image are clear indications of the fact that it was a Jaina image. In the representation of 24 *tīrthaṅkaras* in the Hanumān cave at Khandagiri the *vāhanas* of Sumatinātha, Supārśvanātha and and Anathanātha are *krauñca, svasti* and *śyena* respectively and this is also the direction in Hemacandra's *Abhidhāna-cintāmaṇi.* In this image the *lāñchanas* are the dog, wheel and bear.[2] Most probably the Bengal school followed a different manual in the representation of the *tīrthaṅkaras.*

From stylistic considerations all the Jaina images may be assigned to the Pāla period. The small number of Jaina images in comparison with the large number of the Buddhist and Brahmanical images is perhaps indicative of the fact that Jainism was losing ground in the Pāla period. It is known from the *Vasantavilāsa*[3] that Vastupāla (1219-1233 A.D.), minister of Cālukya Vīradhavala, who went on a pilgrimage, was attended by the *Saṅghapatis* from Lāṭa, Gauḍa, Maru, Dharā, Avantī and Vaṅga. It is important to notice from this incidental evidence that even in the 13th century there were heads of organised associations of the Jainas in Gauḍa and Vaṅga, however small their influence might have been in this period.

Buddhism—Bengal was the last strong-hold of Buddhism in India, but it is very strange that it has been very rarely referred to

---

1. Ibid., 1933-34.

2. This iconographical point of difference was first noticed by Mr. N. B. Sanyal.

3. Vasantavilāsa, Sarga X

in early Buddhist literature. It has been mentioned in the *Saṁyutta Nikāya*[1] that Buddha once lived at Śetaka, a town of the Sumbhas; and it has been suggested that they may be the Suhmas of western Bengal.[2] A Buddhist teacher Upasena has been described as Vaṅgānaputto in the *Aṅguttara Nikāya,*[3] and it has been suggested on the analogy of such epithets as Videhaputto and Mallaputto that Upasena was originally perhaps an inhabitant of Vaṅga. No locality or city seems to have gained high recognition or to have been of much importance to the early Buddhists, and it is also doubtful whether in these two cases there has been really any reference to Bengal.

The story of Sumāgadhā, daughter of Anāthapiṇḍaka, narrates how Buddha came to preach in Puṇḍravardhana at the instance of this pious and devoted lady.[4] According to Yuan Chwang, Buddha is said to have preached in that city for three months and in Samataṭa for seven days and also in Karṇasuvarṇa. In these localities the pilgrim also saw the places where past Buddhas walked. But in spite of these allusions to Buddha's personal ministration in Yuan Chwang's account, it is doubtful whether Budha really came in person, though it may be that Buddhism was making some headway in Bengal during his life-time.

It seems that there were vigorous attempts at proselytising activities during the reign of Aśoka. Yuan Chwang saw many Aśokan topes at Puṇḍravardhana, Samataṭa, Tāmralipti and Karṇasuvarṇa. The vigorous religious propaganda of the Maurya emperor naturally produced its effects. The recently discovered Mahasthan inscription[5] which is to be palæographically assigned to the Maurya period records that oil, tree, paddy and small coins *(gandhaka* and *kākaṇikā)* were ordered to be stored for the *saḍvargikas* in case of emergencies due to

---

1. W. 89, 168-170.

2. Dr Majumdar, Early History of Bengal p. 8.

3. I. XIV. 3.

4. Bodhi-Sattvāvadāna-Kalpalatā Bengali Translation by S. C. Das, pp. 768-779.

5. IHQ., 1934, p. 54. We follow Dr. B. M. Barua's interpretation of this inscription.

water, fire, parrots. Oil was to be conveyed from Puṇḍranagara. This store-house was not far from the Puṇḍravardhana city, the find-spot of this epigraph. Although the fact by whom this order was made is not known, it seems that like the Sohagaura plate this was also an official direction. The *Saḍvargiyas* have been identified with the *Chabhagiyas* of the Vinaya texts, who formed a 'Band of six men with their adherents' and who are said to have acted always contrary to the intent and purpose of the Vinaya discipline. The *Chabhagiyas,* like the followers of Devadatta, might have differed on some points of discipline, which the strict followers of the Vinaya texts did not like and approve. What is important for our purpose is that as early as the Maurya period Puṇḍravardhana became a centre of activity of the *Chabhagiyas,* so much so that provisions were to be made for meeting their emergencies. There are also evidences to show that pious Buddhists from Puṇḍravardhana visited the holy and sacred sites like Sanchi.[1]

A Nāgārjunikoṇḍa inscription[2] which is to be palæographically assigned to the 3rd or 4th century A.D. states that Vaṅga was one of the countries that gladdened the hearts of the Therāvādin teachers. That the Sthavira school flourished in eastern Bengal is also confirmed by Yuan Chwang, when in the description of Samataṭa the Chinese traveller observes that it had 30 Buddhist monasteries and above 2000 Brethren, all adherents of the *Sthavira* school. The Gunaighar plate[3] of Vainyagupta, dated in 508 A.D., records the grant of land to a congregation of Buddhist monks belonging to the *Mahāyāna* sect in the Tippera district.

From Yuan Chwang's account it appears that at the time of his visit the three principal religions, viz. Brahmanism, Buddhism and Jainism, had each a fairly large number of adherents in Bengal. The details about Buddhism left by him may be noted here. In Kajangal (modern Rajmahal) there were six or seven monasteries and above 300 Brethren. In Puṇḍravardhana there were 20 monasteries and above 3000 Brethren and both the Great and Little

1. EI., II, p. 108, 830.
2. EI., XX, p. 23.
3. IHQ., 1930, pp. 40 ff.

10

vehicles were followed. In Samataṭa there were more than 30 monasteries and above 2000 Brethren, all of the *Sthavira* school. In Tāmralipti there were above 10 monasteries and more than 1000 Brethren. In Karṇasuvarṇa there were more than 10 monasteries and above 2000 Brethren who were all adherents of the *Samatīya* school. There were also three monasteries in which in accordance with the teaching of Devadatta milk products were not taken as food. Besides, there were two Universities–one in Puṇḍravardhana and another in Karṇasuvarṇa.

It seems from the accounts of the Chinese travellers that Buddhism was declining in Tāmralipti. In Fa-hien's time there were 22 monasteries in all of which monks resided.[1] In Yuan Chwang's time the number of monasteries were ten and I-Tsing saw only five or six.[2] He has left a graphic account of the University of Bhā-rā-hā in Tāmralipti. But Buddhism increased its influence in Samataṭa. In I-Tsing's time the number of monks rose from 2000 of Yuan Chwang's to 4000. The increasing influence of Buddhism within fifty years was perhaps due to the ardent and vigorous support of the Khaḍga dynasty which ruled in Samataṭa within the period between 625 and 725 A.D. All the known independent kings of Bengal before the middle of the seventh century were followers of the Brahmanical religion. The Khaḍgas were devoted Buddhists, and we are fortunate to have a picture of the flourishing condition of Buddhism and of the part played by Rājabhaṭa[3] in its propagation at the time of Seng-chi. "He was an ardent worshipper of three jewels and played the part of a grand *upāsaka*. His sincerity was profound and faith very great. His glory exceeded that of his predecessors. Every day he made 100,000 statues in moulded clay and read 100,000 stanzas of *Mahāprajñā-pāramitā-sūtras* and made use of 100,000 fresh flowers....." When the royal party went, an image of Avalokiteśvara was placed in the front. His banners and standards concealed the sun, and instrumental

---

1. Legge, p. 100.
2. Takakasu, Intro. xxxiv.
3. Chavannes at first restores the text as Harṣabhaṭa but in a footnote says that it may be constructed as Rājabhaṭa.

music filled the space. The statues of Buddhas, *bhikṣus* and *upāsakas* all marched in front and the king followed behind them. In the capital city there were more than 4000 monks and nuns. All these were entertained by the king. Every morning royal messengers went to them and said, "I am commanded to ask if you have passed a good night." The monks and nuns replied, "We hope His Majesty is in good health. May he live long and his kingdom remain in peace." Only after these messengers had come back and reported, did the king begin to transact the business of the state. The best and most learned *bhikṣus* in the whole of India were assembled in this kingdom, being attracted by the renown of the king, which reached far and wide."[1] Seng-chi himself lived in the royal temple and received extraordinary honour. It is, therefore, no accident that Śīlabhadra, a scion of a royal family of Samataṭa, rose to the exalted position of the head of the Nālandā monastery and under his tutelage Yuan Chwang was placed,[2] and to his learning and liberality the pilgrim pays glowing tribute.

Tantrikism—The *Tantras* claim great antiquity. The Hindu *Tantras* claim origin from the *Vedas*,[3] while the Buddhists trace the Tantrik doctrines to the *Mudrās, Mantras Maṇḍalas, Dhāraṇīs* and *Yoga*, as preached and practised by Buddha.[4] But no avowedly early Tantrik books like the *Guhya-samāja, Mañjuśri-Mūlakalpa*[5] and the *Kaulajñāna-nirṇaya* can be placed before the 7th century A.D. It seems that from the 7th or 8th century onward both the Brahmanical and Buddhist religions were greatly influenced by Tantrikism. It is said in an early Jaina book[6] that Śabaras, Drāviḍas, Kaliṅgas, Gauḍas and Gāndhāras succeed by occult sciences.

1. I am thankful to Dr. R. C. Majumdar for translating the relevant portion from Chavannes' 'Memorie les Religien eminents' pp. 128-29.

2. Beal, Life pp. 158-60.

3. IHQ., IX, pp. 1 ff.

4. Sādhanamālā, Intro. pp. XVI ff.

5. IHQ., IX, pp. 1 ff.

6. SBE., Vol. XLV, Sutrākṛtaṅgas, p. 366.

In the description of the centres of Tantrikism in the *Sammola Tantra*[1] Aṅga, Vaṅga and Kaliṅga are mentioned first.

It is very difficult to define Tantrikism. MM. H. P. Shastri[2] expressed the opinion that "The word *Tantra* is very loosely used. Ordinarily people understand by it any system other than the *Vedas*.... the union of male and female energy is the essence of *Tantra*." Winternitz[3] holds that the term "*Tantra* ought to be restricted to the texts connected with śakti worship." This is, no doubt, one of the main aspects of the Tantrika literature. *Śaivas* look upon this union of male and female energy as that of Śiva and Śakti, the *Sāṁkhyas*, of Puruṣa and Prakṛti, and the Vajrayānists, of Boddhicitta and Nirātmā (śūnya) or Upāya and Prajñā. Besides this abstruse philosophy, we find various other topics discussed in the *Tantras*, viz. the story of the creation, royal duties, social customs, male and female characteristics, curing of deseases, *mantras* for the extraction of snake-poison and even the introduction of the smoking of tobacco in human society. Above all, the *Tantras* are the repository of the esoteric beliefs and practices. In course of time the *Tantras* have become the encyclopædias of knowledge of varied kinds. Tantrika goddesses like Ekjaṭā and Mahācīnatārā seem to be of foreign origin, and it is quite likely that every Tantrika doctrine or practice was not of indegenous growth.[4]

In the *Tantras* the *mantras* have very special significance. Like the muttering of the name of Hari by the modern Vaiṣṇavas, they are thought to be highly efficacious. The *mantras* are the "verbal expression of the idea of god." Almost every god has a *mantra* of his own and to the uninitiated the *mantras* appear to be meaningsless strings of letters. An instance may be taken. The eight thousand couplets of the *Prajñā-pāramitā-śāstra* after successive abbreviations and condensations were reduced to the syllable *'Pra,'* which is the *Bīja mantra* of the goddess *Prajñāpāramitā*. The proper muttering of the *mantras* not only helped spiri-

1. IHQ., VII, p. 8.
2. Intro. to N. N. Vasu's Modern Buddhism in Orissa, p. 10.
3. IHQ., IX, p. 4.
4. Ibid., VII, pp. 1 ff.

tual success but also could prove helpful in mundane affairs, as *māraṇa* (destruction of enemies) and *ākarṣaṇa* (attracting). The *Tantras* advocate the worship of gods and goddesses in *Yantras* (instruments, more properly magic diagrams). Some of the Tantrika *Yantras* in stone with figures of gods and goddesses have come to light. The devotee is to concentrate on the *Yantra* his mind which is fastened to the object of worship. The full correspondence between the mind and the body was aimed at. The intellectual process was supplemented by physical discipline to be attained by *Yogas* of various kinds like the controlling of senses and breathings.

It is quite natural that in such a mystic system the role played by the *guru* (preceptor) was a very important one, and the *Tantras* realise it. For the proper understanding of the *mantras* and for correct application of esoteric practices, initiation by, and the guidance of, a guru were enjoined as absolutely essential. People irrespective of caste, creed and sex were initiated. The use of *Pañca-Makāras*[1] were sometimes advocated for attainment of *siddhi.* There were three distinct stages of *sādhanā*, viz., *śuddhi* (purification), *sthiti* (illumination) and *arpaṇa* (unification), and there were three classes of *sādhakas* (devotees), viz. *Paśu, Vīra* and *Divya.*[2] It was the duty of the *guru* to prescribe to his initiates their mode of *sādhanā* according to their mental and spiritual capacities. If any disciple misused the mode of worship for his physical enjoyment, he was severely taken to task and the *guru* was also held responsible to a certain extent for his degeneration. The disciple was regarded as a spiritual son of his preceptor and was sometimes named after the *guru* after his initiation. In Tantrika *sādhanā* the devotee was identified with the deity and the preceptor enjoyed a higher status than the deity itself.

Divergent views have been expressed as to the valuation of Tantrikism. It has been claimed that it is the greatest contribution of India to the world[3] and that the Tantrika method of *sādhanā*

1. They are madya, māṁsa. matsya, mūdrā and maithuna
2. Dr. N. K. Brahma, Philosophy of Hindu Sādhanā, p. 291.
3. Dr. B. Bhattacharyya, An Introduction to Buddhist Esoterism, see concluding remarks.

combines in it "*yoga, bhakti, mantra, homa* (oblation), *jñāna* and *karma* and can be best studied as the "synthesis of all that was good in the various forms of *sādhanā* in vogue and as such its claim to be the shortest route to the *summum bonum,* and its promise to its adherents of the easy and speedy attainment of the end are perhaps justified."[1] On the other hand it has been condemned[2] as the most revolting and horrible practice that human depravity could think of, and compared with which the worst specimens of Holiwell Street Literature of the last (18th) century would appear absolutely pure. But the plain truth is that the vast Tantrika literature has not been adequately studied with the care and attention that it deserves and it remains yet an enigma to us. We may hope with Avalon that the true spirit of scholarship will endeavour to be just.[3] There remains enough to show that Tantrikism necessitated multiplicity of gods and goddesses and "satisfied everybody, the cultured and the uncultured, the pious and habitual sinners, the lower and the higher ranks of people and devotees."[4]

The Buddhist Pantheon—The study of the later Buddhist religion has been simplified by the publication of the *Sādhanamālā,*[5] a special class of literature dealing with the Buddhist pantheon. This literature was mostly written in the monasteries of Bengal and Bihar, and the Buddhist images so far discovered answer in most cases to their descriptions in the *Sādhanās.* The task is made easier by the fact that the Buddhists were scientific in the classification of their gods and goddesses, most of whom were affiliated to a particular family of the five Dhyānī Buddhas.

Dhyānī Buddhas and Bodhisattvas—The conception of five Dhyānī Buddhas and their association with their female counterparts (śaktis) are for the first time met with in the *Guhyasamāja Tantras*[6] and *Jñānasiddhi*[7] of Indrabhūti, none of which can be at

1. Dr. N. K. Brahma, Op. Cit. p. 275.
2. R. Mitra, Sanskrit Buddhist Literature, p. 261.
3. Tantrik Texts, VII, Foreward, pp. IV-V.
4. Sādhanamālā, intro., p. XXXVI.
5. Our thanks are due to Dr. B. Bhattacharyya for his painstaking work in this direction and we follow him in the main.
6. GOS, No. LIII, Intro., p. XI.
7. BD. Icon., Intro. p. XXV.

present assigned before the 8th century. They are Vairocana, Ratnasambhava, Amitābha, Amoghasiddhi and Akṣobhya. Later on Vajrasattva was added, thus raising the number to six, and in Nepal Vajrasattva is the priest of five Dhyānī Buddhas. Dhyānī Buddhas generally appear as the sires of other gods and goddesses and their separate representatioin is rare. Only two images of Ratnasambhava are known so far.[1] The VRSM. specimen[2] is from Vikrampur and the VSPM. one[3] from Bhagalpur. Only one image of Vajrasattva with an inscription in the tenth century script has been discovered from Sukhavaspur,[4] Dacca. The six Divine Bodhisattvas are Sāmantabhadra, Vajrapāṇi, Ratnapāṇi, Padmapāṇi, Viśvapāṇi and Ghaṇṭāpāṇi and they are affiliated to the six Dhyānī Buddhas. Three images of Vajrapāṇi come from Bihar[5] but none from Bengal. It is quite possible that the images described in the VRSC as Bodhisattva, Lokanātha, Padmapāṇi[6] are those of this Divine Bodhisattva. Images of Maitreya, the Buddhist Messiah, are not very rare in Bihar and Bengal. He is represented separately either standing[7] or seated[8] and also appears in the company of seven mortal Buddhas.[9]

Ādi-Buddha—The conception of Ādi Buddha or Primordial Buddha cannot be traced in literature[10] earlier than the 10th century. In the later Buddhist pantheon he occupies the highest place, for it is said that the five Dhyānī Buddhas originated from him.[11] In Nepal he is called Sayambhū and the *Vṛhat-svayambhū-purāṇa* deals with his cult. Again, some identified Akṣobhya with Ādi-Buddha.[12] According to Getty,[13] Prajñāpāramitā is his Śakti and he is to be

1. JASB., 1926, 169 ff.
2. No. A (a) 6/138.
3. No. C (a) 6/271.
4. DMC., No. 1A (1) a/1.
5. Bd. Icon., Pl. XIIbc ; IM. Nos. 3784, 3785,
6. VRSC. A (b) 6/165.
7. ASIR. 1929-30, Pl. XLIII f, from Jhewari, Chittagong ; VRSC. No. A (b) 13/391.
8. An excellent image from Biswanpur Tandwa, Bihar, ESMS, Pl. XXXIIb.
9. IM, B.G., Nos. 83, 133.
10. Bd. Icon. Intro. pp. XVII-XVIII
11. Ibid.
12. Ibid.
13. Gods of Northern Buddhism, p. 3.

represented as a 'crowned Buddha' with ornaments and princely garments. Many crowned images of Buddha have been found in Bengal and Bihar, and their identification with the saintly Śākyasiṁha in monkish robe has been questioned.[1] According to Mr. N. G. Majummdar, the representation of tne principal incidents of the life of Buddha around the crowned figure is explained by the fact that "*Śākyasiṁha* was given a place in the unreal mythological domain and has been thoroughly identified with the Primordial Buddha" and that eight (or four) important incidents of his life were regarded as signs of his Buddhahood.

Buddha Śākyasiṁha—The images of Buddha illustrate one of the eight principal incidents of his life. Besides (1) the birth (Māyādevī standing under the Śāla tree) and (2) the *mahāparinirvāṇa* (death), we have (3) the enlightenment at Bodh-Gaya in Bhūmisparśa-mudrā, (4) the first sermon at Sarnath in Dharmacakrapravartana-mudrā, (5) the descent from the heaven of 33 gods in Varada-mudrā, where he went to preach to his mother, (6) the submission of the elephant Nalagiri or Ratnapāla in Abhaya-mudrā, (7) the attempt of Devadatta to kill him with the help of assassins and (8) the miracle at Śrāvastī in Vyākhyāna-mudrā. In addition to these incidents, two other events of the master's life are also illustrated in the separate images of Buddha, viz., (1) protection from rains by the hooded canopy of the serpent Mucalinda and (2) the gift of honey by a monkey at Vaiśālī. The images of Buddha in one of the above attitudes are common in Bihar and Bengal.

There is another class of Buddha images in which the central figure is represented by Buddha in Vajrāsana or by a crowned Buddha or Buddha in one of the above eight attitudes, but on the back slab we find all the principal incidents of his life. Sometimes some other additional incidents[2] are also to be found. The additional incidents are (1) the taking of first seven steps by infant Buddha, (2) the casting of the horoscope by the sage Asita Devala,

1. VRSR, 1929-27, pp. 7-10 ; for crowned images, see, IM, B. G. No. 80, Br. No. 68; Nos. 3713, 3703, 3755, 2071 ; VSPC, No. C(c) 2/185.

2. See the huge image of Buddha from Jagadishpur near Nālandā and the Sib-bati Buddha image from Khulna, ESMS, Pls., XIXC, XXA ; also IM, No. Br. 5, pl. XIXb.

(3) the boy Buddha at school,[1] (4) his concern at the sight of an old man,[2] (5) the *mahābhiniṣkramaṇa* or the great renunciation on the back of Kaṇṭhaka followed by the groom Chandaka, (7) the changing of the dress with that of Chandaka, (8) the cutting of hair, (9) the meditation of Buddha, (10) the attack of the Māra's army, (11) allurements by his two daughters and (12) failure of that attempt. After a comparison of the representations of these scenes from the master's life with those of other schools, R. D. Banerjee[3] observes that the Pāla school of sculptures introduced the representations of many incidents which had not been portrayed by the intermediate schools like Mathura and Sarnath after that of Gandhara. The same scholar very appropriately described these scenes on the back slabs as "images bas-reliefs" and the evolution of this style is peculiar to the Pāla school.

Mañjuśrī–The gods, Mañjuśrī and Avalokiteśvara, require special treatment owing to their great importance. Their conceptions are known in early Buddhist literatures like the *Sukhāvatī Vyūha* and *Karaṇḍavyūha* and they are therefore earlier than their parental Buddhas. Mañjuśrī is the god of learning and his worship confers "wisdom, retentive memory, intelligence, eloquence for mastering the scriptures." Two Dhyānī Buddhas claim his allegiance and on some varieties of his images the five Dhyānī Buddhas appear. Besides, there are independent forms. Vāk and Dharmadhātu Vāgīśvara are emanations from Amitābha. Their representations in images are not known. Mañjughoṣa, Siddhaikavīra, Vajrānaṅga, and Nāmasaṅgīti are emanations from Akṣobhya and of them no image is yet reported from Bengal and Bihar. Vāgīśvara, Mañjuvara, Mañjunātha and Mañjukumāra forms bear the images of five Dhyānī Buddhas. The IM. possesses an image of Vāgīśvara.[4] Of this variety Mañjuvara seems to have been popular. His two forms

1. Only in IM. No. Br. 5, the identification is questionable, as it is not very distinct.

2. Ibid.

3. ESMS., p. 44.

4. Bd. Icon, Pl. XIVd.

are prescribed in the *Sādhanamālā*. An image[1] of the simpler form in Dharmacakra-mudrā of the late Pāla period has been discovered at Bara in the Birbhum district. The VRSC. No. A (b) 12/264 describes a six-handed image of Bodhisattva Mañjuśrī surmounted by five Dhyānī Buddhas (one of them missing). The independent forms of Mañjuśrī are Aparcana, Sthiracakra, Vādirāt and Mañjunātha. The *DMC*. No. 9A (ii) b/1 most probably represents Aparcana. He is holding the book against the breast in the left hand, brandishing a sword in the right, and it agrees with the *Sādhana* excepting that it bears the effigies of four Dhyānī Buddhas. The DM. also possesses a wooden image of standing Sthiracakra of high artistic excellence.[2] The *VSPC*. No. C (d) 8/16 also agrees with the *Sādhanā* excepting that the right hand shows Varada-mudrā and the left holds the stem of a lotus on which appears the sword.[3] An image of Mañjuśrī in bronze of the Gupta period has been discovered at Mahasthan.[4] It bears an effigy of Akṣobhya.

Avalokiteśvara–He is the most popular god of the Buddhists and is in charge of the world during the period between the disappearance of Śākyasiṁha and the advent of the future Buddha Maitreya. In the Maccandar Vihāra at Katmandu there are paintings of 108 varieties of Lokeśvara. In the *Sādhanamālā* his fifteen forms have been described. Excepting Vajradhara, all others are emanations from Amitābha. They are Ṣaḍakṣarī, Siṁhanāda, Khasarpaṇa, Lokanātha, Halāhala, Padmanarteśvara, Harihariharivāhana, Trailokyavaśaṅkara, Rakteśvara, Māyājālakarma, Nīlakaṇṭha, Sugatisandarśana and Pretasantarpita. Padmanarteśvara has three sub-varieties and Raktalokeśvara has two other forms. Of these different varieties the images of Ṣaḍakṣarī, Siṁhanāda, Lokanātha and Khasarpaṇa have been found in Bengal and Bihar. A representation of the Ṣaḍakṣarī group (in the company of Maṇidhara and Mahā-

1. Ibid., Pl. XVp.
2. Modern Review, 1938, March issue.
3. Bd. Icon., p. 30.
4. VRSR, 1926-27, Pl. I, fig. 2.

vidyā, broken) has been found in the Birbhum district.[1] The VRSM., DM. and IM. each possesses a fair number of Siṁhanāda images. Images of Lokanātha are very common. The *DMC.* No. IA(ii)a/2 is a fine specimen of Khasarpaṇa and agrees faithfully with the description in the *Sādhana.* It is one of the best products of the Pāla school of art. He is in Ardhaparyaṅka-āsana in Varada-mudrā with his companions Tārā, Sudhanakumāra, Bhṛkutī and Hayagrīva with a lotus stalk in hand. The IM. No. 3808[2] represents another image of Khasarpaṇa. The VRSM.[3] possesses an image of Avalokiteśvara in bronze from Mahasthan and has been assigned on stylistic considerations to the Gupta period.

R. D. Banerjee[4] classifies the Avalokiteśvara images by the number of hands and attributes in them :–

(1). Avalokiteśvara with two hands–the lotus stalk in the left hand and the right in the Varada-mudrā.

(2). With four hands–the two additional ones holding a rosary (*akṣamālā*) and a *kamaṇḍalu* or a book.

(3). With six hands[5]–the other two hands holding a snare (*pāśa*) and a jewel-like substance.

(4). With multiplicity of hands.[6] The *VRSC.* No. A(b)1/47 is a 12-handed image of Avalokiteśvara, but the attributes are not distinct. The *VSPC.* No. C(d)7/9 is also a 12-handed one with the figure of Amitābha over the serpent canopy. The *VRSC.* Nos. A(b)2/37 from Bogra and A(b)3/122 from Vikrampur, Dacca, represent a twelve-handed god and are surmounted by five Dhyānī Buddhas. The VRSC.. No. A(b)4/93 from Vikrampur describes a Bodhisattva Lokanātha surmounted by five Dhyānī Buddhas.[7] No such description is to be found in the *Sādhanamālā.* The presence of five Dhyānī Buddhas on so many images cannot perhaps be explained as "ornamental rather than parental," and it may be that we have not yet

1. ASIR, Eastern circle, 1920-21, p. 27.
2. ESMS, pl. XXXIII.
3. Report, 1927-28, pl. V.
4. ESMS, p. 87 ff.
5. IM. No. 5860.
6. See ESMS, pl. XXXIVa.
7. For another image see ASIR, 1930-34, pl. CXXXIb.

known the *Sādhana* which prescribes Avalokiteśvara as an emanation of five Dhyānī Buddhas.

The *VRSC.* No. A(b)4/124 has been described as Bodhisattva Trailokyavaśaṅkara, corwned with an image of Buddha. It is a three-faced and four-handed figure. In the *Sādhanamālā* Trailokyavasaṅkara is one-faced, two-armed and three-eyed, and therefore, its identification does not seem to be correct. The image may be a representation of Halāhala or Sukhāvatī form but in the *Sādhanas* both are described as six-handed.[1]

Family of Amitābha–He claims complete allegiance of the gods, Mahāvala, Saptaśatika and Hayagrīva and the goddesses, Kurukullā, Bhṛkuṭī and Mahāsitavatī. Kurukullā has four sub-varieties. It is reported that there are three images of Kurukullā among the large Kurkihara finds.[2] No other image of this group is known.

Family of Akṣobhya–He commands the allegiance of a large number of gods and goddesses. His male emanations are Caṇḍaroṣaṇa, Heruka, Buddhakapāla, Vajraḍāka, Hayagrīva, Yamāri and Jambhala. Heruka has three varieties–Dvibhuja Heruka, Heruka in *Yab-Yum* (in close embrace) with his Śakti and Caturbhuja Heruka. The *DMC.* No. IA(iv)b/l is a Dvibhuja Heruka in Ardhaparyaṅka or dancing pose with a horrible look, hurling a Vajra and wearing a garland of skulls. Vajraḍāka has three varieties–Samvara, Saptākṣara and Mahāmāyā. The IM. has recently acquired an image of Samvara from northern Bengal.[3] The *Sādhana* prescribes four heads but this image has three. Otherwise it agrees in details with the description in the *Sādhanamālā.* Yamāri has two varieties–Rakta (red) and Kṛṣṇa (black). Krsnayamāri has again three sub-varieties and one image of the sub-variety, namely, Yamāntaka, has been discovered at Nālandā.[4] Jambhala has another variety called Ucchuṣma-Jambhala.

The female emanations of Akṣobhya are Mahācīnatārā, Jāṅ-

---

1. Bd. Icon. pp. 40, 46, 50.
2. Proceedings and Transactions of the seventh Oriental Conference, pp. 795-796.
3. ASIR, 1934-35. p. 80, pl. XXIVc.
4. Bb. Icon., pl. XxVb,

gulī, Ekajaṭā, Parṇaśavarī, Prajñāpāramitā, Vajracaracikā, Dhvajāgrakeyūrā, Vasuhdarā and Nairātmā. Jāṅgulī has three forms, Ekajaṭā has two and Prajñāpāramitā has four. The IM.[1] possesses a representation of Ekajaṭā who offers a horrible and grim look and flames are gushing out from her person. A broken image of Parṇaśavarī with six hands, three faces and trampling on Gaṇeśa is in the Indian Museum.[2] Prajñāpāramitā is the deification of the spirit of the popular *Mahāyāna* book of that name. The DMC[3] describes an image of this goddess. Vasuhdarā is the Śakti of Jambhala and is the goddess of plenty and prosperity. One image of Vasudharā has been found in the Murshidabad district.[4] The goddess Nairātmā is the deification of the idea underlying Śūnyavāda or Nirātmā (soullessness). The IM. No. 3941 represents an image of Nairātmā. She is dancing in Ardhaparyaṅka attitude on a corpse with a garland of skulls. With angry eyes, canine teeth and burning flames from her person she presents a terrible appearance. A bronze in VSPM.[5] seems to represent this goddess. The only thing that goes against the identification is that her sire Akṣobhya is not to be found on the top.

Family of Vairocana—In the *Sādhanamālā* no male emanation of Vairocana is known. His female emanations are Mārīcī, Uṣṇīṣavijayā, Sitātapatrā, Aparājitā, Mahāsahasrapramardanī and Vajravārāhī. Of these goddesses Mārīcī was very popular. She has six varieties, of which only the images of Aṣṭabhujā Mārīcī are common. She is the Buddhist goddess of dawn and her chariot is drawn by seven pigs. She is four-faced and a *Caitya* appears on her head. In her four faces four sentiments, *bhaya, bībhatsa, raudra* and *śānta* were directed to be expressed. One of the faces is that of a boar. The IM.[6] possesses an image of Uṣṇīṣavijayā which agrees in all details with the *Sādhana* excepting that it bears the effigy of Akṣobhya in

1. Ibid., pl. XXVIId.
2. No. 3957.
3. No IB (1)/1.
4. ASIR, 1927-28, pl. XLIXe.
5. Bd. Icon., p. 91, pl. XXXb.
6. Ibid., pl XXXIc

stead of Vairocana. Vajravārāhī is the śakti of Hevajra and has three varieties.

Though no male emanation of Vairocana is known in the *Sādhanamālā,* a bronze image of Hevajra with this parental Dhyānī Buddha has been discovered in the Tippera district.[1] He is in fighting attitude and in his sixteen hands there are different attributes, mostly weapons. Eight goddesses dance a war dance around him. Another image of Hevajra in *Yab-Yum* has been found at Paharpur.[2]

Family of Amoghasiddhi–Like Vairocana only female emanations of Amoghasiddhi are known and they are Khadirvanī-Tārā, Vaśyatārā, Ṣaḍbhujā Sitatārā, Dhanada-Tārā, Parṇaśavarī, Mahāmāyūrī and Vajraśṛṅkhalā. The images of Khadirvanī-Tārā are very comon. Both standing and seated forms are to be found. She is accompanied by Aśokakāntā Mārīcī and Ekajaṭā. Two fine images of Parṇaśavarī come from the Dacca district.[3] She appears in fighting attitude and presents an angry look. The diseases and pestilences which are represented in human shape flee at her approach.

Family of Ratnasambhava–His male emanations are Jambhla and Ucchuṣma Jambhala. Jambhala is the Buddhist god of wealth and is represented with a pot belly and decked with ornaments. In his right hand he carries a mongoose which vomits jewel. He is a popular god and his allegiance is claimed by Ratnasambhava, Akṣobhya and five Dhyānī Buddhas. The *DMC.*[4] describes two fine images of the present type from Vikrampur.

His female emanations are Mahāpratisarā and Vasudharā. Two eight-handed images[5] from Dacca are generally identified with Mahāparatisarā but they do not belong to this form. Dr. B. Bhattacharyya refers to an independent form of this goddess in the

1. DMC. Addenda, pl. Ia.
2. ASIR, 1927-28, p. 107. pl. XLIXa.
3. DMC. Nos. Pl. XXIII.
4. Nos. pls. XIb, e.
5. Bd. Icon. Pls. XXXVbc.

Sādhanamālā.[1] They agree well with the independent form excepting that they have three faces, while the *Sādhana* prescribes four. One image of Vasudharā from Jhewari, Chittagong,[2] is known but the parental Buddha is lost and it is difficult to say under whose authority (Akṣobhya or Ratnasambhava) she is.

Emanations from five or four Dhyānī Buddhas–The gods included in this group are Jambhala and Mahākāla and the female emanations are Vajratārā, Prajñāpāramitā, Sitatārā and Māyājālakarma Kurukullā. The two images discovered at Majbari (Faridpur) and Patharghata (Bhagalpur) within a full-blown lotus with eight movable petals are generally taken to be representations of Vajratārā. But Dr. N.K. Bhattasali[3] draws attention to the description of an image of Cakra-Mahāsukha in the *Cakra-sambhara Tantra* and is perhaps right in his disagreement in so far as there are no parental Buddhas in the above two instances. The IM. No. 100[4] represents the goddess Prajñāpāramitā of this form. The *VRSC*. No. A(d)2/137 describes an image of Mārīcī and the rim of its chariot roof contains five Dhyānī Buddhas. The only known emanation from four Dhyānī Budhas is the goddess Vajratārā.

Family of Vajrasattva–His two emanations are Jambhala and Cundā.

Independent forms–Under this heading may be included the gods and goddesses who do not claim their origin from any of the five Dhyānī Buddhas or any combination of them. Independent gods are Gaṇapati, Bighnanāṭaka, Vajrahuṅkāra, Bhūtaḍāmara, Vajrajvālāmālākāra, Trailokyavijaya, Paramaśva and Nāmasaṅgīti. One image of Trailokyavijaya[5] from Bodh-Gaya is only known. He is four-faced, eight-armed and tramples on Gaurī and Śiva. The VSPM.[6] possesses an image of Bighnanāṭaka. Its provenance is not known but it seems to be a product of Nepalese workmanship.

---

1. Ibid., p. 117.
2. ASIR, 1927-28, Pl. XLIXb.
3. DMC., p. 51. The reproduction of Vajratārā from Nepal by Dr. Bhattacharyya is of entirely different type. Bd. Icon., Pl. XXXVa.
4. Ibid., Pl. XXXVIc.
5. Ibid., XXXIXc.
6. Ibid., Pl. XXXIXb.

Independent goddesses are Sarasvatī, Aparājitā, Vajragāndhārī, Vajrayoginī, Grahamātṛkā, Gaṇapatihṛdayā and Vajravidāraṇī. The Buddhists seem to have borrowed Sarasvatī, the Brahmanical goddess of learning. That she was highly venerated and very popular is attested by the fact that five of her forms are found in the *Sādhanamālā*, viz., Mahāsarasvatī, Vajravīṇā Sarasvatī, Vajrasāradā,[1] Āryasarasvatī and Vajrasarasvatī. The IM. has an image of Aparājitā.[2] The goddess is in fighting attitude and tramples on Gaṇeśa. Another broken image from Nālandā probably represents her.[3]

Miscellaneous gods and goddesses—Hāritī, protectress and giver of children, is not described in the *Sādhanamālā* but is known from Buddhist mythology. The DM.[4] has an image of this goddess with a fish and bowl in two hands and in the other two she holds a baby. The VRSM.[5] has four specimens. Two images of Hāritī have been found in the ruins of Khāḍi.[6]

The goddesses consisting of the *Tāntrika* Pañcarakṣā Maṇḍala are Mahāpratisarā, Mahāsahasrapramardanī, Mahāmantrānusāriṇī, Mahāmāyūrī, and Mahāsitavatī.[7]

All the Tārā images have not been properly classified. There are many varieties. Dr. B. Bhattacharyya classifies them under two general headings—(1) ordinary and (2) extraordinary. Ordinary Tārās exhibit the Varada pose in the right hand and hold a lotus in the left.[8] Ordinary Tārās are again sub-divided into Green and

---

1. One image from Nālandā has been identified as Koṭiśrī (?) and is, in the opinion of Dr. B. Bhattacharyya, probably that of Vajrasāradā. Both these identifications are questionable. There is no similarity of this image with the Nepalese painting of this goddess reproduced by him. Bd. Icon., Pls. XL de, p. 152.

2. Ibid., Pl. XLIIa.

3. Ibid., Pl. XLId.

4. No. IB (VII)/c

5 A (e) 1/327. A (e) 3/106, A (e) 2/329, A (e) 4/115.

6, VRSR, 1928-29, p. 8.

7. These five goddesses are illustrated in Bd. Icon by miniatures from a manuscript of Pancaraksā.

8. Ibid, p. 135 fn.

White Tārās. Green Tārā has four varieties—Khadirvanī, Vaśya-tārā, Āryatārā and Mahattarī Tārā. Most of the Tārā images belong to this category. White Tārā has two varieties—Mṛtyuvañcana and Aṣṭamahābhaya. Extraordinary Tārās include a large number of goddesses we have described already.

The above account does not exhaust the number of known images[1] and it is also to be noted that all the *Sādhanas* have not been discovered. In spite of some cases of doubtful and questionable identifications it is to be admitted that the Buddhist images as a rule faithfully agree with their descriptions in the *Sādhanamālā*. The extant literature and the number of images hitherto discovered from different quarters make it abundantly clear that Buddhism in its later phase commanded a large following in the Pāla period.

---

1. The following identifications appear to us very doubtful. The VRSC No. A (g) 1/110 describes a ten-handed goddess as Vāgīśvarī, the DMC No. IB (iv) a/1 as Sitapātra and No. 1A (v) a/1 as Piṇḍola-Buddha, God of Medicine. The sixteen-handed image (IM. No. 2076) cannot be identified at all. the eight-handed goddess from Bara (Bīrabhūma-Vivaraṇa, fiig. 30) appears either to be an image of Uṣṇīṣavijayā or Mahāpratisarā. Another image reproduced in the same book (fig. 27) appears to represent a Buddhist god. I am unable to suggest any indentification from the indistinct photograph.

CHAPTER XI

RELIGIOUS CONDITION (CONTINUED)

Brahmanical Pantheon

Vaiṣṇavism—The *Harivaṁsa*[1] narrates the story of a quarrel between Yādava Kṛṣṇa and Vāsudeva of Puṇḍra. The latter was a friend and ally of the Magadha king Jarāsandha and an enemy of Kṛṣṇa. It is said in this story that Pauṇḍraka Vāsudeva considered himself to be the real Vāsudeva, the holder of *śaṅkha, cakra padma* and *gadā,* and regarded Devakīputra Vāsudeva as an impostor. In the battle that ensued on this account the Puṇḍra king lost his life. The story tends to show that at the time of the composition of the *last* part of the *Harivaṁśa* Vāsudeva with his usual attributes was regarded as a fullfledged god, but it may reflect the spirit of a previous age (as we know from the story of Śiśupālavadha in the *Mahābhārata)* when there was a considerable opposition from a section of the people of eastern India to looking upon Kṛṣṇa as an incarnation of Viṣṇu. It may be noted that Pauṇḍraka Vāsudeva was one of the kings defeated by Bhīma in his eastern expedition.

The earliest epigraph referring to Vaiṣṇava worship in Bengal is the Susunia inscription which records the setting up of a wheel of Viṣṇu by king Candravarman. The Vaigram plate of 129 G.E. refers to a temple of Govindasvāmin (a form of Viṣṇu) and the Damodarpur plate No. 4 refers to a temple of Śvetavarāhasvāmin.[2] The Tippera grant of Lokanātha records grant of land to a temple of Nārāyaṇa. The Khalimpur plate of Dharmapāla mentions grant of land to a temple of Nanna-Nārāyaṇa in the Vyāghrataṭī-maṇḍala.

The Brahmanical images and terracotas unearthed in course of

---

1. Vaṅgavāsī edition. Udvṛtta-bhaviṣyat-parva, pp. 439-446.

2. Most probably it means Viṣṇu in Varāhāvatāra. This record also mentions Kokāmukhasvāmin. Dr. R. G. Basak says that Kokāmukha may mean a she-wolf. It cannot be ascertained what god was meant in this case.

excavations at Paharpur are assignable to the Gupta and post-Gupta periods. Stories and exploits connected with the life of Kṛṣṇa are illustrated profusely in panels and they go to show that the Kṛṣṇa cult was popular in Northern Bengal even in the Gupta period. Before the Paharpur excavations our knowledge of Rādhā-Kṛṣṇa cult of ancient Bengal was very poor, the stone representations being the doubtfully identified 'Mother and Child' images as the birth of Kṛṣṇa. His sports with the milk-maids and the part played by him in the *Mahābhārata* have been mentioned in the 4th verse of the Belava plate of Bhojavarman, the last known king of the Vaiṣṇava Varman dynasty. Jayadeva, the court-poet of Lakṣmaṇasena, immortalised the love of Rādhā and Ksrna in his *Gīta-Govinda*. The Kṛṣṇa panels[1] at Paharpur which are possible of definite identification are lifting of the mountain Govardhana, the death of the demons Cāṇura and Muṣṭika in wrestling combat with Kṛṣṇa and Balarāma, the uprooting of two Arjuna trees and the killing of the demon Keśī.[2] An amorous pair[3] with halos round their heads have been identified with Kṛṣṇa and Rādhā. There are separate representations of Balarāma and the river goddess Yamunā. There are various other panels which may be representations of some scenes of Kṛṣṇa's life. Two scenes[4]—a monkey carrying stone on his head for making the bridge in order to cross over to Laṅkā and the fight between Bālī and Sugrīva—show the wide popularity of the *Rāmāyāṇa* stories in that period. Besides the Paharpur finds, a bronze image of Viṣṇu from Rangpur may be assigned to the Gupta period.[5] An ordinary Viṣṇu and Viṣṇu Śeṣa-Śāyin in the Tepa collection at Rangpur,[6] Viṣṇu from Laksmankathi, Backerganje,[7] and another from Jogirsoan, Rajshahi,[8] and a baked clay seal of the god from Sabhar, Dacca,[9] may be assigned to the post-Gupta period.

---

1. ASIR, 1926-27, pp. 142 ff.
2. IC, III, p. 195.
3. ASIR, 1926-27, Pl. XXXc.
4. Ibid., Pl. XXXIVa.
5. Ibid., 1929-30, Pl. XXXVb.
6. VRS. Monograph, No. 4.
7. DMC, p. 87.
8. VRSR, 1930-31, fig. 1.
9. DMC, p. 83.

Viṣṇu images of the Pāla period lie scattered and uncared for all over Bengal, and all the museums and private collections possess a fairly large number. This is a clear proof of the wide popularity of the worship of this god. Viṣṇu is generally represented as standing with his four well-known attributes in four hands. He is accompanied by his two wives Lakṣmī and Sarasvatī, *Vāhana* being the devotee Garuḍa. Sometimes the door-keepers of Vaikuṇṭha, viz., Jaya and Vijaya, also appear. Most of the Bengal images belong to the Trivikrama and Vāsudeva varieties with the order of attributes PGCS and GSCP. in four hands.[1] A specimen of a four-headed bust of Viṣṇu is in the Tepa collection at Rangpur. The central face is normal, the left and right are those of Varāha and lion. The back one is described like that of a Bhairava.[2] The pedestal of a seated image of Viṣṇu *(Yogāsana)* from Itahar, Dinajpur, has been noticed by Mr. S. K. Saraswati.[3] A standing Viṣṇu with a seven-hooded snake canopy has been found in the north-western Sunderbans.[4] A Seṣa-Śāyin image is at Vainyesvara, Murshidabad.[5]

On some Viṣṇu images we find the representation of his ten incarnations on the back slab.[6] The ten incarnations are Matsya, Kūrma, Varāha, Narasiṁha, Vāmana, Rāma (Dāśarathi), (Paraśu)-rāma, (Bala)rāma, Buddha and Kalki. Of these we have some remakable specimens of Matsya, Varāha, Narasiṁha and Vāmana incarnations in separate images. Representation of the Matsyāvatāra in a separate image is not very common in India,[7] and Bengal can claim two—one from Vajrajogini,[8] Dacca, and the other from Serpore,[9]

---

1. For different varieties of Viṣṇu, see Viṣṇumūrti-Paricaya by V. Vidyavinode. So far as we know, varieties of Nārāyaṇa, Hṛṣikeśa and Śrīdhara have been discovered. See VSPC No. F (a) 1/352 ; JASB, 1932, p. 179 ; VRSR, 1928-29, p. 18.

2. VRS, Monograph, No. 4, pp. 30-3/.

3. JASB, 1936, p. 11, Pl. II, fig. 1.

4. VRS. Monograph, No. 4, Pl. III, No. 12

5. Bīrabhūma-Vivaraṇa, fig. 83.

6. DMC., No. 3A (1) a/5 ; ESMS, p. 103.

7. ASIR, 1924-25, p. 154.

8. DMC., No. 3A (1) d/1.

9. Pravāsī, 1338 B. S., pp. 516 ff.

Bogra. On ordinary images of Viṣṇu this form is indicated by a fish. In these two specimens the god is represented as half-fish (lower half) and half-man with usual attributes in four hands and with Lakṣmī and Sarasvatī on his two sides. Images of the Varāha-avatāra are rather common, the VRSM. possessing the largest number. The images of Narasiṁha-avatāra are also fairly common. Three Narasiṁha images[1] in the Abdullapur Vaiṣṇava monastery have six hands instead of four, the two additional ones being in the Abhaya and Tarjanī mudrās. In the images of the Vāmana-avatāra the attempt to chastise the demon king Bali by raising the left foot in order to cover three worlds is cleverly depicted.[2] The image of Paraśurāma is extremely rare in Bengal. The *DMC.*[3] describes one from Ranihati Deul, Purapara in Vikrampur. The only difference from an ordinary Viṣṇu image is that the god holds a *paraśu* instead of the *gadā*.

Many square slabs of stone or metal with the image of Viṣṇu on one side and his ten incarnations on the other in a circular order have been discovered and very appropriately called Viṣṇupaṭṭas.[4] Most probably they are the *Yantras* used by the Tantrika Vaiṣṇavas, The finest specimen is from Khāḍi, Sunderbans.[5]

The images of Balarāma are not very common. The VRSM.[6] possesses one from Dinajpur. The god is standing under a five-hooded snake canopy. The first right hand holds a cup (of wine ?), the second a club and the first left a plough and the other rests on the knee. It may be noted that one image among the Kurkihar

---

1. DMC., Pl. XXXVII bcd.

2. A pot-bellied and comparatively short sized Viṣṇu in IM, in the usual standing posture is described by R. D. Banerjee as Vāmana. We think there is nothing to regard it as an image of Vamana-avatāra except its short size. ESMS, Pl. XLVIIa.

3. Pl. XXXIXb

4. DMC, p. 89.

5. Antiquities of Khāḍi, (Sunderbans) by Mr. K. D. Mitra in VRSR, 1928-29.

6. E (d) 1/386,

(Bihar) finds has been identified with Balarāma,[1] and another of the reign of Devapāla has been found at Nālandā.[2]

Garuḍa appears in Viṣṇu images as kneeling on the right knee with folded hands in adoration. He is sometimes represented as a human being[3] and occasionally as a bird proper.[4] The separate images of two-winged Garuḍa with folded palms are common. They might have adorned the pillars in front of Vaiṣṇava temples. The crowning figure of the Dinajpur Vaiṣṇava pillar is a double-sided Garuḍa. The *DMC.*[5] describes a fine specimen of a double-sided Garuḍa image. The VRSM. specimen[6] from Nagail, Rajshahi, is aslo a good piece of sculpture. The wooden image of Garuḍa from Raghurampur is of fine workmanship.[7]

The images of Lakṣmīnārāyaṇa are not very common and only four of them are known.[8] Representation of Lakṣmī in separate images is not also very common. The *VRSC.* reports the acquisition of three metal images from Bogra and the VSPM.[9] has one from Bhagalpur. Separate images of Sarasvatī are also rare. The DM. specimen comes from Tolbari Bhita near the *Nāstika Paṇḍitera Bhiṭā* (generally supposed to be Atīśa Dīpaṅkara's home) at Vajrayogini, Vikrampur. In the three specimens in VRSM. from Bogra and Rajshahi the ram appears as her *vāhana,* while the known *Dhyānas* direct it to be the swan. Dr. N. K. Bhattasali[10] draws attention to the 7th *Adhyāya,* 12th *Kāṇḍa* of the *Śatapatha Brāhmaṇa,* which connects a ram with Sarasvatī worship. The practice of sacrificing the ram is still observed in some parts of the Dacca district.

---

1. Transaction and Proceedings of the Seventh Oriental Conference, p. 799.

2. ASIR. 1920-21, p. 35.

3. ESMS, p. 106; VRSC, No. E (a) 17/2

4. Ibid, E (a) 1/9.

5. 3A (1) c/2.

6. ESMS, Pl. XCIa.

7. DMC, No. 3A (i) e/1.

8. DMC., No. 3A (i) b/1; Mr. S. K. Saraswati notices three images in his reports of his tours in Malda and Dinajpur. See JASB, 1936, pp. 9 ff. Another image reproduced in Bīrabhūma-Vivaraṇa.

9. K (a) 1/265.

10. DMC, p. 187.

Śaivism—The spread of Śaivism in Bengal is obscure. In the Gunaighar grant of 508 A.D. Vainyagupta is styled as *paramaśaiva,* and in course of the description of the boundary of the donated land to the Buddhist monastery a temple of Pradyumneśvara has been referred to. The existence of a Śaiva temple in the Tippera district in this period indicates that Śaivism had considerable influence by that time. The bull symbol of the coins of Samācāradeva and Śaśāṅka shows that they most probably belonged to this sect. The seal of the Asrafpur plates of the Khaḍgas bears a bull couchant, and the queen Prabhāvatī, wife of Devakhaḍga, consecrated a Śarvāṇī image. In spite of their ardent devotion to Buddhism it seems that the Khaḍgas had Śivaite sympathies also.

Śiva has been represented in various forms at Paharpur and four of them have been described in the report of the Archæological Survey. In these four forms he has the *ūrdhva liṅga (penis erectus)* and has his third eye on the forehead, which along with the presence of *akṣamālā* and *kamaṇḍalu* go to signify his ascetic aspect. (1) The scene of offering poison has been depicted in a simple but dignified way. (2) There is another standing Śiva image with a kneeling bull to his right with a heavy staff *(triśūla?)* in the left hand. (3) In another image his right hand shows *varada* pose and the left holds the *triśūla.* (4) In another there is a halo round the head and his two hands hold *akṣamālā* and *kamaṇḍalu.*

In the Pāla and Sena periods Śiva was worshipped in various forms, of which two-armed Śiva, Sadāśiva, Bhairava, Kalyāṇasundara or Vaivāhikamūrti, Umā-Maheśvara or Umāliṅganamūrti and Naṭarāja types seem to have been popular. Four images of two-armed Śiva are known. They look like Viṣṇu images excepting their characteristic Śaiva symbols, the bull, tridents and *Urdhvaliṅga.*[2] The seal attached to the Sena grants bears the figure of ten-armed Sadāśiva. The VRSM. has three Sadāśiva images and the VSPM.,

---

1. 1926-27, pp. 146-47

2. Two in the VRSM, described in VRSC as Harihara, p. 11; and two in the IM., ASIR, 1930-34, p. 262, Pl. CXXXII. d.

two.[1] Bhairava was originally an attendant of, or emanation from Śiva and instead of the bull, the dog is the *vāhana* of Bhairava. The VRSM. has four,[2] the DM. possesses one and the Nahar collections, Calcutta, contains a fine specimen. Kalyāṇasundara images can be divided into two classes. In one class Gaurī stands in front of Śiva[3] and in another to his left.[4] Umā-Maheśvara images predominate over all other Śiva images, and both metal and stone specimens are common. It is noteworthy that all the known images of Naṭarāja Śiva excepting one from Govindapur in N.W. Sunderbans[5] come from eastern Bengal (Dacca and Tippera districts). The Naṭarāja images can be divided into two classes—ten-handed and twelve-handed varieties.[6]

A rare type of Śiva with a trident and a rosary in two right hands and a skull-head staff and skull bowl in the left two is worshipped at Kasipura, Backerganje. Pārvatī and Gaṅgā stand on two sides and small figures of Ganeśa and Kārtikeya are also noticeable.[7] The eight-armed Aghora images are not common and only three specimens are known.[8] The VRSM. possesses aunique specimen of Ardhanārīśvara from Purapara, Vikrampur, whose images

1. Another image has been discovered recently from Dinajpur and it is reported that it will be preserved in the IM. Mr. H. D. Mitra contributes a very informative paper on Sadāśiva worship in Bengal, see SASB, 1933, pp. 171 ff. Mr. Mitra places the earliest image of Sadāśiva in Bengal in c. 950-1000 A. D. Most probably the ten-handed Śiva in Bīrabhūma-Vivaraṇa, fig. 19. is an image of Sadāśiva. It may be noted that there is none from eastern Bengal.

2. The image described in VRSC. 26, as Revanta seems to be a representation of Bhairava The image illustrated in Bīrabhūma-Vivaraṇa against page 188 appears to be that of Bhairava.

3. DMC., Pl. XLVIIa.

4. Ibid., Pl. XLVIIb.

5. VRS, Monograph, No. 5, fig. 7.

6. DMC., P. 111, Nos, 3A (ii) a/3 are broken.

7. Dr. N. K. Bhattasali calls it Nīlakaṇṭha but admits that the Dhyāna prescribes five heads, while the present image has only four but the attributes in the hands agree. DMC, p. 117.

8. DMC., Pl. XLVII; VRS, Monograph, No. 5, fig. 9, another at Bhardraśila, Dinajpur, JASB, 1936, p. 12.

are of extreme rarity[1] in Bengal. The images from Purapara, Vikrampur, are said to have been worshipped by Vallālasena and one of his queens.[2] It may be mentioned that the Naihati plate of Vallālasena opens with an invocation to the Ardhanārīśvara form of Śiva. The VSPM.[3] has one broken image which appears to represent a seated Śiva *(Dhyānī Śiva ?)*

The worship of Śiva in his phallic emblem was widely popular. The known *Liṅgas* can be divided into four classes. (1). The plain *Liṅga* with *yoni* or *agrapaṭṭa* is represented as plain cylinder with a circular platform around its middle. They are very common and one inscribed in the 7th-8th century script has been found along with the Śarvāṇī image of queen Prabhāvatī.[4]

(2). The cylinder with one face of Śiva is called *Ekamukha Liṅga.*[5]

(3). *Liṅgas* with the bust of Śiva on four sides of the cylinder is called *Caturmukha Liṅga* to which reference has been made in the Bodh-Gaya inscription of the 26th year of Dharmapāla. One specimen is at Aminpur, Dinajpur.[6]

(4). The VRSM. has four *Liṅgas* encircled by four effigies of Devī and a similar one is at Delbandh, Dinajpur.[7]

The bull, the *Vāhana* of Śiva, was generally placed in the outer wall of his temple. The DM. and VRSM. each has a massive bull and another is in the Dinajpur Collectorate.

The images of Gaṇeśa are common. Generally we meet with seated or dancing Gaṇeśa with four or eight hands.[8] The VRSM.

---

1. The VRSC. No. C (e) 2/288 is a fragmentary image from Akṣayavaṭa, Gaya.
2. DMC., p. 131.
3. G (c) 1/341.
4. DMC., pl. LXX.
5. VRSC., No. C (a) 1/82 ; one from Mangolkot, Burdawn. see ESMS. pl. Ela, one at Unakoti, Tippera.
6. JASB, 1932, p. 187 ; for two others see *infra*.
7. Ibid, pp. 188-89.
8. Mr. B. Bhattacharyya describes eight varities of Gaṇeśas. But as the attributes do not agree with his lists, it is difficult to classify them accordingly, see Indian Images, p. 18

has the largest number of dancing Gaṇeśas. The *DMC.*[1] *and VRSC.*[2] each describes a six-handed Gaṇeśa. The *DMC.* describes a unique five-faced and ten-armed dancing Gaṇeśa from Vikrampur, and the learned compiler of the *Catalogue* has quoted a *Dhyāna* from the *Sāradātilaka Tantra,* which enables him to identify it as an image of the Heramba variety of Gaṇeśa. Images of Kārtikeya are not very common. The *DMC.* describes only one and the VRSM. has three, of which No. C(g)1/181 is described as very old. The IM.[4] has acquired a splendid image of Kārtikeya from northern Bengal.

Śaiva and Śākta goddesses—Durgā is the śakti of Śiva and was worshipped in various forms. Her images of different varieties have been discovered but not properly classified. It can well be understood how many different forms she had from the simple fact that the *Devīpurāṇa*[5] alone mentions 62 types. A remarkable image of a goddess is worshipped at Kāgajipāḍā (paper-makers' village), Vikrampur. The lower half is a finely carved *Liṅga* from which she emerges. She holds a rosary and a book in the upper two hands and the lower two are placed one on another in Dhyānamudrā. The goddess has been tentatively identified as Mahāmāyā.[6] Images of Gaurī are common. The *DMC.* describes three and most of the ten images described in the *VRSC.* under the heading Caṇḍī with *Godhikā (mongoose)* as the vehicle are representations of Gaurī.[7] The *VRSC.* N. D(a)7/184 appears to be an image of Umā, as the goddess holds a mirror which differentiates her from Gaurī and Pārvatī.[8]

1. DMC. p. 146
2. G (b) 1/224. For another six-handed dancing Gaṇeśa, see Mediæval Indian Sculptures in the British Museum by R. P. Chanda pl. XXI
3. DMC, pp. 146-47
4. ASIR, 1934-35, pl. XXIVd
5. Vaṅgavāsī edition, Ch. LX, pp 180 ff
6. DMC, pp. 192-3, pl. XIV.
7. Also see the goddess at Mahesvarapasa, Khulna, ESMS, pl. LVIIc and the image illustrated in Bīrbhūma-Vivaraṇa against page 192 (Vol. II) fig. 67
8. Gopinath Rao, Elements of Hindu Iconography, Vol. I, Pt. II, pp. 113, 120

Images of Pārvatī are fairly common. The *Liṅga* along with the rosary in the right hands is her distinctive feature. Three images[1] have been described in the *VRSC.* as Siṁhavāhinī. One has eight hands and the other two have four each. The attributes in them have not been mentioned. But it seems clear that they represent Durgā in one or another form, as the *Vāhana* lion shows. The standing goddess[2] with the lion as *Vāhana* from Mangalbari,, Dinajpur, holds in her upper two hands a *triśūla* and an *aṅkuśa* and the other two are lost. She also represents a form of Durgā. An uncommon type of Caṇḍī[3] of the 3rd year of Lakṣmaṇasena's reign is worshipped in the Dacca town. There is a lion couchant on the pedestal and the goddess has a battle axe in her upper right hand. Two elephants sprinkle water on her and two females with fly-whisks attend her. But for the short inscription which labels her as Caṇḍī, it would have been very difficult to identify her, as it differs from known examples. The metal image of eight-armed Śarvāṇī installed by queen Prabhāvatī was discovered at Deulbadi, Tippera. Two rare and unique images of Devī have been discovered in Jessore and Birbhum, and their identification is far from certain. A six-handed goddess seated on a lotus, which is supported by a lion, is worshipped at Sankhahati, Jessore, as Bhuvaneśvarī.[4] R. D. Banerjee labels it as Pārvatī.[5] She is seated in *ardhaparyaṅka-āsana* with her right foot pendant on the lion and the pedestal contains two other small lions. The two lower left hands hold the *Kamaṇḍalu* and *Triśūla* and the other shows *Abhaya* pose. The two upper right hands hold a lotus and a rosary and the other exhibits the *Varada* pose. The form of Bhuvaneśvarī as described by Mr. Gopinath Rao[6] is four-handed. Otherwise, it agrees with the details. The

---

1. Nos. D(c)1/130, D(c)2/32, D(c)3/29
2. ESMS, pl. LVIa
3. DMC; pl. LXIX.
4. S. C. Mitra, History of Jessore and Khulna (in Bengali) p. 240.
5. ESMS, pl. LVIIIa.
6. Op. Cit., Vol. I Pt. II, p. 37 ; see also Rao's descripiion of Tulasīdevī ; see also the descriptions of Vijayā and Umā in the Devīpurāṇa. pp. 185 ff. But all of them are four-handed. Mr. S. C. Mitra proposes to identify her with Tripureśvarī of the Tantrasāra.

other image[1] at Deuli, Birbhum is a ten-armed goddess, standing in *Atibhaṅga* pose. Three images discovered from that village are said to have been installed by the Sena kings. The *Vāhana* seems to be a lion. The attributes in four left hands are *Triśūla, Darpaṇa, Dhanuḥ,* and *Kamaṇḍalu,* and the attribute or the posture in the lowest left hand is indistinct. The two upper right hands hold *Khaḍga* and *Pāśa* and the attributes in other three are indistinct. The image seems to be a representation of Maṅgalā as described by Gopinath Rao[2] or Mahādevī of the *Devīpurāṇa.*[3] An eighteen-handed goddess seated on a lotus supported by a lion has been discovered at Simla, Rajshahi, and has been indentified with Mahālakṣmī.[4]

The above forms of Devī show, on the whole, beatific countenances inspite of many weapons in her hands and she does not actually fight. Let us now describe her images in fighting mood. Three Vāgīśvarī images are known.[5] The *VRSC.* No. A(g)1/110 and the specimen in Dinajpur Raj palace have eight hands. Six additional hands hold different weapons and one of the normal two shows *Abhaya* pose and the other is engaged in drawing out the tongue of the demon. The specimen from Kachra is a four-handed image.[6] The known images of Mahiṣamardinī can be classified according to the number of hands. Eight and ten[7]-armed varieties are common. A splendid and remarkable six-armed image with an inscription written in seventh century script has been acquired by the VRSM. from Gangarampur, Malda.[8] A specimen of twelve-armed variety in metal was discovered at Kesavpur, Dinajpur.[9] Two specimens of eighteen-handed Mahiṣamardinī are known and the distinctive feature of the image at Vakreśvara,

---

1. Birbhūma-Vivarṇa, Vol. II, illustrated against p. 23
2. Rao, Hindu Iconography, Vol. I, Pt. II, p. 359.
3. p. 185.
4. VRS, Monograph, No. 6, fig. 4, pp. 21 ff.
5. JASB, 7932. p. 183 6. VRSR, 1932-34. pl. IV, fig. 6
7. It is difficult to understand why both R. D. Banerjee and Dr. N, K. Bhattasali think ten-armed variety as rare. The DMC. describes two such images and the VRSM. has three.
8. VRSR, 1931-32, pl. I. 9. ESMS, pl. LIIIc.

Birbhum, is that the goddess is surrounded by other fighting goddesses.[1] Mr. S. K. Saraswati has discovered a remarkable and unique image with thirty-two hands (called by him a form of Caṇḍikā) at Betna, Dinajpur.[2]

Cāmuṇḍā is one of the terrible forms of the Devī in which she appeared to kill the demons Caṇḍa and Muṇḍa. Various forms of Cāmuṇḍā are known. (1) Kṣamā with two hands. The image at Amadi, Jessore,[3] seems to represent this type. It is defaced and broken and the identification is therefore uncertain. The *VSPC*. No. J. (b) 1/345 appears to be an image of this type. (2) The *VRSC*. No. D (d) 9/207 is a four-handed Cāmuṇḍā on an ass with the words *Piśitāsanā* inscribed on it. Dr. N. K. Bhattasali is inclined to identify this image with the variety of Kālikā Cāmuṇḍā of the *Matsyapurāna*. (3) Dhāntura is represented with her left knee pressed against the ground and the right one raised. The left hand is placed on the seat and the right one rests on the raised knee. Three images of this type are known. The earliest is at Katason, Dinajpur, and another at Dinajpur.[4] The best specimen is in VSPM. from Attahasa, Burdwan. (4) Rudra-Cāracikā has six hands. The VRSC. Nos. D (d) 10/280 and D (d) 7/384 represent this variety and on the former the word Cāracikā is actually inscribed. (5). Rudra-Cāmuṇḍā has eight arms. The image illustrated in the *Bīrabhūma-Vivaraṇa,* Vol. II, against p. 124 seems to be an image of this type.[5] (6). Siddha-Cāmuṇḍā has ten arms and images of this type are fairly common.[6] (7) Siddha-Yogeśvarī and Rūpa-Vidyā have twelve arms. The *VRSC*. No. D (d)

---

1. Bīrabhūma-Vivaraṇa, illustrated in Vol. II, against p. 158. The other is at Panighat, Khulna, illustrated in S. C. Mitra's History of Jessore and Khulna against p. 170

2. JASB. 1932, pl. IX, fig. 2

3. Illustrated in the History of Jessore and Khulna, against p. 166

4. JASB, 1932, pl. V. III, fig. 2

5. It is described in the above book as Fulleśvarī Devī

6. The image illustrated in Bīrabhūma-Vivaraṇa against p. 144 appears to be of this class and also VRSC, Nos. 3, 5, 6 and also Cāmuṇḍā at Betna, JASB, 1932, pl. IX, fig. 3

2/252 and *DMC.* No. 3B (ii) h/1 may belong to these two varieties.[1]

A few representations of *Mātṛkās* have been found, but their worship is not prevalent at present. The *VRSM.* has two slabs. No. D (e) 1/7 represents nine Mātṛkās—(1) Brahmāṇī, (2) Raudrī, (3) Kumārī, (4) Vāgīśvarī, (5) Mahiṣamardinī, (6) Varāhī, (7) Indrāṇī, (8) Cāmuṇḍā and (9) Siṁhavāhinī. The other specimen contains seven of them. Besides, the VRSM. has three Varāhīs and one Vaiṣṇavī. The VSPM. has one slab from Devagram, Nadia, representing Brahmāṇī.

Generally, images of Gaṅgā and Yamunā adorn the doors of temples. All the images of Gaṅgā discovered so far are good pieces of sculpture and the *Vāhana* Makara is tastefully represented. The VRSM. has two, and the *Bīrabhūma-Vivaraṇa*[2] illustrates two. One Gaṅgā image is worshipped in the Jaśoreśvarī temple, Khulna,[3] and another at Bhadrasila, Dinajpur.[4] Separate images of Yamunā are rare.

The section on Śaiva images cannot be closed without a passing reference to two important Śaiva centres at Unakoti in Hill Tippera and Deopara in the Rajshahi district. The name Ūnakoṭi is in imitation of the Koṭi-tīrtha (Kāśī) in which place, according to tradition, there are a crore of Śaiva images, and Ūnakoṭi was, as its name implies, second to Koṭi-tīrtha in importance to the Śaivas. There are many sculptures lying scattered here and there on the hill and on the rocky bed of the stream there. What is more interesting is that there are a series of colossal heads and figures carved on the rock. The central figure is a colossal Śiva head of "about 30ft. high, including the high embroidered head-dress which is itself 10ft. in height." There are other gigantic figures of Śiva and Gaṇeśa. A standing figure of Śiva holds the conch and the rosary in the right and left hands respectively. Figures of six and eight-handed Gaṇeśa stand erect with attenuated waists with three and four tusks. There is a Viṣṇu image, resembling that of the Sun-god. Besides, there are images of Hara, Gaurī, Hari-

1. In the description of Cāmuṇḍā images we have followed the Agnipurāṇa

2. Vol. II, against pp. 74, 76

3. ESMS, pl. LXID.

4. JASB, 1936, pl. I, fig. 2

hara, Narasiṁha, Hanumāna, *Ekamukha and Caturmukha Liṅgas.* The site seems to have been sacred to the Śaivas since the 9th century A.D.[1]

The gorgeous and magnificent temple of Pradyumneśvara (Śiva and Viṣṇu combined) at Deopara which has been described by Umāpatidhara in flattering terms is no more. The tank in front of it is called Padumsahar tank and the numerous sculptures found in it in course of excavations and preserved in the *VRSM.* go to show its importance as a religious centre.

Two inscriptions from southern India enable us to form an idea of the esteem and veneration in which the Śaivas of Gauḍa were held there. A Tanjore inscription[2] records that Rājendra Cola built the Rājarājeśvara temple and appointed Sarvaśiva Paṇḍita-Śivācārya as the priest of that temple and further directed that thenceforth the *śiṣyas* and their *śisyas* alone, belonging to Āryadeśa and Gauḍadeśa should be eligible for the office of the chief priest. It is stated in a commentary on the *Siddhānta-Sārāvalī* of Trilocana Śivācārya that Rājendra Cola imported Śaivas from the banks of the Ganges.[3] A record[2] of the fifth year of the Cola king Parakeśarīvarman (Rājādhirājadeva) states that the worship of Śiva by Umāpatideva, *alias* Jñāna Śivadeva, a native of Dakṣiṇa-Lāla in Gauḍadeśa, was responsible for the defeat of an invading Ceylonese army which was desolating the Pāṇḍya country. For this act by which the grace of Śiva was attained, Śivācārya was granted a village, the income from which he distributed among his relations. According to Venkyya, this invasion took place in the 3rd quarter of the 12th century.

Saura images—Next to those of Viṣṇu, the images of the Sun-god are the most numerous in Bengal, but his worship is now dying out. He is generally represented with four hands, the upper two holding lotus stalks. He is dressed in *udīcya-veśa,* ie., northern dress. The upper half of the body is covered with a coat of mail and the lower

1. ASIR, 1921-22, p. 87 2. SII², Pt. I, p. 105

3. Nilakantha Sastri, The Colas, p. 254; an image of Gaṇeśa of the Pāla school has been found in a Tanjore temple, and it has been suggested that it was carried by the army of Rājendra Cola, JIH, 1934, 306-11

4. Rangachariar, Inscriptions of the Madras Presidency, I, p. 388

half is clad in a short skirt tied by an ornamental belt with two daggers on two sides. His legs are covered with boots in accordance with the canonical injunction that they should not be shown bare in any case. This feature is characteristic also of his attendants. His two wives Uṣā and Pratyuṣā stand by his two sides and the third Mahāśvetā in front.[1] His male attendants are Daṇḍa and Piṅgala and his charioteer is half-bird Aruṇa. In some images the Ādityas, the seven Ṛṣis, seven Mātṛkās, the planets and the zodiac signs are represented.[2] The VRSM. has some unique varieties of Sūrya images. The VRSM, No. 693 is a two-handed Sūrya with a circular halo round his head and has been assigned to the late Gupta period.[3] The lower parts of his legs are not shown at all and are covered by the figure of Aruṇa. The only other image[4] of this type has been discovered at Khadi (Sunderbans). In this image the driving of the chariot by holding the reins of the horses is clearly exhibited and has made it more realistic. In these two specimens his three wives are conspicuous by their absence. The VRSM. has acquired a six-handed Sūrya from Mahendra, Dinajpur.[5] The two uppermost hands hold lotus stalks, the intermediate hands have *Akṣamālā* and *Varada-mudrā* and the remaining two have a *Kamaṇḍalu* and *Varada-mudrā*. It has been suggested that it represents the first of the twelve Ādityas, as described in the *Viśvakarmā-śātra*.[6] The only discrepancy is that it prescribes four hands and the two hands showing *Varada* and *Abhaya* mudrās were not perhaps considered essential in the canon. A ten-armed and three-faced (or four faced with the uncarved one at the back) Sūrya has been acquired from Manda, Rajshai. Its existing six hands hold Śakti, Triśūla and Khaṭvāṅga (right) and lotus,

1. According to some description his wives Sureṇu and Nikṣubhā are on two sides, and the other Uṣā in front.

2. DMC, Nos. 3A (iii) a/2, 3 (iii) a/4, and pl. LX, illustrating Sūrya from Sonarang

3. VRSR, 1926-27, fig. I, p. 8.

4. Ibid., 1928-29, fig 17.

5. Ibid., 1932-34, fig I.

6. JASB, 1923, pp. 191-92

Ḍamaru and Sarpa (left). The attributes show, as has been rightly observed, that it was composite image of Sūrya[1] and Bhairava, and it most probably represents Sūrya in his Mārtaṇḍa-Bhairava form, as described in the *Sāradātilaka Tantra.*. But it is to be noted that this *Tantra* prescribes four heads and eight hands. Seated Sūrya images are rare. A metal specimen, dateable in the 7th or 8th century A.D., was found at Deulbadi.[2] A stone image of a seated Sūrya[3] has been discovered at Ekdala, Dinajpur, and the god looks like a *Dhyānī-mūrti.* The pose is unrealistic for one who is mounted on a moving chariot.

A few images of the hunting god Revanta, son of the Sun-god, are known. The VRSM. has two and the DM. has one only and another is at Sonapur, Dinajpur.[4] Navagrahas or nine planets were worshipped. They are the Ravi, Soma, Maṅgala, Budha, Bṛhaṣpati, Śukra, Śani, Rāhu and Ketu. A fine specimen of a Navagraha slab has been discovered at Kankaṇdighi in the Sunderbans.[5] The VRSM. has four slabs. It is to be noted that Gaṇeśa also appears in the company of nine planets.

Other gods and goddesses—Brahmā, Viṣṇu and Śiva constitute the Hindu Trinity. While Viṣṇu and Śiva each has such a large following, the god of creation does not claim the allegiance of many. Even his wife Sarasvatī has been afterwards appropriated by Viṣṇu. A fairly large number of images of Brahmā have been found in Bengal but it is to be noted that not a single specimen from eastern Bengal is known. The VRSM. has about ten images[6] but the best specimen[7] is in the VSPM. from Rajganj, Dinajpur.

---

1. IHQ., 1930, p. 465 ff.
2. DMC, LIX; For another seated Sūrya, see Bīrabhūma-Vivaraṇa, Vol. II, against 140.
3. JASB, 1932, pp. 147 ff.
4. Ibid, 1936, Pl. 2, fig. 4. The IM. possesses four from Bihar.
5. VRSR, 1928-29, fig 5.
6. Ibid., 1930-31, fig 5; 1928-29, fig. 5.
7. VSPC, Pl. VI.

A fair number of a species of bas-reliefs showing mainly the mother and the child have been found in northern Bengal. A controversy is raging about its identification. A lady is represented lying down on a couch in reclining position with her left elbow pressed against a pillow and supporting her head. A child is shown lying down close to the left side. A female shampoons her feet and other females attend her, ministering to her comforts. Gaṇeśa Kārikeya, *Liṅga* and Navagrahas are placed above the couch. According to Dr. N. K. Bhattasali,[1] their presence points to the Śaiva nature of the Mother and Child images and he proposes to identify the child with the Sadyajāta form of Śiva but admits that no appropiate Dhyāna can be cited. Mr. N. B. Sanyal[2] refers to the description of the birth of Kṛṣṇa in the *Bhaviṣyottara Purāṇa* in order to support the view that the Mother and Child images represent that scene. According to him, "the Navagrahas indicate the benign influence of the planets on the newly born baby. *Liṅga* (signifying Śiva) is connected with the birth of Kṛṣṇa, as he (Śiva) is said to have addressed a hymn to Kṛṣṇa when in his mother's womb. The presence of Gaṇeśa means allaying of all troubles".

The worship of the snake goddess Manasā is very popular in Bengal and her images are common. She seems to have overshadowed Sarasvatī and the Buddhist Jāṅgulī who are also destroyers of the snake-poison, so far as that aspect of these two goddesses is concerned.[3] The IM. No. 3950 shows a goddess under a hood of seven serpents with the book and pitcher in her left hands and with the rosary and boon in the right. The goddess Manasā seems to be an importation from southern India and has not been included definitely in any pantheon, Vaiṣṇava or Śaiva. Generaly Manasā is represented with two hands, seated on a lotus under a seven-hooded snake canopy with a snake in her hand. A pitcher is seen underneath her seat on the pedestal. In a *stotra*[4] she is conceived as the spiritual daughter of

1. DMC, pp. 134 ff.

2. VRSR, 1928-29, pp. 19 ff; Transactions and Proceedings of the seventh Oriental Conference, p. 774.

3. The section on Manasā by Dr. N. K. Bhattasali in DMC, is very informative on this point. I think his conclusions are worth accepting.

4. Ibid.

Śiva and in a VRSM. specimen the *Liṅga* appears on the top of the halo[1] The Rangpur Sahitya Parisat collection has a four-handed Manasā with a child on her lap and another specimen of a miniature Manasā has been discovered at Paharpur.[2] Another metal specimen of a Manasā image with a child on her lap has been recently added to the IM. from northern Bengal.[3]

Images of Indra, Agni and Yama have been found in the old Paharpur temples as guardians of quarters. The VRSM. has two images of Yama with the buffalo as his *Vāhana* and has also an image of Agni with the goat as his vehicle. As in the Paharpur specimen[4] of Agni flames are shooting out from his person. An image of Kuvera has been found at Chatrabhog, Sunderbans.[5] Separate images of Nāga and Nāginīs are rare in Bengal, although some specimens[6] of their representations in the IM. come from Bihar. An image of Kāma has been recently added to the IM. from northern Bengal.[7] In the Varāha image[8] in VRSM. from Silimpur the lower parts of the Nāgas and Nāginīs are gracefully intertwined. In the Manasā image[9] from Silghat we find Nāgas and Nāginīs hanging on two sides of the goddess, thus making a suitable back-ground for the snake goddess, the daughter of the Nāgas.

The above account does not exhaust the images of the Brahmanical gods and goddesses and many of them (specially in the VRSM.)[10] remain unidentified. The current dictum that the Hindus

---

1. ASIR, 1921-22, p. 112.
2. VRS, Monograph, No, p. 30. For a Dhyāna of four handed Manasa as Madonna, see DMC, p. 227,
3. ARIR, 1934-35, Pl. XXVb.
4. Ibid., 1926-27, Pl. XXXIId.
5. VRSR, No. 4, fig. 11.
6. The IM has four of them.
7. ASIR, 1934-35, p. 79.
8. VRSR, 1930-31, fig. 3.
9. DMC., Pl, LXXIII.
10. VRSC, pp. 31-33 ; JASB, 1936, Pl, III, fig, 6 ; See the broken image illustrated in Birabhūma-Viyaraṇa, Vol. I, against p. 140.

have thirty-three crores of gods and goddesses may not be actually true but it goes to indicate the richness of their pantheon.

The majority of the sculptures discovered in Bengal belong to the period between the 10th and 12th centuries A.D. Only four Buddhist images[1] can be somewhat confidently assigned to the Gupta and post-Gupta periods. Besides the Paharpur finds, we have noticed a comparatively large number of the Brahmanical images of this period. Very few images of Bengal can be definitely assigned to the 8th and 9th centuries.[2] From the 10th century onward the Brahmanical images far excel in number those of the Buddhists, and of them the images of Viṣṇu and Sūrya predominate. Śaivas and Śāktas worshipped a large number of gods and goddesses, and if none of them singly did command so great and wide popularity like Viṣṇu and Sūrya, their combined strength indicates that they had a great following and were as important in influence as the Vaiṣṇavas and Sauras. It was in this period that we meet gross Tantrik images, and both Buddhist and Brahmanical gods were represented with their respective Śaktis in different poses. The Hindus did not go to excess like the later Buddhists by repesenting their gods and goddesses in *Yab-Yum*.

Relation between different religions and sects—A study of the inscriptions and images reveals some interesting facts on this topic.

---

1. Buddha from Biharail, Manjuśrī and Bodhisattva from Mahasthan and Tārā from Sukhavaspur (in DM.). For references see supra.

2. R. D. Banerjee, "observed in this period there is a great paucity of Brahmanical or Hindu images in south Bihar as well as northern and western Bengal, but such is not the case in eastern Bengal The collection in DM. is specially rich in Brahmanical images of the 9th and 10th centuries and at the same time, it must be admitted that as none of them is inscribed, their attribution is open to doubt." His view was based on the date of the Khaḍgas who, according to him, flourished in the 9th and 10th centuries. This can no longer be maintained and consequently the Śarvāṇī and Sūrya images from Deulbadi of the time of Prabhāvatī cannot be assigned to the 9th century. we do not find any image in the DM. which can be assigned definitely to that period. But it is to be admitted that many Buddhist images of Bihar belonged to this period. (ESMS, pp. 123-24)

The Chittagong plate of Kāntideva offers an instance of the fact that different members of a family followed different religions according to their personal predilections. Bhadradatta, grandfather of Kāntideva, was a Buddhist. His father Dhanadatta was proficient in the Purāṇic literature and his mother was a devotee of Śiva, but he himself was a Buddhist. The Pālas were Buddhists and their seals show *Dharmacakra* (Buddhist wheel of law). It is stated in the Badal pillar inscription that the king Śūrapāla I attended the religious ceremonies of his Brahmanical minister Kedāramiśra and accepted holy sacrificial water with great respect. Mention may be made of the grant of land by Nārāyaṇapāla for providing couches and seats, medicines for the sick to the congregation of Pāśupata teachers at Kalosapota within the *viṣaya* of Kakṣa in *Tīra-bhukti (Tirhut).* He is said to have built hundreds of temples for the Śaiva ascetics. That he had great devotion for Śiva is also proved by the fact that the land donated by the Bhagalpur plate was done in the name of Śiva (Śiva-bhaṭṭāraka), while all other Pāla kings made their grants in the name of Lord Buddha. Madanapāla granted land to a Brahmana in reward for his teaching the *Mahābhārata* to his chief queen Citramatikādevī like the Hindu custom of paying *dakṣiṇā.* It appears that the Buddhist king Śrīcandra, like the Pālas, took part in the Brahmanical ceremony. The Rampal plate of this king was granted in favour of a Śāntivārika (i.e., the priest in charge of propitiatory ceremonies) and his Dhulla grant was issued on the occasion of the performance of a certain propitiatory rite, called *Adhuta-śānti,* during the *Homacatuṣṭaya.* The seal of the Irda plate of the Kamboja king Nayapāladeva shows *Dharmacakra* device like that of the Pālas, but the record opens with an invocation to Śiva. Rājyapāla, the first known member of the family, was a *Saugata* (*Buddhist*). His son Nārāyaṇapāla was a devotee of Vāsudeva and his other son Nayapāla was a Śaiva. From these instances of the different royal families it seems that the line of demarcation between a Buddhist and a Hindu was not very wide. Different members of a family could pay their homage to different gods according to their personal likings without affecting their normal relationship.

There are instances of borrowing and incorporating some gods and goddesses from one pantheon to another. It is admitted that the Buddhists borrowed Sarasvatī and Vighnanāṭaka from the Hindus,

Cāracikā and Mahākāla are common to both. The representations of Yogāsana Viṣṇu and Dhyānī Śiva seem to have been modelled after Dhyānī Buddha. Appearance of small figures of gods on the top of Brahmanical images[1] reminds us of the presence of parental Dhyānī Buddhas. Buddha was regarded as an incarnation of Viṣṇu[2] perhaps at a time when Hinduism had begun to absorb Buddhism, because the importance and popularity of so great a figure could not be neglected. It was positively advantageous to do so in order to gain the support and following of the faltering ones or of those who had no definite and clear-cut religious convictions. It is now admitted that the Hindus have borrowed Tārā from the Buddhists. In the *Rudrayamāla* and *Brahmayamāla* Vaśiṣṭha has been asked to go to learn the secrets of Tārā worship from Buddha in Cīnabhūmi where he has been residing.[3]

Sometimes peculiar images are discovered, and it is diffiult to ascertain whether they are Buddhist or Brahmanical. An image[4] with a four-handed standing figure (looking like Viṣṇu) has been discovered in northern Bengal. Two main male attendants stand on two sides, and two small figures stand close to them. On the top of the main figure is a small figure (looking like a parental Dhyānī Buddha) and on the pedestal there is a small six-handed dancing figure. The attributes in the four hands of the principal figure appear to be Gadā, Padma, Śaṅkha and Cakra but it is to be admitted that these attributes differ from the representation in an ordinary Viṣṇu image. Mr. N. G. Majumdar[5] suggests that these images may represent the conception

---

1. See Viṣṇu from Laksmanakati, Ugratārā from Sikarpur and Gaurī at Mahesvarapasa, Khulna (ESMS, Pl. LVIIc).

2. R D. Banerjee refers to a slab of ten Avatāras at Bodh-Gaya where the figure of Buddha is defaced. According to him, this was intentional and was due to sectarian jealousy. But this may be accidental too (ESMS, p. 103)

3. For full discussion. see Sādhanamālā, Intro. pp. CXXXVII ff; Memoirs, ASI, No. 11; DMC, p. 206.

4. VRSR, 1928-23, p. 28 ff; Modern Review, 1929, February Issue. This image is from Kalandarpur, Bogra,

5. Ibid,,

of Hindu Trinity, the seated figure at the top being Brahmā and the dancing figure representing Naṭarāja Śiva. Again, it has been contended that the god without his Vāhana Garuḍa and without Lakṣmī and Sarasvatī and with the figure of Amitābha on the top should be regarded as a form of Mañjuśrī.[1] Two almost similar images have been found in northern Bengal[2] with the only difference that the god stands under a seven-hooded snake canopy, which, it has been observed, "probably shows that Viṣṇu is conceived here as Ananta, or the Eternal, the hoods of snake Ananta being utilised to give an idea of eternity". Four images illustrated from different parts of Bengal by R. D. Banerjee[3] are regarded as the blending of Avalokiteśvara and Viṣṇu Three of them have a hooded canopy on the head of the god and on two of them we find a seated figure on the top. The upper parts of the other two are broken and most probably they had also the small seated figure on the top. It is difficult to say what particular deity these images represent, as we have no *Dhyāna* to prove their identity. Two other images[4] from Sagardighi, Murshidabad, look like Viṣṇu or Avalokiteśvara and in them the attendants of Viṣṇu are absent. The attributes in hands are not also clear. One represents a standing figure and the other a seated one and both of them have four hands. Whatever god or gods all these images may represent, the predominant Vaiṣṇava element is evident.

In Java there was a Śiva-Buddha cult in which Buddha was completely identified with Śiva.[5] No definite evidence of the existence of such a cult is known. But it may be noted that at present images of Buddha and Tārā are worshipped as Śiva and Durgā by ignorant village-folk.[6] It is now accepted by many that in many of the later Tantras there has been an admixture of Hindu and Buddhistic doc-

1. VRS, Monograph, No. 4, 11 ff.
2. VRSR, 1932-34, fig 4 ; JASB, 1932, Pl. IX, fig. 1.
3. ESMS, Pl. XXVIII. pp. 134, 124. Three of them are twelve-handed and the specimen in metal has six hands. See also Ibid, pp. 95-96.
4. BI. Pls, XXVI, XXVII.
5. IC, I, p. 284.
6. ESMS, p. 45 ; Birbhūma-Vivaraṇa, p. 238,

trines, and it may be noted that the Hindu Tantras are in dialogue forms between Śiva and Pārvatī. The Śaivite Matsyendranātha and Gorakṣanātha were respected by the Buddhist Sahajayānists.

This shows one side of the picture only. There were enthusiasts in every religion to champion and fight for their own. The Chinese tarvellers record many incidents which go to show that there were debates by important personages of different religions, each trying to uphold their own doctrines and tenets and decrying those of the opposite school. Defeat sometimes meant humiliation and conversion to the victor's side. The Bhuvanesvara *praśasti* alludes to the fact that the scholar-minister Bhaṭṭa Bhavadeva was a great enemy of the Buddhists.[2] Saroha-vajra, a follower of Sahaja-yāna, attacks other systems vehemently and glorifies the efficacy of his own.[3] He shows the inherent inconsistency of the caste system, challenges the authority of the Vedas and criticises the conduct of the ascetics who covered their bodies with ashes. He argues if the nudity of the Jainas is capable of leading to the desired goal, the jackals and dogs would easily attain *siddhi.* In his opinion the great *Śramaṇas* with a large number of disciples earn their livelihood by deceiving the people and the Mahāyānists attempt to explain the *Sūtras* without grasping their meaning. Finally he exalts *Sahajayāna,* the best of all paths and the only surest guarantee to salvation.

There is one aspect in the representation of the Buddhist dieties which has not attracted sufficient attention that it deserves.[4] The desire to prove the superiority of their own gods by humbling those of the Hindus is evident in some of the *Sādhanās.* Hariharihari-

---

1. See the accounts of the lives of Yuan Chwang, Sīlabhadra, and Karṇasuvarṇa specially. The History of Indian Logic shows how the Hindus, Buddhists and Jainas tried to disprove the arguments and reasonings of one another.

2. IB, Bhuvanesvara praśasti, Vs. 20.

3. Intro. Baudha-Gāna-O-Dohā, pp. 6-8.

4. Our thanks are again due to Dr. B. Bhattacharyya who for the first time emphasised this point. Bd. Icon., p. 162, Intro. Sāddanamālā, pp. CXXX ff.

vāhanodbhava (a variety of benign Avalokiteśvara) is to be represented as riding on Nārāyaṇa on Garuḍa. Brahmā, Viṣṇu, Śiva and Indra are called the Māras[1] (wicked beings and hence enemies). Siddhidātā Gaṇeśa is often the target of attack and is trampled upon by many gods and goddesses like Aparājitā, Parṇaśavarī and Mahāpratisarā. Śiva is trampled by Daśabhujā Mārīcī, and Śiva and Gaurī by Trailokyavijaya. Indra who holds the parasol of Aparājitā is trampled on by Aṣṭabhujā Mārīcī, Paramaśva and Prasanna Tārā and pays homage to Ubhayavarāhnanā Mārīcī. Indrāṇī is also mishandled by Paramaśva. The severed head of Brahmā is carried by Prasanna Tārā and Ubhayavarāhānanā Mārīcī. Such humiliating position of the Hindu deities served well the purpose of showing the powerfulness of the Buddhist gods and goddesses to the people at large. The Śūnya-purāṇa, admittedly of Buddhist origin but of uncertain date,[2] gives vent to its wrath against the Hindus when Gaṇeśa is identified with Kazi, Brahmā with Muhammad, Viṣṇu with Payagambar, Śiva with Adam, Nārada with a Sheik and Indra with a Maulanā.

The question has been raised : Does the presence of the Hindu deities Śiva, Viṣṇu, Pārvatī, Gaṇeśa and Manaśā in Nālandā (we may add Bodh-Gaya and the Somapurī-Vihāra at Paharpur) testify to the catholicism and eclecticism of the Buddhists and the assertion of Hinduism over Buddhism ? Mr. Sankalia[3] suggests that the desire of the Buddhist to manifest the deity in various modes and forms as found in Vaisnavism and Śaivism and then to show the superiority of their own gods by humbling them was not perhaps absent. If the Hindu gods could have been regarded as manifestations of Buddhistic deities, it is to be admitted that the line of demarcation was also becoming thinner. With the destruction by the Muslims of the monasteries the chief centres of Buddhistic influence and activities

1. See the sādhanās of Prasanna-Tārā, Vajrajjvālānalarka, Vidyujjvālākarālī.

2. It seems to have been composed after the advent of the Muslims, as the subject matter and developed Bengali forms of tne book show. Edited by C. Bandyopadhyaya, pp. 232 ff.

3. University of Nālandā, p. 139.

were almost extinct, and it is an admitted fact that the Buddhists did not claim so much loyalty and discipline from their lay followers as the Brahmanical religion did. Those who could put a fight with the Hindus became scattered. Their strength was broken and resisting power gone. As the Hindu gods had already begun to satisfy them, there was no great difficulty in merging them in the Hindu society, as the history and fate of Buddhism in India show. Therefore the presence of Hindu gods in the Buddhist strongholds may be taken as the sign of the growing popularity, if not of assertion and encroachment, of Hinduism upon Buddhism.

The relation between different sects of Hinduism is not much known. Most probably the combined images of Brahmā-Viṣṇu[1] and Harihara[2] indicate the attempt to show the harmony and amity between the three principal gods constituting the Hindu Trinity[3]. To a Hindu gods are after all gods and inspite of sectarian differences all gods are to be worshipped and respected, to whatever class they may belong. In the Pāla and Sena periods we have already noted the preponderance of Viṣṇu images which tends to show the popularity of his cult also. In the Tippera grant of Lokanātha ((7th century) Nārāyaṇa is adored by the chief gods, the Asuras, the Sun, the Moon, Kuvera, Kinnarīs, Vidyādharas, chief serpent gods, Gandharvas, Varuṇa, the Yakṣas and also by the Brahmanas. The presence of the images of Viṣṇu at Ūnakoṭi and Deopara, two important centres of Śaivism, certainly testifies to its popularity, if not something more. Śiva is regarded now as a devotee of Viṣṇu, so much so that in Bhuvanesvara Śiva in the Liṅgarāja temple is not worshipped until the worship of Viṣṇu has been finished in the adjacent Ananta-Vāsudeva temple and Śiva has no separate culinary department and he gets *prasāda* from Viṣṇu.[4] Lakṣmaṇasena was a Vaiṣṇava and his ins-

1. ASIR, 1934-35, pp. 79-80.

2. Ibid, 1929-30, Pl. XXVIc.

3. It is rather surprising that R. D. Banerjee finds in them difference of opinions between different sects, ESMS, p. 105.

4. We enquired of a Pāṇḍā in charge of a temple how long since this has been the custom. He told me from the beginning of the creation when these two temples were built by Viśvakarmā. The Liṅga-rāja and Ananta-Vāsudeva temples are not far removed in dates.

criptions open with an invocation to Nārāyaṇa. But the seal attached to them bears the figure of Sadāśiva. Vaiṣṇava influence was felt on the *Tantras* also, which are sometimes referred to as *Āgamas* and *Nigamas*. "An Āgama is so called because it proceeds from the mouth of Śambhu (Śiva) and goes to Girijā (Pārvatī), being approved by Viṣṇu, and a *Nigama* is so called because it is emanated from the mouth of Girijā to enter the ear of Girīśa (Śiva), being approved by Vāsudeva."[1]

In the Ṛg Vedic literature Sūrya occupies a more prominent position than Viṣṇu. In the *Śatapatha Brāhmana* Viṣṇu is one of the twelve Ādityas. But afterwards Viṣṇu superseded Sūrya in importance. The large number of Sūrya images discovered in Bengal is indicative of the popularity of the Saura cult but his worship has now-a-days almost fallen into disuse.[2] Iconographically the representation of a standing four-handed Sūrya on a lotus seat with two wives on two sides and with the charioteer Aruṇa closely resembles that of an ordinary Viṣṇu in the company of Lakṣmī and Sarasvatī with his vāhana Garuḍa. Daṇḍa and Piṅgala may be compared with Jaya and Vijaya. Viśvarūpasena and Keśavasena styled themselves *paramasaura* i.e. devout worshippers of the Sun. But their records open with an invocation to Nārāyaṇa. Vijayasena and Vallālasena were Śaivas, Lakṣmaṇasena a Vaiṣṇava, and Viśvarūpasena and Keśavasena Sauras. But the seals of their inscriptions invariably bear the figure of Sadāśiva. This is perhaps an indication of the fact that sectarianism was not carried too far, and that gods of other sects who did not command special reverence from one particular individual were not disrespected, if not actually worshipped.

1. Intro. the Principles of Tantras, XXI, fn.
2. SPP, 1340 B. S., p. 1.
3. B. Bhattacharyya, Indian Images, p 18 for further elucidation of this poi

CHAPTER XII

ART AND ARCHITECTURE

Very few images of Paharpur finds of the Gupta and post-Gupta periods have been illustrated. The illustrated images show soft, fine and lively modelling and easy flow of lines that are characterics of Gupta art. It has been said that Paharpur images "combine in them the broad intellectualism of the Gupta epoch with the emotionalism of Bengal", but it must be observed that they appear to be of inferior workmanship in suggestiveness and refined dignity to the famous panels of the Daśāvatāra temple at Deogadh, Jhansi. The standing Buddha image from Biharoil, Rajshahi,[1] in Cunar sandstone has the common characteristics of a Sarnath Buddha with its diaphanous robe, curly hair, and had not the find-spot been known, it could have easily passed for a Sarnath image. The copper image of Viṣṇu from Kumarpur, Rajshahi,[2] is a crude product and has no artistic pretension. Mahiṣamardinī[3] from Gangarampur, Malda, has an inscription in the seventh century script and is in gray sandstone. It has the majesty and grandeur of the Śaiva panels of Elephanta. Sūrya[4] in black stone from Deora, Mañjuśrī[5] in bronze from Mahasthan, Viṣṇu at Rangpur[6] and at Lakṣmankathi are assignable to the late Gupta period and exhibit quiet, restrained dignity and calm conviction in which, to use Coomaraswamy's words, "the inner and outer life are indivisible." Viṣṇu[8] from Deora (the same find-spot as that of the Sūrya image) is perhaps not earlier than the Baghaura Viṣṇu image of the 3rd year

1. ESMS, Pl. XIXa.
2. Ibid., Pl. LXVIIIa.
3. VRSR, 1931-32, Pl. I,
4. Ibid, 1226-27, fig. 1.
5. Ibid., fig. 2.
6. VRSR, monograph, No 4 ; Rangpur Sahitya Parisad Collection.
7. DMC, Pl. XXXII.
8 ESMS, Pl. XLIVb.

of Mahīpāla I[1] but is the product of Gupta artistic tradition and legacy. Amongst numerous Viṣṇu images of the Pāla period it stands apart in elegance and meditative calm. The position of Garuḍa suggests that a celestial being has condescended to climb down for a purpose and his stay will not be very long, as the bird is trying to rise up with his Lord.

It is now an admitted fact that a new school of art flourished in Bengal and Bihar simultaneously with the establishment of the Pāla power. Tārānātha records,[2] "In the time of kings Devapāla and and Dharmapāla there lived in Varendra an especially gifted artist, named Dhīmān; his son was Bītapāla; both produced many works in cast metal, as well as sculptures and paintings which resembled the works of the Nāgas. The father and the son gave rise to two distinct schools; as the son lived in Bengal, the cast images of gods produced by their followers were called gods of the Eastern style, whatever might have been the birth-place of their actual designers. In painting the followers of the father were called the Eastern school, those of the son, as they were most numerous in Magadha, were called followers of the Madhyadeśa school of painting." We are not concerned with the Madhyadeśa school of painting, the existence of which yet remains to be established. Numerous stone images, bronzes and a few miniatures from Bihar and Bengal go to show the existence of the eastern school of Tārānātha. As its rise synchronises with that of the Pāla power and its main activity was within the Pāla kingdom, it should be properly designated as the Pāla school.[3] In the Sena period too this school continued its activity and does not show any separate and distinctive artistic development. Products of this school have been found in Gorakhpur, Gonda and Basti districts of the United Pro-

1. DMC, Pl. XXXa.

2. IA, IV, p. 102.

3. Coomarasway also calls it Pāla school, see History of Indian and Indonesian Art, p. 113; R. P. Chanda calls it Pāla or Gauḍian school, Medieval Sculptures in the British Museum, p. 48; R. D. Banerjee calls it "Eastern school of Medieval Sculptures".

vinces.[1] Art of Konarak and Khiching, Mayurbhanj,[2] both in Orissa, was influenced by this school, but Assam seems to have stood outside its influence. The art of Nepal and Tibet is regarded as direct continuation of the Pāla school. Its deep influence on some images at Pagan[3] and on Java bronzes[4] has been established beyond doubt. All these go to strengthen the opinion of M. R. Grousset that this school had an influence not inferior to that of the art of Gāndhāra and the Gupta Empire.

Every image of the Pāla period is an interesting study by itself and full justice cannot be done to the subject in a work like this. A great majority of the images are in relief, but the tendency to carve in the round is noticeable when the main figure is separated from the back slab. Pāla art is to be understood in terms of its inheritance and in relation to its environments. Its clear delineation and definition of the features and decorated nimbus can be traced to Gupta art and so also the diaphanous robe of many bronzes. The curly hair, presence of *ūrṇā* and drapery of Buddha images are reminiscent of the Gandharan school as modified by the subsequent schools of Mathura and Sarnath. As in literature, language and religion, so also in art elaboration and ornamentation of old ideas, conceptions and techniques were due to the spirit of the age. In the absence of any inscription it is the richness of ornaments of the deities and the exuberance of decorations on the back slab that help us to determine the comparative date of an image, though it must be admitted that to fix it by the so-called style is always hazardous. The round top and the plainness of the back slab are generally the characteristics of an early Pāla image. But gradually the slab becomes pointed at the top and decorative devices and designs increase lavishly and profusely, which are finally conventionalized. In an ordinary Viṣṇu or Sūrya image we find leographs, scrolls, flying *gandharvas, kinnaras* and *kinnarīs,* swans, cloud-motives

---

1. ASIR, 1906-7, pp. 193-207.
2. ASIR, 1923-24, pl. XXXIV ; 1924-25, Pl. XXV
3. Ibid., 1922-23, pl. XXXIII ; N. Roy, Brahmanical gods in Burma, pp. 80-91,
4. Kempers, the Bronzes of Nālandā and Hindu Javanese Art, pp. 70 ff.

and feather-arabesques. Sometimes the *Vāhanas* and attendant figures are represented as part of decorations (*Haṁsa* in the Sarasvatī of the DM, the bull in the IM. Śiva[1] and the plumage of the peacock of the pleasing and graceful image of Kārtikeya[2] in the IM). In the remarkable image of Ṛṣabhanātha from Surhor the representation of each of the other 23 *tīrthaṅkaras* in a separate temple appears to be a decorative device rather than due to iconographic prescription. The snake in the hands of Naṭarāja Śiva or in one hand of seated Manasā serves both the purposes quite well. The ugly *Kīrtimukha* on the top was perhaps to express more effectively the beauty of the deity beneath it by producing a striking contrast. The æsthetic excellence of Pāla art lies in the combination of its wealth and exuberance of decorative designs with the translation of the inner state of mind of the deity. When worked out by a master hand symmetrically and proportionately, the decorative designs lend an added grandeur and beauty to the whole piece.

Pāla art is emphatically convincing and definite in its purpose. It is a plastic commentary on the *Śilpaśāstras*. What the *Sādhaka* conceived in his inspired moment in *Dhyānas* the artist gave expression to by his chisel, but to do it in numerous shapes and forms with the growth of variegated religious and spiritual experiences is the supreme achievement of the Pāla artists. It is doubtful whether so many *mudrās, āsanas,* poses and postures and attributes can be found in any other Indian school. Every one of them is full of deep meaning and special significance, and when rightly interpreted, they make Pāla art most expressive and suggestive. The Pāla artists could well produce the conception of a Madonna, an ineffable smile, benignity, grace, loveliness, serenity, juvenileness, horror, terror and wrath and almost every sentiment, as the subject matter demanded, and of them *śānta* and *sundara* types predominate. The definition of masculinity and femininity was well understood. The image of Ardhanārīśvara (half-man and half-woman) in round illustrates a clear conception of the physiognomy of the two sexes. In spite of multiplicity of hands in many images the figures are generally organic, and when in fighting atti-

---

1. ASIR, 1930-34, pl. CXXXIId.
2. Ibid., pl. XXIVd.

tude, the whole energy is concentrated in two normal hands. The artists had to perform a difficult task when in different faces of the gods or goddesses (Mārīcī, Parṇaśarvarī, etc.) they had to produce different sentiments. Those who have intimate knowledge of the Pāla sculptures will perhaps admit that the sculptors acquitted themselves creditably. The attendant figures are represented in keeping with the mood of the main figure. A squatting and emaciated figurine with its bones and veins vividly shown offers an appropriate setting for Cāmuṇḍā. The bull dances in ecstasy of joy with Naṭarāja and so also the mice with Gaṇeśa. Liveliness and vivacity that permeate the productions of this school are no less due to the minute carving, high polish and oily finish which are possible because of the non-crystalline grains of the black basalt, the most commonly used material, and even stone sculptures approximate to metal specimens in fine workmanship.

The only specimen of rock-cut carvings found in Bengal are at Ūṇakoṭi, Hill Tippera. Mr. K. N. Dikshit, who examined them *in situ,* observes, "the style betrays a rudimentary and crude conception of the sculptor's art and illustrates in a remarkable way the canons of of primitive art. The anatomical features of the different parts of the body are treated only in broadest aspects without any attempt to to harmonise them."

The large finds of bronzes at Nālandā,[1] Kurkihar,[2] Bihar and at Jehwari, Chittagong, and the actual remains of bronze-casting discovered at Nālandā[3] and Paharpur show the high degree of excellence and wide currency of this art. The Indian name of the metal is *aṣṭadhatu* and from that point of view as well as from the chemical point of view the coining of the term *Octo-alloy* is happy and appro-

1. ASIR, 1930-35, pls. CXXXIV-CXI.

2. Amounting to 218, see Proceedings and Transactions of the Seventh Oriental Conference, pp. 791 ff.

3, ASIR, 1930-34, pp. 130 ff.

4. Ibid. p. 122.

priate[1] The bronze Mañjuśrī from Mahasthan and the Sarvāṇī image from Deulbadi were gold-plated, and a silver image of Viṣṇu of very fine workmanship[2] has been discovered at Curain, Vikrampur, (now in the art-gallery of the IM.). Other important finds are Sūrya from Candimundu,[3] Lokanātha[4] from Sylhet, Piṇḍola from Sonarang,[5] a Buddhist goddess (Sitapātra Tārā ?) from Tippera,[6] Vajra Tārās (?) from Faridpur and Bhagalpur,[7] four Viṣṇu images from Rangpur[8] and four Viṣṇu or Avalokiteśvara images from Sagardighi, Murshidabad,[9] three miniature images from Comilla[10] and Manasā from Rajshahi in the IM.[11] This last one was set with precious stones. The *VRSC.* describes about eleven and so also the *VSPC.* and the *DMC.* supply the whereabouts of about a dozen more. The bronzes show finer workmanship than their stone prototypes and the figures appear more sensitive and sensuous.

Temples there were many in ancient Bengal and we have already referred to some for whose maintenance provisions were made by kings and other important personages. The finds of many images from certain localities of the Dacca, Tippera, Rajshahi, Dinajpur, Bogra and Birbhum districts suggest that there had been temples in those sites. The discoveries of door lintels and jambs go sometimes to confirm it. Plinths and walls of many temples have been exposed by the Archæological Department. The recent excavation at Vaigram, Dinajpur, has perhaps laid bare the remains of the temple built by Śivanandin, which has been mentioned in the Vaigram plate of 128 G. E. All that can be surmised is that it had a *garbhagṛha,* a

---

1. DMC., Intro, p. XX.
2. Ibid., pl. XXIX
3. Idid pl. KIX
4. Ibid., pl. IV
5. Ibid., IA (V) a/1
6. Ibid., IB (IV) a/1.
7. Ibid., pls, XV, XVI, XVII.
8. ASIR, 1911-12, pp. 104 ff.
9. ESMS, pls. LXVIII, LXXIVa.
10. Rupam, 1928, p. 26.
11. ASIR. 1934-35, pl. XXIVb.

circumbulatory passage enclosed by a wall and on four sides there was an open terrace adjoining the wall.[1]

The most important and imposing structure hitherto unearthed is the temple of Paharpur, Rajshahi. It is described thus by its principal excavator, Mr. K. N. Dikshit,[2] "The temple is one of the most extensive buildings of antiquity ever unearthed in India, its length from north to suth being 356′ 6″ and its breadth from east to west being 314′ 3″. The ground plan consists of a colossal square cross with projecting angles in each corner, the number of such projections being four each in the north-east and north-west sectors and three each in the remaining two. The upper terraces were apparently reached by a stair-case on the north, opposite which was the quadrangular enclosure. The temple rose in three terraces above the basement in the first and second terraces. The plan of each terrace was more or less parallel to the ground plan, but the number of recessed angles between the arms of the cross naturally grew smaller at each higher terrace. The first and second terraces have each a spacious verandah or circumbulatory passage for worshippers, walking round the main shrine. At the second terrace level there are halls or *maṇḍapas,* with stone pillars and antechambers behind them at each of the cardinal points. The main shrine at the summit was probably a square chamber with a verandah all round.

"The most striking feature of the monument is the scheme of decoration of the walls of the basement and those flanking the circumbulatory passages. The walls are of fine-jointed masonry of well-burnt brick in mud. The plainness of the surface is relieved at intervals by projecting cornices of ornamental brick, bands of terracotta panels and stone sculptures at the corners and in recessed niches in a lower part of the basement. The artistic level of the terracotta plaques and some sculptures leaves no doubt as to their age, which cannot be far removed from the best period of Gupta art and must be relegated approximately to the 5th and 6th centuries.

---

1. Ibid., p. 42,

2. ASIR, 1225-26, 1626-27, 1927-28, pp. 107-113. pp. 140-69 and pp. 101-111 respectively. Also ASIR, 1928-29, 1929-30 and 1930-34, pp. 98-99, pp. 98-99, pp. 138-142 and pp. 113-128 respectively.

"It is quite probable, as it has been suggested from the find of the Paharpur plate of 159 G.E.[1] recording grant of land to the Jaina *Vihāra* of Vaṭa-Gohāli, that the temple was originally associated with Jainism and its shape may be traced to a Caturmukha Jaina temple with probably an antechamber on each side forming what may be called a *Sarvatobhadra* (equal on all sides) temple.[2] It seems quite clear that both Buddhism and Brahmanism were amply represented in the scheme of reconstruction and decoration adopted in the fifth or sixth century, when the present outline of the monument must have come into existence. The reconstruction of the pillared halls on the second terrace, the repairs to some of the verandah walls and the provisions of cloisters for monks on a large scale, marked the establishment of the *vihāra*. There must have been at least 200 cells in the entire establishment, occupying a quadrangle of about 900 square and providing accommodation for about a thousand monks. No single monastery of such dimensions has yet come to light in India."

The temple unearthed at Satyapir Bhita to the east of the Main Temple of Paharpur has been identified with the one referred to in the Nālandā inscription of Vipulaśrīmitra.[3] It had a sanctum, pillared hall, circumbulating passage and vestibule, surrounded by rows of votive *stūpas*. There were residential blocks for the monks to the south of the central temple.

Excavations of the mound at Bairagi Bhita, Mahasthan, have revealed the remains of temples of three distinctive periods, Gupta, early and late Pāla. At Govinda Bhita the remains of a huge temple have been unearthed and constructions of late Gupta and early Pāla periods are discernible.[2] At Medh or Lakhindarer Medh, about a mile to the south of Mahasthangar, a group of small brick-built chambers, ranging themselves in parallel rows and rising in tiers or terraces, together with a huge and massive wall, have been unearthed. On the top of the mound a shrine, polygonal in plan, has

---

1. EI, XX, pp. 55 ff.
2. ASIR, 1927-28, pp. 38-39.
3. Ibid., 1930-34, pp. 122-26
4. Ibid, 1928-29, pp. 90 ff.

been found. The structure has been assigned on grounds of the style of the ornamental bricks to the late Gupta period.[1]

Traces of an ancient city have been found at Rangamati in the Murshidabad district, and the remains of a structure of different periods of constructions have been unearthed, of which the lowest was probably a Buddhist monument of the 6th-7th century A.D.[2]

Other noteworthy remains are of a stūpa-mound of the Gupta period at Bharat Bhayana[3] in the Khulna district and of a large temple measuring 195′ by 150′ with four gateways, a porch and *maṇḍapa* at Bairat in the Rangpur district. The shrine was provided with a beautiful black basalt pedestal with a spout.[4]

Most interesting are the temples at Dihar in the Bankura district, which have been assigned to the eleventh century A.D. They are built of conglomerate and are cruciform in shape. The *śikharas* are lost. "It seems that the lower parts were plastered and whitewashed. Over the plinth mouldings there is plain with the exception of the portion lying over the lintels of each opening. Above this portion begin the numerous cornices supported by elephant dwarfs, acting as brackets in different attitudes or brackets containing different animals."[5]

The extant stone temples at Barakar, (known as Begunia temples), at Chatna and at Harmashra, (Bankura) bear close similarity to the Jaina temple of Chotanagpur but do not seem to fall within our period and so also is the small stone temple at Gauri near Asansol.[6]

The extant examples of brick-built old temples are at Siddhesvari (Bahulara,) Bankura, Ichai Ghose's temple in Burdwan,[7] at Govindapur, Deulbari and Jatar Deul in 24-Parganas[8] and at Sat-Deul, Burdwan.[9] Their attribution to the Hindu period in the absence

1. Ibid., 1930,34, pp. 40-42.
2. Ibid., 1128-29, pp. 98 ff.
3. Ibid., 1921-22, p. 26.
4. Ibid., 1925-26, p. 113.
5. ESMS, p. 150
6. ASIR, 1922-23 pp. 180.111 ; ESMS, p. 150,
7. IMC, pl. XXXIIbc.
8. VRS, Monograph, No. 5, figs, 1, 3, 4, 5, 6,
9. ASIR, 1934-35, pl. XIXa,

of some positive data is questionable. Coomarswamy assigned the Bahulara temple to the 10th century,[1] but Mr. K. N. Dikshit[2] cautiously observes that "it is possible that the earlier (10th century) date is a century or two early, but there can be no doubt that these two examples (Bahulara and Jatar Deul) cannot be far removed in date from their stone prototype so well-known from the Bhuvanesvara style of architecture, the latest example of which is dated in the 12th century A.D." Their *śikharas* are slightly curvilinear, the *garbhagṛha* square in size and the entrance has a triangular corbelled arch over it. They seem to have been surmounted by *āmalakas.*

We are somewhat on surer grounds as regards the age of the temples represented on the images of the Pāla period. The most common is the *Bhadra* type of temples, the roofs of their receding terraces being surmounted by a dominating *śikhara.* The trifoil arch is supported by pillars.[3] The crowning *āmalaka* on the *śikhara* is very prominent in the image of Ṛṣabhanātha from Surhor.[4] It appears that this type was most popular in ancient Bengal. The miniature beautiful temple from Bangar (now in Maharaja's palace at Dinajpur)[5] deserves more than a passing notice. It shows the use of Caitya-windows on each facade which bears a niche, containing a figure of Buddha or Bodhisattva.

Stone pillars were extensively used in temples, the best examples of which are one from Sonarang[6] in the DM. and four from Pabna.[7] The old practice of erecting monumental columns as in the Maurya and Gupta periods was continued. Best examples are one from Rajmahal[8] (originally at Gauḍa), the Kamboja king's pillar from Bangar,[9] two inscribed pillars from Paikore,[10] Birbhum, Badal pillar of Gurava Miśra[11] and the pillar in the *Dhībar Dighee*[12] in

---

1, History of Indian and Indonesian Art, p. 108
2, ASIR, 1927-28, p. 41.
3, IMC/pl. LXXXI.
4. VRSR, 1232-34, pl, III.
5. ESMS, pl. LXXXVIc.
6, DMC, LXXVa.
7. Ibid., pp. 157-58, XCIVD.
8. Ibid., pls. LXXXIXa XCd.
9. Ibid., pl. LXXXIXc.
10. Ibid., pls. LXXXIXbc,
11. ASIR, 1927-28, p. 140.
12. Gaudarajamālā, against p. 49.

Dinajpur associated with the name of the Kaivarta king Divya. The carvings on the first two are of exquistite workmanship and they perhaps belong to the tenth century A.D. The carvings on the two Paikore pillars are not of much artistic excellence. The finial on Vijayasena's pillar is a broken image of Manasā. The Śaiva pillars had bulls, while the Vaiṣṇava ones had Garuḍa. The Kaivarta king's pillar is almost equal in height to the highest Aśokan column and has not been examined with the care that it deserves.

A large number of terracottas have been found at Paharpur, Mahasthan, Rangamati and Sabhar (Dacca). They were generally used to embellish the exterior of the temples of the Gupta and post-Gupta periods in Bengal. Of the pre-Gupta finds mention may be made of a few at Tāmralipti,[1] one from Murshidabad in the VSPM.[2] and a few from Mahasthan.[3] Very few terracotta plaques of the Pāla period are known, while the Paharpur finds of the pre-Pāla period alone amount to about 3,000, of which about 1,800 are *in situ*. It has been remarked that if all of them are arranged in a line, they would cover a distance of about a mile. The subject-matters dealt with in the plaques are most varied and of absorbing interest.[4] Of gods we have representations of Brahmā, Viṣṇu, Śiva, Gaṇeśa, Buddha and Avalokiteśvara; Vidyādharas, lion-faced, bird-winged men and men with short tails belong to the class of semi-human beings; various classes of men like soldiers, musicians, ascetics, amorous couples and others have been represented. The animal world is also well represented by elephants, deer, buffaloes, foxes, horses, tigers, dogs, cows, to mention a few only, and of the birds the common are parrots, peacocks, cocks and geese. More interesting are the representations of the stories from the *Pañcatantra* like *Vānara-kīlaka-kathā* and *Siṁha-śaśaka-kathā* and scenes depicting inborn animosity between mongoose

1. ASIR, 1921-22, pp. 74-75.
2. SPP, 1342 B. S, pp. 209 ff.
3. ASIR, 1930-34, p. 128.
4. All of them have not been described; a detailed monograph on Paharpur with the full description of the terracottas is a pressing necessity and will add much to our knowledge of the life of ancient Bengal.

and snake, the peacock devouring the snake, and of daily life and work. It has been rightly observed that "the delineation of homely subjects, everyday scenes of rural and out-of-door life must have made the artist in terracotta keen of observation and fully responsive to his environment. As a folk art of the soil to which it belongs the terracotta plaques of Bengal hold a very distinct and important position." Of other important specimens of potters' art found at Paharpur, mention may be made of several thousands of miniature votive *stūpas,* made of clay, and three remarkable pieces of glazed polychrome pottery with chocolate coloured and white floral ornament or white and green foliated leaves on a brown background.[1] At Medh ornamental bricks bearing floral patterns and a motif simulating the window have been found.[2]

Painting—Eight Mss. of the Pāla period, illustrated with miniatures, are known. They are—(1) Ms. of the *Aṣṭasāhasrikā-Prajñāpāramitā,* dated in the 15th year of Gopāla II and copied in the *Vikramaśīla*[4]*-deva-vihāra,*[3] (2) Ms. Add. 1464 of the same book in the Cambridge Library, dated in the 5th year of Mahīpāla I,[4] (3) Ms. of the same book copied in the 6th year of Mahīpāla in Nālandā,[5] (4) Ms. of the same book in the Ghose Collection, Calcutta,[6] probably of the 10th century, (5) Ms. Add. 1688 of the *Pañca-rakṣā* copied in the 14th year of Nayapāla (in the University Library of Cambridge),[7] (6) Ms. of the *Aṣṭasāhasrikā-Prajñāpāramitā* copied in the 39th year of Rāmapāla[8] in the collection of Vandenburg, (7) Ms. of the same book, copied probably in 1136 A.D.[9] in the Boston Museum

1. ASIR, 1930-34, p. 126, PI. LIIIcd.
2. Ibid., pl. XVIII.
3. JRAS, 1910, pp. 150-41.
4. Bendall, CBMC, pp. 106-01.
5. Des. Cal. of Sans. mss. in Asiatic Society of Bengal, pp. 1-2.
6. Rupam, 1929, p. 78.
7. Bendall, Op. Cit., b. 100.
8. Rupam, No. 1, p. 9.
9. Intro. to Indian Art, p. 110; History of Indian and Indonesian Art, p 141.

and (8) damaged last leaf of a Ms. of the same book copied in the 18th year of Govindapāla.[1] Miniatures in a few Ms. copied in Nepal also show the same style of painting.[2] The miniatures are "not organically and decoratively associated with the script but they occupy spaces left by the scribe to be filled by the painter." "The technique is calligraphic. The draughtsmanship is unusually strong and having regard to the material–fragile and soft plam leaf–on which the drawing is made, the beauty of line and colour evokes our admiration."[3] The miniatures illustrate the divinities of Tantrika Buddhism. Figures are extremely sensuous and even the male figures have feminine grace.[4]

1. H.P. Shastri, Des. Cat. p. 6
2. Rupam, 1929, 78ff.
3. Ibid.
4. For some good illustration, see DMC, Pls, I, II.

APPENDIX G

COINAGE

The earliest known coins of Bengal are *gaṇḍaka* and *kākaṇika*[1] mentioned in the old Brāhmī inscription of Mahasthan. Many punch-marked coins have been discovered from different localities. The Tamluk High School preserves 350 coins of which the rectangular cast type predominates. The obverse of the rectangular cast coins shows Taurine, tree-in-railing and *caitya* with three windows, and the reverse shows square cross, elepahant, svastikā and triangular-headed symbol. The obverse of the round cast ones shows three arches with crescent, and the reverse, elephant.[2] Six rectangular copper coins have been found at Beracampa, 24-Parganas.[3] The DM. cabinet has recently acquired a large number of them from Bhairavbazar, Mymensingh, but they have not yet been classified. One silver punch-marked coin was discovered at Jakra,[4] 24-Parganas, and another at Tamluk.[5] Thirty-five silver coins have been found near Manda, Rajshahi and of them five are in the IM. cabinet.[6]

It seems that gold coin was current in the beginning of the Christian era. Alluding to the foreign trade of Bengal, the author of

---

1. There are differences of opinion regarding the weight of Kākaṇī. Prof. Bhandarkar is of opinion that half-Kākaṇī was equal to 1. 14 grains at the most (Carmaichael Lectures, 1921, p. 112), while Dr. S.N. Chakravarti holds that it was heavier than that (A Study of Ancient Indian Numismatics, p. 112).

2. ASIR, 1921-22, pp. 74-74.

3. Ibid, 1922-23, p. 109

4. JASB, 1879, p. 245.

5. Ibid, 1882, p. 112

6. ASIR, 1930-34, pp. 255-56.

the *Periplus* says that there is a gold coin which is called Caltis.[1] About six gold coins of the Kushana kings, Kaṇiṣka, Vāsudeva I and Vāsudeva II have been discovered from Midnapore, Murshidabad and Bogra.[2]

A large number of Gupta gold coins have been found in almost every part of Bengal, and besides important recorded finds and collections, there are many private collections too. In 1783 a large hoard of about 200 gold coins were discovered. at Kalighat and they were transmitted to the Directors of the East India Company. Unfortunately many of them were melted down. Only a few coins of Candragupta II, Narasiṁhagupta, Kumāragupta II (?) and Viṣṇugupta are in the possession of the British Museum, Hunterian and Bodelian Collections.[3] In the same year 13 gold coins were found near Hooghly,[4] and they consisted of 1 Standard type of Samudragupta, 5 Archer type of Candragupta II, 3 Archer, 3 Horeseman, 1 Lion-slayer types of Kumāragupta I. The other notable finds are from Muhammadpur, Jessore,[5] and Mahanad, Hooghly.[6] At the last mentioned place one unique coin of Kumāragupta I of the Elephant-rider type has been found. R. D. Banerjee notices a number of coins of Candragupta II,[7] Kumāragupta I[8] and Skandagupta[9] from Burdwan, Midnapore, Hooghly and Faridpur. In all probability Gupta gold coins are *dināras,* so often mentioned in the land-sale documents of the period, the word being derived from the Greek Denarius.

Silver and copper coins were also used in the Gupta period. R. D.

---

1. Benfy thought that it was derived from Sanskrit Kalita, meaning 'numbered'. Vincent Smith mentions one class of Bengal coins, called Kallais. Schoff is inclined to indentify it with Kallais of southern India. (Schoff, Periplus, p. 259). Rai Bahadur K. L. Barua observes that the Kalita merchants of Assam used the gold coins called Kaltis (Early History of Kāmarūpa, p. 189.)

2. BI, pp. 88-89 ; JASB, 1933, pp. 127ff.

3. Allan, Catalogue of Indian Coins, Gupta Dynastics, Intro. p. cxxvi.

4. Ibid , p. cxxviii.

5. Ibid., p. cxxvii.

6. BI, pp. 67 ; ASIR, 1934-35, p. 43.

7. BI, pp. 59ff

8. Ibid. pp. 65ff,

9. Ibid., pp. 71ff.

Banerjee[1] refers to two copper coins from Katwa, Burdwan, with the legend *samudra.* It is reported that silver coins of Candragupta II, Kumāragupta I and Skandagupta were found at Muhammadpur, Jessore.[2] *Rūpakas* have been mentioned in the Vaigram plate of 128 G. E., from which it is known that three *kulyavāpas* and two *droṇas* of land were purchased by paying 6 *dināras* and eight *rūpakas* at the rate of two *dināras* per one *kulyavāpa.*. It is certain from the Paharpur plate that eight *dronas* were equal to one *kulyavāpa.* From this it has been concluded by Dr. R. G. Basak[3] that 16 *rūpakas* were equivalent to 1 *dināra.* But it is to be noted that in the Vaigram plate three *kulyavāpas* of *khila* (uncultivated) land were bought by paying 6 *dināras,* and two *droṇavāpas* of *vāstu* (homestead) land were bought for 8 *rūpakas.*. Prices of *khila* and *vāstu* lands might have varied and in that case the above ratio between *dināra* and *rūpaka* does not seem to be correct.

Gold coins were current in Bengal after the fall of the Imperial Guptas; the coins of Śaśāṅka and Jaya (nāga?) have been found not in inconsiderable number. Two coins of Samācā (radeva?) should also be taken into consideration. The unattributed 'Imitation Gupta' coins[4] from Muhammadpur, (Jessore), Kotalipara in Faridpur, Sabhar in Dacca and from Rangpur are crude in execution and have no pretension to artistic excellence. The legend on the reverse of four of them reads *Sudhanyāditya,* and the figure is that of a six-handed goddess.

It is strange that while coins of the Gupta and post-Gupta periods have been found in large numbers coins of Pāla and Sena periods are very rare. But it would be a mistake to conclude that there was no metalled currency in that period. The Bodh-Gaya stone inscription or Keśava *praśasti* records that Keśava excavated a tank at a cost of 3,000 *drammas. Dramma* is derived from the Greek word Drachma, and Prof. Bhandarkar[5] has shown that its weight approxi-

1. The Age of the Imperial Guptas, p. 214.
2. Allan, op. cit,, p. cxxvii,
3. EI, XXI, p. 78ff.
4. Allan, Op. Cip., p. 154; JASB, N. S., pp. 58-64.
5. Carmaichael Lectures, 1922, pp. 206-11.

mates to 65 grains of silver. Five copper coins have been found at Paharpur and they have been assigned to the early Pāla period and a silver coin (*dramma*) found there has been attributed to Vigrahapāla I.[1] Three silver coins of the Sassanian type with the legend *Śrī Vi* or *Vigraha* from Bihar have been attributed to Vigrahapāla III by V. A. Smith.[2] Twenty-five silver coins from eastern Magadha with the same legend and of the same type have been mentioned in the *Supplementary Catalogue*[3] of the IM. It is very curious that of all the Pāla kings the coins of the Vigrahapālas have come to light. In the grants of Lakṣmaṇasena,[4] Viśvarūpasena and Keśavasena the income yielded by the donated land has been mentioned in terms of *purāṇas* and *kapardaka-purāṇas,* but we do not know any specimen of them. Prof. Bhaṇdarkar[5] suggests that *"kapardaka-purāṇa* is a *purāṇa* which is shaped like *kapardaka* or *kauri."* This is perhaps strengthened by the statement of Minhaj when he values the gifts and charities of Lakṣmaṇasena in terms of *kauris.*

1. ASIR. 1927-28, pp. 101ff.
2. Catalogue of the Coins in the Collection of the IM. 1, pp. 233, 239.
3. Pp. 56-57.
4. See Ch. on Administration.
5. Op. Cit., pp. 139-40.

APPENDIX H.

THE GAUḌAS AND GAUḌA

The division of the Brahmanas from broad geographical point of view into *Pañca-Gauḍa* and *Pañca-Drāviḍa* is well-known. The five Gaudas are the (1) *Sārasvatas,* (2) *Kānyakubjas,* (3) *Gauḍas* (4) *Utkalas* and (5) *Maithilas.* It is evident that they derive their names from the countries in which they settled and about the location of four (excepting the Gauḍas) there is no doubt whatsoever. There were more than one Gauḍa. Firstly, Gauḍadeśa meant north-western Bengal in ancient and mediæval times. It was by far the most famous of all the countries of that name. Secondly, it is known from the *Rāmāyaṇa* and the *Vāyupurāṇa*[1] that there was a Gauḍa in Uttarakośala. It has been contended by Dr. R. G. Basak[2] from the passage, *"nirmitā yena Śrāvastī Gauḍadeśe dvijottamāḥ* (or *Mahāpurī*)" in the *Matsya, Kurma* and *Liṅga Purāṇas* that this Śravastī is to be located in Bengal. If we accept that there was a Gauḍa in Uttarakośala, which has been identified with the Gonda district and the neighbouring tracts, this Mahāpurī Śrāvastī may be identified with the famous city of Śrāvastī of the Buddhist literature or present Sahet-Mahet. In the *Sahyādri* section of the *Skandapurāṇa,* in which the division of the Brahmanas into *Pañca-Gauḍas* and *Pañca-Drāviḍas* has been mentioned, *Gauḍas* figure after *Sārasvatas* and *Kānyakubjas* and before *Utkalas* and *Maithilas.* It seems that they have been described in the geographical order from the west to the east, and if by the *Gauḍas* the Brahmanas of Bengal were meant, *Gauḍas* would have figured after the *Maithilas.* It is to be noticed that in the *Bṛhat-Saṁhitā*[3] of Varāhamihira the territory of Gauḍa is placed along with Matsya, Pāñcāla, etc. in the middle section of India.[3] Thirdly,

---

1. EI, XIII, p. 200; the passages discussed by Dr. R. G. Basak in connection with the location of Śrāvastī of the Silimpur stone inscription.

2. Ibid.

3. XIV, 3.

there was a Gauḍa between Khandesa and Orissa, and Cunningham identified it with the districts of Betul, Chindwara, Seoni and Mandal.[1] The five Drāviḍas are the (1) *Mahārāṣṭras,* (2) *Tailaṅgas,* (3) *Drāvidas* or of the country of the Tamil language, (4) *Karṇāṭakas* and (5) *Gurjaras.* It is difficult to say when the Brahmaṇas came to be known by these names. Yuan Chwang speaks of Harṣavardhana as the *king of five Indies.* It cannot be precisely stated what the pilgrim meant by this expression, but from the extent of Harṣa's empire it does not seem improbable that it extended over five Gauḍas. It is stated in the *Rājataraṅgiṇī* that the Kāśmīra king Jayāpīḍa made his father-in-law Jayanta, king of Puṇḍravardhana, the emperor of *Pañca-Gauḍas.* The romantic element in the story of Jayāpīḍa's visit to Puṇḍravardhana has led many scholars to doubt the veracity of the whole episode, and no king of Puṇḍravardhana, ruling in the 8th century over such a vast kingdom, is known. In one southern Indian inscription the epithet *Pañca-Drāviḍeśvara* has been applied to Rājendra Cola.[2]

The *Gauḍa Brāhmaṇas* are scattered over different parts of India. Writing in 1887, Wilson notices 17 classes of them.[3] A careful search will reveal still great many other varieties. Among the *Kāyasthas* there is a section called *Gauḍa-Kāyastha* living near modern Delhi. Again, among the Rajputas there is one section called *Gauḍa-Rājaputas.* There is a separate caste called *Gauḍatagās* who claim their origin from *Gauḍa Brāhmaṇas.*[4] The distribution of *Gauḍa Brāhmaṇas* over almost all parts of India and the existence of *Gauḍa-Rājaputas, Gauḍa-Kāyasthas* and *Gauḍa-tagās* cannot be very easily explained.

---

1. Cunningham, ASIR IX, p. 150 ; see also VJI, I, in the Chapter on Pañca-Gauḍa. Dr Roy Chowdhury is of opinion that Gauḍa in the Matsya, Kurma, Liṅga Mss. may be inserted as a Sanskritised form of Gonda. He cited the example of the Central Provinces where the name Gond is very often Sanskritised into Gauḍa (PHAI, p. 439) But Cunningham concluded just the opposite of it.

2. SII, I, p. 118.

3. Wilson, Indian Castes, Vol. II, p. 64-66.

4. See Viśvakoṣa on Gauḍa-Rājaputas, Gauḍa-Kāyasthas and Gauḍa-ṭagās.

By way of analogy an explanation can be suggested. The issues raised by Prof. D. R. Bhandarkar in his illuminating paper on the *Nāgara Brāhmaṇas and Kāyasthas of Bengal*[1] are various and many, but his conclusion that there was a tribe called *Nāgara* in ancient India which in course of time spread over different parts of the country is perhaps to be accepted. The same also seems to be the case with the *Gauḍas.* The Gauḍa tribe seems to have migrated to different parts and entered into the Rajput and Kāyastha societies. It may be noted that the *Āgarwalā Vaṇikas* utilise the services of the Gauḍa section of the Brahmanas and it may be that this mercantile community might have some remote connection with the *Gauḍas.*

It is not known where was the earliest home of the *Gauḍas.* The *Sārasvatas* called themselves *Ādi Gauḍas,* and it may be that their first settlement was in the region watered by the river Sarasvatī.[2] Again, Gauḍa in Uttarakośala might have been also the original land, because it seems that it has preserved the name of the tribe. There are epigraphic evidences to show that even in the historical period the Brahmanas from Uttara-kośala migrated to different provinces.[3] Therefore the claim of Gauḍa in Uttarakośala as the original home of the Gauḍa tribe cannot be brushed aside.

But of all the settlements of this tribe, Gauḍa in the east was undoubtedly the most famous and important. It was certainly an ancient country. Pāṇini associated it with the east.[4] It rose in great importance under Dharmapāla and Devapāla, and it is not unlikely that the title *Pañca-Gauḍeśvara* is "reminiscent to the Gauḍa empire under them because it cannot be equated with the ancient realm of Gauḍa kingdom in the early centuries of Christian era.[5]" With the great importance of the Gauḍa kingdom in mediæval India the title of *Gauḍeśvara* had some imperial glamour around it and it was difficult for the kings of Bengal to part with it when they had no authority

1. IA., 1932, pp. 41, 61.
2. For Adi Gauḍas see Wilson, op. cit.
3. Vide Supra. Brahman Immigrations in Bengal.
4. VI, II, 99.
5. Dr. Roy Chowdhury, op. cit.

over Gauḍa. Keśavasena and Viśvarupasena, sons of Lakṣmaṇasena, ruled over eastern Bengal after the conquest of north-western Bengal by the Muslims but they retained the title of Gauḍeṣvara. Govindapāla is generally taken to be of the Pāla dynasty but it is doubtful whether he had had any authority over northern and western Bengal; yet the title *Gauḍeśvara* was applied to him. This proud title was assumed by the kings of Cuttack in the 16th century.[1] Like the story connected with the reported immigration of five Brahmanas at the instance of Ādiśūra, one tradition is current among the *Gauḍa Brāhmaṇas* and *Gauḍatagās* of Delhi region that the services of their ancestors from Gauḍa in Bengal were in great demand by the epic king Janamejaya at the time of his snake sacrifice and hence their migration there. It is doubtful if Bengal itself was Brahmanised at the time of Janamejaya and therefore much weight cannot be attached to this story.

It may, then, be concluded that the Gauḍas were an important tribe in ancient times. They settled in different parts of the country and on account of their settlements many places were named after them. In the Brahman, Rajput, Kāyastha and Gauḍatagā societies many men of this tribe had entered and formed separate sections in these castes. Of all the settlements of this tribe, Gauḍa in Bengal outshone all in view of its great importance under the Pālas and many Gauḍas try to establish some connection with this famous country.[2]

---

1. IA, XLII, p. 49.

2. French says that there is strong and continuous tradition among the Panjab Hill tribes that the ruling families in certain states are descended from the Rājās of Gauḍa in Bengal. These are Sukhet, Keonthal, Kastwar and Mandi. See Art of the Pāla Empire, p. 19 ; Journal of the Panjab Historical Society, Vols. III, IV, VI.

Early History of Bengal.

WORD INDEX, Vol. II

A

Abdullapur 93
Abhaya 99, 100, 104
Abhidānachintāmaṇi 71
Abhinanda 10,11
Ācāraṅgasutta 45
Ācaras 10
Ācārya 7, 27
Ācāryaśāntideva 27
Ācārya Jitasena 27
Adam 113
Adavadi 46, 47
Adbhutasāgara 9
Adbhutaśānti 109
Ādi Buddha 79
Ādi Dharmapāla 42
Ādi Gauḍas 135
Ādideva 14
Ādinātha 70
Ādiśiṁha 35, 36, 48
Ādiśūra 10, 31, 34, 35, 42, 44, 46, 47, 48, 55, 57, 136.
Ādityas 104
Advayasidhi 8
Advya-vajra 17, 18, 21, 30
Advyavajra-saṁgraha 21
Āgamas 15, 115
Āgarwalā Vaṇikas 135
Agastya Saṁhitā 6
Aghora 96
Agni 107
Agnihotra 40
Agrahāra 39
Ahichatra 39, 41
Aitreya Āraṇyaka 40
Aitareya Brāhmaṇa 40
Aja 23
Ajayagar 37
Ājīvika 68, 69
Ajivikism 38
Akarṣaṇa 77
Akṣamālā 95, 104
Akṣobhya 79, 81, 82, 86, 87
Ālamyaṇa 44
Amadi 101
Āmalakas 125
Amarakoṣa 3
Amātya 8
Ambaṣṭha 59
Amgachi 48
Aminpur 97
Amitābha 79, 81, 82, 83, 84, 111
Amoghasidhi 79, 86

Aṁśa 55
Ananta 111
Ananta Vāsudeva 114
Anandapura 41
Anantanātha 71
Anantanārayaṇa 41
Anargha Raghava 1
Anāthapiṇḍaka 72
Aṅga 66
Aṅguttara-Nikaya 66, 72
Aniruddha-Bhaṭṭa 9, 52
Āhnika 10
Antyajas 60
Antaraṅga 6
Antarvyapti 22
Annunyāsa 2
Apabhraṁśa 23, 24
Apārajita 85, 88, 113
Aparcana 82
Arabic 5
Ardhanārīśvara 96, 97, 119
Ardhaparyaṅkāsana 83, 99
Arjuna 91
Arthasastras 42
Arthavyakti 4
Ārti 55
Aruṇa 104, 115
Aruṇadatta 7,
Ārya-Buddha-bhūmi-vyākhyā 18
Ārya Govardhana 12
Āryadeva 23
Āryapaṭṭa 97
Āryas 39
Āryasarasvatī 88
Āryasaptaśatī 12
Āryāvarta 14, 39
Āsanas. 119
Asansol 124
Āścarya-caryā-caya 24
Asita Devala 80
Aśoka 68, 72
Aśokan 126
Aśokānta māricītt 86
Aśokaśrimitra 29
Asrafpur 28, 95
Assam 7, 16, 118
Aṣṭadhātu 120
Aṣṭāṅga-hṛdaya 6
Aṣṭa-sahasra-Prājñā-pāramitā 25, 30, 127
Asura 114
Atīśa 22, 30
Atīśa Dīpaṅkara 26, 94
Atibhaṅga 100
Attahasa 101
Audumbara 36
Āvallika 9
Avalokiteśvara 3, 14, 81, 82, 83, 113, 121, 126
Avantī 71
Āvasathika 9
Avadutapāda 21
Āvṛti 54, 55,
Āyāraṅgasuatta 65, 66
Āyurveda 5
Āyurveda-dīpikā 6

B

Backerganje 91, 96
Badal 109, 125
Badura 60
Bagchi Dr. P.C. 20
Baghaura 116
Bahulara 124, 125
Bairagi Bhita 123
Bairat 124
Bālabhadra 13
Bālāditya 25
Bālādityarāja 24
Bālagrāma 15, 37, 91, 93, 94
Bālaputradeva 24
Balāvatāra-tarka 21
Bālī 91, 93
Bāṇakuṇḍa 36
Bandyaghāti 47

Baṅgāla 17, 18, 19, 21, 22, 30
Bangarh 37, 125
Bankura 20, 124
Banerjee 61
Banerjee R.D. 32, 70, 81, 83, 99, 111,
Barabar –68
Barakar 124
Bargaon 26
Barakuṇḍa 36
Barrackpore 37, 70
Barua B. M. 69
Basak R.G. 131, 133
Basti 117
Baudh 37
Baudhāyana 39, 40
Begunia 124
Belava 37, 91
Benares 66
Bengali 24
Betna 101
Bhade 23
Bhādra 125
Bhadrabāhu 65
Bhadrapāda 23
Bhadraśilā 102
Bhadreśvera 6
Bhaduri 46
Bhagalpur 26, 79, 94, 109, 121
Bhagavatī 68
Bhagavati Sutta 66
Bhairava 95, 96
Bhairab-bazar 129
Bhamaha 4
Bhandarkar, D. R. 41, 131, 132, 135
Bhānu 6
Bhānumatī 6
Bharadvāja 15, 36, 37, 59
Bharadvāja gotra 10, 34
Bharadvāja Gautama 44
Bharadvājas 35
Bha-ra-ha 14, 28, 79
Bharat Bhayana 124
Bhāsavṛti 3
Bhāskaravarman 5, 41, 42
Bhasu-vihāra 27
Bhaṭṭa 15
Bhaṭṭa Bhavadeva 8, 14, 35, 47, 52,
Bhaṭṭanārāyana 5, 10
Bhattacarya, Dr. B. 86, 88
Bhattasali, N. K. 41, 87, 94, 101, 106
Bhava-bhumi-vārtā 58
Bhababhuti 5
Bhabiṣyottara Purāṇa 106
Bhikṣu 21
Bhikṣus 69, 75
Bhīṁa 11, 57
Bhīṁapāla 6
Bhiharoil 116
Bhojavarman 37, 91
Bhoṅgāla 22
Bhṛkuti 83
Budhaguptarāja 24
Bhupendravarman 45
Bhutadāmāra 87
Bhūriśreṣṭha 14
Bhuriśeṣṭhī 7
Bhursut 14
Bhusuka 23
Bhuśūra 46
Bhutivarman 41
Bhuvanesvara 112
Bhuvanesvara prasasti 47
Bhuvaneśvarī 99
Bibhuti Candra 30
Bighnanāṭaka 87
Bihar 26, 79, 80, 94, 107, 117, 120, 132
Bijjala 23
Bīrabhūma-Vivaraṇa 101, 102
Birbhum 13, 36, 65, 70, 83, 99, 100, 101, 121, 125
Biruwa 23
Bītapāla 117
Biṭṭiga 39
Bodelian Collection 130
Bodh Gaya 29, 80, 87, 97, 113, 131
Bodhibhadra 29
Bodhi-citta 76

Bodhideva 52
Bodhi-sathva 82, 84, 125
Bogra 38, 83, 93, 94, 121 130
Boses 61
Brahmā 14, 105, 111, 113, 126
Brahmā-Viṣṇu 114
Brahmagupta 9
Brahmakṣatriyas 51
Brāhmaṇa-Sarvasva 10, 45, 52, 59
Brahmaputra 7
Brahmayamāla 110
Brāhmī 129
Bṛhaddharma Pūrāṇa 59
Bṛhaspati 105
Bṛhat-Samhitā 133
British Museum 130
Bstan-hgyur 16, 17, 18, 19, 21, 22, 30
Bubhuksa 22
Buddha 3, 21, 81, 105, 109, 111, 126
Buddhism 38, 40
Buddhists 108, 109, 110
Burdwan 36, 101, 124, 130, 131
Buston 17

C

Caitya 85, 125, 129
Cakra 110
Cakradatta 6
Cakra-mahāsukha 87
Cakrapāṇi 6
Cakrapāṇdatta 5
Cakra-samvāra-Tantra 87
Calcutta 96, 127
Caltis 130
Cālukya 71
Cambridge Library 127
Campanagar 26
Campahiṭṭi 47
Campati 47
Cāmmuṇḍā 101, 102, 112
Caṇḍa 101
Cānura 91
Caṇḍāls 60
Caṇḍarasanā 84
Candella 14
Caṇḍī 98, 99
Caṇḍikā 101
Caṇḍīmuṇḍu 121
Candra 1
Candradvīpa 2, 20
Candragarbhā 21
Candragomin 1, 18
Candragomins 17
Candragupta 65
Candragupta II 130, 131
Candragupta Maurya 66
Candraketu 34
Candrakirti 2
Candramukhī 34
Candravarman 90
Cāracikā 101, 110
Caraka 6
Carmakāra 60
Cāsī-Kaivartas 60
Cāṭila 23
Caturmukha 103,123
Caturmukha Liṅga 97
Central Provinces 14
Ceylon 2, 22
Ceylonese 103
Chakravarti, M. 8, 12
Chanda, R. P. 32
Chandaka 81
Chando-Ratnākara 22
Chandogya 8
Chatra 124
Chatrabhog 107
Chatterjee 46
Chatterjee Dr. S. K. 23
Chabhagiyas 73
Cheedivlasa 45
Chindwara 134
Chinese 18, 67, 73, 74, 112

Cīnabhūmi 110
Chittagong 16, 21, 30, 87, 109, 120
Chotanagpur 124
Choyandaka 29
Cikitsā-sāra-saṁgraha 6
Cirantana-Śaraṇa 12
Citramatikā-devī — ?
Cola 103
Coomarswamy 116, 125
Colgong 26
Comilla 121
Cunar 116
Cuṇḍā 87
Cunningham 27, 38, 134
Curain 121
Cuttack 136

D

Dacca 16, 83, 79, 91, 99, 121, 126, 131
Dakṣiṇā 109
Dakṣiṇā-Lāla 103
Dakṣiṇa-Rāḍha 14
Damayantī 12
Ḍamaru 105
Damodarpur 40, 90
Damodarsena 2
Dānasāgara 9, 53
Dānaśīla 30
Daṇḍa 4, 5
Daṇḍa 104, 115
Daṇḍin 4, 5
Danujamādavdeva 61
Darbhapāṇi 15, 52
Dārika 23
Daśabhujā mārīci 113
Daśakarma-paddhati 8, 10
Daśaratha 68
Daśarathadeva 46
Dāsas 60
Daśāvatar 116
Dāyābhāga 9, 52, 97
Delbandh 97
Delhi 136
Denarius 130
Dendhāna 23
Deora 116
Deogadh 116
Deopara 12, 102, 103, 114
Deulbadi 99, 105, 121
Deulbari 124
Deuli 100
Devadatta 69, 73, 80
Devagaṇa 6
Devagrāma 102
Devakhaḍga 27
Devakīputra 90
Devakoṭa 65
Devala-Brahmana 60
Devapāla 10, 24, 25, 29, 94, 117, 135
Devendravarman 45
Devī 97, 100, 101
Devīpurāṇa 98, 100
Dhanadatta 109
Dhanaidaha 40
Dhanañjaya 9
Dhanaturā 101
Dhārā 11, 71
Dharma 75
Dharāśūra 47, 49, 53
Dharmas 46
Dharmacakra 109
Dharmacakramūdrā 82
Dharmādharmaviniścaya 21
Dharmadhātu 81
Dharmādhikāra 9
Dharmagāthās 15
Dharmakāra 30
Dharmakṛtya 21
Dharmapāla 10, 18, 19, 20, 24, 26, 29, 38, 48, 90, 97, 117, 135
Dharmaśāstras 9, 15

Dharmavijaya 52
Dhātupradīpa 2
Dhīmāna 117
Dhibar Digheer 125
Dhīvaras 60
Dhoyī 13
Dhruvānandamiśra 55, 61
Dhulla 109
Dhvajāgra Keyura 85
Dhyāna 98, 106, 111
Dhyānas 119
Dhyānamurti 105
Dhyānamudrā 98
Dhyānī Buddhas 78, 79, 81, 82, 83, 84, 87, 110
Dhyānī Śīva 97, 110
Digambaras 67, 70
Dipar 124
Dighwa-Dubhali 37
Diksit K. N. 120, 122, 125
Dinajpur 38, 40, 66, 71, 92, 93, 94 97, 99, 100, 101, 102, 104, 105, 121, 125, 126
Dināras 130, 131
Dīpaṅkara 20, 21, 22, 27
Dīpaṅkara Buddha 29
Divvoka 57
Divya 77, 126
Divyāvadāna 69
Dohās 23
Dolāvāhis 60
Ḍombī 23
Drachma 131
Dramma 131
Drammas 131
Drāviḍas 75, 134
Dravya-guṇa-Saṁgraha 6
Droṇa 131
Droṇavāpas 131
Dudhpāṇi 35
Dūrgā 99, 111
Dūrgottara 30
Dūtakāvya 13
Dvijāhnika-paddhati 10
Dvija-nayana 52

E

East India Company 130
Eḍumisra 61
Ekdala 105
Ekajaṭā 76, 85, 86
Ekamukha 103
Ekamukhaliṅga 97
Elephanta 116

F

Fahien 13, 74
Faridpur 35, 45, 58, 87, 121, 130, 131

G

Gadā 110
Gadhādhar-vaidya 6
Gaṇakas 60
Gaṇapati 70, 87
Gaṇapatihṛdaya 88
Gandhaka 129
Gāndhāras 75, 81, 114, 118
Gāndharvas 118
Gandha-Vaṇikas 59
Gaṇeśa 7, 85, 88, 96, 97, 98, 102, 105, 106, 113, 120, 126
Gaṅgā 39, 46, 96, 102
Gangarampur 100
Ganges 15, 30, 103

Gaṇita 15
Garbhagṛha 121, 125
Garbhapāda 20
Garga 52
Garuḍa 92, 94, 110, 113, 115, 117 126
Gauḍa 4, 7, 11, 13, 14, 21, 36, 38, 46, 71, 75, 103, 125, 133, 134, 135, 136
Gauḍābhinanda 11
Gauḍa Brahmanas 134, 136
Gauḍadeśa 103, 133
Gauḍa-Rājaputas 134
Gauḍapāda-Kārikā 7
Gauḍa-Rājajutas 134
Gauḍatagās 134, 136
Gauḍe-Brahmana 62
Gauḍeśvara 136
Gauḍī 5
Gauḍīrīti 3
Gauṇa 50
Gauṇakuliṇa 49
Gaurī 87, 96, 98, 102, 113, 124
Gautama 44
Gāyatrī mantra 50
Getty 79
Ghaṇṭāpāṇi 79
Ghaṭakas 57
Ghaṭṭajīvis 60
Ghose Collection 127
Ghose J. C. 41
Ghṛta Kauśika 44
Girījā 115
Gīta-Govinda 13, 91
Girīśa 115
Gochandi-kula 9
Godāsagaṇa 66
Godhikā 98
Gouda 38, 117, 133
Gopāla I 19
Gopāla II 37, 127
Gopas 60
Gorakhpur 117
Gorakṣanātha 20, 23, 112
Gosāla 68
Goṣṭhikathā 43, 61
Gotras 41, 43, 44, 57
Govardhana 2, 12, 65, 91
Govinda Bhitā 123
Govindacandra 6
Govindapāla 25, 128, 136
Govindapur 124
Govindarāja 8
Govindasvāmin 90
Grahamatṛkā 88
Greek 130, 131
Gṛhis 60
Ghrya-mantra bhāsya 10
Grousset M. R. 118
Guhanandin 66
Guhya-Samāja 75
Guhya-Samāj Tantra 78
Gunaighar 73, 95
Guṇaviṣṇu 10
Gundari 23
Guñjarī 23
Gupta 14, 40, 42, 82, 91, 104, 108, 116, 117, 118, 122, 123, 124, 125, 126, 130, 131
Guravamiśra 15, 35, 52, 125
Gurjaras 134

H

Halāyudha 8, 9, 14, 45, 53, 59
Halahala 84, 82
Haṁsa 117
Hanumāna 71, 103
Hara 102
Haraha 5
Hāralatā 9
Hārita 30

Hāravarṣa 10
Hari 76
Haribhadra 20, 30
Harihara 102, 103, 114
Harihariharivahar 82, 112-13
Harikāladeva 30
Harikoṭi 36
Harimiśra 61
Hāritagotra 39
Harivaṁśa 90
Hāritī 88
Harivarmadeva 14
Harivarman 52, 58
Harṣa 134
Harṣapura 29
Harṣavardhana 24, 37, 134
Haṣtīnibhaṭṭa 14
Hastipāda 37
Hayagrīva 83
Hazaribagh 65
Hemcandra 71
Hemādri 6
Heramba 98
Heruka 84
Hetu-tattvopadeśa 2
Hevajra 86
Hevajratantra 20
Hill Tippera 102, 12[illegible]
Himālaya 7
Himāvat 39
Hoerule 6
Holiwel Street 78
Homacuṭaya 109
Hooghly 14, 130
Horaśāstra 15
Hoysala 39
Hunterian 130

I

Ichai Ghose 124
Itahar 92
Indus 134
Indra 107, 113
Indrāṇī 102
Indrapāla 38
Indumitra 2
It-Sing 14, 28, 74
Irda 37, 109
Īśāna 10, 52
Īśānavarman 5

Jagaddala 23
Jagaddala-vihāra 30
Jajilpara 37
Jālandharipā 23
Jāiikas 60
Janamejaya 136
Jaiminī 8
Jaiṇa 7
Jainas 44, 45, 46, 47, 49, 53, 66, 67, 69, 70, 112, 123, 124
Jainism 38, 40, 65
Jakra 129
Jalalabad 25
Jambhāla 84, 85, 86, 87
Jambucatvāra 36
Jāñgulī 85, 106
Jarāsandha 90
Jasoreśvarī 102
Jatar Deul 124, 125
Jātis 60
Jāti-saṅkara 61
Java 2, 25, 118
Jaya 92, 115, 131
Jayacandra 12, 58

Jayadeva 12, 13, 91
Jayanagara 35
Jaya-nandī 23
Jayanta 134
Jayantabhaṭṭa 11
Jayapāla 15
Jayapīḍa 134
Jessroe 16, 99, 101, 130, 131
Jetāri 20, 21, 26
Jhansi 116
Jhewari 87, 120
Jimūtavāhana 8, 9, 52
Jñānapākasamuccya 3
Jñānasiddhi 78
Jñānaśivadeva 103
Jñānaśrīmitra 21
Jogirsoan 91
Jyāviṣa 15

K

Kachra 100
Kādambarī-Kathāsāra 11
Kagajipada 98
Kāgrāma 36
Kaivarta 11, 56, 57, 126
Kajangal 73
Kākaṇika 129
Kakkasas 60
Kakṣa 109
Kāla-viveka 9, 52
Kalki 92
Kālidāsa 1, 10
Kalighat 130
Kālikā 101
Kaliṅga 67, 75, 76
Kalosapota 109
Kalpasūtra 66
Kalyāṇamitra 25
Kalyāṇaśrī 21
Kalyāṇasundara 95, 96
Kāma 107
Kāmākhyā 16
Kāmakoti 36
Kamālaśīla 20
Kamauli 23
Kamaṇḍalu 83, 95, 99, 100, 104
Kambalapara 23
Kamboja 37, 60, 109, 125
Kāmarūpa 15, 20, 38
Kaṁsa-Vaṇikas 59
Kanaka-stūpa-vihāra 30
Kanauj 36
Kandi 36
Kanha 23
Kaṇiṣka 130
Kaniṣka-vihāra 25
Kāñjikā 6
Kaṅkagrāma 36
Kankana 23
Kaṅkandighi 105
Kanouj 34, 36
Kanṭhaka 81
Kānti 4
Kāntideva 109
Kānya-Kuvja 8, 12, 133
Kapardaka-purāṇa 132
Kara 5
Karaṇa 59
Karaṇḍovyuha 81
Karmakāras 60
Karmānuṣṭhāna-paddhati 8, 52
Karṇa 21
Karṇasuvarṇa 27, 69, 72, 74
Karṇāṭa 51, 134
Kārikās 61
Karnatic 48
Karṇāvatī 58
Kārtikeya 15, 96, 98, 106, 119
Karuṇāśrīmitra 29
Kāryakāraṇa-bhāva-siddhi 21
Kāśī 34, 58, 102
Kāśikā 2, 3

Kāśīkāvivarṇa 2
Kasipura 96
Kāśmīra 11, 26, 134
Kāśyapa Suṣena 44
Kāśyapa gotra 34
Kāśyapas 35
Kaṣṭa-Śrotriya 47
Katak 37
Katason 101
Kathuma-Śākhā 8
Katmandu 82
Katwa 131
Kalna 20
Kaulajñāna-nirṇaya 20, 25
Kaulinya 56, 57, 59
Kaundanya 44
Kaundanya gotra 43
Kauri 132
Kauśāmbī 25
Kauśikagotra 43
Kāva 22
Kāvyamimāṁsā 15
Kāvyas 11
Kāyastha 7, 41, 45, 134, 135, 136
Kazi 113
Kedāra-miśra 15, 52, 109
Keilhorn 36
Kendubilva 13
Keśava 131
Keśavasena 11, 115, 132, 136
Kesavpur 100
Keśī 91
Ketu 105
Keur 26
Kewar 46
Khaḍga 74, 95, 100
Khadi 93, 104
Khadirvani-Tārā 86
Khalimpur 90
Khandagiri 71
Khaṇḍana-Khaṇḍa-Khādya 8, 12
Khandesa 134
Kharvāṭa 66
Kharas 60
Kharvela 66
Kharveṭa 66
Khasarpaṇa 29, 82, 83
Khaśas 60
Khaṭvāṅga 104
Khiching 118
Khila 181
Khodulaśarman 46
Khri-Sron-den-tsan 19
Khulna 102, 124
Kinnarīs 114, 118
Kīrtirmukha 119
Kīrtivarman 14
Kodivarśiya 66
Kolāñca 34, 36, 37, 38
Konarak 118
Katalipara 58, 131
Koṭi-tirtha 102
Koṭivarṣa 66
Koṭivarṣa-viṣaya 40
Kroḍāñca 37
Kraḍāñja 37, 38
Kṛṣṇa 70, 90, 91, 106
Kṛṣṇamiśra 14
Kṣemiśvara 5
Kṣamā 101
Kṣitiśa 34
Kudavas 60
Kukkurī 23
Kula 49 55
Kulācala 47, 49
Kulagranthas 31, 33, 47, 58, 59
Kulamañjarī 49
Kulāñca 37, 38
Kulapañjikās 31, 32, 33, 36, 44, 46, 49, 62
Kulārṇava 61
Kulaśāstras 31, 32, 35, 36, 37, 38, 39, 44, 45, 47, 48, 53, 54, 56, 57, 62
Kulatattvārṇāva 33, 34, 43
Kulīna 54, 55, 61
Kulinism 32, 45, 48, 50, 51, 53, 54,
Kulinism 61

Kulinistic 49
Kulyavāpas 131
Kumāracandra 30
Kumāradevī 12
Kumāragupta I 24, 130, 131
Kumāra 102
Kumarila 52
Kumārila Bhaṭṭa 8, 15
Kumarpur 116
Kumbha-Kāras 60
Kuntīra 37
Kurukulla 19, 87
Kurkihar 93, 120
Karma 92, 133
Karmapurāṇa 38
Kushana 130
Kuvera 107, 114

L

Lāḍha 66
Lahore 16
Lalitāditya Muktāpīḍa 11
Lakhindarer medh 123
Lakṣmaṇa Sena 3, 8, 9, 11, 13, 36, 455, 51, 54, 55, 61, 91, 114, 132
Laksmankathi 91, 116
Lakṣmī 92, 93, 111, 115
Lakṣmīnārāyaṇa 94
Lalitaparibhāsa 3
Lallācārya 7
Laṅkā 91
Lāṭa 71
Lāṭa-Brahmanas 42
Later Guptas 36
Dr. B. C. Law 38
Legione de Honours 56
Liṅga 98, 99, 106, 107, 133
Liṅgarāja 114
Lohāpaddhati 6
Lokanātha 5, 41, 79, 82, 90, 121, 83, 114
Lokeśvara 82
Lomaśa 7
Latsavas 22, 30
Lucknow Museum 37
Lui-pā 20, 23
Lui-pāda 16, 19

M

Maccandar vihār 82
Madanapāla 109
Mādhavakara 5
Mādhavasena 11
Mādhavabhaṭṭa 8
Madhu 13
Madhuvan 37
Madhyadeśa 37, 39, 41, 117
Madhyadeśa-vinirgata 37, 38, 39
Madhyamaka-Ratna-pradīpa 30
Madhyāṁśa 55
Madhyama-Saṅkaras 60
Madhyaśreṇī 50
Mādhurya 4
Madhyamika 21
Madonna 119
Madra 36
Madyadoṣī 50
Magadha 18, 24, 36, 48, 56, 57, 59, 66, 90, 117, 132
Magadhādhirāja 35
Magadhanātha 36
Mahābhārata 96, 109
Mahābhāṣya 3
Mahābhiniṣkramaṇa 81
Mahābodhi 29
Mahācārya 27
Mahācīnatārā 76, 84

Mahādevī 100
Mahākāla 87, 110
Mahākāvya 11
Mahālakṣmī 100
Mahāmātra 9
Mahanad 130
Mahāmāṇḍalika 13
Mahāmantrānusārinī 88
Mahāmāyā 84, 98
Mahāmayurī 86, 88
Mahāpaṇḍita 29
Mahāpauma 68
Mahāprājña-pāramitā-sūtras 74
Mahāpratisarā 86, 88, 113
Mahārāstras 134
Mahāsahasrapramardanī 88
Mahāsāradā 88
Mahāsiddhas 23
Mahāśivagupta II 37
Mahaśivagupta-yayāti 37
Mahāsahasra-pramardinī 85
Mahasthana 27, 62, 72, 82, 83, 116, 121, 123, 126, 129
Mahasthangar 123
Mahaśvetā 104
Mahāsitāvati 88
Mahāvaṁśa 55, 61, 62
Mahāvidyā 82, 83
Mahāvīra 65, 66, 67, 68
Mahāyāna 20, 21, 27, 29, 73, 85
Mahāyānists 112
Mahendra 104,
Mahendrapāla 37
Maheśamiśra 61
Maheśvara 4
Mahindrapāla 25
Mahinta 23
Mahīpāla I 21, 37, 117, 127
Mahiṣamardinī 100, 102, 116
Mainamati 30
Maithilas 133, 24
Maitra 46
Maitreya 2, 79, 82
Maitreyanātha 20
Maitrīśrīmitra 29
Majbari 87
Mahākhaliputta Gosāla 67
Majumdar N. G. 80, 110
Makara 102
Mālākaras 60
Malda 100, 116
Malla 60
Mallikārjunasūri 7, 69
Māmmaṭa5
Manahali 47
Manasā 106, 107, 113, 119, 121, 126
Manbhum 36, 65
Manda 104, 129
Maṇḍapas 122, 124
Mandla 134
Maṇḍalas 75
Mandasor 5
Mandhātā 14
Mandi 16
Maṅgala 100, 105
Mangalbari 99
Mandhara 82
Mañju Ghoṣa 81
Mañjukumāra 81
Mañjunātha 81, 82
Mañjuśrī 116, 81, 82, 11, 121
Mañjuśrī-Mūla-Kalpa 75
Mañjuvara 81
Mantras 45, 75, 76
Mantra-bhāṣya 10
Manu 39, 60
Manusaṁhitā 8
Mārtanda-Bhairava 105
Māra 71, 81, 113
Maraṇa 77
Māricī 85, 87, 120
Mathurā 81, 66, 118
Mātṛkās 102, 104
Matsāśī 47
Matsavāsa 47
Matsya 92, 133
Matsyapurāṇa 38, 101

Matsyāvātāra 92
Matsyendranātha 20, 23, 112
Mauḍāṅga 57
Maulānā 113
Maurya 65, 68, 72, 73, 125
Māyādevī 80
Māyājalakeyura 82
Mayurbhanj 118
Medhātithi 34
Medh 123
Meghadūta 13
Maṇidhara 23
Midnapore 36, 50, 130
Milikka 66
Mīmāṁsā 15
Mīmāṁsaka 7
Mīmāṁsā-sarvasva 8
Mīṅanātha 20
Mīṅapāda 20
Minhaj 132
Mitra K. D. 70
Mleccha 60, 66
Modakas 60
Mokṣakaragupta 30
Mongyr 48
Mṛtyunvañcana 89
Mucalinda 80
Mundrās 75, 119
Muhammad 113
Mohammadpur 130, 131
Mukherjee 46, 61
Mukhyakulīna 49
Muṇḍa 101
Muktāvastu 37
Murāri 5
Murshidabad 36, 92, 111, 121, 126, 130
Muslim 32, 54, 59, 113, 136
Muṣṭika 91
Mymensingh 129

N

Nadia 30, 102
Nāga 107, 30
Nāgabodhi 19
Nagail 94
Nagara 134
Nagara Brahmanas 41, 134
Nāgārjunas 17, 19, 26, 20
Nāgarjuni 68
Nāgarjunikoṇḍa 73
Nāginīs 107
Nag-tso 27
Nahar 96
Naihati 97
Nairatmā 85
Naiṣadhiya 11, 12
Nala 12
Nalagiri 81
Nālandā 5, 18, 19, 23, 25, 25, 26, 28, 29, 75, 84, 88, 94, 120, 123, 127
Nandī 62
Nanna-Nārāyaṇa 42, 93
Nāmasaṁgiti 81, 87
Nāpitas 60
Napoleon 56
Narasiṁha I 39
Narasiṁha 92, 103
Narasiṁhgaupta 130
Nārāyaṇa 5, 90, 113, 114, 115
Nārāyaṇapāla 15, 109
Nārāyaṇavarman 42
Naṭa 60
Naṭarāja 95, 96, 120
Naṭarāja Śiva 111, 119
Nātha 20
Nāthapanthis 23
Navagrahas 105, 106
Navagrāma 14
Nāyapāla 5, 21, 22, 26, 37, 109, 127
Nemīnātha 70
Nepāla 16, 23, 79, 118, 128
Nepalese 22, 87
Nidāna 5

4

Nidhanpur 5, 35, 41, 45
Nilakaṅṭha 58, 82
Nirodoṣa-Kula-Pañjikā 61
Nirgrantha 65, 68, 66, 67, 70
Nirvāṇa 65
Niścalakara 7
Nigamas 115
Nirātmā 76
Nula Pañcānana 61
Nyāsa 2, 3
Nyāya-Kandalī 7, 8, 14
Nyāyamañjarī 11

O

Odantapurī 26
Ojas 4
Orissa 10, 37, 39, 50, 118, 134
Oriya 24

P

Pabna 61, 125
Pādīśvara 6
Padma 110
Padmanartteśvara 82
Padampāṇi 79
Padumsahar 103
Pagan 118
Pag-Sam-Jon-Zang 17, 2, 29, 18, 19, 21, 30
Paharpur 29, 69, 95, 66, 86, 91, 107, 108, 113, 116, 120, 122, 123, 126, 127, 131, 132
Paikore 125, 126
Pāka-yajña-paddhati 10
Pālakāpya 7
Pañca-Drāviḍa 133
Pañca-Drāviḍeśvara 134
Pañca-Gauḍas 34, 133, 134
Pañca-Gauḍeśvara 135
Pancakhanda 41
Pancakoṭi 36
Pañca Makaras 77
Pañca-rakṣā 127
Pañcarakṣā Maṇḍala 88
Pañcastūpa 66
Pañcatantra 126
Paṇḍita 19, 26, 27
Paṇḍita-sarvasva 10
Paṇḍita-vihāra 21, 23, 30
Pañjikā-kāra 7
Pṇāḍya 103
Pāṇini 2, 68, 135
Paṇitabhumi 68
Pañjikā 7
Pañjikā-kāra 7
Panjab 16
Parākeśarīvarman 103
Paramāra Bhoja 11
Paramśva 87, 113
Parāśara 44
Paraśurāma 93
Pareshnath Hill 65
Parṇasavarī 85, 86, 113, 120
Paribhādriya 8
Pārśvanātha 70
Pārvatī 96, 98, 99, 112, 113, 115
Paryāga 55
Pāśa 83, 100
Pāścātyaprakaraṇa 52
Pāścātya Vaidikas 31, 51, 58
Paśu 77
Pāśupata 109
Paśupati 10, 52
Patharghata 26, 87
Patna 37
ṭṭike
Puṇḍ...
Pauṇḍravard...
Paurastya 4
Pavanadūtam 13
Payagambar 113
Periplus 130

Phala-Saṁhitās 15
Piṇḍola 121
Piṅgala 104, 115
Piśācas 30
Piṭakas 21
Po-chi-po 27
Pomvardhaniya 66
Prabhavatī 21, 95, 97
Prabodhacandrodaya 14
Pradoṣaśarman 41
Prāḍaviveka 8
Prādyumneśvera 95, 103,
Prahāsa 35, 37, 52
Prakṛit 76
Prājña 76
Prājñāvarman 22
Prājñāpāramitā 29, 76, 85, 87
Prājñāpāramitasūtras 76
Prakṛta 3
Prasanna Tārā 113
Praśasti 5
Pratihāra 25
Prahāsa 104
Prāyaścitta-nirūpaṇa 8
Prayāga 39
Pretasantirpita 82
Pulindas 60
Puṇḍa 68
Puṇḍra 90
Puṇḍravardhana 45, 65, 66, 67, 68, 69, 72, 134
Puṇḍravardhanabhukti 40
Purāṇas 9, 60, 132
Purapara 93, 97
Puruṣa 76
Puruṣottamadeva 3
Puspapura 25
Prutreṣṭi 33

R

Raktalokeśvara 82
Raktaviti 27
Rāma 11, 92
Rāmacarita 10, 11, 62
Rāmāyaṇa 133
Rāmapāla 6, 11, 25, 30, 38, 109 91, 127
Raṇabhañjadeva 37
Raṇavaṅkamallḁ 30
Rangamati 124, 126
Rangpur 91, 92, 116, 121, 124, 131
Rangpur Sahitya Parisad 107
Ranipati 93
Rao Gopoinath 99, 100
Rāra 66
Ratnākara Śāntideva
Ratnākara Śāntideva 22
Ratnamālā 5
Ratnapāṇi 79
Ratnapāla 80
Ratnasambhāva 79, 86, 87
Ratnavajra 26
Raudra 85
Raudrī 102
Ravi 105
Revanta 105
Ṛg-Vedic 115
Ṛṣabhanātha 70, 71, 119
Rabhāṅga 57, 125
Ṛāḍha 7, 9, 13, 14, 16, 43, 45, 46, 48, 59, 65, 66, 68
Rādhā-Kṛṣṇa 91
Rāḍhīya 8, 31, 44, 45, 46, 47, 49, 54, 42, 59, 61
Raḍhīya-kula-mañjarī 61
Raghurampur 94
Rāghavendrakaviśekhara 58
Rāhu 105
Rāhulabhadra 18
Rāhulagupta 21
Rāhulamitra 28
Rājabhaṭa 74

Rājagṛha 67
Rājādhirājadeva 103
Rajakas 60
Rājaputas 60
Rajmahal 73
Rājshahi 1, 94, 100, 104, 102, 121
113, 122, 129
Raiganj 105
Rājarājeśvara 103
Rājarājabhaṭa 27
Rājapaṇḍita 9, 10.
Rājaśekhara 5, 13
Rājataraṅgiṇi 134
Rājendracola 103. 134
Rajmahal 125
Rajput 134, 135, 136
Rājyapāla 109
Rakṣita 2
Ṛṣis 104
Rudra-Cāracikā 101
Rudra-Cāmmuṇḍā 101
Rudraṭa 4
Rudrayamāla 110
Rugvinistcaya 5
Rūpakas 131
Rūpavidyā 101

S

Śabara 18, 23, 75, 60
Subaripa 19
Śabarisvara 19
Sābarṇa 36, 59
Sābarṇagotra 34
Sābarṇas 35
Sābarṇa Parāśara 44
Śabda-Canḍrikā 6
Śabdapradīpa 6
Sabhar 16, 91, 126, 131
Sadakṣarī 82
Sadāśiva 95, 115
Sādhaka 119
Sādhana 22, 30, 77, 78, 82, 84, 89, 112
Sādhanamālā 19, 82, 83, 86, 87, 88,
89
Saduktikarṇāmṛta 6, 11, 12, 13
Saḍvargikas 72, 73
Sadyajāta 106
Sagardighi 111, 121
Sāgnika 34
Sahaja 23
Sahajayāna 112
Sahajayānists 112
Sahet Mahet 133
Sahore 16
Sahyādri 133
Śaiva 20, 26, 98, 102, 106
Śaiva-sarvasva 10
Saivism 95, 113
Śākadvipi 60
Śāktas 98, 108
Śakti 76, 104, 108
Śakrādītya 24
Saktipur 36
Śaktivarman 11
Śākyasiṁha 80, 82
Śalikanātha 7
Samāca 131
Sāmalavarman 33, 52
Sāmantabhadra 79
Samantasara 58
Samatata 18, 29, 67, 70. 72, 73, 74
75
Samatiya 74
Sāmaveda 8
Sambandha-Nirṇaya 62
Śambhu 115
Sametasikhara 65
Samīkaraṇa 55, 61
Samudra 131
Sāṁkhyas 76
Sammola Tantra 76

Sāmpradāyika 42
Samudragupta 130
Samvara 84
Saṁyutta Nikāya 72
Samvari 34
Sanātana 20
Sāndhivigrāhika 14
Sandhyākarnandi 5, 11, 62
Śāṇḍilya 15, 35, 36, 46, 47, 58
Śāṇḍilyagotra 10, 34
Śāṇḍilya Nārāyaṇa 44
Saṅghārāma 27
Śāni 108
Sankalia 113
Saṅkha-Vaṇikas 60
Sankhahati 99
Śāntarakṣita 17, 19
Śānti 23
Śāntideva 17
Śāntinātha 70
Śāntivārika 109
Sanyala N. B. 106
Sapādalakṣma 41
Saptākṣara 84
Saptasātī 43, 44, 45
Sāradātilakatantra 98, 105
Saraha 17, 18, 23
Sarahabhadra 18
Śaraṇa 12
Saraṇadeva 3
Sārasvata 33, 43, 133, 135
Sarasvatī 39, 58, 88, 92, 93, 94, 105, 106, 109, 119, 115, 135
Saraswati, S. K. 101, 111, 92
Sarda Act 54
Sarnath 12, 80, 81, 116, 118
Saroha-vajra 112
Sarpa 105
Sarvānanda 3
Śarvāṇī 95, 97, 99, 121
Sarvotabhadra 123
Śāsana 14
Śāśāṅka 95, 131
Sassanian 132
Sat-Deul 124
Satānanda 11
Satapatha Brāhmaṇa 94, 115
Satśatī 43
Sat-Śrotriyas 47
Satyapir Bhita 29, 123
Saugata 109
Sauhmas 60
Sukumarya 4
Śaunaka 58
Śauṇḍika 60
Saura 103
Saurasenī 23
Sāvakas 60
Śayambhu 79
Seng-chi 75
Seoni 134
Serpore 92
Śeśa-Śayin 91, 92
Setaka 72
Shastri, H. P. 3, 7, 16, 23, 51, 76
Siddhas 17, 23
Siddha-Cāmuṇḍā 101
Siddhācārya 19
Siddhaikavīra 81
Siddhala 14
Siddhānta 14
Siddha-Śrotriyas 57
Siddha-Yoga 6
Siddha-Yogeśvarī 101
Siddhesvari 124
Siddhi 112
Śikharas 124, 125
Śīlabhadra 18, 75
Śilāditya 24
Śīlas 26
Silimpur 15, 35, 37, 107
Siṁhanāda 82
Siṁhapura 48
Simha-Śaśaka-Kathā 126
Siṁhavāhinī 99, 102
Simla 100
Singhbhum 65

Śiṣtas 39
Śiṣyadhi-mahātantra 7
Śiṣya-lekhadharma 18
Śitapātra 85
Śītatārā 87
Sitapatra Tārā 121
Śiva 87, 95, 96, 97, 102, 103, 105, 106, 107, 109, 112, 113, 115, 119, 126
Śiva-bhaṭṭāraka 109
Śiva-Buddha 111
Śivācārya 103
Śivadāsasena 6
Śivanandin 121
Siyambaka 15, 37
Skandagupta 130, 131
Sumāgadhā 71
Skandapurāṇa 133
Smith, V. A. 132
Smṛti 9, 31, 46, 52, 60
Sohagura 73
Solośa-mahājanapada 66
Soma 105
Somapura-vihāra 69
Somapurī-māhavihāra 29, 113
Someśvaradeva 37
Sonarang 121, 125
Sonpur 37, 105
Śradhākṛtya-paddhati 10
Śrādhāpaddhatiṭikā 52
Śramanas 112
Śrāvastī 15, 38, 80, 133
Śrāvastiianapada 37
Śrāvastīdeśa 38
Śrāvastīmaṇḍala 37, 39
Śrāvastībhukti 37, 39
Śrāvastī-viṣaya 39
Śrīcandra 109
Śrīdharācarya 14
Śrīdharadāsa 7, 13, 52,
Śrīharṣa 5, 8, 11, 12, 16
Śrīkanṭha 7
Śrīkuṇṭha 12
Śrījñāna Atiśa 21
Śrīvāstava 37
Śrotriyas 50
Śrotriyagāīñs 49
Śrutakevalī 65
Śrutis 46
Śruti 15, 31, 52
Sthavira 73, 74
Sthiracakra 82
Strota 106
Stūpas 123, 127
Subbabhumi 65
Śubhakaragupta 30
Sudaksiṇā 38
Sudhāvakumāra 83
Sudhānakumāra 131
Śuddhi 77
Śuddhi-viveka 9
Sudhānidhi 34
Śūdra 56, 43
Sugatisandarsana 82
Sugrīva 91
Sukhavaspur 79
Sukhāvatī 84
Sukavatī-vyuha 81
Śukla-Yajurveda 10
Śukra 105
Sumāgadhā 72
Suparśvanātha 71
Sumatra 25
Sumbhas 72
Sunderbans 70, 92, 93, 104, 105, 107, 113
Śūnyavāda 20
Suparśvrnātha 71
Śūra 47, 48, 56
Śūrapāla 109
Sureśvarācārya 7
Surhor 71, 125
Suri 36
Sūrya 104, 105, 108, 115, 116, 118, 121
Sūrya-siddhānta 7
Sushilā 58
Sushila 58

Surasta 6
Susunia 90
Sūtras 2, 60, 102
Suvaṅga 41
Suvarṇadvipa 21, 24, 25
Suvarṇavaṇikas 50, 56, 60
Suvarṇavihara 30
Svastikā 129
Svetāmvaras 70
Śvetavarāha Svāmin 90
Suviṣada-samputta 20
Swat Valley 16
Sylhet 16, 41, 42, 121
Śyāmalavarman 33, 58

T

Tadaka 23
Tāḍita 36
Tailaka-pāda 17, 21, 30
Tailakāras 60
Tailaṅgas 134
Tailakas 60
Takṣa 60
Tāmbulī 60
Tāmila 134
Tamluk 129
Tamluk High School 129
Tāmralipti 13, 14, 28, 66, 72, 74, 126
Tāmalithya 66
Tanjore 103
Taṅkadāsa 20
Tantra 14, 75, 76, 105, 111, 112, 115
Tantrapradīpa 2
Tantramūlavṛtti 21
Tantravārtikā 8, 52
Tāntrika 1, 3, 5, 108, 128
Tantuvāyas 60
Taponidhi 15
Tārā 29, 30, 83, 86, 88, 89, 110, 111
Tārānātha 17, 21, 22, 29, 117
Tarkāri 15, 37
Tarkārikā 37
Tathāgatagupta 24
Tattvabodhasaṁgrahaṭikā 8, 20
Taurṁe 129
Tautātimataṭikā 8, 52
Tepa 92, 91
Therāvādin 73
Tibet 21, 23, 118
Tibetan 2, 17, 19, 22, 26, 30
Ṭikā-sarvasva 3
Tiladaka 25
Tilopa 21
Tippera 5, 30, 41, 45, 73, 90, 95, 99, 114, 121
Tīrabhukti 109
Tirhut 109
Tīrthaṅkaras 65, 70, 71, 119
Tirumalai 6
Traikūṭa-vihāra 60
Trailokya-vijaya 113
Trailokyavasaṅkara 82, 84
Trailokyavijaya 87
Triśūla 99, 100, 104
Trivikrama 92
24 — Parganas 124, 129

U

Ubhayavarahanana māricī 113
Udāna-varga 7, 22
Udayana 13
Udayanācārya 58
Uddiyana 16, 17, 18, 21

Udicya-deśa 103
Ugra 59
Ujjayinī 9, 11
Umā 98
Umāliṅgana-mūrti 95
Umā-maheśvara 95, 96
Umāpatīdhara 12, 103
Umāpatīdeva 103
Unādavṛti 2, 3
Unakoti 102, 114, 120
United Provinces 117,-18
Upaveda 5
Upādhyāya 27
Upāṅgas 66
Upa-Purāṇa 60
Upāsakas 74, 75
Upasena 72
Upāya 76
Uposatha 28
Upper Gangetic 40
Urdhavaliṅga 95
Uṣā 104
Uṣṇīṣavijaya 85
Utkala 57, 133
Uttamasaṅkaras 59, 60
Uttarakośala 38, 133, 135
Uttara-Rāḍha 10, 14
Uvaṭa 10

V

Vācaspatimiśra 61
Vadirat 82
Vādnagar 41
Vāgabhaṭa II 6
Vāgīśvara 81
Vāgīśvarī 25, 100, 102
Vāhana 107
Vāhanas 119
Vaidharbha 4
Vaidharbhī 4
Vaidharbhī-rīti 11
Vaidika 44, 46, 59
Vaidikas 48
Vaigram 38, 40, 90, 121, 131
Vaikuṇṭha 92
Vainyagupta 27, 73, 95
Vainyeśvara 92
Vairocana 79, 85, 86
Vaiśālī 67
Vaiṣṇavas 13, 76, 91, 106, 111
Vaiṣṇavasarvasva 10
Vaiṣṇavī 102
Vaisnavism 113
Vaivāhikamūrti 95
Vājaseneyī Kaṇvaśākhā 10
Vajjabhumi 65, 68
Vajra 24
Vajracāraçikā 85
Vajraḍāka 84
Vajradhara 54
Vajrahumkāra 87
Vajragāndharī 88
Vajrāṅga 81
Vajrapāṇi 79
Vajrasāradā 88
Vajrasattva 79, 87
Vajraśrhkhalā 86
Vajratāysā 87, 121
Vajravalamālākāra 87
Vajravarāhī 85, 86
Vajravidāraṇī 88
Vajravīṇā 88
Vajrayāhists 76
Vajroyoginī 88, 92, 94
Vāk 81
Vakreśvara 100
Vallabhānanda 56
Vallālacarita 50, 56
Vallālasena 9, 11, 32, 33, 35, 45, 47, 48, 49, 50, 51, 57, 58, 97
Vāmama 4
Vandenburg 127

Vandyaghāṭiya 3
Vānarakilakakathā 126
Vaṅga 7, 12, 14, 33, 66, 69, 71, 72, 73, 76
Vaṅgaja 45, 46
Vaṅgāla 29
Vaṅganaputta 72,
Vaṅgasena 6
Vaṇikas 56, 57
Vappaghośavata 35
Vaśadra 88, 107
Varadarāja 7
Varada-mudrā 82, 83, 104
Varāha 15, 92, 107
Varāhamihira 9
Varāhavatāra 93
Varāhī 102
Varajīvīs 60
Vardhamāna 65
Varendra 8, 10, 11, 15
Vārendra 8, 10, 11, 15, 20, 26, 31, 37, 42, 43, 44, 45, 46, 47, 57, 58, 59, 61, 117, 115
Varendrakulapañjikā 34, 36, 61
Varman 48, 59, 51, 91, 92
Varṇas 48, 60
Varṇa-Saṅkara 61
Varuṇa 114
Vasantavilāsa 71
Vaśiṣṭha 39, 44, 59, 110
Vāstu 131
Vastupāla 71
Vasu N. N. 33, 61, 62
Vāsudeva 90, 92, 109, 115
Vāsudeva I, 130
Vāsudeva II, 130
Vasudharā 85, 86, 87
Vaṭa-Gohāli 66, 123
Vaṭagrāma 36
Vaṭeśvarasvāmī 47
Vātsyas 35, 36
Vātsyagotra 10, 34
Vaṭudāsa 13
Vāyupurāṇa 38, 133
Vedas 3, 15, 41, 43, 46, 76, 75, 112
Vedāṅgas 46
Vedic 40
Veṇa 60
Veṇīsaṁhāra 10
Venkyya 103
Videhaputta 72
Vetāla 13
Vidyādharas 74, 114, 126
Vidyanidhi L. 62
Vidyās 15
Vighnanāṭaka 109
Vigraha 132
Vigrahapāla 48, 132
Vijaya 92, 115
Vijayarakṣita 7
Vijayasena 8, 11, 12, 33, 37, 70, 115, 126
Vijñānavāda 20
Vijñāpti-mātrāsidhi 22
Vikartana 49
Vikramaṇipura 21
Vikrampur 46, 79, 83, 86, 93, 94, 96, 97, 98, 121
Vikramapurī 23
Vikrampurīvihāra 30
Vikramaśīla 10, 21, 22, 23, 27, 26
Vikramaśīladeva-vihāra 127
Viṇāpāda 23
Vināsana 39
Vināya 73
Vindhya 39
Viñjhā 68
Vipula 67
Vipulaśrīmitra 29, 124
Vīra 77
Vīradeva 25
Vīrasena 12
Vīradhavala 71
Vīrasiṁha 37
Virupa 23
Vīryendrabodhi 29

Viśākhadatta 1
Viṣṇu 7, 70, 92, 93, 94, 102, 103, 105, 108, 111, 113, 114, 116, 117, 118, 121, 126,
Viṣṇugupta 130
Viśvakarmaśāstra 104
Viśvapāṇi 79
Viśvarūpasena 9, 11, 115, 136, 132
Vītarāga 34
Vitāśoka 68
Vrata 34
Vṛhatkathākoṣa 65
Vṛnda 6
Vvavahāramātṛkā 9 52
Vaṛhat-Svayambhupurāna 79
Vyāgratātīmaṇḍala
Vyāsa 19

W

Wilson 134
Winternitz 76.

Y

Yab-Yum 108
Yakṣas 114
Yama 107
Yamari 84
Yamāntaka 84
Yamunā 91, 102
Yantras 77, 93
Yaśodharamiśra 58, 59
Yaśovarman 5, 24
Yaśovarmapura 25
Yavadvīpa 24
Yavanas 60
Yoga 75, 77
Yogācāra 21
Yogadeva 52
Yogāsana Viṣṇu 110
Yogī 50, 57
Yogavasīṣṭha-Sāra 11
Yogeśvara 13
Yoni 97
Yuan Chwang 5, 13, 18, 24, 27, 66, 69, 70, 72, 73, 74, 75, 134

Z

Zahore 16, 17, 19, 22

———

Errata list

Page I	Heading	Learning	for Learing
„ 4	line 15	omit	In before Dandin
„ 8	fn, 5	read	JBORS for JBOSB
„ 16	fn, 3	„	Dr. B. Bhattacharyya for Dr. V. Bhattacharyya
„ 22	line 25	insert	a, before contemporary
„ 28	„ 16	read	priests for priest
„ 30	„ 8	„	Yakṣas for Yokṣas
„ 48	„ 30	„	Like for lkie
„ 88	„ 17	„	Mahāsahasrapramardāne for Mahāsaharapramardāin
„ 96	fr. I	„	JASB for SASB
„ 99	line 20	„	at for as
„ 104	„ 22	„	Viśvakarmāśāstra for Viśvakārma-satra
„ 105	„ 2	Insert	a after was
„ 106	„ 8	read	Kārtikeya for Kārikeya
„ 107	„ 10	Omit	As after vehicle
„ „	fr. 3	read	ASIR for ARIR